SPORT IN AFRICA

Sport in Africa

ESSAYS IN SOCIAL HISTORY

*Edited by William J. Baker
and James A. Mangan*

AFRICANA PUBLISHING COMPANY
a division of Holmes & Meier
New York · London

First published 1987 by
Africana Publishing Company
a division of Holmes & Meier Publishers, Inc.
30 Irving Place
New York, N.Y. 10003

Great Britain:
1–3 Winton Close
Letchworth, Hertfordshire SG61 1BA England

Book design by Gloria Tso

Library of Congress Cataloging-in-Publication Data

Sport in Africa.

   Contents: Games and sport in pre-colonial
African societies / John Blacking—The wrestling
tradition and its social functions / Sigrid Paul—
The biggest game of all / Thomas Q. Reese—[etc.]
   1. Sports—Africa—History.   I. Baker,
William J. (William Joseph), 1938–
II. Mangan, J. A.
GV665.S66   1987   796'.096   87-1804
ISBN 0-8419-0906-7
ISBN 0-8419-0940-7 (pbk.)

Manufactured in the United States of America

Contents

Introduction

History is the handmaiden of the present. The imperialist view of African history is undergoing fundamental revision as newly emerged nations require fresh perspectives on the political, cultural, and economic dimensions of their past. Whereas European colonizers saw in "darkest Africa" merely a host of peoples to be subdued, exploited, and enlightened by European standards, historians today are seeing an altogether different Africa—complex indigenous institutions, cultural values, and commercial patterns that were disturbed and redirected but not wholly destroyed by alien powers. In the contemporary rewriting of African history, the stability, self-confidence, and future development of new nations are at stake.

While political and economic historians set about their essential task, social historians have an equally important story to tell: of the way in which Africans have lived and died, fought and loved, worked and played. Sport is a central but neglected part of that story. Today organized sport is developing rapidly throughout Africa; its antecedents, evolution, and cultural and political significance need to be understood. This volume of twelve essays by anthropologists, educationists, historians, political scientists, and sociologists explores the origins, diffusion, and permutations of African sport; its importance as a factor in social stability, status, cohesion, and control; its relation to various educational values and ethical norms; and its recent usefulness in achieving international visibility and prestige for independent African nations.

We have organized these essays under three headings that roughly approximate the precolonial, colonial, and postcolonial phases of African history, but we are keenly aware of the impossibility of imposing a strict chronological scheme on the African saga. Africa is a vast continent of many peoples, innumerable tongues, and diverse climates and topographies. The course of African development is uneven from one region to another, and all the more between rural and urban communities. In the countryside, inherited attitudes and patterns of behavior persist tenaciously with scarcely a hint of modernity. Colonial institutions adapt and survive in new guises under bullishly anticolonialist governments. Ancient traditions, colonial customs, and modern urban styles exist side by side. Occasionally they overlap. Today's African athletes might travel by jet aircraft to compete before a huge crowd in a concrete stadium, but some athletes still wear magic armbands and practice rituals that would be wholly recognizable to their ancient forebears. Although we have divided this book into traditional, colonial, and modern sections to convey a sense of real change over time, we know these categories to be imprecise.

Our use of the term *sport* similarly lacks specificity, and purposely so. Following the *Oxford English Dictionary,* our definition is liberal and comprehensive, embracing sedentary recreations like gambling as well as spontaneous play and pastimes, the hunting of game, traditional athletic contests involving both individuals and groups, and those activities now recognized throughout the world as the modern sports of track and field, cricket, and soccer. We instructed our contributors to consider sport in inclusive rather than exclusive terms, covering a wide range of recreational and competitive activities.

As John Blacking suggests in the opening essay, *sport* is a relatively modern term that might well be an ill-fitting category when applied without qualification to traditional African forms of dance, play and contests. Yet throughout pre-colonial Africa, ritualistic dances and games were long performed with a seriousness akin to sport in modern industrial societies, and for purposes not altogether different: the striving for status, the assertion of identity, the maintenance of power in one form or another, and the indoctrination of youth into the culture of their elders. Sigrid Paul and Thomas Q. Reefe, in explaining the age-old character and social purpose of wrestling and gambling respectively, underscore the various usages of ancient rituals and recreations.

Of no small importance for the evolution of sport in Africa, the high point of European imperialism in the late nineteenth century coincided with the rise of organized sport throughout the industrialized world. In Victorian Britain, the birthplace of most modern games, athleticism flourished on the playing fields of the so-called public (private) schools, on the rivers Cam and Isis, at Lord's and Wimbledon, on race courses and athletic tracks, and in omnipresent rugby and soccer clubs. At the hands of Anglo-Saxon enthusiasts, modern sports and the games ethic made their way to the rapidly industrializing nations of Europe and North America, and to the less developed continents of South America, Asia, Australia, and Africa.

In the second section of this book, Anthony Kirk-Greene documents the significance of the district administrator as a carrier of Britain's athletic culture to Africa, Anthony Clayton charts the consequences of the sporting enthusiasms of the imperial soldier, and James A. Mangan analyzes the moral imperatives allegedly inherent in public-school games and their espousal by colonial educationists. On a somewhat different note, John

MacKenzie considers the hunt in its transformation from a mere food-gathering function to a "sporting" endeavor at the hands of late nineteenth-century European imperialists, while Terence Ranger's treatment of urban pugilism in Southern Rhodesia provides an appropriate conclusion to the colonial era and also introduces one of the many kinds of sporting options available to Africans today.

In the spirit of the "timely reminder" in Blacking's opening essay that sport is "never neutral or apolitical, as some people imagine," our contributors to the third and final section all focus on the sociopolitical ramifications of modern African sport. Ali A. Mazrui relates indigenous sub-Saharan traditions, Islamic customs, and alien Western values to the question of African women in sport. Robert Archer considers the intricate interplay of sport and politics in South African towns, and Baruch Hazan explains the manner in which the Soviet Union works through sporting channels to pursue its political interests in Africa. Finally, William J. Baker assesses the national, pan-African, and global implications of sport for newly independent African nations.

Despite the variety of perspectives and themes represented in this book, some omissions are evident. We decided not to include an essay on South Africa and apartheid per se because that issue is already well covered in the literature; it is, in fact, the only topic sufficiently documented in the history of African sport. Regrettably we were unable to provide essays on colonial French Africa and the universally popular modern game of soccer. Reams of correspondence simply never produced publishable essays.

As yet, too few academics have recognized the social significance of sport, particularly for African studies. We are therefore all the more grateful to our contributors, several of whom turned momentarily away from other research interests to attend to the subject at hand. We are also grateful to Max Holmes and Barbara Lyons of Holmes & Meier Publishers for their commitment to this project; and to Phyllis Martin of Indiana University, whose careful, critical reading of the entire manuscript saved us from some egregious errors of fact, form, and terminology.

The future of African sport history is rich in promise. No doubt there will be speedy correction to the lack of attention characteristic of the past. We invite other scholars to amend and extend this exploratory effort. We are content to have begun the process of documentation, analysis, and reflection.

William J. Baker
James A. Mangan

Notes on Contributors

ROBERT ARCHER works for the Catholic Institute for International Relations in London, primarily on programs relating to Southeast Asia. With degrees from Cambridge University and London University, he has contributed to the *Guardian* (Manchester) and various Third World periodicals. He is the author of *Madagascar depuis 1972, la marche d'une révolution* (1976), *Sport et Apartheid, sous le maillot la race,* with Antoine Bouillon (1981, translated as *The South African Game: Sport and Racism,* 1982), and *Vietnam, the Habit of War* (1983).

WILLIAM J. BAKER, Professor of History at the University of Maine, concentrates on modern British history and sports history. Educated at Furman University, Southeastern Seminary, and Cambridge University, he is the author of *Beyond Port and Prejudice: Charles Lloyd of Oxford, 1784–1829* (1981), *Sports in the Western World* (1982), and *Jesse Owens: An American Life* (1986). He also edited *America Perceived: A View from Abroad in the Nineteenth Century* (1974), *Sports in Modern America,* with John M. Carroll (1981), and *Sports and the Humanities,* with James A. Rog (1983), and has served on the editorial boards of *The Journal of Sport History* and the *British Journal of Sport History.*

JOHN BLACKING has been Professor and Head of the Department of Social Anthropology at the Queen's University of Belfast since 1970. After his education at Cambridge University, he taught at the University of the Witwatersrand, South Africa, and Makere University, Uganda. His chief publications are *Black Background: The Childhood of a South African Girl* (1964), *Venda Children's Songs: A Study in Ethnomusicological Analysis* (1967), *Process and Product in Human Society* (1969), *How Musical Is Man?* (1973), *Man and Fellowman* (1974), and two edited volumes, *The Anthropology of the Body* (1979) and *The Performing Arts* (1980). Forthcoming is *A Commonsense View of all Music: Reflections on Percy Grainger's Writings on Ethnomusicology and Music Education.* In 1984 Blacking was elected a member of the Royal Irish Academy.

ANTHONY CLAYTON, Senior Lecturer at the Royal Military Academy, Sandhurst, was educated at the University of Paris. He then served in the Kenya Civil Service from 1952 to 1965, being appointed to Sandhurst after Kenya's independence. In 1970 he received his doctorate from St. Andrews University. He is joint author with Donald C. Savage of *Government and Labour in Kenya 1895–1963* (1975), and author of *The Zanzibar Revolution and Its Aftermath* (1981), *Counter-Insurgency in Kenya 1952–56* (1984), and *The British Empire as a Superpower 1919–39* (1986). Clayton is now engaged in a study of the French colonial military system in Africa.

BARUCH A. HAZAN is a Lecturer at the Institute of European Studies, Vienna. Trained at the Hebrew University in Jerusalem and the Maxwell School of Public Affairs at Syracuse University, he concentrates on Soviet and East European governments, propaganda, subversion, and terrorism. His publications include *The Government of the USSR* (in Hebrew, 1973), *Soviet Propaganda—The Case of the Middle East* (1976), *Olympic Sports and Propaganda* (1982), *Soviet Impregnational Propaganda* (1983), *The East European Political System* (1985), and *The Kremlin—from Brezhnev to Gorbachev: Infighting in the Kremlin* (1986).

ANTHONY KIRK-GREENE, Lecturer in the Modern History of Africa and Fellow of St. Antony's College, Oxford University, is a former district officer in northern Nigeria and professor at Ahmadu Bello University in Nigeria. Trained at Cambridge, he wrote *The Principles of Native Administration in Nigeria, 1900–1947* (1965), *Crisis and Conflict in Nigeria,* 2 vols. (1971), *A Biographical Dictionary of the British Colonial Governors in Africa* (1980), and with Douglas Rimmer, *Nigeria since 1970* (1981). He also edited *The Transfer of Power in Africa: The Colonial Administrator in the Age of Decolonization* (1979), and is currently working on a history of British colonial administrators in Africa.

JOHN M. MACKENZIE is Senior Lecturer in History at the University of Lancaster. His graduate degree is from the University of British Columbia, and his publications include *Partition of Africa* (1983), *Propaganda and Empire* (1984), editor of *Imperialism and Popular Culture* (1986), and co-author of *The Railway Station: A Social History* (1986). In addition to his central focus on the economic and social history of Zimbabwe, he is interested in British imperial attitudes and propaganda. He is the general editor of the "Studies in Imperialism" series for Manchester University Press, and is currently working on late-nineteenth century Orientalism and a wider study of hunting.

J. A. MANGAN, Head of the Department of Education at Jordanhill College of Education, Glasgow, studied at the universities of Durham, Oxford, and Glasgow. He was the inaugural chairman of the British Society of Sports History, and is the founder and general executive editor of the *International*

Journal of the History of Sport (formerly the *British Journal of Sports History*). He is the author of *Athleticism in the Victorian and Edwardian Public Schools: The Emergence and Consolidation of an Educational Ideology* (1981) and *The Games Ethic and Imperialism: Aspects of the Diffusion of an Ideal* (1986); editor of *Pleasure, Profit and Proselytism: Sport and British Culture at Home and Abroad* (1987), and co-editor of *Manliness and Morality: Middle Class Muscularity in Britain and America 1800–1950* (1987), and *From Fair Sex to Feminism: Sport and the Socialization of Women in the Industrial and Post-Industrial Eras* (1986). A fellow of both the Royal Historical Society and the Royal Anthropological Institute, Mangan is now researching liberal education and the games ethic at Oxford and Cambridge in the Victorian and Edwardian eras.

ALI A. MAZRUI holds dual appointments in Political Science at the University of Jos, Nigeria, and the University of Michigan. Having served on the editorial boards of fifteen international journals, in 1979 he delivered the Reith Lectures for the BBC on "The African Condition," which appeared in book form as *The African Condition: A Political Diagnosis* (1980). His other books include *Towards a Pax Africana* (1967), *Violence and Thought* (1969), *Cultural Engineering and Nation-Building* (1972), *Soldiers and Kinsmen in Uganda* (1975), *The Political Sociology of the English Language* (1975), *A World Federation of Cultures: An African Perspective* (1976), *Political Values and the Educated Class in Africa* (1978), and *Nationalism and New States in Africa* (1984). He is currently involved in the UNESCO general history of Africa.

SIGRID PAUL, Associate Professor of Cultural Science at the University of Salzburg, Austria, was trained in cultural anthropology at Uppsala, Sweden, and did research on fundamental, formal, and informal education at the University of the Saar, West Germany. She is the author of *Begegnungen: Zur Geschichte persönlicher Dokumente in Ethnologie, Soziologie und Psychologie*, 2 vols. (1979), *Afrikanische Puppen* (1970), and *Gemeindeentwicklung in Indien: Zur Kontinuität eines Problems* (1981), and the editor of *Ethnomedizin und Sozialmedizin in Tropisch-Afrika* (1975) and *Kultur, Begriff und Wort in China und Japan* (1984). Her works represent her major fields of interest in methodology, life history approaches, socialization, play and games, folktales, and ethnomedicine.

TERENCE RANGER, Professor of Modern History at the University of Manchester, received his D. Phil. from Oxford and concentrates on the history of religion, rural consciousness, colonial culture, and protest in East, Central, and southern Africa. His published work includes *Revolt in Southern Rhodesia, 1896–97* (1967, 1971, 1979), *Dance and Society in Eastern Africa* (1975), *The Invention of Tradition*, with Eric Hobsbawn (1983), and *Peasant Consciousness and Guerilla War in Zimbabwe: A Comparative Study* (1984). He is now engaged in a comparative study of Matabeleland and the Makoni district in Manicaland during the colonial period.

THOMAS Q. REEFE is the Director of Career Services at the University of California at Santa Cruz, and was formerly Associate Professor of African History at the University of North Carolina at Chapel Hill. Educated at Middlebury College and the University of California at Berkeley, he has taught as a Fulbright Scholar at the University of Yaoundé, Cameroon. In addition to numerous articles on precolonial and colonial Central Africa and on various methodological and pedagogical aspects of African history, he is the author of *The Rainbow and the Kings: A History of the Luba Empire to 1891* (1981).

SPORT IN AFRICA

PART ONE

INDIGENOUS TRADITIONS

1

Games and Sport in Pre-Colonial African Societies

JOHN BLACKING

This chapter is concerned with games and sportlike activities in precolonial Africa. Many of these activities are still practiced, especially in rural areas, and their existence provides a challenge to contemporary uses and abuses of sport and to arguments about its function in modern industrial societies. Physical activities that have been variously described by ethnographers as "play," "games," "sports," "pastimes," "physical education," "recreations," and "dances" were generally classed together as extensions of human aesthetic and ludic capabilities, and integrated into social life and the continuing education of all members of a community—not only as reflections and reinforcements of cultural tradition, but also as means of enhancing people's creativity and adaptation to changing circumstances.

There are three sections: in the first I ask to what extent "sport" is a transformation of human institutions that are probably as old as human society and as fundamental to its existence as kinship and economic organization. This view was implicitly held by some writers on African physical activities, and especially by Geoffrey Gorer. The second section contains a brief survey of some of the references to games and sports in sub-Saharan Africa. The third section explores some common patterns in the available evidence. I suggest that precolonial African models of games and sport treat them as forms of play in ways that may help us to understand better the nature of modern sport and to appreciate the creative "open-mindedness" of true play as a series of techniques of the body.

The general distinctions between the concepts of "play," "games," and "sport," which have been summarized by Harris and Park,[1] have been adopted as a rough guide to uses of the words in this chapter. But many of the authors quoted use them in different ways.

Is "Sport" a Transformation of Ancient Human Institutions or a Modern Invention?

During the half-century from 1933 to 1983, there was a massive increase in the quantity and sophistication of social anthropological fieldwork carried out in sub-Saharan Africa. Unfortunately, there was a corresponding decrease in the attention that fieldworkers gave to play, games, sport, dance, music, and the arts. Whereas most early monographs contained brief descriptions and illustrations of such activities, recent works have rarely carried more than a few passing comments in the text and perhaps one or two entries in the index.

This does not reflect the interests of the members of the societies studied, for whom these activities have always been sources of emotional satisfaction and signs of the distinctiveness, creativity, and imagination of their cultures. It reflects rather the professional and material interests of the fieldworkers. Religion and kinship were traditional and highly respectable areas of theoretical discourse for social anthropologists; political and economic organization and problems of development assumed importance later and were reflections of the colonial and postcolonial interests in sub-Saharan Africa of governments, political parties, and commercial enterprises, on whose patronage the provision of research grants depended directly or indirectly. The few scholars who turned their attention to dance, music, games, and what most of their colleagues regarded as marginal areas of anthropological interest in sub-Saharan Africa soon found that these areas were not considered marginal either by the members of African societies or by the national governments and educationists who have assumed responsibility for their future development.

The study of "sport" in traditional African societies therefore poses two major problems: first, there is a critical lack of information about what might be described as "play, games, and sport"; and second, there must be considerable debate as to whether any activity in traditional African societies corresponded to what is now understood by the Western concept and practice of sport. The lack of information will no doubt be rectified by African scholars, who can collect oral testimony about the past as well as describe current practice of what Coakley has defined as "spontaneous play" and "informal games."[2] Perhaps some anthropologists from Europe and North America could also assemble hitherto unpublished field data on these topics. The second problem is fundamental to any anthropological discussion of sport and is the theme of this chapter. It has practical implications as well as being theoretically interesting.

Africa provides particular cases that relate to the general problem: is sport a transformation of institutions and patterns of action that existed in most, if not all, societies of horticulturalists and hunter-gatherers? Or is it a comparatively modern invention that arose in response to social and cultural changes in feudal, capitalist, and industrial societies? Unless we accept Joseph Mazo's somewhat idiosyncratic definition of dance as a contact sport,[3] there were very few activities that could be described in terms of modern concepts of sport. Moreover, even though traditional wrestling seems to have its modern counterparts, we cannot assume that because of similarities of product there are continuities of meaning and significance. We cannot, for example, automatically define Nuba wrestling in the same way as Olympic wrestling as part of a group of activities called "sport" because the contexts and processes involved are very different.

On the other hand, certain types of experiences and the subjective meanings assigned to those experiences, as well as certain general patterns of physical movement and interaction, are not necessarily limited to the contexts and practice of modern sport. They could well be found through other activities in societies that, strictly speaking, had no sport, just as people in societies with sport make sense of it in many different ways. Although there are clearly significant contrasts between the structures of tennis, boxing, running, football (soccer), and gymnastics that must influence the experiences of their practitioners, there is also evidence that people share attitudes to sport and interpretations of their experiences that are not restricted to any particular sport or group of activities. They may even "vacillate in and out of" say, "a state of playfulness during the course of almost any activity,"[4] as within a single game of football.

I am not convinced that sport is a novel human phenomenon, and I suggest that many processes of practicing and making sense of sport had their analogues in traditional African societies. If my guess is right, then there ought to be two interesting consequences for contemporary societies. First, analyses of the equivalents of sport in traditional African contexts might enable us to arrive at more flexible evaluations of sport in general, as well as particular sports, in industrial societies. And second, if some sport-like activities were more characteristic of certain cultural configurations rather than others, it may be better for African nations to invest in sports that are more appropriate for their development and in which their citizens are most likely to succeed and find satisfaction, than to succumb to the pressures and fashions of the Euro-American–dominated sports world.

Sport and excellence in sport are social facts, and the bodies of people when they first engage in sport are not infinitely plastic. They have been molded by motives, habits of posture and gesture, and patterns of movement that are as much a product of enculturation as of individual variation. We should be asking what cultural factors could have influenced the performances of Olympic athletes like Abebe Bikila, Kip Keino, and Ben Jipcho. We should be asking what kinds of modern team games might be the best equivalent of a dance that fulfilled a vital role in the past. Perhaps some kinds of sport might be positively harmful in certain contexts and innocuous in others. R. G. Sipes's study[5] of correlations between war and combative sports was a timely reminder that sport can never be neutral or apolitical, as some people imagine. Sipes argued that war and combative sports were not alternative discharge responses to accumulated aggression, but rather complementary institutions that were part of a general culture pattern. The two institutions were in a proportionate, and not an inverse, relationship: in societies in which war and violence were present, there was also combative sport; but where war was relatively rare, combative sports tended to be absent. In other words, aggression was institutionalized in some societies, but not others, as a component of a cultural pattern, and combative sports were not a "healthy" guarantee of peaceful behavior.

One has to go back to 1921, to Basden's study *Among the Ibos of Nigeria,* to find a chapter entitled "Sports and Pastimes." George Basden was a committed British missionary, and although some of his remarks are patronizing, his respect for the Ibo encouraged him to make a thorough study of their traditional life. The opening paragraphs reveal his concept of sport:

> Ordinarily the Ibo is a very serious person. At the same time he has a well-developed humorous side to his nature and he can, on occasion, give play to his emotions with complete abandon, so much so that he becomes totally oblivious of things around him.
>
> The games commonly played by boys and girls have been described in Chap. V [turning somersaults in the air, shooting with bows and arrows, wrestling and dancing]. In the case of adults it is not always easy to distinguish between recreation and serious occupation; sometimes the two are combined, as in shooting. In the case of dancing it is often difficult to differentiate between that which is simply recreative and that which is the physical expression of religious enthusiasm. Shooting, wrestling, dancing and swimming are the sports of men; comparatively few of the women swim, but all indulge freely in dancing. The national game of Okwe is common to both sexes.[6]

Basden went on to describe archery competitions, wrestling contests, dancing, swimming, and the *Okwe* board game, which is widely known as *mancala* and found in many different forms in sub-Saharan Africa. In Igbo it was often played for high stakes, so that some people accumulated large debts. Wrestling was practiced by boys and unmarried men, and Basden was distressed at the lack of "sporting instinct,"[7] because athletes preferred to retire rather than lose. He comments on their dancing:

> The twistings, turnings, contortions and springing movements, executed in perfect time, are wonderful to behold. Movement succeeds movement in rapid succession, speed and force increasing, until the grand finale is reached. . . . For these set dances . . . the physical strength required is tremendous. The body movements are extremely difficult and would probably kill a European. The whole anatomy of the performer appears to be in serious danger, and it is a marvel that his internal machinery is not completely thrown out of gear. The practice of such dancing leads to a wonderful development of the back and abdominal muscles. Moreover the movements are free, there is nothing rigid about them, and they produce

no sign of "physical exerciser" stiffness. Every movement is clean, sure and decided, showing absolute control of the muscles.[8]

This kind of dancing, often performed by professionals, was very different from the dancing connected with religious festivities, in which women played a leading part. That consisted of "strange sinuous movements of the limbs and body," which Basden thought superior to contemporary dancing in England and America. He also observed an important feature of African dancing that was frequently ignored by later writers: "in all native dances each man (and woman) acts independently of his fellows and yet fits into his proper place in the general scheme."[9] The importance of individuality and creative originality in African societies is too often overlooked by those who emphasize the formal and corporate elements of their traditional life. It was, and still is, in dancing that people were able to combine most successfully the education and integration of mind, body, emotion, and sensitivity, and the development of social consciousness and self-actualization.

Traditional African performing arts were equated with modern physical education in a study by an American mission worker, Gladwyn Murray Childs. He wrote an account of Umbundu kinship and character in Angola in the 1930s, whose point of view he described as "a composite of practical anthropology, progressive education, and the newer approach to Christian missions." [10] He concluded that "the dance is of great importance to Umbundu life: social, educational, and ceremonial,"[11] and in commenting on what he described as "physical education and recreation" he wrote:

> The dance is very good physical exercise but it is much more than that. It is more than mere [*sic!*] recreation. . . . There is nothing which can take its place. It is doubtful whether the solidarity of any group of Ovimbundu can be firmly established or long maintained without the dance. They do adopt various foreign forms of recreation, but the dance meets a deeper need. Whatever new exercises and games may be introduced the physical educator cannot afford to neglect indigenous forms.[12]

Writing of his travels in West Africa in 1934, Geoffrey Gorer described amateur wrestling as "by far the most popular, indeed almost the only West African sport,"[13] and he deplored the introduction of compulsory organized games and sports as a puritanical substitute for dancing.[14] His book, originally published in 1935, contained the first descriptions of many African dances, but it was not until the 1950s that researchers began to make systematic studies and recordings, in West Africa and other parts of the continent.

Most writers have implicitly or explicitly agreed with Basden, Childs, Gorer, and earlier ethnographers that modern African sports are a substitute for ceremonial and recreational dancing, and that many modern games are extensions or elaborations of traditional games and activities. Since these changes are largely the result of colonial systems of education and of subsequent experience of the hegemony of European and North American cultural styles in international politics, they can hardly be described as transformations. That is, a modern African society's prowess in international sport may have little or no direct connection with its traditional concern for dancing. On the other hand, the possibility that much sport is a transformation of dancing is of great theoretical interest and of particular relevance to educational development in African societies. Could there be a connection between the dance styles of the Teso of Uganda and the fact that "the Uganda record for the high jump has been held for several years by Iteso and an Etesot gained second place for Uganda in the high jump at the Empire Games in Vancouver in 1954?"[15]

Play, Games, and Sports in Sub-Saharan Africa

Some of the earliest ethnographic accounts of southern African games were included in Dudley Kidd's *The Essential Kaffir* in 1904 and *Savage Childhood: A Study of Kaffir Children* in 1906, and George Stow's *The Native Races of South Africa* in 1905. The first two covered a variety of Bantu-speaking peoples in the southeast from the Cape to the Zambezi, and the latter was concerned with the so-called Bushmen and Hottentots as well as Nguni and Sotho-Tswana societies. As in most subsequent accounts, the descriptions of games are not as detailed as one could wish, and there is little indication of the extent to which recruitment and social organization were spontaneous and informal or influenced by the players' membership of other social groups.

Stow described two types of ball game of the San but classified them as "dances":

> Some of their dances required considerable skill, such as that which may be called the ball dance. In this a number of women from five to ten would form a line and face an equal number in another row, leaving a space of thirty or forty feet between them. A woman at the end of one of these lines would commence by throwing a round ball, about the size of an orange, and made of a root, under her right leg, and across to the woman opposite to her, who in turn would catch the ball and throw it back in a similar manner to the second woman in the first row; she would return it again in the same way to the second in the second, and thus it continued until all had taken their turn. Then the women would shift their positions, crossing over to opposite sides, and again continue in the same manner as before; and so on until the game was over, when they would rest for a short time and begin again.
>
> Another ball dance was played merely by the men. A ball was made expressly for this game out of the thickest portion of a hippopotamus' hide,

cut from the back of the neck; this was hammered when it was perfectly fresh until it was quite round; when finished it was elastic, and would quickly rebound when thrown upon a hard surface. In this performance a flat stone was placed in the centre upon the ground, the players or dancers standing around. One of them commenced by throwing the ball on the stone, when it rebounded; the next to him caught it, and immediately it was thrown again by him upon the stone in the same manner as by the leader, when it was caught by the next in succession, and so on, one after the other passing rapidly round the ring, until the leader or one of the others would throw it with such force as to send it flying high and straight up into the air, when during its ascent they commenced a series of antics, throwing themselves into all kinds of positions, imitating wild dogs, and like them making a noise "che! che! che!" but in the meantime watching the ball, which was caught by one of them, when he took the place of leader, and the game was again renewed.

The play was sometimes varied by two players being matched against each other, each throwing and catching the ball alternately, until one of them missed it, when it was immediately caught by one of those in the outer ring, who at once took the place of the one who had made the slip, and thus the play continued.[16]

Henri Junod described boys', girls', and adult games of the Shangana-Tsonga of Mozambique in 1912.[17] He included as adult games the pastimes of beer drinking, hemp smoking, and the Tsonga version of the *mancala* game, *tshuba*. Hemp smoking was not as common as beer drinking, and it was accompanied by a saliva-squirting contest, whose rules Junod described.[18] He attributed the craze for playing *tshuba* to the enforced decline of the 'great sports' of fighting and hunting, which had absorbed the Tsonga in earlier times.[19]

Forty years later, when writing of the southern Sotho in the 1930s, Hugh Ashton declared that fighting and cattle raiding had been "their major sports."[20] Stick fighting was as important among the Red Xhosa in the 1950s[21] as it was for the Mpondo in the 1930s. Monica Hunter described it as follows:

Fighting with sticks is as constant an occupation of the Mpondo as is playing with a ball of the English. I have seen a mother playing with her son of 2 or 3, pretending to hit him so that he put up one arm for defence and tried to hit back; boys of 4 and 5 have their knobkerries, and begin to scrap. When out herding the elder boys arrange contests, pairing off couples and forcing them to fight; the combats between individuals are constant; the boys of one umzi [homestead] fight those of another, the herds of one set of imizi, the herds of another, one district another. Often two neighbouring districts are in such a state of war, that if a boy from one enters the other he is immediately "attacked." The borderline between a game and a serious fight between districts, in which several may be killed, is undefined.[22]

Professor Hunter's implied comparison of Mpondo and English sporting activities is rather unfair on the Mpondo, as it suggests that violence was more endemic in their society. In fact, stick fighting as a combative sport was not as lethal and damaging to the body as boxing, or as punishing as ice hockey and American football, or indeed as many other accepted Euro-American sports that do violence to the body. It is perhaps significant that, with the notable exception of dancing, most of the traditional African activities that have been described as sport or might qualify as such according to modern definitions, were aggressive and combative and often associated with warfare. Moreover, their distribution in sub-Saharan Africa was uneven, unlike that of many games that were played almost everywhere. In other words, sport was no more a mere pastime than it is in contemporary industrial societies. It was psychologically and sociologically related to the exercise and maintenance of power and to the enculturation and social control of young people. If a comparative study of traditional African sport were undertaken, its incidence in different societies would almost certainly be seen to vary proportionately with the incidence of certain modes of political and economic organization and patterns of intergroup relations.[23] On the other hand, I would expect that dancing, for reasons I shall discuss later, would follow significantly different patterns.

Ashton mentioned the peaceful Sotho sport of racing, whose distribution in other parts of Africa is limited by environment and the availability of animals. Lindblom had reported in 1931 that oxen were widely used in Africa as riding animals,[24] and it was common for herdboys to ride and sometimes race their animals home. In the mountains of Lesotho, riding was the major means of transport, and few people rode "for pleasure, except at race meetings. Racing is an old sport. Formerly special oxen were raced over arduous courses of many miles, but they have now been replaced by horses."[25] Tobogganing was another sport of limited distribution, which I have seen only in Karamoja, Uganda, where youths sat perched on stones and set off down the side of suitably smooth hills of bare rock. O. F. Raum reported that Shira children used "the hard fruits of the *Kigelia* tree, which are the shape of a large cucumber. The boys cut seats into them" and rode "down steep grass-covered slopes."[26]

The comparatively limited practice of racing and tobogganing contrasts with the widespread distribution of the rolling target (hoop-and-pole) game[27] and the *mancala* game, both of which have already been cited. Junod gave a detailed description of the rules and course of the Tsonga version of the game,[28] and his example was followed by Smith and Dale for the *chisolo* of the Ila of northern Zambia,[29] by Stayt for the *mufuvha* of the Venda,[30] and by others. The themes of the *mancala* game varied but the style and characteristics of the different versions were broadly the same.

Not all games that were structurally similar, however, were given even remotely similar meanings and uses. For example, the curious movements that Dorothy Bleek described for the Great Water Snake game of the Naron of the central Kalahari[31] were the same as those that all Venda novices had to perform during their premarital *domba* initiation. But in the latter the movements were accompanied by a song about the labors of the dung beetle and the rite was designed to warn the girls of the pains of childbirth.[32] In 1958, I observed another distinctive dance movement for novices at the Venda girls' puberty rites, with a song referring to religious worship.[33] The same movements were observed among the Ila of Zambia between 1902 and 1915, as a boys' game imitating a battle fought on marshy ground. Boys formed up in two lines, kneeling on one knee, and advanced, changing from one knee to the other and clapping hands.[34] Even within the same Venda society, standing on one's head had different meanings as a boy's singing game and a girl's initiation dance.[35] I hope that those who are involved in the revival of interest in the anthropological study of play and games will not neglect to consider the diffusion of African games and structured movement or the transformations of meaning that have been assigned to them. Such information can be valuable both because of the light it can throw on the analysis of play and ritual in contrasting cultural systems, and because of what it may contribute to historical studies of different African groups.

A great opportunity was missed in the ethnographic survey of Africa sponsored by the International African Institute in the 1950s and 1960s. Very few of the volumes contain any references to play, games, dances, or the affective, aesthetic, and imaginative aspects of African life, let alone accounts of what forms they took. And yet, when one scans the information that is available, it becomes clear that the differences in the forms and meanings of the repertoires of games, sports, and dances in particular societies are more interesting than the recurrence of certain games to which many writers have drawn attention. I agree very much with the general argument of Helen Schwartzman that we need to look at the imaginative, creative, and transformative aspects of children's play and use of games, and I have been convinced at least by my own children and others whom I have known well that they are active participators and manipulators, rather than passive receptors, almost from birth. Schwartzman's conclusion is persuasive:

> Play is an activity that is very much alive and characterized always by *transformation* and not preservation of objects, roles, actions, and so forth. By emphasizing the preservative quality of play texts, researchers have ignored the transformative quality of play contexts. And, similarly, by

emphasizing the socialization function of play contexts, researchers have ignored the satirical, critical, and interpretative qualities of play texts.[36]

Nevertheless, the congeniality of the social and cultural environments in which children can exercise their creativity varies greatly, and the frameworks of games, sports, and discourse through which play can be channeled can impose limits on transformation. Thus variations in repertoire suggest significant contrasts in the patterns of cultures as well as the more obvious consequences of different environments.

Not surprisingly, the Reverend John Weeks found in 1909 that the Boloki of the Upper Congo River had three water games,[37] and in 1958 Burssens added that they had canoe races,[38] in addition to children's games that are found all over Africa. For them, wrestling was more of a ritual than a sport, and it was accompanied by dances, music, songs, and magical acts.[39] They also played a gambling game, "a sort of hopscotch," and often became so involved that they wagered tools and even wives. For the Wolof of Senegambia, wrestling was the favorite sport,[40] with intervillage competitions during the period from harvest in October to the trade season in December and January. But when Gerhard Lindblom worked among the Akamba south of Mount Kenya from 1910 to 1912, he found no wrestling and no games of chance, and gambling was rare. In fact, he stated that "no real sport" existed, though there were many dances, games, and pastimes, such as spearing the hoop, and various thought-reading games, walking on the hands, standing on the head, and the Kamba version of *mancala*.[41] Jean La Fontaine found no riddles or riddle games among the Gisu,[42] which was most unusual, and Walter Goldschmidt found no games of chance and no games of skill except jackstones among the Sebei,[43] who live to the east of the Gisu on the slopes of Mount Elgon. He provided illustrations of childhood play but reported that contests formerly associated with boys' seclusion after circumcision—throwing spears, throwing clubs, and wrestling—had gone.

Games and Sport As Play: African Challenges to Conventional Wisdom

A cursory survey of forms of play, games, and sport in Africa reveals many common patterns of *behavior,* which at first invite easy comparison and generalizations. For example, the informal play of children was often sex-specific and modeled on the activities of adults: girls pounded earth, cooked mud, or formed "families" for the distribution of wild fruits that they had collected; and boys shot beetles with miniature bows and arrows, made model houses with discarded maize cobs,[44] built miniature cattle kraals, and exchanged "cattle." Children's counting games and songs, games of touch, and varieties of five-stones or jacks seem to have been as widespread as different types of riddle contests and of the game of throwing "spears" at moving objects—whether they were the rolling hoops of the Karomojong or the tubers of the Venda.[45] Relay songs and dances were a common pastime, especially on moonlit nights, and the common call-response (solo-chorus) structure of much African music allowed players to succeed each other in taking over the solo parts.[46] Youths exhibited and challenged others' individual skills and physical prowess in the *mancala* game, and in different types of boxing and stick fighting. Teams of dancers, representing ethnic groups, chiefdoms, neighborhoods, or voluntary associations, rehearsed and performed for the benefit of their own group or in friendly competition with others.[47]

As soon as one begins to inquire into the meaning of such activities and their significance as action to the people involved, then a different picture emerges. As I suggested in the last section, the meanings, uses, and functions of apparently similar types of play and games vary considerably according to the attitudes and statuses of individuals and contexts of different institutions and sociocultural systems, and it would be wrong at this stage to make any generalizations about play, games, and sport in sub-Saharan Africa on the basis of available ethnography. For example, children's games are sometimes said to "establish social control" by "reinforcing" major themes of life in a society,[48] and it is tempting to interpret in the same way similar situations in all societies. Frank Salamone argued that children's games are generally "mechanisms for socialization" whose forms can be expected to "reflect underlying cultural patterns."[49] But this does not mean that in all societies and social situations there are necessarily causal relationships between the forms of games, their reinforcement of major themes, and their effectiveness in establishing social control. Nor does it mean that there must always be a distinction between games and the real world beyond games.

For example, in traditional Venda society, children's life was considered to be part of the real world, and they could be present at adult activities as often as they wished. Play and games were as much an appropriate and integral part of children's life as were singing, dancing, and beer drinking. Although some games were used for political purposes (see the description of *bepha* below), and they were always vehicles for social interaction and identity maintenance, they were not expected to reinforce values or establish social control. In any case, although they were available for use by all, there was no sense of compulsion, or even fear of social sanctions, that drove all to join in. Some people enjoyed riddle contests, while others were not particularly interested: knowing riddles was not regarded as a key to knowledge and understanding, but as a game that could bring a good player some recognition.[50] The word for "game" or "play," *mutambo*, could have different significance according to context. If I asked children or adults about the meaning and uses of some children's games, my question was usually treated with some amusement and amazement: *"Athi divhi. Ndi mutambo fhedzi!"* [I don't know. It's only a game!] A rather different attitude was taken to similar questions about the boys' and girls' team dances *tshikanganga* and *tshigombela,* which were also called "games" (*mitambo*). And the games of the *domba* initiation school were taken seriously as an essential part of the education of every young Venda.

These attitudes were only partly reflected in Venda classifications and terminology, and the intended meanings of the verb *tamba* (to play) and its derivatives depended on the context referred to and often the status of the speaker as well. This should not surprise anyone who has considered the extraordinary variety of interpretations of the concept of sport in almost any symposium on the subject,[51] and so I make no apology for failing to take a stand and declare what I mean by sport. As a result of my experiences as an enthusiastic participant in sports and gymnastics at school and in the army, and of subsequent irritation as an observer of the uses and abuses of sport and sportsmen, sportswomen and children, I am unable to arrive at an anthropological definition of sport that is not severely limited by the bias of my cultural experience and acquired prejudices. Marie Hart and some other authors whom she included in *Sport in the Sociocultural Process,* such as the late Allan Tindall, were quite right to stress the need to study the categories and meanings of those involved in sport.[52] But this enterprise is from the start complicated by the fact that the very phenomenon they wish to interpret in a variety of contexts is defined in their own terms. This is methodologically acceptable as long as *sport* is treated as a gloss word that covers a variety of activities that may appear similar or be given the same name, or if the researcher is simply concerned to examine the contexts and distribution of activities that fit precisely his/her definition of sport. But it is unacceptable and unhelpful if the concept of sport is treated as un-problematic, and it is assumed that we know what we mean by sport, and therefore only have to look at this phenomenon in a variety of contexts in order to understand better its range of uses and significance.

I suggest emphatically that although we may have very clear ideas about the significance of what we choose to call sport in particular contexts, we do not yet know what sport is as a human phenomenon. For example, sport has been compared with ritual, and it has been asked to what extent games, athletic contests, sports, and dramas are secular rituals. The anthropologists Mary and Max Gluckman responded to this:

> After wavering toward thinking they might profitably be so considered, we have decided that they do have similarities with rituals, but have also elements which are so very different, that it is wiser to keep them distinct. . . . This statement does not deny that on occasions games or masquerades formed parts of ritual ceremonies; nor does it deny that ceremonies of one kind or another can be attached to the playing of games

or the staging of dramas. It does deny that all—perhaps most—games and dramas can be so regarded, without putting them out of context and distorting the means by which they exhibit moral values.[53]

Similarly, we cannot accept the suggestion that sport is, or should be, a transformation of the dancing of traditional societies, as was implied by the comments of Basden, Childs, Gorer, and others who provided ethnographies of what they called variously "play," "games," "sports," "pastimes," "physical education," and "dances." The very reasons that the Gluckmans gave for distinguishing games and athletic contests from ritual must also be applied to distinctions between different kinds of dances: there were dances whose progress, like the main activities of ritual, was "always known in advance, and conformity to rule and tradition" was "important,"[54] and there were dances that were like games and athletic contests, because the actors had "a series of choices open to them."[55] Dances could therefore be play, games, sport, and/or physical and moral education, depending on context, use, and user.

In some African societies, distinctions between different styles and purposes of "dance" movements were expressed with special terminology. In Venda, for instance, there was a general verb *tshina* that referred to all kinds of dancing, but particularly to the characteristic communal dancing in a circle (*-mona*), which was alternated with display dancing (*-gaya*) by solo dancers or by groups of two, three, or four together. Men's and boys' communal dancing differed in style from that of women and girls; but although everybody recognized this, both styles were called *-tshina*. Old ladies danced in a stately way (*-tanga*) on important occasions, or sometimes they and older men danced excitedly for joy (*-pembela*). The characteristic movements of girls' initiation (*vhusha*), which might be compared to gymnastic routines, were called *-thaga*.[56]

Venda communal dances were classified as either *mutambo* (game, from *-tamba*, to play) or *ngoma* (literally large bass drum, hence sacred). The latter included the most important dance *tshikona*, the main initiation dances of *vhusha* and *domba*, and the "possession" dance *ngoma dza midzimu*. A further distinction was made between "the song of *vhusha*" and "the song of *domba*," which referred to the central choral dance of each initiation, which were repeated several times daily for the duration of the schools, and the different *ngoma* rites and accompanying songs and movements, which all novices had to perform at least once to qualify as graduates. There were other songs and dances at *domba*, performed in a lighter vein in contrast to the sacred choral dance, and these were described as "game songs" (*nyimbo dza mitambo*). Although they were sometimes arrangements of the games of childhood such as dance songs of the class *dzhombo*, their meaning in the context of initiation was much more serious.

The other Venda games of childhood and youth, the dances *tshikanganga* and *tshigombela,* also became serious affairs because of their use for the networks of *mabepha* (musical expeditions) that chiefs and prominent headmen sent to each other, to express sympathy after a death, to greet or visit a newly established ruler, to ask for tribute, and to greet humbly or pay homage.[57] In 1962, I compared the musical expeditions that I had observed in Venda to the school rugby matches that I had experienced in England, and I think the comparison remains valid, although the political significance of the Venda institution was clearly greater:

> *Bepha* has a variety of meanings according to the status of the individual. For members of the team it is entertainment of the same order as preparing for, and participating in, an away-match to another school, without the anxiety of being dropped from the team [all who were prepared to attend rehearsals and improve their performance were allowed to serve in the team]. . . . The journey to another district is important not so much for the extension of young people's geographical knowledge, nor for the association with strangers, as for the consolidation of existing relationships based on locality rather than kinship. . . . From my own similar experiences of away matches at school, I remember how the journey gave us an excellent opportunity of cementing friendships, especially when we came from different Houses, and how we had an impression of an association of Headmasters and senior staff, whose solidarity was expressed in the friendly rivalry between a group of schools. . . .
>
> *Bepha* is, therefore, an agreeable means by which a ruler can cultivate indirectly the continued loyalty of his people and remind them of his position. . . .
>
> Above the entertainment and prestige value and the consolidation of district loyalties, are the links which *bepha* expeditions reinforce between the widely scattered members of ruling clans . . . their chief political function is to consolidate both locally recruited groups and the widely dispersed, and predominantly consanguineous, families who rule those groups.[58]

Several kinds of behavior and action that would seem to come under the general rubric of sport in modern industrial societies were present in traditional Venda society. But I cannot say whether or not they could be accurately described as analogues of sport, and whether or not the essential characteristics of modern sport were present in traditional Venda and other African societies. My own impression is that, apart from some games and the more obvious activities such as wrestling, certain nonritual aspects of dancing will provide the most likely sources for useful analogies with sport. Studies of dance from different parts of Africa seem to corroborate this, as well as observations such as those of the Bohannans about the role of dancing and its relationship to work in the context of Tiv markets,[59] and of M. d'Hertefelt about the Rwanda use of dance as an appropriate sport for conduct in warfare. During their military training, the young men learned war dances in which new figures were continually being created. Their purpose was to portray the changing fortunes and uncertain outcome of battle and final victory.[60] I am reminded of the role of golf in modern business, and again of my own school experiences, where the purposes of sport and officer cadet training were often hard to disentangle, and the military instructor and games coach were often one and the same person!

It is not too late to find out more about the concepts and uses of games and sport in traditional African societies, although much of the research must inevitably be historical rather than sociological. It is not too late to learn from African societies something about the origins and essence of modern sport, and perhaps as a result to understand contemporary trends in such a way that the abuses of sport may be diminished and its positive social, educational, and emotional benefits be increased.

Above all, the kind of study that is required must investigate play, games, and sportlike activities as parts of the shared conceptual system of interacting individuals and social groups. A fine example of how this can be done has been provided by Dr. Charles Adams, who investigated concepts of play and games in Lesotho and the ways in which these concepts were realized in practice.[61]

Dr. Adams pointed out that many of the analytic distinctions contained in models that are widely used in discussions of play, ritual, and expressive behavior "frequently reflect more our own concerns, our own social and intellectual histories, than they do the phenomena which are their purported objects of analysis."[62] The Basotho domain of *games,* however,

> includes ways of behaving that are expressive, performative, dramatic, and processual. *Games* and *playing* refer to behaviour and aspects of behaviour that are not only "play" and "ritual," but "art" as in playing music and dancing, and "science" in the sense of procedures for knowing and understanding, experimentation and learning, hypothesizing and testing. The graphic and plastic arts, such as architecture, pottery design, and painting, as well as technological crafts, such as carpentry and making toys and models, are excluded from the domain of *games. Playing* ranges from the simple spontaneous activities of telling jokes and riddles to the rehearsed, proscribed, rule-governed events of the nine-months process of men's initiation and inter-village dancing competitions."[63]

Playing and *games* were not categorically differentiated activities. Hopscotch, soccer, competitive dancing, and playing poker belonged to the domain of *games,* or things that were *played,* as much as judicial hearings, herding cattle, curing the psychosocial effects of witchcraft, and gift exchanges. "The concept of *game* contains . . . the notion of 'making things parallel or commensurate,' and *games* are applications of, or ways of creating, comparisons, similitudes, identities, analogies, and metaphors."[64]

The Sotho concept of *games* as described by Adams differed in several respects from the Venda concept and uses that I observed. Nevertheless, Adams's main conclusion could be applied to the Venda data and, I suspect, to data from many other African societies: "The most challenging issue raised by the Basotho model is that concerning the integration of artistic, ludic, scientific, and ritualistic performative activity and domains."[65]

This is also a challenge to the aims and purposes of modern sport, which the Sotho and the Venda have now incorporated into their traditional category of games. It recalls the observation of Gregory Bateson that "the evolution of play may have been an important step in the evolution of communication,"[66] namely, the ability to recognize that a signal is a signal and not necessarily a mood. Play combat is not real combat, just as the "pseudo-love and pseudo-hate of therapy are not real love and hate."[67] The paradoxes of play allow for creative changes in people's habits of communication, which are essential in psychotherapy and generally desirable in social life. Sport has the potential to be socially therapeutic and to enhance creativity, but only when it really is play and is not merely a reflection or reinforcement of the status quo, as Sipes argued in his analysis of combative sports and aggression. The traditional Sotho and Venda concepts coincide with the arguments of Bateson. Together with similar evidence from other African societies, they suggest that a more integrated concept of games and sport as techniques of the body and as extensions of aesthetic and ludic capabilities[68] may help us both to understand better the nature of modern sport and to turn it to more creative social uses.

Notes

1. Harris and Park, 2–3.
2. Coakley, passim.
3. Mazo, passim.
4. Harris and Park, 3.
5. Sipes, passim.
6. Basden, 127.
7. Ibid., 129.
8. Ibid., 132.
9. Ibid., 133.
10. Childs, viii.
11. Ibid., 114.
12. Ibid., 144.
13. Gorer, 48.
14. Ibid., 176.
15. Lawrence, 106.
16. Stow, 113–14.
17. Junod, I, 66–70, 172–76, and 340–51.
18. Ibid., 344.

19.   Ibid., 350.

20.   Ashton, 98.

21.   Mayer and Mayer, passim. Stick fighting between age sets and between clans was a favorite activity of the Murle of the Upper Nile (see Lewis, 93–94 and 121). They wore special clothing and chest protection and their performances were "stylized and highly conventional." Serious wounds were seldom inflicted.

22.   Hunter, 160. Guttman quotes a similar situation, 7: "The line between the mediaeval tournament and the mediaeval battle was not very finely drawn. At the Battle of Brémule in 1119, three men were killed; at the tournament at Neuss in 1240, sixty died."

23.   Studies that point toward this conclusion are, for example, Roberts, et al., and Roberts and Sutton-Smith.

24.   K. G. Lindblom, passim.

25.   Ashton, 98.

26.   Raum, *Chaga Childhood,* 265.

27.   Raum, "The Rolling-Target Game," passim.

28.   Junod, 345–50.

29.   Smith and Dale, II, 232–37. See also M. Sanderson.

30.   Stayt, 364–66.

31.   Bleek, 18–21.

32.   Blacking, "Songs, Dances, Mimes," 154 and plate 1D.

33.   Ibid., 27, song no. 45.

34.   Smith and Dale, II, 246.

35.   Blacking, *Venda Children's Songs,* 43–44, plate 12.

36.   Schwartzman, 328–29.

37.   Weeks, 408.

38.   Burssens, 90.

39.   Ibid.

40.   Gamble, 77.

41.   Gerhard Lindblom, 407–28.

42.   La Fontaine, 61.

43.   Goldschmidt, 264.

44.   Blacking, *Venda Children's Songs,* 20, plate 1.

45.   Ibid., 36–37.

46.   Ibid., 25, 139–54.

47.   E.g., Ranger, and Blacking, "Musical Expeditions."

48.   E.g., Salamone.

49.   Ibid., 202.

50.   Blacking, "Venda Riddles," passim.

51.   For example, Gerber, passim.

52.   See also Harris and Park, 514–15.

53.   Gluckman and Gluckman, 191–92.

54.   Ibid., 197.

55.   Ibid., 201. Cf. also Ranger, passim.

56.   Blacking, "Songs and Dances," 92; and "Venda Traditional Dances," passim.

57.   John Blacking, "Musical expeditions," 5–6.

58. Ibid., 8–9, 10.
59. Bohannan and Bohannan, 72, 146.
60. D'Hertefelt, et al., 74–75.
61. Adams, "Ethnography of Basotho Evaluative Expression," passim.
62. Adams, "Distinctive features," 1. Dr. Adams referred to analytic distinctions between "*play* and *games, ritual* and *play* (and bricolage), *symbols* and *signs, fantasy* and *reality, activity* and *passivity, routinization* and *revolution, work* and *leisure, integration* and *innovation, serious* and *non-serious, anxiety* and *boredom, structure* and *process.*"
63. Ibid., 3.
64. Ibid.
65. Ibid., 14.
66. Bateson, 316.
67. Ibid., 324.
68. Blacking, *Anthropology of the Body,* "Introduction" and "Towards an Anthropology of the Body."

Bibliography

Adams, Charles R. "Ethnography of Basotho Evaluative Expression in the Cognitive Domain *Lipapali* (Games)." Unpublished Ph.D. dissertation. Indiana University, 1974.
———. "Distinctive Features of Play and Games: A Folk Model from Southern Africa." Unpublished manuscript, 1978.
Ashton, Hugh. *The Basuto.* London: Oxford University Press for the International African Institute, 1952.
Basden, George. *Among the Ibos of Nigeria.* London: Seeley, Service and Co., 1921.
Bateson, Gregory. "A Theory of Play and Fantasy." From *Approaches to the Study of Human Personality,* pp. 39–51, Psychiatric Research Reports, no. 2, 1955.
Blacking, John. "The Social Value of Venda Riddles." *African Studies* 20 (1961): 1–32.
———. "Musical Expeditions of the Venda." *African Music* 3 (1962): 54–78.
———. *Black Background.* New York and London: Abelard Schuman, 1964.
———. *Venda Children's Songs.* Johannesburg: Witwatersrand University Press, 1967.
———. "Songs, Dances, Mimes and Symbolism of Venda Girls' Initiation Schools." *African Studies* 28 (1969): parts 1–4.
———. *The Anthropology of the Body.* ASA Monograph no. 15. London: Academic Press, 1977.
———. "An Introduction to Venda Traditional Dances." In R. Lange, ed. *Dance Studies,* vol. 2, 1977.
———. "Songs and Dances of the Venda People." In David Tunley, ed. *Music and Dance.* Papers from the Fourth National Symposium of the Musicological Society of Australia. Perth: Department of Music, UWA, 1982.
Bleek, D. F. *The Naron: A Bushman Tribe of the Central Kalahari.* Cambridge: Cambridge University Press, 1928.
Bohannan, Paul, and Laura Bohannan. *Tiv Economy.* Evanston, Ill.: Northwestern University Press, 1968.

Burssens, H. *Les peuplades de l'entre Congo-Ubangi*. Ethnographic Survey of Africa. Central Africa, Congo, part IV. International African Institute, 1958.

Caillois, R. *Man, Play, and Games*. Trans. M. Barash. New York: The Free Press, 1961.

Childs, Gladwyn Murray. *Umbundu Kinship and Character*. London: Oxford University Press for the International African Institute, 1949.

Coakley, Jay J. "Play, Games, and Sport: Developmental Implications for Young People." *Journal of Sport Behaviour* 3 (1980): 99–118.

Comhaire-Sylvain, Suzanne. Jeux Congolais. *Zaire* 6 (1952): 351–62.

D'Hertefelt, M., A. Trouwborst, and J. Scherer. *Les anciens royaumes de la zone interlacustre*. ESA, part XIV. London: International African Institute, 1962.

Doke, C. M. *The Lambas of Northern Rhodesia*. London: George G. Harrap, 1931.

Earthy, E. Dora. *Valenge Women*. London: Oxford University Press for the International African Institute, 1933.

Gamble, David. *The Wolof of Senegambia*. ESA, West Africa, part XIV. London: International African Institute, 1957.

Gerber, Ellen W., ed. *Sport and the Body: A Philosophical Symposium*. Philadelphia: Lea and Febiger, 1982.

Gluckman, Mary, and Max Gluckman. "On Drama, and Games and Athletic Contests." 1977. Reprinted in Janet C. Harris and Roberta J. Park, eds. *Play, Games and Sports in Cultural Contexts*, 1983.

Goldschmidt, Walter. *Culture and Behaviour of the Sebei*. Berkeley: University of California Press, 1976.

Gorer, Geoffrey. *Africa Dances*. Rev. ed. London: John Lehmann, 1949.

Guttman, Allen. *From Ritual to Record: The Nature of Modern Sports*. New York: Columbia University Press, 1978.

Harris, Janet C., and Roberta J. Park, eds. *Play, Games and Sports in Cultural Contexts*. Champaign, Ill.: Human Kinetics Publishers, Inc., 1983.

Hart, Marie, ed. *Sport in the Sociocultural Process*. 2d ed. Dubuque, Iowa: Wm. C. Brown, 1976.

Hunter, Monica. *Reaction to Conquest: Effects of Contact with Europeans on the Pondo of South Africa*. London: Oxford University Press, 1936.

Junod, Henri A. *The Life of a South African Tribe*. 2 vols., 1912, 1926. 2d ed. New York: University Books, 1962.

Kidd, Dudley. *The Essential Kaffir*. London: Adam and Charles Black, 1904.

———. *Savage Childhood: A Study of Kaffir Children*. London: Adam and Charles Black, 1906.

La Fontaine, Jean. *The Gisu of Uganda*. ESA, part X. London: International African Institute, 1959.

Lawrence, J. C. D. *The Iteso*. London: Oxford University Press, 1957.

Lewis, B. A. *The Murle: Red Chiefs and Black Commoners*. Oxford: Clarendon Press, 1972.

Lindblom, Gerhard. *The Akamba in British East Africa*. 2d ed. Uppsala: Appelbergs Boktryckeri Aktiebolag, 1920.

Lindblom, K. G. *The Use of Oxen as Pack and Riding Animals in Africa*. Stockholm, 1931.

Mayer, Philip, and Iona Mayer. "Socialization by Peers: The Youth Organization of the Red Xhosa." In P. Mayer, ed. *Socialization: the Approach from Social Anthropology.* Tavistock, London: ASA Monographs no. 8. 1970.

Mazo, Joseph H. *Dance Is a Contact Sport.* New York: Dutton, 1974.

Meek, C. K. *A Sudanese Kingdom: An Ethnographical Study of the Jukun-speaking Peoples of Nigeria.* London: Kegan Paul, Trench and Trubner, 1931.

Ranger, T. O. *Dance and Society in Eastern Africa 1890–1970: The Beni Ngoma.* London: Heinemann, 1975.

Raum, O. F. *Chaga Childhood: A Description of Indigenous Education in an East African Tribe.* London: Oxford University Press for the International African Institute, 1940.

———. "The Rolling-Target (Hoop and Pole) Game in Africa." *African Studies* 12 (1953): 104–21, 163–78.

Read, Margaret. *Children of Their Fathers: Growing up among the Ngoni Nyasaland.* London: Methuen, 1959.

Roberts, J. M., M. J. Arth, and R. R. Bush. "Games in Culture." *American Anthropologist* 61 (1959): 597–605.

Roberts, J. M., and B. Sutton-Smith. "Child training and game involvement." *Ethnology* 2 (1962): 166–85.

Salamone, Frank A. "Children's Games as Mechanisms for Easing Ethnic Interaction in Ethnically Heterogeneous Communities: A Nigerian Case." *Anthropos* 74 (1979): 202–10. Reprinted in Janet C. Harris and Roberta J. Park, *Play, Games and Sports.*

Sanderson, M. G. "Native Games of Central Africa." *Journal of the Royal Anthropological Institute* 43 (1913): 726–36.

Schwartzman, Helen B. *Transformations: The Anthropology of Children's Play.* New York: Plenum Press, 1978.

Sipes, R. G. "War, Sports and Aggression: An Empirical Test of Two Rival Theories." *American Anthropologist* 75 (1973): 64–85.

Smith, Edwin W., and Andrew Murray Dale. *The Ila-Speaking peoples of Northern Rhodesia.* 2 vols. London: Macmillan, 1920.

Stayt, H. A. *The Bavenda.* London: Oxford University Press, 1931.

Stow, George W. *The Native Races of South Africa.* London: Swan Sonnenschein and Co., 1905.

Weeks, John H. "Anthropological Notes on the Bangala of the Upper Congo River. Part III." *Journal of the Royal Anthropological Institute* 40 (1910): 360–427.

2

The Wrestling Tradition and Its Social Functions

SIGRID PAUL

According to innumerable reports of early travelers and missionaries, and more recently of anthropologists, sociologists, and linguists engaged in field research on traditional African cultures, precolonial Africans participated in many types of ball play, target games, top spinning, foot races, and jumping contests.[1] They also frequently and fiercely wrestled.

Generalizations about forms, functions, and ceremonial settings of wrestling, and about age, sex, and legal status of wrestlers should be made cautiously. Foreign observers have invariably approached African cultures with alien outlooks and varied interests, motives, and methods of interpretation. They have worked at different times, mostly within limited sections of societies, and with specific categories of informants. This uneven literature on precolonial wrestling must not be too readily glossed over in order to present an undifferentiated picture. Nor can games and sports activities be considered in isolation from their total sociocultural contexts. Unfortunately, however, many of the literary references to games are isolated from the social organization, the socialization process, and the local worldview of the societies being scrutinized.

Names of African ethnic groups or societies cause problems, especially for readers not well versed in African studies. Ethnonyms appear in the literature with varying connotations. Some are self-chosen; others have been given by neighbors, often with ethnocentric assumptions. Sometimes they are collective terms for a cluster of internally related groups with names of their own. To assist the nonspecialist reader, ethnonyms are used as rarely as possible in this chapter.[2]

From ancient Egypt[3] to the Canary Islands (whose population contains Berber and Negro elements),[4] wrestling was a traditional sport, but our focus will be primarily on Black Africa. Reminding the reader of the difficulty of locating ethnic groups with reference to modern political boundaries, we will proceed with a survey of the continent from the northwest down to West Africa, then into the central and Congo regions, and finally to southern and East Africa.

Along the Senegambian coast and throughout its hinterland, wrestling has long been a favorite activity for various ethnic groups. A vivid description from Guinea-Bissau/Gambia, given in 1958, contains many items that recur in reports from other parts of the continent:

> Intervillage contests among the Diola were organized annually after harvest, earlier in the year young men trained on their way to their fields. On special occasions, such as the construction of a fetish or the King's Festival at Oussonye, ritual matches took place.

> Wrestlers were mostly boys between 16 and 20. They entered the ring according to age, the youngest first. When girls wrestled, especially at royal festivals, they kept to the same rules as boys. Not infrequently a male champion got married to a female one, so that their children might surpass them in performance.

> Champions were designated representatives of their kinship or local groups. They did not compete as individuals. Before an intervillage match took place, these groups carefully prepared their champion: he was fed liberally while confined to his hut for several days. During that time he was expected to abstain from sexual intercourse. When the day arrived, the whole village approached his flower-decorated hut, and sang songs of encouragement. Next people enlarged the door using a farmer's hoe to demonstrate how much their favorite had gained in weight during seclusion. Then they led him to a large open space, where a bunch of fibres, fastened to a high pole, advertised the match to strangers. Drums had sounded from early morning; girls had dressed up; a lot of food had been prepared; elders had sacrificed to their local spirits to guarantee good luck. When the champion arrived within the ring of spectators, trumpets were sounded.

> If the wrestler deemed his opponent to be stronger than himself, he was entitled to refuse a challenge, because groups aimed at putting up well-matched contestants. In such a case elders, who had absolute authority, could even pull their representative out of the ring.

> The wrestlers started in a bent position, one knee on the ground, trying to catch hold of each other's hands. Suddenly one of them would jump up and push his head, chest or waist against the other's body, try to grab his leg, lift him up and throw him to the ground. There were many different holds, all aimed at putting the opponent flat on his back and thus scoring a point.

> Often a bout only lasted a few minutes: either one wrestler was on the ground, or the two had proved to be well matched and this sufficed for the moment. After each bout the elders, who functioned as judges, pronounced the outcome. A special announcer sounded his trumpet once for each score. The drums were moved into the center, and the victor's kinsmen danced frenetically, Young girls dried the fighter's body, shook his hand and knelt before him in encouragement for the next bout.

On return from the arena, the victor was carried through the village, accompanied by war-shouts and derisive songs addressed to the loser's party. The crowd stopped at the hut of the wrestler's betrothed who handed him a symbol of victory. The couple could only marry after the man had been decisively defeated in a match.

In order to gain a credit for their kin-group, wrestlers sometimes even took to "doping". They swallowed stimulants both before and during a match, used magic devices, and called on their protecting spirit for supernatural support. Credit was also given for an exhibition of fairness. Beating and tearing clothes during a match was forbidden. There had to be no ill-will, neither between individuals nor contending groups.[5]

In Senegal wrestling has been traditional for over three centuries. Our first reference dates back to 1689. A few weeks after Ramadan the boys were circumcised, and at the subsequent festivals the strongest boys and men were matched to wrestle in the marketplace. *Griots*—a term used in former French West Africa for professional bards, musicians, and keepers of kin-group traditions—summoned the participants. As late as the 1950s *griots* were still extant, but matches were now advertised in the newspapers. And modern wrestling fans give their favorite sportsman cash rewards instead of animals, the customary gifts of former years.[6]

European observers among traditional farmers and fishermen in this region spoke of unrestricted and brutal wrestling.[7] But those Fulani who had given up cattle raising and settled down in Senegal expected a high standard of fair play:

In the dry season boys roamed about the fields, organized into boys' societies, each with a young "president." He was the strongest among them and carried a whip to correct the rulebreakers. With due dignity he directed the contestants: 'Don't lift your opponent's feet, don't take him by treachery, don't let him fall brutally, don't lean against each other like trees . . . take each other in a fair manner! The victor will be my successor, and you will have to respect him as you respect me now!"

Toward the end of the dry season, first village and then regional champions were chosen. After the final contests leaders of all age groups or children's societies prepared a big meal, the girls rivaling the boys in the arrangement of festivities.[8]

Wrestling was also popular across the river Senegal.[9] In Guinea, among the Malinke, Soninke, and other related groups, wrestling was the national sport. Adults, boys between ten and twenty, and girls around ten years old took part. They competed with their equals from other villages on festive occasions, or chose special, ritual dates for their matches. A victor was called *chef des jeux* and had to defend this title within a week.[10]

In Liberia public wrestling between young men and occasionally women was practiced. When Mano adolescents had finished their rice harvest, they met their rivals originally at local marketplaces and later in towns, where representatives were nominated for each section of town.[11] At Niafunke in Mali, Bambara and Songhai people had great wrestling festivals. An observer in colonial times has described them thus:

> At first a boy of about twelve walked around in the arena, first slowly, then faster, jumping while running and clapping his feet in the air. He was heard shouting threats like: "To-night the other world will receive guests!" Then he chose a strong opponent among his followers, who had been lying down while he rounded the arena. . . . Stronger and older wrestlers followed after this initial match, finally even adult men, some of them already married and widely known. They came with a number of followers. In real Homeric style they even praised their men and offered to exchange them for others.

The rules of wrestling in this region are said to have been simple and the performance brutal. In some Bambara villages such as Bla in the district of Koutyala, where the eldest uncircumcised boys wrestled toward the end of the dry season, contestants used an extremely dangerous wrestling bracelet with a cutting edge.[12]

South of the Niger Bend, among the Voltaic peoples, we find the culturally close neighbors of the Bambara, the Dogon:

> In one of their regions the religious and political chief had a field of his own which was situated between two villages. After millet-harvest boys and youngsters would clear the straw from this field and sing various songs in anticipation of their coming wrestling matches.

> During the following four dry months, the boys' village societies would meet on this field by moonlight. Each would form a half-circle while their representatives met in the center. Boys who refused to take part in the preparatory work were mocked and not allowed to wrestle on the first day. A boy who refused to wrestle at all, was treated with contempt, unless his challenger had turned up with an iron bracelet, for although this bracelet had no cutting edge like the Bambara one, it could cause great pain.

> In former times boys from the whole region participated in the contest between the two villages near the chief's field, but many other contests took place, between traditionally rival villages or quarters.[13]

The consequences of being a good wrestler are well documented. Among the Lobi and Bobo, both clusters of ethnic groups in Upper Volta, boys began their training at a tender age and continued within a children's society. Since the strongest at wrestling had a chance to become group leader, legend tells of several conquerors of this region who had started on the road to success by being chiefs of such societies. These societies met by moonlight, surrounded by a host of young male and female spectators. Elders watched from a distance to prevent serious fights, which were apt to arise after particularly exciting matches. Girls were enthusiastic observers and sometimes left their boyfriends for better wrestlers.

Presumably wrestling and sexual activity were considered to be mutually exclusive even here. Among the Lobi, however, wrestling formed a part of the marriage ritual:

> During the wedding-night a bride who had been well brought up by her parents, was supposed to cry out when overcome by her husband. In the morning the bridegroom's friends summoned him to a wrestling match. His knees were carefully scrutinized. If the bride had resisted his advances, they were expected to show signs of his efforts. Sore knees were interpreted as a proof of the young man's good upbringing.
>
> If the bridegroom threw his comrades in wrestling, they pulled him down saying: We have caught you a wife . . . and now you throw us? This is not fair. The elders confirmed these reproaches. If on the other hand the bridegroom was thrown, each of his friends challenged him in order to tire him out completely.[14]

In northern Nigeria wrestling must once have been of considerable importance, but Islamization devalued sporting activities, which are closely bound up with "pagan" rituals, ancient social institutions, and the consumption of beer. Yet even among the Islamic Hausa peoples wrestling has been observed. In the past, butchers' sons arranged a contest in front of a king's or nobleman's house in the hope of being presented with a goat.[15] Wrestlers used magic charms prepared by a traditional specialist or even by an Islamic priest or both.[16] In old Hausa folktales men are said to have wrestled with spirits, even with the devil himself.[17] But, as we shall see below, some Hausa, stressing their dignity, abstain from participating in such activities or emphasize at least that to them wrestling is mere fun.[18]

Also the following evidence, from Nupe country, suggests that wrestling as a traditional social institution diminished in importance under Islam. In 1911 the famous German historian of African culture, Leo Frobenius, while residing in Mokwa, inquired about the old game of *eko-chechi*. His old Nupe friends told him that they had not practiced it since in the middle of the nineteenth century the Islamic Fulani had established themselves as rulers of the country and had smashed the *eko-chechi* drums. In nearby Bokani, however, people had preserved their drums, so they were sent for, and a grand spectacle was arranged in honor of the guest:

> People from all over Nupe country arrived. Agricultural work was interrupted. Beer was brewed, cattle slaughtered. No caravan departed as planned. Market-women withdrew to a corner of the square. Mats were spread on the ground and the dignitaries seated.
>
> But none of the wrestlers entered the arena, although drums sounded and

Nupe wrestling match. Photo taken during the German Inner African Expedition IV (1910–12). With permission of the Frobenius Institute, Frankfurt/Main. No. 5271.

the seconds challenged each other in preparation of the wrestlers' challenge. Finally the old man who had arranged the fight stirred up the young fighters, reminded them of olden days, when elders had to beat those too eager to wrestle. At last one youth threw off his clothes, fastened three times his loincloth, bowed to the drum and touched it. Then he danced and raised his fist until another wrestler had made up his mind and joined him. Each man put his left foot behind his line; their seconds, posted to their left, watched that no rule was transgressed. Upon their signals both wrestlers jumped into the space between the lines, pointed their fists at each other, jumped back, teased, mocked, incited each other, danced, mimicked. . . . Suddenly one player took hold of the other's neck, lifted him, hit him with the sole of his foot . . .

The drummers raged, the spectators cheered, the seconds jumped up and down until the holds became too tight. All at once the seconds jumped behind their protégés and pulled them away from each other. . . . More bouts followed, victors were congratulated, very small boys came forward, then adult men. Wrestling had no end until far into the night. Only the hosts abstained from it.[19]

In contrast to this highly colorful, dramatic description we find more analytical remarks about the functions of wrestling in a much later article by Salamone about the Gungawa in the Yauri Division of the Nigerian Plateau.

Although the author did fieldwork as late as 1972, his observations and interpretations are applicable to the traditional scene.[20] The Gungawa and some neighboring groups had a distinct wrestling style, he noted, while some other clusters within the same division adhered to different rules. Thus wrestling styles served as a means of group identification. Furthermore, the mere presence of wrestling activities distinguished traditional ethnic groups from Islamic Hausa, who, for reasons already mentioned, rejected them. Consequently, when a Gungawa rose to the politically and economically superior position of "Hausa," his new status prevented him from taking part in wrestling matches.

In addition to differentiating between ethnic or social groups, wrestling among the Gungawa served other functions as well. Intravillage wrestling, organized during the latter part of the rainy season, was a festive event with drumming, dancing, and beer drinking. But it was also a means of establishing internal rank order, male leadership roles, and friendship bonds as well as promoting social solidarity within the village. Utmost care was taken in such intravillage wrestling that nobody was hurt.

Inter-village wrestling, on the other hand, was a serious affair:

> Its aim was to hurt the opponent, with or without the dangerous wrestling bracelet. It was a test of manhood and thus a means of courting. Therefore religious and magic support was indispensable. Delays of matches and refusals to fight were not uncommon. Dancing was prolonged to size up the adversary. This kind of wrestling symbolized the strained, if not hostile relationship between exogamous villages and thus between men and their potential "foreign" wives. To impress a specially desired woman from the opposite village supplemented a champion's prestige. Thus both the young, potential marriage partners, and the old people arranging marriage alliances between the villages, had a stake in these matches.

In promoting intervillage contact, wrestling helped in the formation of alliances, fostered interaction among otherwise isolated Gungawa villages, and impressed upon their members that all were Gungawa. Conversely, collective contention against other villages bred group solidarity and served as an "ethnic boundary marker" within a larger unit of cultural homogeneity.[21]

Among the Mafa in the Mandara Mountains of Northern Cameroon, one of the non–Islamic ethnic groups, boys chose as their play-group leader the one excelling in wrestling.[22] In the Cameroon grassland and the adjoining Central African Republic, both men and women have been known to wrestle, for the settling of disputes, or for stakes such as cattle and money.[23]

Several writers have reported intergroup wrestling contests among the Ibo in Southeast Nigeria. Basden wrote about young boys training to represent their villages at ceremonial matches. According to Adams, men of one compound wrestled those of another, and women challenged those of a rival village at the annual festival of *Oru Owerri,* at the end of which new yams were eaten.[24] Wrestling is an ancient Ibo institution described in such etiological folktales as "The Origin of Man's Furrow-behind":

> Once upon a time, human beings and spirits were neighbours and had many things in common. One of the bonds holding them together was the annual wrestling contest held in the land of the spirits. This particular annual event was much anticipated by all concerned because each community fielded its best wrestlers. The human society sent six stout men . . . with Akpi as their leader. The special feature of this contest was that any contestant whose back touched the ground died instantly.
>
> Akpi was the one to open the competition; his opponent was a three-headed but one-legged spirit. The wrestlers appeared to be evenly matched. . . .
>
> Akpi killed the leader of the spirits and defeated the rest of them, but all his companions were killed. Akpi stole a magic horn from the spirits, restored his men to life, and they fled.
>
> Akpi was on the verge of crossing the boundary between the lands of the spirit and human beings when the spirit caught up with him and scratched his back with his claws. This accounts for man's furrow-behind or the hollow at his back.[25]

In the district of Savalou (Benin), wrestling was practiced by various ethnic groups, but of special interest is the following example:

> On the seventh day of seclusion at her first menstruation a Fon girl handed her girl-friends perfumed ashes from her hut-fire. The girls ran out and smeared this mixture on the face of anyone they met in the village. The remains were offered to the girl's betrothed, an invitation to wrestle her publicly. In the evening the two, but also their friends, met in a serious contest. If the girl in question was thrown, bystanders made coarse remarks and laughed at the boy, who caressed his fiancee's breasts to console her. But if the boy was thrown, he could be sure of male contempt and female rejoicement.[26]

Ritual wrestling between young men and women having been initiated into the first age-grade after puberty has also been reported from the Yala in southern Nigeria. But among the Iso-Edo in this region a male candidate to the initiation ceremony had to wrestle a still younger boy. Even if the latter was known to be the stronger one, he still had to feign defeat and thus symbolize his inferiority.[27]

In the Crossriver region of southern Cameroon, wrestling was a means of settling quarrels.[28] In the most important society of this region, called Ekoi, people wrestled in a ritual fashion, used drums, and appealed to their ancestors for support. Here the age classes were in charge of arranging festivals and games of various sorts.[29]

Also, east and west of the river Mungo, in the Cameroon forest, wrestling was a ceremonial institution.[30] In 1887 Buchner spoke of public intervillage matches among the Duala, with strict rules and severe judges. In 1953 Ittmann similarly observed that champions represented their villages alternately at home, or in the rival village. They had high status both within their group and beyond its boundaries.[31] Likewise, among the Kole,

> boys who had trained on the beach so that they could throw at least some of their best rivals were in high esteem within their lineages. Only they were allowed to wrestle publicly.
>
> Village champions qualified by excelling in age-group matches. Elders then sent them to inter-village events.
>
> Big matches were arranged between two parts of a village and between different sub-groups of the tribe. The latter took place on specific dates and required a lot of training. Victors in such matches were not only highly honored—more than learned persons—but also feared. Often they became insolent and "swallowed" another's possessions completely.

Here too, wrestling symbolized the rivalry between marriage groups: when a bride was taken away, the bridegroom's age group relatives fought with those of the bride.[32]

Sexual rivalry was also expressed in contests among the Fang in Gabon. Grebert observed a wrestling spectacle, in which women, men, and even small boys took part.[33] Other observers reported on ceremonial intervillage matches which included all the elements mentioned above.[34]

Among the various groups in the Congo region, wrestling contests between individuals of both sexes, age classes, and villages were common:

> During peanut-harvest Njabi men and women were summoned to form groups. In the middle of the field one after the other wrestled, a man matched to a woman. The winner was presented with two or three baskets full of peanuts. When more men than women had won, the "master of the field" announced that from now on only men were to wrestle. After this more serious contest all people returned to the village. The victors were honored by songs and a large reward of peanuts, even if they had not been very willing to take part in harvesting toils.[35]

In other places in this region adult men challenged still younger ones, and boys each other; occasionally girls of the same age fought. Before a young Ndibu was accepted into an age class, he had to wrestle during the rainy season on slippery ground. Reports on the groups occur from the nineteenth century to the 1970s.[36]

When the former mayor of Brussels, Charles Buls, made a boat trip up the river Congo in 1898, he had to stop at Stanley Falls. There the local chiefs honored him with dance festivals and a big wrestling contest.[37]

Lindeman, who made a fine study of Congolese games around this time, described *liwanda* as the most favorite sport around Lisala:

> Twice a year, at the time of inundation, villages met in contests, although in between wrestling was a common practice within the villages. The challengers, coming from another village, walked through the streets, signalizing their intention by drumming. When the two parties had lined up opposite to each other, judges in the centre, they started by singing and matching contestants so they might exhibit equal capacities. Of such importance was equality in strength that seconds tried to prevent a second bout, in case the opponent had proven to be too strong for his man.
>
> After the match the victor's party toured the village. The old women sang and waved green branches to be given to the champion, while the men carried their best knives. The victor's mother wore her son's head-dress, carried his knife in her girdle and another one in her hand. His wife had given him her beads and put a knife in his hand, while he himself painted himself and powdered his hair with a red substance.[38]

Lindeman observed that usually the people coming from afar lost the match and wondered if possibly etiquette had demanded thus. Some miles below Stanley Falls, Bentley had made similar observations about the Lokele. There is no mention of quarters or villages contending, but there is a description of inhabitants with different tattoos wrestling, which might indicate that various sections of the people challenged each other. "The match, customs, and elaborate rules were very exciting," he noted, "but the general tone of good humour and self-control was still more remarkable; it was excellent." In this region wrestling was, at the turn of the century, the "national" sport.[39]

There are more casual heterogeneous references to wrestling in the eastern, central and southern regions of Zaire[40] and Zambia.[41] According to Colle, wrestling was rare among Luba adults in Katanga. Nevertheless, Luba mothers and those of the neighboring Sanga proclaimed their young sons' victories with the greatest pride, and the most successful wrestler was selected group leader.[42]

Ethnic groups in Angola, Mozambique, Zimbabwe, Malawi, and South Africa provide further evidence not only of the extensiveness but also of the variety of the indigenous custom of wrestling.[43] In his description of the Bantu peoples of Southeast Africa, Kidd describes a match in which one wrestler, larger than his opponent, uses only one arm and adopts a kneeling position.[44] In the same region both boys and men have been observed wrestling in a sitting position.[45]

When the traveler Alexander visited the kraal of the Namaqua chiefs Jan and Henrick Buys in the early nineteenth century, the young men wrestled, danced and practiced shooting games in his honor.[46] Even the Bushmen knew this kind of athletic competition. Their contests often resulted in

Lokele wrestling match at Yakusu (Stanley Falls), 1896. From W. H. Bentley, *Pioneering on the Congo,* II (London 1900).

bloody fights,[47] which was in marked contrast to the controlled matches in many other regions.

One of the most fascinating studies of African children and their activities deals with the Chaga of Kilimanjaro. Competitive activities such as wrestling were a distinctive process of social selection—the contest's outcome determined an individual's status. A boy's emergence as a leader was the result of his physical, mental, and social qualities rather than his parental or family position. An opportunity to display such qualities was offered in early boyhood when the yet uncircumcised youngsters, herding their fathers' cattle, met in public wrestling matches. These included the well-known elements such as the matching of contestants, right to refuse, avoidance of ill will in case of defeat, and increased honors for a victor in district or interlineage contests.[48]

When Gusii elders in west Kenya were asked about traditional sports, they mentioned young warriors wrestling for fun.[49] Also concerning the Luyia (Kavirondo), we hear of large annual festivals in earlier times to which people traveled long distances to see matches and enjoy the efforts of the best wrestlers.[50]

Reports from each of the East African "interlacustrine kingdoms" (such as Buganda, Bunyoro, Toro, Ankole, etc.) also mention wrestling as a traditional sport. Early visitors to Buganda praised the skillful local contestants.

In later years more detailed descriptions became available. In 1902 Roscoe described how the Kabaka (king) had his own wrestling hall and occasionally even took part in matches himself, although nobody was allowed to throw him on penalty of death. As late as 1934 Sir Apolo Kagwa, himself a Ganda, mentioned that especially amusing champions were in great favor with the Kabaka. The chiefs, seated on skins, acted as judges, and both wrestlers knelt before their king and gave their thanks after a round.[51] Toro boys too were encouraged by their king and chiefs to enter the ring. In the kingdom of Bunyoro young and old enjoyed this sport, and from the age of seven male wrestlers met in large public contests. Boys wrestled in Rwanda and both Tutsi and Hutu girls imitated them.[52] Small wonder that the Pygmies in the Kivu region were also familiar with this sport.[53]

In Northeast and North Africa we find sparse references to wrestling among boys and young men.[54] But then we have entered or are close to Islamic countries again. Surrounded by Arab or Arabized groups, however, is a cluster of hill tribes in Kordofan, commonly called Nuba by Arabs and anthropologists. Here, where people have preserved many old customs, we again find that wrestling is a significant element of social structuring. Evidence is available for the northern patrilineal as well as the southern matrilineal communities. Some of the northern hill communities organized their youth into age classes or age grades. Each lasted three years, after which time its members were corporately promoted to the next grade. The first started at puberty and the last ended with the attainment of marriageable age. It was the duty of members of the first grade to work on the fields belonging to the boys' fathers or future fathers-in-law, while adolescents belonging to the next grade supervised them:

> It was in connection with this field work that wrestling took place. The second grade started the matches, and then the novices practiced, being supported by members of the third grade. Exceptionally courageous and ambitious boys belonging to the junior grade sometimes challenged a senior boy, a move which was acclaimed by juniors and seniors alike.

In the dry season intervillage matches were arranged for their own sake:

> During these public matches boys of the lowest grade had a chance to show what they had learned, while members of the older grades competed for a champion's trophy. A victor in such matches was honored with praise-songs composed by his peers and the girls. The fame of an especially expert wrestler could spread beyond his home community and hill.

Among one of these northern groups, the Nyima, boys of the third age grade were circumcised in their late teens. Before circumcision wrestling was one of their prominent activities. After circumcision, however, boys who had gone through this ceremony could never again meet on the wrestling ground. While waiting for circumcision the boys had to work the fields of the spirit priest and the rainmaker, both responsible for the fertility of the soil. (In 1928 Nadel observed newly circumcised boys wrestling in front of the political chief's house!)

On the southern hills wrestling also belonged to the phase of puberty and early adolescence although there were no rigid age classes. Each boy was promoted to the first informal age group individually, when his family considered him to be mature enough. Initial wrestling was part of this confirmation.

> But when the boy was to be promoted to the next higher age level, families saw to it that many boys of the same age gathered for the festivities. A boy's father or mother's brother furnished him with all necessary parts of a wrestler's outfit. A lot of beer was brewed, and many people were invited either by the boy's relatives, or by a representative the boy had chosen himself. This was the time for a boy to enter the ring in an inter-village match for the first time.

Among the Masakin Qisar, whose wrestling traditions have been well documented in various films, every village chose one special champion who was elected for a three-year period. His rich outfit was donated by his father, mother's brother, or the whole community, and it was kept in a special hut all through the wrestler's life. This village representative was given a special diet of milk, honey, and sesame. He was exempted from most communal work and had the responsibility of training a successor. Even after his resignation such a representative was highly honored. At his funeral a special—and particularly severe—wrestling contest was arranged by members of the eldest group of young men. It should be mentioned, perhaps, that among the Nuba wrestling was one of two important types of sport, the other being stick duels or spear fighting. Usually wrestling was practiced by members of the younger grades, while fights of the other kind were carried out by the older ones. To change over from wrestling to spear or stick fighting was sometimes interpreted as a sign of waning prowess due to married life, hence the aphorism: "If you marry, you cannot wrestle anymore." It does not mean, however, that youths had to observe celibacy![55]

A final brief reference to Madagascar completes our survey. In this outpost of black African influence, wrestling scenes such as those described for the continent have been portrayed with reference to the Betsileo.[56]

It is clear from the extant evidence that wrestling was known all over traditional Black Africa. But wrestling in ceremonial settings with symbolic significance was an institution restricted to certain ethnic groups or societies. A theory of the role of traditional African wrestling would have to be based on a careful classification of the characteristics of the societies in question. Then possibly variables explaining both common and distinctive elements of traditional wrestling practice could be located. But, as mentioned earlier, documents are too heterogeneous and too often isolated from their sociocultural contexts to allow reliable generalizations. The best we can do is to make a few general remarks about some conspicuous elements of these societies.

The majority of ethnic groups, in which wrestling was of importance to individuals and the groups they represented, can be labeled agricultural. Generally wrestling people were sedentary and lived in compounds, villages, or town quarters that were often inhabited by members of one kinship group and their dependents. Frequently these social units were exogamous. This implies a sense of identity among those who commonly gave away marriage partners and received others of the same sex in return.

Almost all societies that practiced wrestling as a competitive sport between rival social or local groups were organized on patrilineal principles, as were those in which men and women or children wrestled within their community or kinship unit. Only where girls, on reaching puberty, wrestled boys or where they met girls in ritual contests, were matrilineal as well as patrilineal principles involved. Probably the way descent was reckoned was not decisive, as male vitality was equally desirable and necessary in patrilineal and matrilineal societies. Nevertheless, the fact that in some matrilineal societies girls were expected to demonstrate physical strength and agility might be an indicator of women's somewhat stronger and freer position in societies of this kind. The dangers of generalization, however, are underlined by the fact that girls have not been observed wrestling in a matrilineal community such as the Masakin Qisar in the Nuba hills.

It has been maintained that wrestling and stick duels are types of sport characteristic of a "paleonigritic cultural substratum."[57] This would imply that in such areas men were engaged also in agricultural routine work, whereas in many other African regions women were traditionally responsible for this kind of activity. We have seen, indeed, that many young wrestlers were in charge of farm work. Another element considered paleonigritic is the dominance of the principle of seniority: the elder brother, son, age class, and so forth being of higher status than the younger. The wrestling scenes illustrate this principle.

Some of the societies discussed here were divided into regular age classes, members of which were bound to each other for life. Age classes served as symbols of mutual identification. It has been reported that ability in wrestling was a prerequisite of initiation into such a formal class, but in regions without age classes, age, age group or legal status often determined the activity of wrestlers. In West and central Africa wrestling was an institution in areas where secret societies and cult groups exercised an important disciplining function, and yet there is no evidence of wrestling having been associated with initiation into such groups.

Whether paleonigritic or not, wrestling is seen to exist in some regions characterized by the existence of political states. It must be remembered, however, that such states included various ethnic groups with cultures of greater antiquity. Heads of such states usually functioned as mediators between the human and the superhuman levels of existence. Kings, like local chiefs, were in charge of the soil, responsible for the vitality of nature and people.

African ancestors, as "living elders," belonged to their lineage as long as they were remembered by their offspring. They protected and punished those on earth and were expected to guarantee nourishment, health, and fertility. When beer was consumed in connection with wrestling matches, when drums and trumpets were sounded, these activities might very well have been used as a means of establishing contact with the deceased. Where Islam had a firm hold, however, the ancestors were supposed to have become shadows of the past. God or his representatives on earth were appealed to directly. Furthermore, acceptance of Islam was often a means of stepping up the social ladder. If participation in wrestling contests was considered to be "heathen" because of beer drinking and associated worship, followers of Islam tended to abstain from it.

Next there is the question of wrestlers' sex and age. In the majority of cases, contestants were boys or adolescents. Married men wrestled on rare occasions as coaches, to amuse spectators, to settle disputes, and against women at harvesting times. The Ganda king's wrestling might have been of ritual significance. Adults, however, supported the young wrestlers in a number of ways: the men by inciting, by encouraging, by coaching, by paying for a victor's token or a champion's outfit, by serving as judges, by confirming a match's outcome and shouting a victor's praise, even by presenting him with a gift of food, money, or a wife. Adult women, especially mothers of champions, contributed their enthusiasm and pride. Organized wrestling with all its festive and ritual preparation, and the establishment and maintenance of a successful wrestler's prestige, could not be visualized without the support of elders.

Initiation or public acceptance into preadult society was a crucial point in a wrestler's life. In some places this upgrading was a prerequisite for participation in public matches; in others it ended a wrestling career. Where circumcision was practiced, either adolescents already circumcised did not wrestle any more, or this sport was a part of circumcision festivities, or it was particularly engaged in by those who had recently been upgraded by this ritual operation. In other places membership in an age class or age group entitled marriageable young men to wrestle on public occasions.

Marriage normally ended a wrestler's career, but sometimes marriage of a champion was postponed until he had been defeated conclusively in the arena.

As we have seen, wrestling was not solely a male affair. Women sometimes wrestled each other in order to settle a personal dispute, but women or girls also fought with each other on other occasions. Among the Ibo in Nigeria, women of one village would challenge those of a neighboring one at a particular annual festival. And Diola girls sometimes exhibited wrestling champions who were desirable marriage partners for their male counterparts. Occasionally women also wrestled men, for instance, at harvest time. These instances can be interpreted as a formalization of the traditional tensions between the sexes. They should also be considered in relation to the sexual division of work. Where women had a heavy work load and a right to the products of their labor, it would not be surprising if more female groups contended with men in playful wrestling matches. Rivalry between the sexes may also account for girls wrestling boys in puberty rites: here their future sexual intimacy in marriage was also foreshadowed.

In African climatic conditions, sports like wrestling had a natural season, the dry one, when players could find a smooth sandy or grass-grown open space, a firm foothold, and a large gathering of spectators. This season began with harvesting and ended with preparations for a new agricultural period. During this period people had more leisure time and more food at their disposal. They had also to see to it that the soil—or the spirits taking care of it—had new vitality. Although none of the observers made this assumption, wrestling might once have been considered to vitalize the earth, especially if young, sexually potent (and perhaps celibate) people engaged in it.[58]

Although the dry season was the main period for public ceremonial and ritual wrestling, young people trained and performed also at other times of the year, unless it was feared that heated contests disturbed the spirits. On the rare occasions that wrestling occurred in the rainy season, there was a specific reason for it. For example, the Ndibu used slippery ground to make candidates for an age group liable to fall, thus emphasizing their immaturity. In cases in which wrestling was part of circumcision/initiation or girls' puberty rites, or where people challenged each other on wedding days, appropriate dates were usually set in the dry season. There is no specific information regarding other dates, although they were said to have been chosen for particular, ritual reasons. The reference to more recent public wrestling in Senegal shows that traditional dates or seasons are no longer observed once competitive sports have become commercialized amusements.

Regarding facilities, only the Kabaka of old Buganda has been reported to have had a special wrestling hall. For their part the Masakin Qisar in the

Nuba hills kept a storeroom for a champion's wrestling paraphernalia. This is reminiscent of the storing of masks and costumes in other places. In West Africa the marketplace, the traditional meeting place for different social groups, was frequently chosen for intervillage matches. In modern towns stadiums have often replaced the old venues. Two historical locations are of particular interest: Dogon boys wrestled in a field, strategically situated between the two villages from where the rival wrestlers came, and which was at the disposal of their common political and religious chief. Nyima boys in the Nuba hills, waiting for circumcision, had to work the fields of the spirit priest and those of the rainmaker. Both priest and rainmaker were responsible for the fertility of the soil, which offers support for the hypothesis that wrestling among the young was considered to assist or strengthen natural forces.

Not much needs to be said about the setting and nature of ceremonial, public matches, since the earlier descriptions often speak for themselves. Some aspects recurred in many places. There was the open space, mostly circular, sometimes square, around which spectators assembled in local, kinship, sex, or age groups. The sitting or standing order was in accordance with social status. Colorful costumes and elaborate preparations of food and beer were all means of emphasizing the special nature of the festive occasion. Often several age groups wrestled one after the other, usually begun by the youngest one. Each group was represented by particularly skilled wrestlers, for individual victories were interpreted as group victories. Each group supplied referees, who were older than the contestants. In a number of cases, seconds have been reported.

A public match usually had a prelude and a postlude. The former consisted of preparing the festival and the champions, matching contestants, and heightening the tension through ritualistic means of incitement. In many cases sacrifices to benevolent spirits, drumming, vocal and instrumental music, and individual and collective dancing announced the beginning of the contests. Music and dance also commonly served as interludes. Postludes tended to be marked by aggression, but this tendency was often well handled and neutralized by the elders. Victors were honored within their groups, but although observers have reported on the victors' praise tours, privileges, and subsequent high status, little mention has been made of the loser and his party. In some cases they were reported to have assaulted more successful opponents, even to the extent of attacking them with dangerous weapons. This was wholly unacceptable, of course. Sanctions that were expected and tolerated, however, were verbal aggressiveness, mockery, and ridicule. Because of the tension involved, the sublimation of potential ill feelings—turning them into socially acceptable formalized behavior—was frequently a central concern in the training of the young for their contests.

Wrestling in Black Africa traditionally served several social functions for individuals and groups. Salamone has pointed to the fact that, at least among the Gungawa, intravillage wrestling helped to establish a male rank order.[59] Intragroup wrestling may often have been mere children's play without any serious connotations, but what has sometimes been called "children's rolling about" or "wrestling in a haphazard fashion" might in reality have been a struggle of children belonging to rival maternal or paternal households to attain or confirm their own rank and that of their family unit. Similarly, remarks about wrestling to settle disputes, either between men or women or adults of the opposite sex, may refer to such attempts to underline rank relationship, for instance between wives of one common husband, or adult sons of one father but different mothers.

Several reporters have emphasized that the strongest or most skillful wrestler attained a leading position within local play groups, formal age classes, or boys' societies. In this context Centner has reminded us of the significance of vital force in traditional African societies,[60] but this force is not congruent with muscular strength alone. Raum has dealt with the criteria for according a high rank in a more subtle way. He has noted of the Chaga[61] that age group leaders emerged on account of their individual qualities, which had become manifest in competitive games such as wrestling. These qualities were not merely physical but social, such as a keen sense of justice and a sense of socially appropriate behavior. A good illustration of the importance of such qualities is provided by the Fulani teacher Traoré. The best wrestler, who was leader of the formal boys' society, would exhort his followers to observe fairness in the game, to be ambitious for leadership, and to emulate his social skills. But he also organized a big meal for them at the end of the wrestling season, thereby establishing his role as a host.[62] This behavior exemplifies a widespread African practice: namely, that the one being honored because of his social qualities has to support and entertain his followers.

A boy exhibiting special wrestling capacities gained high prestige within his family, kinship group, and community. Mothers were proud of their sons; fathers and mother's brothers had to pay for a son's or nephew's outfit, or for a substitute working on the father-in-law's farm. Men of the age group of a wrestler's father (or even grandfather) served as judges of a youth's readiness to take part in intervillage matches. The community prepared its champion by feeding him well, keeping him in seclusion before a match, and helping him to get the appropriate costume. The young man at the top, the star wrestler, enjoyed special privileges. He could be exempted from normal responsibilities for the time of his being a champion. In short, he had an enviable position in the community. The fact that a village representative could at times be honored beyond his death among the Masakin Qisar, that a Ganda chief sometimes presented a successful wrestler with a wife, and that modern Senegalese offer high rewards in cash to their favorites all suggest the social significance of superiority in wrestling. Moreover, apart from promoting to high rank within the age group and a high prestige within family and community, wrestling efficiency also served the purpose of upgrading individuals singly or collectively to higher status levels on the basis of age. In exceptional cases single boys could be promoted to a senior age group earlier than others of their age.

Most of what has hitherto been said about the function of wrestling as an aid to an individual's social mobility is pertinent to the collective attainment of rank, status, and prestige. Thus wrestling matches between different local populations had a number of functions. Planning and organizing the festival was a means of strengthening solidarity between members of the local group. In different roles, all or at least many of the community had to contribute time, effort, or goods; they had to organize themselves and prepare for meeting opposing groups with proper hospitality and in collective harmony. During the match each party displayed its potential in strong young men, who, at least in former times, could have been viewed as an army of future warriors. But these wrestlers and their judges also had an opportunity to demonstrate fairness, expert command of rules, and readiness to compromise, thus exhibiting qualities sought after in potential marriage partners and allies in economic or martial enterprise. Public credit was given to elders for having brought up their children in an attractive way and to the young people for having endeavored to live up to their elders' ideals. Thus, whereas intervillage wrestling on the one hand functioned to establish and stress internal, local solidarity, on the other it both emphasized rivalry between contending groups and their mutual interdependence and potential solidarity at a wider regional level. The fact that wrestling rules had to be the same for all groups emphasized their identity in contrast to other ethnic units with no traditional intergroup relationships and probably different wrestling rules.

A special function of wrestling was the dramatization of ambivalent male-female relationships. Covert male-female hostility was expressed in ritualistic wrestling between girls in puberty and their betrothed among the Fon-Ewe. Fang and Njabi women had a chance at harvest time to display their strength. But while Njabi men were said to take revenge on behalf of their vanquished kinswomen, Fang women revenged themselves for a defeat by assaulting a man when he happened to walk by their fields defenseless. Wrestling across the sexes could thus have served to strengthen a sense of identity among members of one or the other sex.

In summary, wrestling is an old and important institution in Black Africa. Traditionally it served the functions of endowing a person with prestige, establishing his personal rank, and ascribing and enhancing his social status. An individual's victory brought honor to his reference group. Intergroup wrestling reinforced each group's internal solidarity and sense of identity, and all the while it accentuated ambivalent group relationships. Apart from these social functions wrestling activities were apparently considered to reinforce the fertility of the soil, although wrestling and sexual activities were mutually exclusive.

Notes

1. Cf. Otto F. Raum, "The Rolling Target (Hoop-and-Pole) Game in Africa: Egyptian Accession Rite or Multiple Ritual Symbolism," *African Studies* 12 (1953): 104–21, 163–80; Sigrid Paul, "Afrikanische Ballspiele," *Baessler-Archiv* N.F., 18 (1970): 155–251 and "Afrikanische Kreiseltypen und Kreiselspiele," *Veröffentlichungen aus dem Übersee-Museum in Bremen,* Reihe B, 2, Heft 4 (1971):237–72. Apart from regional monographs on traditional games referred to below see sport games that have survived up to this day in Fritz Klepzig, *Kinderspiele der Bantu* (Meisenheim/ Glan, 1972).

2. See for ethnonyms and general data on ethnic groups referred to George P. Murdock, *Africa: Its Peoples and Their Culture History* (New York, 1959).

3. A. Wiedemann, "Das Spiel im alten Ägypten," *Zeitschrift des Vereins für rheinische und westfälische Volkskunde* 9 (1912): 174 et seq.; and E. W. Lane, *Manners and Customs of the Modern Egyptians* (London, 1908), 357.

4. René Verneau, *Cinq années de séjour aux Iles Canaries* (Paris, 1891), 223.

5. Louis-Vincent Thomas, *Les Diola: Essai d'analyse fonctionelle sur une population de Basse-Casamance,* I, Mémoire de l'Institut Français d'Afrique Noire 55 (Dakar, 1958): 297–301; cf. Cligny Rambaud Lasnet, *Une Mission au Sénégal* (Paris, 1900), 163–64; Charles Béart, *Jeux et jouets de l'Ouest Africain,* I, Mémoire de l'Institut Français d'Afrique Noire 42 (Dakar, 1955): 295; and Hermann Baumann and Dietrich Westermann, *Les peuples et les civilisations de l'Afrique* (Paris, 1957), 378.

6. Gaby, *Rélation de la Nigritie contenant une exacte description de ses Royaumes et de leurs Gouvernements, la Religion, les Moeurs, Coustumes et Raretez de ce Pais* (Paris, 1689), 43–44; Béart, I, 299.

7. Cf. G. Balandier and P. Mercier, "Les pêcheurs Lébou du Sénégal," *Etudes Sénégalaises* 3 (1952): 59 et seq.; cf. Béart, I, 300 et seq.

8. Mamadou Traoré, "Jeux et jouets des enfants foula," *Bulletin de l'Institut Français d'Afrique Noire* 2, no. 1–2 (Dakar, 1940): 237–38.

9. L. J. B. Bérenger-Féraud, *Les peuplades de la Sénégambie* (Paris, 1879), 78.

10. Béart, I, 295 et seq.; and G. Boyer, *Un Peuple de l'Ouest Soudanais: Les Diawara,* Mémoire de l'Institut Français d'Afrique Noire 29, no. 1 (Dakar, 1953):119.

11. George Schwab, *Tribes of the Liberian Hinterland,* Papers of the Peabody Museum of American Archeology and Ethnology, Harvard University 31 (Cambridge, Mass., 1947):158 et seq.; Béart, I, 297.

12. Béart, I, 297; and Marcel Griaule, *Jeux Dogons,* Travaux et Mémoires de l'Institut d'Ethnologie 32 (Paris, 1938):118.

13. Griaule, 118 et seq. Cf. also J. C. Froelich, *La Tribu Konkomba du Nord Togo,* Mémoire de l'Institut Français d'Afrique Noire 37 (Dakar, 1954). Konkomba

refused to wrestle because of pride; they would not be able to stand the disgrace of defeat.

14.   Henri Labouret, *Les Tribus du Rameau Lobi,* Travaux et Mémoires de l'Institut d'Ethnologie 15 (Paris 1931):176–77, 273.

15.   A. Mischlich, *Über die Kulturen im Mittel-Sudan* (Berlin, 1942): 107; cf. also Kurt Krieger, "Knabenspiele der Hausa," *Baessler-Archiv,* N.F. 3 (1955): 229.

16.   A. J. N. Tremearne, *Hausa Superstitions and Customs* (London, 1913), 414–15.

17.   A. J. N. Tremearne, *The Ban of the Bori* (London, 1914), 211–12, 241.

18.   Paul Staudinger, *Im Herzen der Haussa-Länder* (Berlin, 1889), 367. This traveler had watched Hausa wrestling Yoruba despite their differing styles.

19.   Leo Frobenius, *Und Afrika sprach . . .* (Berlin, 1912), 387 et seq. Cf. also his information on the Dakakari in Diary no. 5 of DIAFE 3, 1910–12, Archives of the Frobenius Institut, Frankfurt/M., Fed. Rep. of Germany; and P. G. Harris, "Notes on the Dakakari Peoples of Sokoto Province, Nigeria," *Journal of the Royal Anthropological Institute* 68 (1938):135–36. The Frobenius diary also contains notes on circumcised boys' wrestling in Borgu, at Nikki, Bussa, and Gungana.

20.   Frank A. Salamone, "Gungawa Wrestling as an Ethnic Boundary Marker", *Afrika und Übersee* 57, Heft 3 (1973–74): 193–202.

21.   Cf. Salamone, "Persistence and Change in Ethnic and Religious Identity: Yauri Emirate, NW State, Nigeria," unpublished Ph.D. dissertation, Buffalo, N.Y., 1973.

22.   Richard Mutsena, informant to Paul Hinderling in "Les Jeux des enfants Mafa," unpublished manuscript, 1965.

23.   Günther Tessmann, "Die Mbaka-Limba, Mbum und Lakka", *Zeitschrift für Ethnologie* 60 (1928): 345; G. Tessmann, *Die Bafia* (Stuttgart, 1934), 156; and G. Tessmann, *Die Baja,* I (Stuttgart 1934), 209–210.

24.   G. T. Basden, *Niger Ibos* (London, 1966), 347 et seq.; Adams, "Ibo Texts," *Africa* 7 (1934): 453–54; cf. J. I. Harris, "Papers on the Economic Aspect of Life among the Ozuitem Ibo," *Africa* 14 (1943–44): 18.

25.   Rems Nna Umeasiegbu, *Words Are Sweet: Igbo Stories and Storytelling* (Leiden, 1982), 122–23, cf. 130–31.

26.   Béart, I, 296–97, 301–2.

27.   Baumann and Westermann, 339; H. L. M. Butcher, "Some Aspects of the Oto System of the Isa Sub-Tribe of the Edo People of Southern Nigeria," *Africa* 8 (1937): 156.

28.   Alfred Mansfeld, *Urwald-Dokumente. Vier Jahre unter den Crossflussnegern Kameruns* (Berlin, 1908), 117.

29.   A. Talbot, *In the Shadow of the Bush* (London, 1912), 285.

30.   E. Zintgraff, *Nord-Kamerun* (Berlin, 1895), 33; cf. later notes on wrestling in this region in Klepzig, 166.

31.   Max Buchner, *Kamerun: Skizzen und Betrachtungen* (Leipzig, 1887), 35; and Johannes Ittmann, "Volkskundliche und religiöse Begriffe im nördlichen Waldland von Kamerun," *Afrika und Übersee* Beiheft 26 (Berlin, 1953): 5.

32.   Johannes Ittmann, "Spiele der Stämme rings um die Ambasbucht (Kamerun)," *Afrika und Übersee* 43 (1959): 37 et seq.

33. F. Grebert, *Au Gabon* (Paris, 1928), 109.

34. Günther Tessmann, *Die Pangwe,* II (Berlin, 1913), 318–19. Tessmann had never seen women wrestling among the southern Fang, but he referred to G. Zenker, "Yaúnde," *Mitteilungen aus den deutschen Schutzgebieten* 6 (1895):36–70, who apparently had. Cf. also the Fang saying "Do not wrestle anyone stronger than you" in V. Largeau, *Encyclopédie Pahouine* (Paris, 1901): 433.

35. Klepzig, 165.

36. W. Holman Bentley, *Dictionary and Grammar of the Kongo Language* (London, 1887), 253; John Whitehead, *Grammar and Dictionary of the Bobangi Language* (London, 1899), 229; E. Torday and T. A. Joyce, *Notes éthnographiques sur les peuples communement appelés Bakuba, ainsi que sur les peuplades apparentés, les Bushongo,* Annales du Musée du Congo Belge, sér. 3, 2, no. 1 (1910): 95; Karl Laman, *The Kongo,* vol. I (Uppsala, 1953): 68, vol. II (Uppsala, 1957): 20; and Klepzig, 165–66, 291–92.

37. Anonymous, "Du Stanley-Pool aux Stanley-Falls," *Bulletin de la Société Royale de Géographie d'Anvers* 23 (1899): 236.

38. M. Lindeman, "Les jeux au Congo," *La Belgique Coloniale* 4 (1899): 317–18; and M. Lindeman, "Les Upotos," *Bulletin de la Société Royale Belge de Géographie* 30 (1906): 24–26.

39. W. H. Bentley, *Pioneering on the Congo,* II (London, 1900), 289–93. Cf. also John H. Weeks, "Anthropological Notes on the Bangala of the Upper Congo," part III, *Journal of the Royal Anthropological Institute* 40 (1910):408; M. C. Van Overbergh, *Les Bangala,* Collection de Monographies Ethnographiques 1 (Bruxelles, 1907): 93; and Frederic Starr, *Congo Natives: An Ethnographic Album* (Chicago, 1912): plate 78b.

40. M. C. Van Overbergh, *Les Mangbetu,* Coll. de Monogr. Ethnogr. 4, (Bruxelles, 1909):145; Ch. Delhaise, "Chez les Wasongola du Sud," *Bulletin de la Société Royale Belge de Géographie* 33 (1909): 189; Ch. Delhaise, *Les Warega,* Coll. de Monogr. Ethnogr. 5 (Bruxelles, 1909): 63; Joseph Halkin, *Les Ababua,* Coll. de Monogr. Ethnogr. 7 (Bruxelles, 1911): 125; Ch. Delhaise, "Les Bapopoie," *Bull. de la Société Royale Belge de Géogr.* 36 (1912): 99–100; and A. Engels, *Les Wangata* (Bruxelles, 1912), 94–95. For later descriptions of boys and girls wrestling in this region, see again Klepzig, 291–92.

41. D. W. Stirke, *Barotseland: Eight Years among the Barotse* (London, 1920), 131; D. Campbell, *In the Heart of Bantuland* (London, 1922), 174; and C. M. Doke, *The Lambas of Northern Rhodesia* (London, 1931), 143.

42. R. P. Colle, *Les Baluba,* Coll. de Monogr. Ethnogr. 10 (Bruxelles, 1913): 87; and Th. H. Centner, *L'enfant africain et ses jeux dans le cadre de la vie traditionelle au Katanga,* Collection Mémoires CEPSI no. 17 (Elisabethville, 1962): 175–76.

43. Hugh S. Stannus, "Notes on Some Tribes of British Central Africa," *Journal of the Royal Anthropol. Institute* 40 (1910): 332–33; H. S. Stannus, *The Wayao of Nyasaland,* Harvard African Studies 3 (Cambridge, Mass., 1922): 357; Wilfred D. Hambly, *The Ovimbundu of Angola,* Field Museum of Natural History Publ. 329, Anthrop. Series 21, no. 2 (Chicago, 1934): 220; Mattenklodt, "Die Kisama," *Wiener Beiträge zur Kulturgeschichte und Linguistik* 6 (1944): 104; E. Casalis, *Les Bassoutos,* new ed. (1859; Paris, 1930), 245; Monica Hunter, *Reaction to Conquest* (London, 1936), 160; Günther Spannaus, *Streiflichter aus dem Leben der Kinder und Jugendlichen bei den Ndau,* Jahrbuch des Linden-Museums, N.F. 1 (Stuttgart, 1951): 124; and

Victor Lebzelter, "Das Betschuanendorf Epukiro (SW Afrika)," *Zeitschrift für Ethnologie* 65 (1933): 69–70.

44. Dudley Kidd, *Savage Childhood: A Study of Kaffir Children* (London, 1906), 200–201.

45. J. Macdonald, "Manners, Customs and Superstitions of South African Tribes," *Journal of the Royal Anthrop. Institute* 19 (1890): 292; and Dudley Kidd, *The Essential Kaffir* (London, 1904), 337–38.

46. James Edward Alexander, *An Expedition of Discovery into the Interior of Africa, through the Hitherto Undescribed Countries of the Great Namaquas, Boschmans, and Hill Damaras,* I (London, 1838), 264–65; and George McCall Theal, *Ethnography and Condition of South Africa before A.D. 1505* (London, 1919):122.

47. Hans Kaufmann, "Die Auin," *Mitteilungen aus den deutschen Schutzgebieten* 23 (1910): 150; Joachim Helmuth Wilhelm, "Die !Kung-Buschleute," *Jahrbuch des Museums für Völkerkunde* 12 (Leipzig, 1953): 178.

48. Otto F. Raum, "Some Aspects of Indigenous Education among the Chaga," *Journal of the Royal Anthrop. Institute* 68 (1938): 219; O. F. Raum, *Chaga Childhood* (1940; London, 1967), 267. Cf. also Otto Reche, *Zur Ethnographie des abflusslosen Gebietes Deutsch Ost-Afrikas,* Abhandlungen des Hamburger Kolonialinstituts 17, Reihe B, Heft 11 (Hamburg, 1914): 67.

49. Robert A. LeVine and Donald T. Campbell, *Gusii of Kenya* II, Ethnocentrism Series, HRAFlex Books, FL 8-001 (New Haven, Conn., 1972), 316, 349.

50. John Osogo, *Life in Kenya in the Olden Days: The Baluyia* (Nairobi, 1965), 2; cf. also John Roscoe, *The Northern Bantu* (Cambridge, 1915), 193; John Roscoe, *The Bagesu and Other Tribes of the Uganda Protectorate* (Cambridge, 1924), 124; and E. D. Embley, "The Turkana of Kolosia District," *Journal of the Royal Anthrop. Institute* 57 (1927): 195.

51. C. T. Wilson and R. W. Felkin, *Uganda and the Egyptian Soudan* I (London, 1883), 216; R. P. Ashe, *Two Kings of Uganda; Six Years in East Equatorial Africa* (London 1889), 292; John Roscoe, "Further Notes on Manners and Customs of Baganda," *Journal of the Royal Anthrop. Institute* 32 (1902): 72; John Roscoe, *The Baganda* (London, 1911), 78; and Apolo Kagwa, *The Customs of the Baganda,* trans. Kalibala, ed. May Mandelbaum, Columbia University Contributions to Anthropology 22 (New York, 1934): 136–37.

52. A. L. Kitching, *On the Backwaters of the Nile* (London, 1912), 225; John Roscoe, *The Bakitara or Banyoro* (Cambridge, 1923), 260; John Roscoe, *The Banyankole* (Cambridge, 1923), 116; John Roscoe, "The Bahima," *Journal of the Royal Anthrop. Institute* 37 (1907): 118; Lukyn Williams, "Hima Cattle," *Uganda Journal* 6 (1938–39): 102; R. Bourgeois, *Banyarwanda et Barundi,* I, Académie Royale des Sciences Coloniales, Classe des sciences morales et politiques, Mémoires, N.S. 15 (Bruxelles, 1957): 621; P. M. Pauwels, "Jeux et divertissements au Ruanda," *Annali Lateranensi* 24 (1960): 242. Cf. for Rwanda-Burundi also Klepzig, 292.

53. P. Schumacher, *Expedition zu den Zentralafrikanischen Kivu-Pygmäen,* II, Mémoires de l'Institut Royale Colonial Belge 5 (Bruxelles, 1950): 106. For wrestling of forest hunters elsewhere cf. Paul Schebesta, *Bambuti, die Zwerge vom Kongo* (Leipzig, 1932), 56 and his book *Die Bambuti-Pygmäen vom Ituri,* II (Bruxelles, 1941), 238.

54. G. Marin, "Somali Games," *Journal of the Royal Anthrop. Institute* 61 (1931):

500; Francis Nicolas, *Tamesma, les Ioullemmeden de l'Est ou Touâreg "Kel Dinnîk,"* Cercle de T'awa—Colonie du Niger (Paris, 1950): 184; and Jean Chapelle, *Nomades Noirs du Sahara* (Paris, 1957), 268. Cf. for Ethiopian wrestling Marcel Griaule, *Jeux et Divertissements Abyssins,* Bibliothèque de l'Ecole des Hautes Etudes, Sciences Réligieuses 49 (Paris, 1935): 58.

55. S. F. Nadel, *The Nuba: An Anthropological Study of the Hill Tribes in Kordofan* (London, 1947):132–37, 230–35, 296–300, 406–11; A. Kronenberg und R. Husmann, *Ringerfeste der Masakin (Ostsudan, Kordofan); and Masakin Übungsringkämpfe; Masakin Einkleiden eines Ringers,* texts accompanying films made by H. Luz and W. Herz, Encyclopedia Cinematographica D 920/1966, E 705/1964, E 1097/1967 (Göttingen, 1976). Cf. also Friedrich-Karl Rothe, "Die Welt des Kindes und des Jugendlichen bei dem Nuba-Stamm der Mesakin-Qusar," dissertation (Hamburg, 1967), 22 et seq. Both Rothe and Kronenberg mentioned that sometimes young women, carried away by their enthusiasm, started to wrestle after a male match. But none of the fieldworkers confirmed Hermann Baumann's earlier opinion that girls' wrestling among the Nuba stood for a puberty ceremony (Baumann and Westermann, 304).

56. H. M. Dubois, *Monographie des Betsileo (Madagascar),* Travaux et Mémoires de l'Institut d'Ethnologie 34 (Paris, 1938): 537–39, 545; cf. J. Faublée, *L'Ethnographie de Madagascar* (Paris, 1946), 65.

57. Baumann and Westermann, 69.

58. Cf. these ritualizing ideas associated with various ball and hockey games in Paul, *Afrikanische Ballspiele;* and with spinning tops in Paul, *Afrikanische Kreiseltypen und Kreiselspiele.*

59. Salamone, 197.

60. Centner, 176.

61. Raum, *Chaga Childhood,* 267.

62. Traoré, 238.

3

The Biggest Game of All:
Gambling in Traditional Africa

THOMAS Q. REEFE

Biggest Game, Invisible Game

Gambling is play, a universal human function, and like the other forms of play gambling can be a most serious undertaking. As drama it is acted out in the arenas of public and sacred life: marketplaces, courtyards, cult centers, etc. What people in the West call games of chance are hardly that elsewhere in the world. They are games of intent and discovery in which specialists divine the future, the desires of the ancestors, or the malice of one's neighbors. What can be bought, sold, or abducted can be wagered. Gambling is nonreciprocal exchange, a form of expropriation, which is why it is so closely associated with the potential for disorder, blood feuds, and warfare. Priceless things can be won and lost, and when the prestige of players is at issue the stakes are high indeed.

On the other hand, high stakes and intense gambling have not been ubiquitous in human history. Many people play games of chance without gambling on the outcome. There is no correlation between societies of risk and the propensity to gamble. Eskimos, who live a most precarious existence, do not symbolically assert that reality through gambling any more than do Kalahari Desert hunter-gatherers. There is no easy correlation between gambling and the complexity of society, for it can be intense in some small-scale, segmentary societies and some industrial societies and not in others. Rather, gambling clusters in certain zones and regions of the world, the product of local cultural selection and long-term historical evolution. Vedic India and Rome were two such areas of antiquity. Gaming was particularly intense across West and Central Africa.[1] Gambling was the biggest game of all along the Guinea Coast before this century, and slaves were among the most common commodities wagered. In the precolonial

I wish to thank several people for their willingness to discuss gambling and to share with me their personal insights and information. These include Herbert Bodman, Jack Censer, Elisabeth Colson, Robert Harms, David Itzkowitz, Ira Lapidus, Paul Lovejoy, Michael McVaugh, Jean Mfoulou, Anthony Oberschall, John Price, and Allen Roberts.

era the small-scale and highly competitive societies of the rain forest, stretching from southern Nigeria to the East African lakes, constituted a separate zone within the larger African gambling region. In the zone people bet high and human stakes, and symbols of social and religious expression were embedded in gaming forms.[2]

Gambling has been virtually invisible in the analytical literature about Africa. Indeed, we know more about the material culture of gaming and how group membership shaped betting behavior and staking strategy among American Indians than among Africans.[3] For one thing the theoretical base for the study of gambling is weak. Psychological studies all too often tilt toward analysis of aberrant behavior where the gambler becomes *"a neurotic with an unconscious wish to lose."*[4] However, recent research into the betting habits of eighteenth-century Virginia gentry and the British working class show that constant gamblers were responding to normative class values.[5] The truly compulsive individual has always existed on the fringe of gambling culture, and in Africa what is most interesting is gaming's unexceptional nature. Gambling has been subsumed almost exclusively under play rather than under economics or religion where it also belongs, and the overwhelming majority of material on play in Africa concerns children's games.[6] The theoretical literature about play has been constrained by a misguided concern to explain the development of civilization, particularly Western civilization, through the evolution of play forms. The inspiration comes initially from Huizinga's *Homo Ludens,* but it is repeated even in *Les jeux et les hommes,* Caillois's more provocative work on games of chance.[7] The need for field inquiries about gambling in non-Western societies has been shown not in Africa but by Geertz in Indonesia. His work on Balinese cockfighting illustrates how the act of two chickens chopping each other to pieces is transformed into high drama expressing a society's most profound view of itself.[8] The toss of a handful of carved gambling chips or cowrie shells in Africa has been an act of similar import expressing a rich matrix of symbolic associations and social values.

Research into gambling in Africa has presented its own problems. While the Middle East and Muslim West Africa have been regions of gambling activity for centuries, the Koran specifically forbids the practice. As a result Islamic sources report little about this sin and are frequently difficult to interpret when they do.[9] Most primary source material on high-stakes African gambling is scattered as incidental comment in eyewitness accounts from the early colonial period. After that missionaries inveighed against it, and colonial authorities attacked it as a threat to public order.[10] As institutions of slavery died out or were suppressed during the colonial period, gambling of rights in people disappeared. By the interwar period, when the first social anthropologists began to enter the field, high-stakes gambling either was not as prevalent as it once had been, or, what is more likely, it was simply less visible. As a result there is a lack of detailed information about the social setting of gambling.[11]

This does not mean that gambling is unimportant today in Africa. Betting is done in marketplaces and gambling dens. Soccer pools exist on the continent as they do elsewhere. A post–World War II study of gambling in industrial South Africa described a thriving numbers racket run by Chinese for African workers.[12] However, the bibliography on gambling in modern Africa is meager in the extreme. This is one reason why gambling in traditional Africa has been chosen as the theme for what follows. The concept is sufficiently broad to allow the use of most of the available material. There can be a tilt toward gaming in the precolonial era. The theme permits an examination of what are very complex and in many cases very ancient patterns of play. In the end the best tack is to be encyclopedic about the gambling categories used and to be exemplary with eloquent primary data chosen from societies scattered across the continent.

The National Games of Africa

The number of gambling games played in precolonial Africa was limited, but they were widespread. Thus, one betting game of skill has been dubbed "The National Game of Africa."[13] Distinctions must be made about gambling forms and their continental distribution. For example, modern playing cards were probably first developed in Fatimid or Mamluk Egypt. Their dissemination through the Mediterranean Basin and into Europe during the Renaissance is clear.[14] Card games were introduced to sub-Saharan Africa at various times during the slave-trade era, and it is possible that by the beginning of the nineteenth century they had penetrated as far inland as southern Zaire.[15] Nonetheless, the popularity of playing cards in Africa is a twentieth-century phenomenon. Square-shaped bones from the feet of humans and animals are ideally suited for pitch-and-toss games. They have been used for millenia north of the Sahara. Called *astragali* in antiquity and knucklebones more recently, they were precursors of modern dice.[16] Although used in southern Africa for divination, knucklebones were not a standard gaming instrument in black Africa, and dice are not used extensively.[17]

Pitch-and-toss games are probably very old in West and Central Africa as they are elsewhere in the world where gambling has been intense. Wood, seeds, bark, and the like are shaped into two-faced gambling chips. A handful of chips are tossed in the air and gamblers bet on the combination landing up or down, open or closed, by displaying their own chips in the anticipated winning positions.[18] The *abbia* game played by the farmer-trappers of southwestern Cameroon is the best-known example of wood chip gambling. The chips are pointed and oblong, usually under four centimeters in length, and carved from the hard nut of a common rain forest

Abbia Gambling Chips

Man

Antelope

Fish

Bird

Snakes

Bird

Flintlock

Crossbow

Blacksmith
Bellows

Mvet
Musical Instrument

Knife

Ideograms

Source: Drawings by Agnes Beschnitt in Morris Siegel, *The Mackenzie Collection: A Study of West African Carved Gambling Chips,* American Anthropological Association Memoir no. 55 (Menasha, Wis., 1940), plates I–VI.

tree. Nuts are split in two and the stylized images of the important objects, activities, and symbols of life are carved on the polished outer convex surface of the chip. Thus, the images of animals in movement and in traps, of warfare, material culture, and ideograms are statements of cultural values and priorities, and the chips serve as primary source material for the study of African art.

Abbia gambling was suppressed early in the colonial period, and if it were not for the placement of a colonial capital we would know much less about the game. The Germans established an administrative post in the midst of the *abbia* gambling region before World War I, and this post, Yaoundé, became the capital of French and later independent Cameroon. Political control generated German and then French academic and popular interest in the groups around the capital. The *abbia* game was studied as it was declining, and chips were collected and placed in Western museums as examples of African miniature carving.[19] The chips are sold today on the tourist market and made into jewelry. The populations of the Yaoundé area were among the first to respond to the challenge of colonialism and now constitute a significant part of the business and political elite of the country. Because of this the gambling chip, an important symbol of the elite, has become one of the images of national life in Cameroon. The shape of the chip is represented on the large mural overlooking the altar of the Catholic cathedral in the capital and is integrated into designs on the robes of priests. Chips have been commemorated on postage stamps, and *Abbia* is the name of a movie theatre in Yaoundé as well as the title of the country's major academic and cultural journal.[20] Thus, while the game has atrophied, the gambling chip has endured to take on new meaning in a larger context.

Minted coins are flipped and tossed in the West; cowrie shells were the trader's and the gambler's currency in Africa. Cowries have an open or female side, and their back or closed side can be cut open and shaved flat for balance. Wax is often added for weight. The most popular type of shell was harvested on the Maldive archipelago in the middle of the Indian Ocean. It was first imported into the Niger Bend of West Africa via the Middle East and North Africa during the medieval period. Beginning in the sixteenth century European slavers brought cowries to the West and Central African coasts in huge quantities, and the primacy of the cowrie as a gambling device dates at least to that century.[21] Since then cowries have become part of local symbolic systems and have entered the gambler's lexicon. In northern Nigeria, where five types of cowrie gambling have been recorded, two shells landing in the closed position are called "cat's eyes," evoking that animal's baleful stare.[22] The number of shells tossed depended upon what numbers were sacred or of import to the local culture. Cowrie gambling was named for the action in southeastern Nigeria: pitch-and-toss. Four or twelve shells were used. As George Basden, an early colonial observer, noted, gaming could be fast and furious:

> 'Pitch and Toss' . . . is . . . one of the fastest ways of winning and losing money ever devised by man. It demands smart alertness and exceptional eyesight to become an expert at the game.
>
> Immediately the calls cease, the challenger gives a peculiar twist to his hand from back to front, causing the shells to spread as they fall. Quick as lightning, the players note the positions and forfeit their stakes or collect their gains. The play becomes exceedingly fast, and soon a cloud of dust encircles each group of gamblers. I have watched players at this game, and it has always been quite beyond me to note the positions of the fall; the cowries have been counted and snatched up again long before I could begin to count.[23]

Africa's most commonly played game of skill is best labeled *wari-solo* for its West and Central African archetypes. Also known by the Arabic name of *mancala,* this game is popular among gamblers. Percy Talbot, writing about

Wari Boards—West Africa

Dogon Board (from Griaule and Dieterlen)

Yoruba Board (from Murray)

Fang Board (from Culin)

Source: Edouard Foa, *Le Dahomey* (Paris, A. Hennuyer, 1895), plate VI.

Ibo Board (from Basden)

Source: G.T. Basden, *Niger Ibos* (1938; reprint edition, New York, Barnes & Noble, 1966), p. xxx.

Patterns of *Wari-Solo* Play

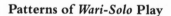

Two Row *Wari* Play

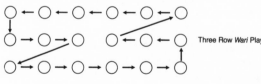

Three Row *Wari* Play

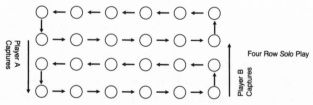

Four Row *Solo* Play

Distribution of *Wari* and *Solo* in Africa

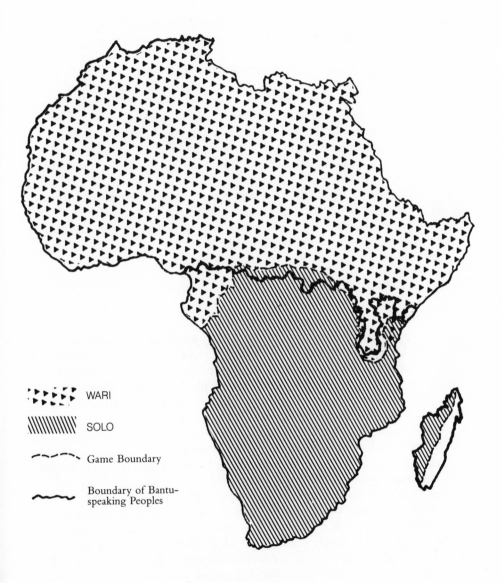

Adapted from Deledicq and Popova, *Wari et solo, le jeu de calculs africain* (Paris, CEDIC, 1977), 107.

the populations of southern Nigeria earlier in this century, characterized *wari-solo* as "a great gambling game, and may be said to take the place of betting and cards in England."[24] It is a board game of calculation and capture in which players on opposite sides of two (*wari*), three (*wari*), or four (*solo*) rows of cups or depressions deposit and capture each other's seeds and beans. Cups in each row can vary from as few as three to eight or more; six is the norm. The goal is to capture all or a prescribed quantity of an opponent's seeds. An equal number of seeds is distributed in each cup; usually four in *wari*-type games and two in *solo* versions. Certain gambits are considered aesthetic for their flow. How the initial distribution begins and where it ends up influences the course of actual play. Free play begins with one contestant lifting all the seeds from a cup on his side of the board and distributing them one by one, usually in a counterclockwise direction. The completion of a lap is followed, depending upon the quantities of seeds in the final cup and in the cup on the adjacent row, by capture and/or another lap. At this point rules for individual games become complex and need not concern us here, for the literature on play abounds with detailed descriptions of the game.[25] Rather, generalized patterns have something to tell us about history and gaming.

Wari-solo is the world's most widely distributed board game. It is played from Manchuria across South Asia to the Middle East and throughout Africa.[26] It was brought to the New World by slaves and is known in Guyana as a "sweet game"—one that is wholly gratifying to play.[27] Unlike chess, backgammon, checkers, and other board games that have evolved toward standardized rules acknowledged across many cultures, *wari-solo* is known in almost a thousand variants.[28] Individual rules are the product of highly localized evolution and adaptation from a common board design. In Africa the game is known by dozens of names, usually a local or regional word for the board or the seeds used.[29]

The first written mention of the game comes from an Arabic source of the tenth century A.D., but it is obviously of much greater antiquity. It evolved in one region of the world and slowly diffused, perhaps along trade routes. While various origin points have been suggested, there are reasons to believe that the game first developed somewhere on the African continent. Here one finds the greatest variety of the gross forms of the game indicating the longest period of in-place evolution. There are two basic cycles of play. In *wari*-type games seeds are distributed in a single cycle around the board. Two-row single-cycle play is the most common in the world and presumably the oldest. Three-row single-cycle play has only been known in parts of Ethiopia, the Horn of Africa, and Arabia. It is a newer, regional variant of a two-row play.

Solo-type games are undoubtedly an African invention and are closely associated with one of the continent's important historical processes: the diaspora of the Bantu-speaking peoples. The games are played with four rows of cups and in twin cycles. Each contestant distributes seeds only in the two rows on his side of the board with capture occurring across the center rows. These games are played exclusively by Bantu speakers of East, Central, and southern Africa and a few of their neighbors. It is worth emphasizing that much controversy surrounds the early history of the Bantu-speaking peoples, and hypotheses come and go with some rapidity. Nonetheless, information about *solo* variants is compatible with what is generally accepted about the diaspora. For example, the game type is not played in the northwest corner of the Bantu zone along the Nigeria-Cameroon border, where the oldest languages of the group are spoken. This suggests that the development and diffusion of *solo* games may have occurred after ca. 700–500 B.C., the latest possible dates for the beginning of expansion. The East African highlands, where the game is strong, may have been an area of innovation. Non-Bantu and Bantu speakers have interacted here, and the highlands adjoin the Horn of Africa, where three-row *wari* games developed. *Solo*-type games are a play overlay in some areas, indicating subsequent diffusion. They seem to have been a relatively recent addition to a preexisting tradition of two-row *wari* in the Central African rain forest. Four-row play occurs in western Madagascar, the area of longest cultural interchange with the East African coast, while in eastern Madagascar an older board game of Asiatic origins is popular.[30] Clearly the forms and history of *wari-solo* are clues to the larger issues of Bantu expansion and need to be considered in future research.

Life is a game; play is life. *Wari-solo* expressed both sides of this reality with myriads of domestic and agrarian images. Rows of cups can be carved out of soft rock in less than an hour to become permanent play locations along trade routes and at river crossings. At one spot in Uganda the sculpting of cups in rocks was associated in oral tradition with the arrival of an ancestral rainmaker, and to touch the cups was to guarantee early rains.[31] Seeds are normally "sown" or "planted" in cups, but in southern Zambia, where rainfall is uncertain, to draw seeds from a cup was "to draw water."[32] Along the Zaire River the course of play was likened to marriage. The game passed from a woman's preparation for marriage through courting and the stages of bridewealth exchange to marriage ending in permanent residence with the husband's kin.[33] Cattle keepers of East Africa called the seeds "cows." Cups became cattle camps, and a cup holding four cows was a "bull." To capture an opponent's seeds was "to eat the goat," and when a move was made that left one vulnerable it was said that one had "eaten his own goat."[34]

Game boards were usually made from wood, and some woods provided a more satisfying or aesthetic sound than others when seeds were dropped into them.[35] The board could be rough-hewn or the finest example of the wood-carver's art. In either case it was a matrix of powerful symbols. Frequently there was a single village board. As it was the symbol of village vitality in parts of Zaire, to desecrate a board by sitting on it required ritual cleansing by the village notable responsible for protecting the board.[36] In northern Gabon the alignment of square cups on the board reproduced exactly the layout of huts in a village, and the board was played as an expression of the village's competitive spirit.[37] Coastal and riverine populations carved boards in the shape of boats and canoes.[38] In the nineteenth century chiefs along the Liberian coast paid with slaves for ivory boards or ones ornamented with gold.[39]

Wari-solo is neither a contemplative exercise nor a counting game. The challenge comes from confronting the rapidly evolving complexities of seed distribution. The game is usually played with such speed that there is not time to count seeds and barely time to consider the implications of a move. In this century one challenging Central African variant has been called "The Airplane," for a whirling propeller evokes the appropriate image of the speed of distribution around the board.[40] There are training regimens for youths who start off with simpler versions of the game. In Rwanda boys are taught a game of *solo* solitaire emphasizing memorization, for if 119 consecutive moves are done correctly in the course of twenty-four laps the board is cleared of all seeds.[41] Only by frequent play over many years can one learn to spot at a glance the implications of certain seed patterns and to chose instantaneously the proper riposte.[42] Skills developed are similar to those of the chess master who learns to identify and respond to a wide variety of classical gambits without thinking through all the moves. Some *wari-solo* masters have been known to play the game blindfolded, and in Burundi the loser in a special blindfold pursuit game played around the outer holes of a *solo* board gave up a cow or had to deliver up a daughter in marriage without requiring bridewealth in exchange.[43]

Despite the speed of play, denouement can be a long time coming. For example, in a common *solo* game there is a contradiction, an irony about the rhythm of competition. The more seeds a person successfully accumulates in the more cups the greater the number of targets he offers his opponent. Conversely, an apparent loser has fewer and more widely scattered seeds on the board and is actually less vulnerable to attack.[44] The flow of *wari-solo* play is made up of a series of electrifying moments: power surges, strategic withdrawals, and dramatic comebacks. Usually, one cannot gain all the seeds of an opponent in a single game, and lengthy match play is normal.[45] This means that *wari-solo* is undertaken when time is available and is perfected by those groups in society that have the time to play. Competition is often seasonal, enjoyed during the idle times after harvest, for example. The game is integrated into rituals, especially those that have periods of rest or inactivity like circumcision or postnuptial seclusion.[46] Leisure, then, is a critical element of play and gambling, and M. B. Nsimbi, a Ugandan commentator on the game, has suggested that the game declined in the colonial era because increasing labor demands cut into free time.[47]

Prestige Gambling, Deception, and Joking Relationships

Pastoralists in northern Uganda staked what seemed to be major assets when playing *solo* games: quantities of cows and rights in one or several girls. Misunderstandings about who staked what with whom were a matter of heated postgame debate. Yet nothing tangible was ever exchanged between loser and winner; cows and young women did not move from one compound to another. Staking was a symbolic act in which the final betting tally became an index of the skill of the victor. Prestige had, in fact, been measurably lost and won.[48] This matter was not inconsequential. Gambling was an integral part of adult play even where goods and rights in people were not exchanged, for the prestige of players was always on the line.

Experience comes with age, and *wari-solo* is the ideal sedentary competition in which elders can express their dominance over younger and more physically able males. Competitive *wari-solo* skills can be appreciated as almost equal to but separate from skills requiring youthful vigor:

> It is the one intellectual test possible, and a skilled player has more than local prestige. It is, moreover, a very real prestige, almost comparable with prowess in hunting, and an outstanding player may even be celebrated in song; he acquires a social status by his skill in the game, and, other things being equal, this intellectual ability may serve to decide the succession of a chieftainship between rival candidates.[49]

Ritual humiliation becomes the first act when gambling for prestige. In Coptic Ethiopia *wari*-style play was accompanied by competitors taunting each other with invective and well-known phrases of contempt. The loser was jeered at by the victor, who contemptuously attempted to make the sign of the cross on the loser's forehead with a seed. "He ate the rat" was the unappetizing metaphor used to describe defeat.[50] A player who won a *solo* match with a single stroke either was extremely skillful or faced an inept opponent. In Uganda defeat from a single stroke meant total and permanent loss of prestige. The victor upset the board, scattering the seeds about, and then demanded that the loser turn the board over and pick up and replace the seeds with his teeth. The loser invariably refused and was denied a rematch.[51]

Cheating, deception, and trickery are skills appreciated in gaming cultures. Cheating was common throughout the Islamic world, and as the popularity of card playing grew among the aristocracy of the ancien régime in France, so did the techniques of deception.[52] In Africa, where the trickster is often exalted in folktales, deception and prestige gambling were interrelated:

> The mental attitude toward cheating is interesting. It is not reprobated, but no one likes being discovered. To be discovered carries no penalty and does not disqualify the player, for he is only called to order and has to make his move again. But to be discovered involves a loss of prestige. It is not the act of cheating, but inept cheating which is discreditable, and often one will hear of an exceptionally brilliant player that he is a most accomplished cheat, as he is never found out. A consistent winner is presumed to be an able cheat, and a player may be congratulated on his powers of cheating even when the compliment is undeserved.[53]

The ability to deceive was a necessary skill of the *wari-solo* player.[54] Seeds can be palmed and dropped in or picked up from incorrect cups with a variety of deft moves.[55] The wooden game board itself has been named "the trickery tree," and at least one version of the game is called "cheating." Competitors are often allowed to conceal their side of the board with arms and hands. So much dust can be kicked up by players and excited spectators when the game is played with holes dug in the ground that visibility is obscured. There are practice games of pursuit played on *solo* boards that are boring if played by the rules, for the outcome is foreseeable from the first move. The challenge comes when players try to deceive each other.[56]

Trickery brings a skill factor to pitch-and-toss gambling that reduces the element of chance. Cowrie shells can be weighted to fall to one side or the other. Altered cowries draw an elevated price in northern Nigeria. There, blind men are assumed to be especially cunning, and a proverb warns, "If you gamble with [cowries], do not do so with a blind man, for he is certain to hide one under his feet."[57] Speed allows deception. It is one reason why pitch-and-toss and *wari-solo* are played with such haste. If a contestant were to slow the pace of play, he might find himself replaced by a spectator. While there are many interdictions about nocturnal play and gambling that deal with respect for supernatural powers, there is also the practical matter that reduced visibility gives the trickster an unnatural advantage.[58]

Distraction is the public side of deception. Spectators kibitz, attempting to turn a competitor's attention or unnerve him so that his opponent can cheat. Children are warned in Lagos about the danger of becoming too fond of *wari* play with the following tale of concentration and distraction:

> One day a man who spent all his spare time playing [*wari*] was deeply engrossed in a game when a messenger came running to tell him that his house was on fire. The player addressed did not take the report seriously, and was so little alarmed at the news that whenever his opponent was slow

to play he twitted him saying: . . . Play! They say your house is burning! Later, when the game was over, and the speaker went to his house, he found it burnt to the ground.[59]

As stakes rose and as larger groups became involved the tone of competition changed. Deception and distraction became issues of danger, raising the threat of violence.[60] Formal umpiring was rare in precolonial Africa, but when it occurred it was in conjunction with high-stakes gambling. Chiefs were expected to control gambling and adjudicate disputes during long and raucous competitions in the Liberian interior.[61] *Abbia* gambling was a most serious business, and a recognized master of the game with no direct interest in the outcome of a contest was recruited to throw the chips, proclaim the victor, and regulate disagreements.[62]

Competition and violence were so closely related when adults played that many times people were literally gambling with the peace. Joking relationships have long been recognized as a mechanism by which individuals and groups both express and control the tensions that exist between them. Humor, joking insult, and friendly abuse were institutionalized in the play arena as a counterpoint to the antagonisms built up by competition for things, people and prestige.[63] Raillery was an element essential to strategies of distraction and deception. Ritual insult was part of *wari*-type play in southwestern Nigeria. A newly arrived spectator would ask who was winning by declaring, "I greet the novice and I greet the adept." The person who was winning would respond, "The adept is answering, the novice dares not answer."[64] In northern Uganda pastoralists and agriculturalists met to trade in a highly charged atmosphere. Watchfulness and distrust were the mood until someone started up a *solo* match, and before the day was out ambiance and trust had been created out of bantering and boasting. Only then could trade begin. In the same area groups that had been at war might have to meet from necessity. After a few *solo* games they would be discussing amicably a number of topics including former raids against each other.[65]

Antigambling Sentiment

Gambling is rarely condoned in those societies where high-stakes betting is intense. At a minimum it is characterized as a moral caution. The message is embedded in African oral literature. The people who played *abbia* at the beginning of this century told a story about lightning and the animals. An impartial man was chosen as umpire, then the chimpanzee, lion, and gorilla gambled high stakes with lightning. They played against lightning individually; they pooled their bets and played against him collectively. They won. At the end of competition, however, *crack!* Lightning struck! All the animals were killed; only the umpire was left alive to referee the future. Lightning scooped up the winnings and departed.[66] This tale is a metaphor about the life-threatening quality of gambling and warns one to be careful in the choice of gambling adversaries. Proverbs from northern Nigeria strike a similar cautionary note. "A [cowrie] gambler is not a man" suggests that gaming diminishes the one involved.[67] "Gambling soon estranges a person from his relatives" emphasizes the threat to individuals and their kin and client networks.[68]

Gambling was a compelling cultural option in those rain forest societies lacking centralized authority structures. The opportunity to accumulate goods, prestige, and rights in people was open to all men who had or could beg, borrow, or steal the stakes to play. Mothers teaching moral precepts in the *abbia* zone of the forest advised their sons not to play the game, as well they might, for women were frequently the stakes.[69] However, maternal precepts had little effect in a society where there was no institution to contain or limit gaming. When centralizing structures did exist attempts were often made to suppress gambling, because it was an obvious threat to peace and order. For example, in the late nineteenth century emperor Menelik II of Ethiopia forbade gambling. Apparently he was successful, for it has not been pervasive in the Ethiopian highlands in this century.[70] Elsewhere local chiefs acted independently. Antigambling measures of village chiefs in the Kwango River valley of Zaire were sufficiently standardized that the placing of a special palm leaf in the village center was recognized by all to mean No Gambling Allowed![71] In the nearby Kuba Kingdom the commemorative statue of a king who ruled in the second quarter of the seventeenth century was the symbol of royalty's attempt to control gambling. A *wari-solo* board was placed in front of the stylized figure of the seated king as a mnemonic marker, for oral traditions say he taught his people this game of skill to divert them from their passion for games of chance. However, the reform did not endure, as *wari-solo* subsequently became a popular betting game.[72]

Islam is its own case. The Koran is clear about gambling:

> They will ask thee about wine and games of chance: Say, "In them is sin and profit to men; but the sin of both is greater than the profit of the same." [Sura II, verse 216]
>
> "O believers, verily, wine and games and statues and divining arrows are only an abomination of Satan's work; therefore, avoid them, that haply ye may prosper. Satan only desires to place enmity and hatred between you by wine and game; and to turn you from the remembrance of God and from prayer; but will ye not desist, and obey God?" [Sura V, verses 92f][73]

On the other hand, as many as twenty-seven types of games may have been used for betting in the medieval Middle East.[74] The apparent contradiction between Koranic injunction and the popularity of gambling in Muslim West Africa has not gone unnoticed.[75] Given the history of Islam in the region, the antigambling provisions of the Koran were hard to implement. Up to the beginning of the nineteenth century Islam existed in an atmosphere of cultural pluralism and accommodation with non-Islamic traditions. Even when the Muslim reformist regime of the Sokoto Caliphate attempted to suppress gambling in nineteenth-century northern Nigeria it was unable to do much more than limit what was a deeply engrained practice.[76]

There has always been an undertone of cynicism in Muslim societies about the gambling interdiction. As one sultan of Morocco, who was known for his high-stakes betting at cards, said when reminded of the interdiction, "I do not gamble, I cheat."[77] Gambling was an exchange system that became entangled in Koranic complexities about commerce and moneylending. Legal accommodation and outright subterfuge pertaining to usury were transferred, by close analogy, to gambling. Sura II verses 276–77 states, "Surely they say, usury is like sale. But God has made sale lawful and usury unlawful." Gambling was seen as a form of usury in which the "use value" of money was risked in an immoral transaction for unproductive gain. Usury and gambling were, in the sense of Sura II verse 216 quoted above, "sin and profit to men." However, commerce entails risk, especially the short- and long-term risking of money and goods in trade. This necessary risk was recognized and permitted under Muslim law, and it was the analogous risk factor of gambling that came to be tolerated.[78]

Despite accommodation, subterfuge, and cynicism, gambling remained a sin provoking in the devout a sense of metaphysical guilt. The metaphysical element has proven a more enduring strain of antigambling feeling in monotheistic cultures than the edicts of holy books and the musings of theologians and lawyers. Gambling challenges monotheism implicitly as metaphysics and explicitly as ritual. It is about chance, luck, and fate, even in areas where the effort is made to minimize chance and maximize skill through cheating and deception. Gambling is a mockery and a heresy to belief systems that emphasize the existence of a world with a purpose directed by a single omniscient being. A gambler makes a public effort to change the course of the future by willfully entering the play arena. It is only a short step from thinking about gambling to considering a deeply threatening issue: free will. Medieval Muslim poets linked fate and gambling in metaphor, and in the ninth century A.D. gambling was used as a metaphor for the discussion of free will.[79] There are also Christian reasons to take seriously gambling's metaphysical challenge to monotheism. Gambling was rife in polytheistic Rome, and it was only the Christian emperors who made a concerted effort through law to suppress it.[80] It seems no coincidence that the Coptic Church of Ethiopia, heir to the monophysite tradition in Christianity, was opposed to the use of games in divination and forbade priests from playing *wari-solo*.[81] However, in non-Coptic and non-Muslim Africa the gods and the ancestors were far more tolerant of gambling.

Gambling with the Gods

The connection between games, gods, and gambling is intimate. The outcome of a contest is a matter of doubt. The future is uncertain without the intervention of the ancestors and their supernatural powers. Sensible people do not risk precious things without first seeking the assistance of the forces that influence or predict the future. Like trickery and deception, the ability to invoke the gods or manipulate the supernatural was an essential gambling skill. The outcome of play was dramatic proof of the winner's association with powers that went beyond the normal ken. The reality of the random event encouraged the doctoring of the player and his gaming instruments, and Levy-Bruhl's general observation about non-Western gamblers holds for Africa: "It is often observed that before the native gambles he goes through a series of methodical preparations. He fasts, he purifies himself, he dances, he seeks to procure himself certain dreams and only risks his stake when he has obtained them."[82]

The random event is described in terms of luck in the West; in Africa it was a question of power being rubbed on and even ingested. For example, Liberian gamblers rubbed their hands on personal medicine hidden under their sitting mats before they scooped up the cowries for a toss.[83] An *abbia* gambler was one of the best-prepared gamesters on the continent. In his culture the physical properties of plants and animals were transferable to himself and his gambling chips. This gave him direct access to the powers embedded in the biologically congested rain forest. Each player laid out disks carved from a specific gourd to indicate the anticipated winning combination of chips in an *abbia* toss. The night before the contest a gambler ate a special meal prepared from the seeds of the gourd. The folk pharmacopeia was part of his arsenal. He was warmed up and fortified by as many as eight different medicines made from spicy plants or ones that burned. Burrs were mingled with the stakes to snare a win.[84] Women did not gamble, but some men were fortunate to be married to "good luck wives" whose presence at a match inspired victory.[85]

The mystique of the gambling chip was part of the culture. The nut from which the chip was carved as well as the fruit surrounding the nut were said to be poisonous. The tree itself was a danger to gamblers, and they had to get nuts for carving from women and children who collected the fruit.[86] Each chip was a power unit, and nongamblers were known to carry or wear a chip as a protective charm. The power was derived from the force of the object or ideogram carved on the face of the chip, and the efficacy of the power was warped and shaped by the personality and force of the owner.

Abbia chips were stored in a bag that was suspended from a tree hidden in the forest far from the village, for the sack contained too malevolent a jumble of conflicting forces to be kept near people. An experienced gambler possessed dozens, even hundreds of chips, and, if losing heavily, he staked those possessions last. The expert knew which of his chips were best used against opposing chip patterns. He was aware of how his chips interacted with the seasons, the rains, and the hour of the day.[87] In reality the numerous powers to which the *abbia* gambler had direct access increased his choices and thus his difficulties. He added to the uncertainty of the random event the complex task of manipulating a myriad of forces in environmental combat.

Gambling and divination are part of the same ideological matrix. Each is, in its own way, an attempt to address the future and to gain insight into the affairs of men. Symbolic associations between the two are close, and often the gamester and the diviner manipulated the same devices. The Roman gambler cast four *astragali* as did the priest in the temple.[88] Cowries were the instruments of the gambler and the diviner in west Africa. Four were commonly used in pitch-and-toss gambling, and, as with cowrie divination, four up or four down were preferred combinations. There are sixteen possible outcomes when four cowries are thrown, and sixteen is often a power number.[89] In southwestern Nigeria and neighboring Benin sixteen cowries were thrown in divination, and the practice was brought to the New World by slaves.[90]

Diviners have adapted the *wari-solo* board to their needs here and there across the continent. An oral tradition from southwestern Cameroon tells how a clan ancestor introduced *wari* play to his people as a means of detecting who was at fault when he judged disputes.[91] War is always a gamble, and diviners and magicians were essential components of the precolonial order of battle. *Wari-solo* is a war game. Play is "battle," and losers are "killed" or have their "heads cut off."[92] In the Kingdom of Benin one version of the game was played in a mnemonic sequence recalling the great wars of the past.[93] It is only a short step from playing the war game to using it to predict the outcome of combat, and warriors in Afars and Issas played it precisely for this purpose.[94]

The knowledge that competition among men is the mirror of combat between supernatural forces has endured from the precolonial era to postindependence. It is a fact accepted by one group living on the Zaire River upstream from Kinshasa that each team in a soccer match starts out with a preordained number of goals. In the days preceding the match, team magicians do battle with medicine and supernatural force to steal the opponent's points and to defend their own. Actual play is the public enactment of what the magician's combat has already determined.[95] Cameroonian soccer players kick up the ground around their opponent's goal in an effort to uncover the magic that keeps the ball from going in, and the magician's salary is a normal operating expense for many Kenyan soccer teams.[96] We can only guess at the scope and power of the supernatural forces that permeate nighttime play in a lighted soccer stadium.

If play reflects the will of the gods, one could play God too. If he dares, the litigant in Uganda can compete at *solo* before he goes to court, but his loss at play can become his verdict in court.[97] Furthermore, *wari-solo* is widely associated with power numbers. As with pitch-and-toss gambling, the number four is important. It is the women's number for fertility. The game was frequently associated with fertility and played with clusters of four seeds and with multiples of four. Many *solo* games call for an initial distribution of forty-eight seeds, a sacred number in ritual and cosmology.[98] There is a special game of *wari* played by women on the Ivory Coast in order to influence the sex of the unborn. A pregnant woman plays with a girl or a boy, depending upon which sex she wishes for her child. If she wants twins, a fortuitous pairing, then she plays with twins.[99] Play literally makes the world go round for the populations of the Niger Bend. Priests there said that a *wari*-type game was given to man to allow him to influence the cosmos. The heavens were conceived of as a celestial ark with twin arches running its length. Holes in arches were analogues to the rows of cups in the game. Play allowed man diurnal and nocturnal control of celestial bodies. The board was oriented on an east–west axis, and play made possible the movement of the sun on the same axis. Pebbles were stars, and the circulation of pebbles around the board facilitated the movement of the stars around the heavens. The game provoked movement through time as well as space, for each cup represented a month.[100]

The Unexamined Exchange System of Africa

The economics of gambling has rarely been a subject of study outside the West. It is argued that one man's gambling loss is simply another man's gain. The amount of goods circulating in a society as a whole is unchanged, and services do not increase. Gambling, therefore, is an unproductive system and by extension the economics of gambling is unimportant.[101] Such reasoning begs many issues. Who gambles, who wins, and what is won are important. One man's gains can be many men's losses, a fact of consequence to the winner's and losers' kin and clients. Gambling can stimulate production, for "gambling debts, like the economic debts accrued in gift and ceremonial exchange and the tax and tribute of advanced societies, require households to produce beyond their needs."[102]

Gambling has been the unexamined exchange system of Africa. In some societies it ranked just behind bridewealth as a nonmarket mechanism for transferring goods, services, and rights in people. Food, salt, iron tools and weapons, beads, and cowries were commonly staked. Cattle were redistributed through gambling in East Africa. Land was bet in Ethiopia.[103] In the nineteenth century Zaire River gamblers, operating from dugout canoes, wagered quantities of money and trade goods in cowrie games.[104] Professional gamblers who supported themselves solely on their winnings were not unknown in West Africa. Sometimes it was the gambler who accumulated wealth, political office, and tribute. In African history gaming was perhaps at its most spectacular during the slave-trade era. For example, Ouidah was a major West African port with a rated annual export capacity of one thousand to six thousand slaves in the eighteenth century.[105] William Bosman, writing in 1704, described the residents of Ouidah: "They are great gamesters, and willingly stake all they are masters of in the world at play; and when money and goods are wanting, like the Chinese, they stake first wife and children, and then land and body."[106] Early in the eighteenth century gambling became such a problem that one Ouidah king banned it. However, his weak successor turned a blind eye to the practice to avoid popular resistance from his subjects.[107] A king of Dahomey, one of Ouidah's suppliers, banned gaming and threatened to sell violators directly into the slave trade.[108] A similar passion for gambling and betting with human lives was noted nearby at Accra.[109]

When rights in people were wagered gambling became involved with the most pivotal factors of production in agrarian noncapitalist economies: labor and human reproduction. What struck observers most was the frequency with which rights in people were staked. The exchange of these rights through gambling was a complex issue intertwined with many non-market mechanisms. Judicial ordeal is gambling with the gods, and in one Ivory Coast society cowrie gambling determined who was right and wrong in a dispute with the victor enslaving the loser.[110] Gambling was one way for elders to gain access to the labor and produce of more physically fit juniors. Older men have been known to cajole and goad less experienced and younger men into *solo* play in Zaire to get them to bet their labor, and it seems no coincidence that professional gamblers were noted for their age in Upper Volta.[111] A meager material stake was quickly depleted, forcing the poor to gamble their freedom. Thus, high-stakes gambling was open to many people, if only once or for a brief period in their lives.

Men gambled but women generally did not, for men usually controlled the stakes in society. Cowrie shell gambling seems to have been exclusively a male enterprise. There were men's versions of *wari-solo,* and there were women's versions. Only under the most exceptional circumstances did one play with members of the opposite sex. In some societies women did not play at all, forbidden by formal interdiction. Adult play and gaming reflected the realities of the sexual division of stakes and labor, and as public ritual it affirmed and reinforced the division. The accepted wisdom is that women did not play or played infrequently because they lacked leisure time.[112] While undoubtedly true in many cases, the argument does not explain the full dimensions of female play and of women's role in gambling. Women have been known to take up *wari-solo* as a serious pastime. Royal women played the game in Uganda.[113] De Golbéry reported that *wari* was avidly pursued in the mid-1780s by women of the Senegambia area, for "young Fulani, Wolof and Mandingo women have a passion for a game they call *ouri;* it is a game of combination that they play frequently and they glory in being skillful at it."[114]

Women's play can tell us about women's culture and about economic relationships. For example, men may gamble, but they were not always worth gambling for. The point is made in a women's *solo* game from northwestern Tanzania in which a single seed in a cup cannot be played, suggesting the aphorism, "Males are not productive." Two seeds in a cup are playable and are known as "woman," for "women are productive."[115] Men gambled for the productive and reproductive capacity of the opposite sex, and in this sense women were instrumentalities of gambling culture. In the *abbia* zone of southwestern Cameroon people were gathered around re-sourceful lords of the forest who established their primacy through all the manly arts: hunting, combat, and gambling. Rights in women were wa-gered frequently, and in one reported case a particularly successful forest lord acquired ninety-seven women exclusively through gambling.[116] By loaning women to bachelors the chieftain guaranteed the loyalty of these single men. This system is symbolized in the very name of the *abbia* gambling chip, which means both "gambling pawn" and "loan woman."[117]

In Africa much of what has been described as enslavement through gambling was actually debt pawning, and the possibility of debt redemption helps explain the willingness to gamble away rights in people. The loss of rights in a woman or a child was not necessarily irrevocable. One was also betting that in case of a gambling loss one could, with time, redeem the debt pawn. The arrangement was well understood along the western shore of Lake Tanganyika: "[The gambler] stakes without the least regret his whole fortune, the woman he married, a slave and even his child, with the tacit understanding that he can buy them back.[118]

Eyewitness accounts from the *abbia* zone explain graphically what it meant to be a living symbol of a bad bet. In 1889 a German trader came upon two *abbia* losers who had been held for three months in the stocks of the victor's village, where they were slowly starving to death for lack of anyone to redeem them.[119] Pawns and slaves alike were mutilated to mark them. When there was an active slave trade, pawns could be exported if debt redemption did not occur promptly. A pawn might be held for as little as a day in the Yaoundé area of Cameroon in the mid-1890s and then be sold to traders for ten to fifteen pounds of salt.[120]

Gambling was compatible with precolonial African class structure. If political regimes could suppress gambling among commoners, their ruling groups could also co-opt it as their own class-exchange system. *Wari-solo* gambling was a visible affirmation that the aristocracy had the free time to play and the assets to wager. Across the continent the game board was a symbol of the leisured ways of courtly life. The king of Ashanti played on a gold board; bronze boards were used in Benin.[121] Board and seeds were royal insignia in the interlacustrine kingdoms of East Africa. There the new king of Buganda plucked the seeds for future royal play from a sacred tree as part of his investiture ritual, and games were played by court notables and distinguished visitors in the corridors and thatched antechambers of the royal enclosure.[122] The power of kingship and the malevolence of gambling are closely associated in the oral lore of Rwanda. When kings gambled with the gods they threatened the lives of *solo* players. A proverb warns that "the king who, in the morning, consults with diviners kills the one who, in the morning, is playing *(solo)*." Gambling was a source of dissension and violence between members of royal families just as it was between commoners. The Rwandan origin myth states that the wandering hero who founded the kingdom had been forced to migrate because his brother had expropriated all his cows and goods in *solo* gambling. Vengeance was later achieved when the victorious brother was murdered while playing the game.[123] *Solo* was so closely associated with the Rwandan ruling class that the game went into eclipse following the overthrow of the aristocracy in the 1960s.[124]

Gambling the realm was a prerogative of the ruling class. The aristocracy could win and lose goods and people, and kings and chiefs could literally gamble away their right to rule and collect tribute. Expropriation through play was far less disruptive than the violent expropriation of war. Thus, in northwestern Tanzania kings have been known to stake tributary rights to villages when gambling with each other. Here the king was the champion gamester of the state, and theoretically he could lose his right to rule to a more able opponent, even if the opponent was a commoner. However, there was too much at stake in terms of prestige and tribute for his notables to allow that to happen. If someone arrived at court whose playing skills were not known, he was tested first. Should his ability appear superior to that of the king, the court notables brushed aside his challenge.[125] Nocturnal play was always a danger, because so many supernatural forces operated after sundown. Nighttime gambling was an affair for magicians and those willing to play for the very highest stakes. It was the ideal environment in which to gamble with the gods. Pretenders to a chiefship in Upper Volta played a *wari* game at night. The winner ruled, for nocturnal play was known to reveal the will of the ancestors.[126] Kings and courtiers took great risks in managing the affairs of state, and this last example of the politics of play is presented to show how risk-taking integrates with the dramatic historical moment. In southern Ghana awareness of danger was hidden behind a facade of indifference displayed through royal play, for rulers engaged in *wari* in full view of their court when most threatened.[127] The collapse of the kingdom of Denkyira at the end of the seventeenth century was a pivotal episode in the rise of the Ashanti confederation, and "[the Denkyira king] was said to have been found by the Ashanti . . . army sitting shackled with golden fetters and playing *wari* . . . with one of his wives. They were beheaded and the golden fetters . . . became part of the insignia of the [Ashanti] Golden Stool.[128]

End of the Beginning

The purpose here, quite baldly put, was to make a case for the systematic study of gambling in Africa. A continental-wide survey was necessary because there are no complete local studies. Articles and bits and snippets on *abbia* are as close as we get, but even here the more that is learned the more questions there are to ask. *Abbia* gambling was just one expression in one locale of a type and style of competitive life characteristic of many Central African rain forest societies. Competition sprang from the nature of social organization and the disparities in wealth and prestige. Gambling was one way for a man of no consequence to upgrade his economic condition and to revolutionize his social status in a single coup. It was a necessary act of social desperation by a class of have-nots or have-littles, and as we have seen the penalties for failure could be grim in the extreme. On the other hand, the lords of the forest had to gamble to assert their prowess and potency. It was also a way, if they were skillful, well doctored and deceptive, to exploit the underclass. Gambling must be understood against the backdrop of compelling competition before it can be placed in its proper economic context.

Gambler's wealth could be bridewealth as the following two *abbia* episodes indicate. A seventy-five-year-old woman testified to a researcher in 1967 that in her youth she had been pawned against a gambling debt. She became a loan woman passed from hand to hand until redeemed by her father who, apparently, paid with the bridewealth provided him by the man she did marry.[129] Conversely, in 1907 a successful *abbia* gambler loaned his winnings to a friend so that the friend could pay bridewealth.[130] Competitive gift-giving was another pervasive system of exchange. This potlatch-type mechanism operated in place of or alongside trade systems across a broad forest belt. It was a form of very public risk taking, for the lords of the forest had to deliver up their wealth to one another in ceremonies where goods became the gambling instruments and prestige was the stake.[131] We need to know how gambling and bridewealth meshed with competitive gift-giving to form a total system of nonmarket exchange. Once we do a fuller dimension of African economic history will be revealed.

Gambling created debt, and debt encouraged production in a general sense. More specifically gambling was a component of precolonial trade and commercial relations whose significance has not been appreciated. This is especially true in the gaming regions touched by Africa's many slave trades. If we take eyewitness accounts seriously, it would appear that on the Slave Coast debt pawns and gambling debtors were one of several constant sources of sustaining the transatlantic trade in between the supply surges fed by prisoners of war coming from inland conflicts. Gambling was often the socioeconomic activity of traders, and cowrie gaming and *wari-solo* play enhanced computational skills and business acumen. Turning back to the slave port of Ouidah, an early eighteenth-century observer followed up lengthy remarks about gambling there with a comment that has a familiar ring:

> It must be said in their praise that there are few people who know as well as they their business, who know it with so much skill and finesse, who see it so clearly, and who know better how to take advantage of time and opportunity. Without knowing the rules of arithmetic they can compute in their head the price of merchandise and do it more quickly than an accountant can do it with quill and tally sheet, and one need not fear that they will be mistaken or that they will forget the least thing whether it be commissions or charges.[132]

Gambling becomes the political economy of play when leaders and ruling groups wager. Kings and chiefs had to grapple with the fact and the threat of gambling by their subjects. African polities were ingenious in the ways they channeled the potential for disorder into symbolic expression. Ritual rebellion is one example. Ritual sport is another, for the champion of the king of Benin wrestled with the champions of his territorial chiefs as an expression of the tensions that existed between superior and subordinates in a charged political atmosphere.[133] Gambling operated in the same manner at courts. Kings and their minions staked people, goods, and even their realms, status, and rights to tribute. The examples on record are sufficient to suggest that gambling was one of the important transactions in precolonial African political economies, and high-stakes gaming among today's African administrative and commercial bourgeoisie is worth investigating for similar reasons.

Gambling is deep play; it is deeply symbolic. People take risks for reasons that transcend the economic utility of the bet. With or without high material stakes men risk prestige, honor, and esteem in the play arena. The value of money and goods exchanged is often of less import than the meaning of the words exchanged between contestants. The art of verbal abuse and joking insult is as integral to status gambling as it is to war and peace. The diminishing physical capacity of elders is overshadowed by their displays of dexterity, skill, and intellect at *wari-solo*. The gaming board, shell, and seed offer access to the powers that shape and warp the lives of men and women. Gambling with the gods is more than simple metaphor; it becomes a vital function of life itself. Not to gamble would be irrational, for one would then be open to all the uncertainties of life. Thus, the instrumentalities of play—both objects and ideologies—need to be studied for a deeper understanding of the meaning of life in African gaming cultures.

We lack a detailed study of how kin and corporate group membership constrained and directed who gambled with whom in Africa. Geertz, writing on the Balinese case in Indonesia, points out that the more distantly related or connected were two gamblers the more likely they were to wager high stakes. Villages backed their own champions.[134] Presumably similar factors operated in Africa, but we lack proof from a good case study. The issue is especially important where rights in people were staked. Did rules of exogamy mean that women were gambled out, and were they more likely to be gambled between groups that normally intermarried? If so, did this sour existing intergroup relations, or did previous intermarriage between groups take the bite out of the fact that gambling was nonreciprocal exchange? To whom was one more likely to give a debt pawn?

Recent writing makes clear that lineage and kinship ties in many African societies were not as rigid and binding as once thought. Lineage was an ideology regulating and legitimizing webs of complex and often quite fluid social relationships.[135] Nowhere was this truer than among the gambling cultures of the central African rain forest. What was once believed to be an extensive zone of segmentary societies is now more accurately seen to be an area where an open-ended "house system" prevailed. Houses were corporate groups organized around lords of the forest, expanding and contracting in relationship to the changing fortunes of these men. House relationships rarely endured beyond the lifetime of the forest lord, offering little inter-generational continuity.[136] Gambling was well adapted to such a situation as we have seen. We might then speculate that people came together more or less willy-nilly to gamble. This happened in the *abbia* zone, where gambling festivals drew people from the surrounding countryside.[137] Gambling parties lasted for weeks, even months in the Liberian hinterland.

> Such a game means an event for the village, even for the whole region; spectators are found in crowds, women and girls are provided by their owners to serve as dancers, singers, vendors of liquor and food . . . ; drums, songs and yells fill the place. Friends encourage and reward the players with shouts of applause, so that soon an unrestrained excitement takes hold which carries the players into the greatest imprudences . . .[138]

In these cases the exchange of goods, services and people seems to have been determined more by the outcome of *abbia* chip and cowrie toss than by kin, clan or corporate group interests. If this was so in other areas where gambling was widely practiced, then the term *random event* comes to have great meaning in the processes of history.

Notes

1. John M. Cooper, *Temporal Sequence and the Marginal Cultures,* Catholic University of America, Anthropological Series no. 10 (Washington, D.C., 1941), 67; Rodolfo Lanciani, "Gambling and Cheating in Ancient Rome," *North American Review* (1892): 97–105; John A. Price, "Gambling in Traditional Asia," *Anthropologica,* n.s. 14, no. 2 (1972): 162–63; and Franz Rosenthal, *Gambling in Islam* (Leiden: E. J. Brill, 1975), 67, 69.

2. W. Holman Bentley, *Dictionary and Grammar of the Kikongo Language* (London: Baptist Missionary Society, 1887), 495; Charles Delhaise, *Les Warega (Congo Belge),* Collection de Monographies ethnographiques 5 (Brussels: Albert de Wit, 1909): 277; Joseph Halkin and Ernest Viaene, *Les Ababua (Congo Belge),* Collection de Monographies ethnographiques 7 (Brussels: Albert de Wit, 1911): 452; Philippe Laburthe-Tolra, trans. and ed., "Yaoundé d'après Zenker (1895)," *Annales de la Faculté des Lettres et Sciences Humaines de Yaoundé* 2 (1970): 92–93; Joseph Mertens, *Les Ba Dzing de la Kamtsha* (Brussels: Marcel Hayez, 1933), 289; Robert Schmitz, *Les Baholoholo (Congo Belge),* Collection de Monographies ethnographiques 9 (Brussels: Albert Dewit, 1912): 431–32; Morris Siegel, *The Mackenzie Collection: A Study of West African Carved Gambling Chips,* American Anthropological Association Memoir no. 55 (Menasha, Wis., 1940): 20–21; Frederick Starr, *Ethnographic Notes from the Congo Free State: An African Miscellany,* Proceedings of the Davenport Academy of Sciences 12 (Davenport, Iowa, 1909): 144–46; Emil Torday, *Camp and Tramp in African Wilds* (London: Seeley, Service & Co., 1913), 137; Cyr. van Overbergh, *Les Bangala (Etat Ind. du Congo),* Collection de Monographies ethnographiques 1 (Brussels: Albert de Wit, 1907): 317; Cyr. van Overbergh and Ed. de Jonghe, *Les Mangbetu (Congo Belge),* Collection de Monographies ethnographiques 4 (Brussels: Albert de Wit, 1909): 427; A. M. Vergiat, *Moeurs et coutumes des Manjas* (Paris: Payot, 1937), 137; Samuel Verner, *Pioneering in Central Africa* (Richmond: Presbyterian Committee of Publications, 1903), 127–28; John H. Weeks, *Among Congo Cannibals* (London: Seeley, Service & Co., 1913), 154; and John H. Weeks, *Among the Primitive Bakongo* (London: Seeley, Service & Co., 1914), 127.

3. Burt W. and Ethel G. Aginsky, "The Pomo, A Profile of Gambling among Indians," in Morris Ploscowe and Edwin J. Lukas, eds., *Gambling, Annals of the American Academy of Political and Social Sciences* 269 (1950): 108–13; Stewart Culin, *Games of the North American Indians* in *Twenty-Fourth Report of the Bureau of American Ethnology 1902–1903* (Washington, D.C.: Government Printing Office, 1907), 44–225; G. R. Desmond, *Gamblng among the Yakima,* American Anthropological Association Anthropological Series no. 14 (Washington, D.C., 1952); and Regina Flannery and John M. Cooper, "Social Mechanisms in Gros Ventre Gambling," *Southwestern Journal of Anthropology* 2, no. 1 (1946): 391–419.

4. Edmund Bergler, *The Psychology of Gambling* (New York: Hill and Wang, 1957), vii (italics by Bergler). See also William R. Eadington, ed., *Gambling and Society, Interdisciplinary Studies on the Subject of Gambling* (Springfield, Ill.: Charles C.

Thomas, 1976), part 4; and Robert M. Lindner, "The Psychodynamics of Gambling," in Ploscowe and Lukas, 93–107.

5. T. H. Breen, "Horses and Gentlemen: The Cultural Significance of Gambling among the Gentry of Virginia," *William and Mary Quarterly* 3d ser. 34, no. 2 (1977): 239–57; and Ross McKibbin, "Working-Class Gambling in Britain, 1880–1939," *Past and Present* 82 (1979): 147–78.

6. Charles Béart, *Jeux et jouets de l'ouest africain,* Mémoires de l'Institut Français d'Afrique Noire no. 42, 2 vols. (Dakar, 1955); Th. H. Centner, *L'enfant africain et ses jeux dans le cadre de la vie traditionnelle au Katanga,* Mémoires du Centre d'Etudes des Problèmes Sociaux Indigènes no. 17 (Elisabethville, Katanga, 1963); Marcel Griaule, *Jeux Dogons,* Travaux et Mémoires de l'Institut d'Ethnologie no. 32 (Paris, 1938); and Fritz Klepzig, *Kinderspiele der Bantu* (Meisenheim am Glan: A. Hain, 1972).

7. Johan Huizinga, *Homo Ludens: A Study of the Play Element in Culture* (Boston, Beacon Press, 1955); and Roger Caillois, *Les jeux et les hommes* (Paris: Gallimard, 1958) trans. by Meyer Barash as *Man, Play and Games* (New York: Free Press, 1961). See also Charles Béart, *Recherche des éléments d'une sociologie des peuples africains à partir de leurs jeux* (Paris: Présence Africaine, 1960). For a more provocative theoretical analysis of play see Victor Turner, "Liminal to Liminoid, in Play, Flow, and Ritual: An Essay on Comparative Symbology," in Edward Norbeck, ed., *The Anthropological Study of Play, Rice University Papers* 60, no. 3 (1974): 53–92.

8. Clifford Geertz, "Deep Play: Notes on the Balinese Cockfight," in *The Interpretation of Cultures: Selected Essays by Clifford Geertz* (New York: Basic Books, 1973), 412–53, reprinted from *Daedalus* 101 (1972): 1–37.

9. Rosenthal, 6–7.

10. Béart, *Jeux et jouets de l'ouest africain* I, 421–22, 425; Paul Bohannan, *Justice and Judgment among the Tiv* (London: International African Institute, 1957), 115; Henri A. Junod, *The Life of a South African Tribe,* 2 vols. (Neufchatel, Switz.: Attinger Frères, 1912), I, 318; Laburthe-Tolra, "Yaoundè d'après Zenker (1895)," 93 n. 5; Siegel, 21; and Verner, 128.

11. Siegel, 23. It should be pointed out that *Notes and Queries on Anthropology,* 6th ed. (London: Routledge and Kegan Paul, 1951), one of the standard references for field inquiries in Africa, makes only passing mention of gambling, 335.

12. Laura Longmore, "A Study of Fah-Fee," *South African Journal of Science* 52, no. 12 (1956): 275–82.

13. Stewart Culin, "Mancala, The National Game of Africa," *Report of the U.S. National Museum 1894* (Washington, D. C.: Government Printing Office, 1896), 595–607, reprinted in Elliott M. Avedon and Brian Sutton-Smith, eds., *The Study of Games* (New York: John Wiley & Sons, 1971), 94–102.

14. Rosenthal, 62–63, 172; and Roger Tilley, *A History of Playing Cards* (London: Studio Vista, 1973), chaps. 1–2.

15. Harry H. Johnston, *George Grenfell and the Congo,* 2 vols. (London: Hutchinson & Co., 1908), II, 708.

16. Th. Capidan, "Le jeu aux osselets chez les Roumains, les Slaves et les Albanais," *Revue internationale des études balkaniques* 1 (1934–35): 211–31; and F. N. David, *Games, Gods and Gambling* (New York: Hafner Publishing Co., 1962), 2–20.

17. Béart, *Jeux et jouets de l'ouest africain* I, 350, 424; and Jacques-Olivier Grandjouan, *L'astragale et le pari* (Paris: G.-P. Maisonneuve et La Rose, 1969), 30–32.

18. Béart, *Jeux et jouets de l'ouest africain* I, 424ff; Delhaise, 277; Halkin et Viaene, 451; and Vergiat, 137.

19. Simone Delarozière et Gertrude Luc, "Une forme peu connue de l'expression artistique africaine: l'*Abbia*. Jeu de dés des populations forestières du sud-Cameroun," *Etudes camerounaises* 49–50 (1955): 3–52; Luitfrid Marfurt, "Abbia, un jeu des Beti du sud-cameroun," *Abbia* 25 (1971): 69–80; Maurice Pervès, "Parmi les Fang de la forêt équatoriale: le jeu de l'abbia," *Revue de géographie humaine et d'ethnologie* 1, no. 3 (1948): 26–41; Frederick Quinn, "Abbia Stones," *African Arts* 4, no. 4 (1971): 30–32; Otto Reche, *Das Abia-Glückspiel der Jaunde und die Darstellungen auf den Spielmarken*, Mitteilungen aus dem Museum für Völkerkunde in Hamburg no. 9 (Hamburg, 1924); and Siegel, 26–28, 35–74.

20. *Abbia, Revue culturelle camerounaise/Cameroon Cultural Review* (Yaoundé: Ministre de l'Information et de la Culture and L'Université du Cameroun, 1963–); and *Scott Standard Postage Stamp Catalogue, 1978*, 4 vols. (New York: Scott Publishing Co., 1977), II, 337, nos. 492–96.

21. Marion Johnson, "The Cowrie Currencies of West Africa, Part I," *Journal of African History* 11, no. 1 (1970): 17–20, 26–27, 32–34.

22. Roland S. Fletcher, comp. and ed., *Hausa Sayings & Folk-Lore* (London: Oxford University Press, 1912), 111–12.

23. George T. Basden, *Niger Ibos* (1938; reprinted New York: Barnes & Noble, 1966), 352–53.

24. Percy A. Talbot, *The Peoples of Southern Nigeria,* 4 vols. (London: Oxford University Press, 1926), III, 817.

25. Culin; A. Deledicq and A. Popova, *Wari et solo, le jeu de calculs africain* (Paris: CEDIC, 1977); J. H. Driberg, "The Game of Choro or Pereaüni," *Man* 27 (1927): 168–72; "Les mankala africains," special section of *Cahiers d'études africaines* 63–64, vol. 16, nos. 3–4 (1976), 431–97; Harold J. R. Murray, *A History of Board-Games Other Than Chess* (Oxford: Clarendon Press, 1952), chaps. 7–8; M. B. Nsimbi, *Omweso, A Game People Play in Uganda*, African Studies Center Occasional Paper no. 6 (Los Angeles: University of California, 1968); A. O. Odeleye, *Ayo, A Popular Yoruba Game* (Ibadan: Oxford University Press, 1977); Richard Pankhurst, "Gabata and Related Board Games of Ethiopia and the Horn of Africa," *Ethiopia Observer* 14, no. 2 (1971): 154–206; and Philip Townshend, *Les jeux de mankala au Zaïre, au Rwanda et au Burundi*, Cahiers du CEDAF no. 3, Ser. 1: Anthropologie (Brussels: Centre d'Etudes et de Documentation Africaines, 1977).

26. Assia Popova, "Les mankala africains," *Cahiers d'études africaines* 63–64, vol. 16, nos. 3–4 (1976), 436.

27. J. Graham Cruickshank, "Negro Games," *Man* 29 (1929): 179–80; Melville J. Herskovits, "Adjiboto, an African Game of the Bush-Negroes of Dutch Guiana," *Man* 29 (1929): 122–27; and Melville J. Herskovits, "Wari in the New World," *Journal of the Royal Anthropological Institute of Great Britain and Ireland* 72 (1932): 23–37.

28. Deledicq and Popova, 11.

29. Ibid., 110. The game is known as *wari* along the West African coast from

Senegal to Ghana and as *solo* in southern Zaire, Zambia, and parts of Tanzania. Some of the better-known names of the game are *awele* (Ivory Coast), *ayo* (southwestern Nigeria and Benin), *mweso* (Uganda), *gabata* (Ethiopia) and *bao* (East African coast).

30. Deledicq and Popova, 10, 23–32, 72, 106–7; and Townshend, *Jeux de mankala,* 6–7, 21, 31, 63.

31. Culin, 602; and E. C. Lanning, "Rock-cut *Mweso* Boards," *Uganda Journal* 20, no. 1 (1956): 97–98.

32. Edwin W. Smith and Andrew M. Dale, *The Ila-Speaking Peoples of Northern Rhodesia,* 2 vols. (1920; reprinted New Hyde Park, N.Y.: University Books, 1968), II, 234.

33. Townshend, 14–15.

34. Walter Driedger, "The Game of Bao or Mankala in East Africa," *Mila* 3, no. 1 (1972): 10; and Alan P. Merriam, "The Game of *Kubuguza* among the Abatutsi of North-East Ruanda," *Man* 53 (1953): 170–72.

35. Philippe Laburthe-Tolra, *Les seigneurs de la forêt,* Publications de la Sorbonne, Série N.S. Recherche no. 48 (Paris, 1981), 315.

36. Townshend, 44, 55, 65.

37. R. Sokolsky, "Structure," in Douglas Fraser, ed., *African Art as Philosophy* (New York: Interbook, 1974), 119.

38. G. N. Collins, "Kboo, A Liberian Game," *National Geographic Magazine* 21 (1910): 944–45; and Townshend, 24, 53, 57.

39. Culin, 603.

40. Townshend, 35.

41. Merriam, 172.

42. R. J. Newberry, "Some Games and Pastimes of Southern Nigeria: Part III—Ayo," *Nigerian Field* 8, no. 2 (1939): 79.

43. Merriam, 171; Pankhurst, 192; and Townshend, 61–62.

44. Merriam, 171.

45. R. Avelot, "Le jeu des godets, un jeu africain à combinaisons mathématiques," *Bulletin et Mémoires de la Société d'Anthropologie de Paris* Ser. 5, vol. 7 (1906): 269–70; and Deledicq and Popova, 33, 79, 80.

46. Deledicq and Popova, 34–35; Pankhurst, passim; and Townshend, 66.

47. Nsimbi, 4–6.

48. Driberg, 170.

49. Ibid., 169.

50. Pankhurst, 156, 174–76.

51. Nsimbi, 10–11.

52. H. Plantet, "Joueurs et tricheurs," *Revue de deux mondes* (1 May 1952): 170–75; Rosenthal, 154–56.

53. Driberg, 169.

54. Townshend, 68–69.

55. Nsimbi, 12.

56. Pankhurst, 166, 176, 183, 186, 191; Marie-Martine and Serge Tornay, "Le jeu des pierres chez les Nyangatom (s.-o. éthiopien)," *Journal de la Société des Africanistes* 41, no. 2 (1971): 257; and Townshend, 29, 39, 60.

57. Fletcher, 112; Arthur J. N. Tremearne, *Hausa Superstitions and Customs* (London: John Bale, Sons & Danielsson, 1913), 46.

58.   Driberg, 169; Merriam, 171; Frederick W. H. Migeod, *A View of Sierra Leone* (New York: Brentano's, 1927), 282; and Odeleye, *Ayo*, 14.

59.   Newberry, 75.

60.   Townshend, 66.

61.   David F Lancy, "Work, Play and Learning in a Kpelle Town," Ph.D. dissertation, University of Pittsburgh, 1977, 223; and George Schwab, *Tribes of the Liberian Hinterland*, Papers of the Peabody Museum of American Archaeology and Ethnology, Harvard University 31 (Cambridge, Mass., 1947): 160 n. 28.

62.   Marfurt, 74.

63.   Breen, 257; Laburthe-Tolra, *Seigneurs de la forêt*, 315; and Popova, 455.

64.   Odeleye, 14–15.

65.   Driberg, 168–69.

66.   M. Heepe, ed., *Jaunde Texte von Atangana und P. Messi*, Abhandlungen des Hamburgischen Kolonial-Instituts 24 (Hamburg, 1919): 279–80, translated in Siegel, 29–30.

67.   Fletcher, 114, n. 1.

68.   R. C. Abraham, *Dictionary of the Hausa Language* (London: University of London Press, 1962), s.v. *cācā*.

69.   Laburthe-Tolra, *Seigneurs de la forêt*, 293.

70.   P. Mérab, *Impressions d'Ethiopie* (Paris, 1921–1929), III, 270, cited in Pankhurst, 156.

71.   Torday, 137.

72.   E. Torday and T. A. Joyce, *Notes ethnographiques sur les peuples communément appelés Bakuba, ainsi que sur les peuplades apparentées. Les Bushongo*, Musée Royal du Congo Belge, Ethnographie, Anthropologie, ser. 3, vol. 2, fasc. 1 (Brussels, 1910), 26, 97; Jan Vansina, *The Children of Woot: A History of the Kuba Peoples* (Madison: University of Wisconsin Press, 1978), 245; and Jan Vansina, "*Ndop*: Royal Statues among the Kuba," in Douglas Fraser and Herbert M. Cole, eds., *African Art & Leadership* (Madison: University of Wisconsin Press, 1972), 42–43.

73.   Robert Roberts, *The Social Laws of the Qorân* (London: Curzon Press, 1971), 114-15. See Rosenthal, 77–85, for a philological discussion of the Koranic prohibition of gambling. For a general discussion about interdictions against play and forms of amusement see "La'ib," *Encyclopedia of Islam* (Leiden: E. J. Brill, 1982), V, 616–17.

74.   Rosenthal, 27–66.

75.   Polly Hill, *Rural Hausa, A Village Setting* (Cambridge: Cambridge University Press, 1972), 249; and Mary Kingsley, *Travels in West Africa, Congo Français, Corisco and Cameroons* (1897; reprint London, Frank Cass, 1965), 18.

76.   Fletcher, 111; and Tremearne, 58.

77.   Béart, *Jeux et jouets de l'ouest africain*, I, 421, n. 2.

78.   Majid Khadduri and Herbert J. Liebesny, *Law in the Middle East*, vol. 1, *Origin and Development of Islamic Law* (Washington, D.C.: Middle East Institute, 1955), 88; Charles K. Meek, *Land Law and Custom in the Colonies* (London: Oxford University Press, 1949), 232–35; and Rosenthal, 138–40.

79.   Rosenthal, 158–71.

80.   Lanciani, 105; and Charles S. Rayment, "Roman Anti-Gambling Measures," *Classical Weekly* 43, no. 8 (1950): 121–22.

81. Pankhurst, 154.

82. Lucien Levy-Bruhl, "Primitive Mentality and Gambling," *Criterion* 2 (1923–1924): 189.

83. Schwab, 159.

84. Delarozière and Luc, 50; and Guenter Tessmann, *Die Pangwe,* 2 vols. (Berlin: Ernst Wasmuth, 1913), II, 317 cited in Siegel, 23.

85. Laburthe-Tolra, *Seigneurs de la forêt,* 317.

86. Reche, 4ff, quoted in Siegel, 27.

87. Delarozière and Luc, 50–51; and Marfurt, 73–75.

88. Davids, 15.

89. Claudia Zaslawsky, *Africa Counts: Numbers and Patterns in African Culture* (Boston: Prindle, Weber and Schmidt, 1973), 113.

90. William Bascom, *Sixteen Cowries, Yoruba Divination from Africa to the New World* (Bloomington: Indiana University Press, 1980), 3; and Bernard Maupoil, *La géomancie à l'ancienne Côte des Esclaves,* Travaux et Mémoires de l'Institut d'Ethnologie no. 42 (Paris, 1961), 265–68.

91. Laburthe-Tolra, *Seigneurs de la forêt,* 315. For a similar story see also Assia Popova, "*Isolo,* jeu royal des Sukuma," *Cahiers d'études africaines* 73–76, vol. 19, nos. 1–4 (1979): 120–21.

92. Deledicq and Popova, 39; and Townshend, 44.

93. Jacob U. Egharevba, *Concise Lives of the Famous Iyases of Benin, Benin Games and Sports . . .* (Nendeln: Kraus Reprint, 1973), 9–12.

94. Pankhurst, 180.

95. Robert W. Harms, *River of Wealth, River of Sorrow: The Central Zaire Basin in the Era of the Slave and Ivory Trade, 1500–1891* (New Haven: Yale University Press, 1981), 199.

96. Rémi Clignet and Maureen Stark, "Modernisation and Football in Cameroun," *Journal of Modern African Studies* 12, no. 3 (1974): 416.

97. Nsimbi, 4.

98. Deledicq and Popova, 78, 81; Driedger, 10; and Townshend, 16.

99. Deledicq and Popova, 34–35.

100. Marcel Griaule, "L'arche du monde chez les populations nigériennes," *Journal de la Société des Africanistes* 18, 1 (1948): 117–26.

101. Caillois, 5, 10.

102. Price, 161.

103. Pankhurst, 167.

104. Harms, *River of Wealth,* 152–53, 184–85, 199.

105. Philip D. Curtin, *The Atlantic Slave Trade, A Census* (Madison: University of Wisconsin Press, 1969), 227.

106. William Bosman, *A New and Accurate Description of the Coast of Guinea* (1705; reprinted London: Frank Cass, 1967), 354.

107. Jean Baptiste Labat, *Voyage du chevalier Des Marchais en Guinée, îles voisines, et à Cayenne, fait en 1725, 1726 & 1727,* 4 vols. (Paris: Charles Osmont, 1730), II, 214–220.

108. Edouard Foa, *Le Dahomey* (Paris: A. Hennuyer, 1895), 249.

109. Paul E. Isert, *Voyages en Guinée et dans les îles Caraïbes en Amérique* (Paris: Maradan, 1793), 204–5.

110. Béart, *Jeux et jouets de l'ouest africain,* I, 426.

111. Henri Labouret, *Les tribus du rameau Lobi,* Travaux et Mémoires de L'Institut d'Ethnologie no. 15 (Paris, 1931), 174; and Townshend, 55.

112. Driberg, 170; Nsimbi, 4; and Townshend, 26, 48, 52, 65–66.

113. Nsimbi, 4.

114. Sylvain M. X. de Golbéry, *Fragments d'un voyage en Afrique: Fait pendant les années 1785, 1786 et 1787,* 2 vols. (Paris, 1802), II, 480.

115. Popova, 113, 122.

116. Marfurt, 71.

117. Laburthe-Tolra, *Seigneurs de la forêt,* 442, n. 11.

118. Schmitz, 431.

119. Curt von Morgen, *A travers le Cameroun du sud au nord, voyages et explorations dans l'arrière pays de 1889 à 1891,* trans. Philippe Laburthe-Tolra, 2 vols. (Yaoundé, Archives d'Histoire et de Sociologie de l'Université Fédérale du Cameroun, 1972), I, 108.

120. Laburthe-Tolra, "Yaounde d'après Zenker (1895)," 92–93.

121. Thomas E. Bowdich, *Mission from Cape Coast to Ashantee,* 2d ed. (London: Griffith & Farran, 1873), 249; and Felix von Luschan, *Die Altertümer von Benin* (1919; reprinted New York: Hacker Art Books, 1968), 427.

122. Nsimbi, 2–3.

123. Townshend, 28.

124. Zaslavsky, 125.

125. Popova, 121–22.

126. Béart, *Jeux et jouets de l'ouest africain,* II, 477.

127. Bowdich, 249.

128. R. S. Rattray, *Ashanti* (Oxford: Clarendon Press, 1923), 290.

129. Jeanne-Françoise Vincent, *Traditions et transitions, entretiens avec des femmes beti du sud-cameroun,* Office de la Recherche Scientifique et Technique Outre-Mer, L'Homme d'Outre-Mer n.s. no. 10 (Paris: Berger-Levrault, 1976), 71.

130. Heepe, *Jaunde Texte,* 299–301, cited in Laburthe-Tolra, *Seigneurs de la forêt,* 318.

131. Georges Balandier, *The Sociology of Black Africa,* trans. Douglas Garman (London: Andre Deutsch, 1970), 185–87, 486–95; Georges Dupré, "Le commerce entre sociétés lignagères: les Nzabi dans la traite à la fin du XIXe siècle (Gabon-Congo)," *Cahiers d'études africaines* 48, vol. 12, no. 4 (1972): 629; Laburthe-Tolra, *Seigneurs de la forêt,* 360–61; Jean-Emile Mbot, *Ebughi bifia, "Démonter les expressions,"* Mémoires de l'Institut d'Ethnologie no. 13 (Paris, 1975), 84–87; and Ch. Zoll'owambe, "Visage africain d'une coutume indienne et mélanésienne," *Bulletin de la Société d'Etudes Camerounaises* 19–20 (1947): 55–60.

132. Labat, 221.

133. Joseph E. Sidahome, *Stories of the Benin Empire* (London: Oxford University Press, 1964), 3–5.

134. Geertz, "Deep Play," 437–38.

135. For general discussions of this complex issue see Jane I. Guyer, "Household and Community in African Studies," *African Studies Review* 24, nos. 2–3 (1981): 87–137; and Shula Marks and Richard Rathbone, "The History of the Family in Africa: Introduction," *Journal of African History* 24, no. 2 (1983): pp. 145–161.

136. Jan Vansina, "The Peoples of the Forest," in Phyllis Martin and David Birmingham, eds., *History of Central Africa,* 2 vols. (London: Longman, 1983), II.

137. Marfurt, 73.

138. Diedrich Westermann, *Die Kpelle, ein Negerstamm in Liberia* (Leipzig: J. C. Hinrichs, 1921), 70–71, translated in Siegel, 34.

**PART
TWO**

COLONIAL WAYS

4

Imperial Administration and the Athletic Imperative: The Case of the District Officer in Africa

ANTHONY KIRK-GREENE

Introduction

In the examination of the link between athletic ability and Britain's imperial administrators,[1] two prototypes of British social history converge. One is the role of the mid-Victorian and Edwardian public (i.e., private) schools as the nursery of Britain's men on the imperial spot, training up cohorts of gentlemen fit to administer the empire. The other is the lofty reputation of those public schools as deriving from the code of muscular Christianity—a creed that, as time went by and Christian virtues made way for more secular values of excellence in education, tended to become more agnostic without, at least until the contextually revolutionary admission of girls into the sixth form (U.S. grade twelve) at boys' schools from the 1960s, necessarily losing anything of its athletic rationale. Fused together, the image has ineluctably—and often accurately—emerged, particularly in the era of post-colonial revisionism, of the youthful imperial administrator ruling his black or brown subjects with the same manifestation of benign yet autocratic paternalism and the same self-expectation of instant and unquestioning authority as had been the case barely a few years earlier when he was basking in the triumph of being head prefect and thrilling to his brief glory as Captain of Bigside.

"Never since the heroic days of Greece," enthused the Spanish-American philosopher George Santayana of the British colonial administrator, "has the world had such a sweet, just, *boyish* master."[2] It was the school that made the man yet kept the boy. Nor did as initially a hostile critic of empire as the French traveler Odette Keun doubt for long the beneficial *rites de passage* of a public school education, based on the athletic imperative, in turning boys into men and transforming the generally inconsiderate and irresponsible English graduate into a paragon of civilized behavior as soon as he was put to "governing Africans":

> They are all drawn from the British universities. They are all appointed when very young. The Commissioners who examine them personally in England make a point of knowing their athletic record, and their physique

81

is taken into consideration. Many of these civil servants [in Africa] were in their time . . . well-known cricketers and football players.[3]

Arguably, then, the experience of public school prefectship and team captaincy led neatly and effectively into the successful practice of "indirect rule" as the art of governing native races.[4] With differences, the district officer acted the housemaster, the chief and his senior counselors or officials played the part of the prefects, and the chief's subjects filled the role of the "lower school." In the opinion of a notable historian of Britain's colonial civil servants, the Briton abroad was fundamentally an underpaid schoolmaster set over an overpopulated school. "He lived in the house and took a full part in its life, without ever crossing the line. He knew the boys well and liked them and sympathized with their problems. His discipline was unyielding and fair."[5] Dr. Jeffrey Richards, the historian of the cinema as empire, has observed how

> all the relationships in the imperial system, between masters and servants, officers and men, are imitations of the headmaster-pupil relationship of the old School. In the last resort, the Empire was Eton and Harrow writ large. . . . For many of them their school life was the most important part of their lives, and for many of them it ran through their later lives.[6]

And echoes of the fundamental public school ethos of "Play up! Play up! And play the game!"[7] were recalled, consciously or instinctively, by many a rosy-cheeked subaltern up the Khyber Pass or many a pink-kneed district officer (DO) beside the Zambezi as he brought his training to bear on his first challenge in the real world.

Such, too, was the noble vision that Lord Lugard, the most influential African proconsul of the twentieth century, recalled when he emphasized the merits of the public schools in turning out "the class which has made and maintained the British Empire": "They have produced an English gentleman with an almost passionate conception of fair play, of protection of the weak, and of 'playing the game.' They have taught him personal initiative and resource, and how to command and obey."[8] Arguing that the tropical administrator's code is to be found in no handbook of regulations, Lugard went on to cite Winston Churchill's conviction that all was said that needed to be said in the assurance that at all times and under all circumstances the colonial administrator could be relied on to act in accordance with the unwritten traditions of an English gentleman.

Probing this stereotype a little further, of the school prefect and captain of his house or college (intramural) team turned colonial administrator, one soon perceives a complementary set of stereotypes at work. The imperial cadet was selected for his stern responsibilities because he had convinced a worldly wise (and generally similarly educated, at least until the latter-day addition of a trade union member) Colonial Service Appointments Board (CSAB) that he possessed, among others, the quintessential qualities of responsibility, initiative, and integrity, together summed up as "character." Exactly what all these virtues entailed, at the age of twenty-one or -two, was often less susceptible to evaluation than the fact (feeling?) that the candidate had them—or else plainly did not. Somehow they were, in the eyes of the Colonial Office (CO) selection board, just as they had been in those of the housemaster and the college tutor (academic supervisor) a few years earlier, bound up with the desirable and admired capacity for "leadership" (again, exactly what this meant was hard to define and therefore rarely needed to be defined since it could so easily be recognized). Margery Perham, supreme colonial authority in her academic right, noted in her diary when visiting Nigeria in 1931, "from England we have sent some of our best men to Africa, and whatever the faults of our public school system, though it may neglect the arts and tend to stereotype the personality, it does foster standards of character that may have value in the Africa of today."[9]

Nor has the search for "character" diminished over the years, even though nowadays its indicators may be less athletic. The latest (1983) of a series of post–World War II reports on the way the United Kingdom Civil Service selects candidates for fast-stream entrance formulates the complaint that there are too few applicants "of marked originality or pronounced character."[10] The emphasis on "character" was even commended in the United States, when that country moved into the African personnel field in the 1960s. Dr. Nelson of Columbia University urged on Americans selected for the TEA (Teachers for East Africa) scheme that "'coping' is a trait unanimously valued as the prime virtue by British headmasters. . . . The British colonial ideal has been 'a person of character' who has coped with whatever comes his way,"[11] while in selecting candidates for its highly competitive graduate work program overseas, the Maxwell School of Government at Syracuse University set up a mini-CSAB in Oxford, complete with Colonial Office personnel and one or two serving DOs on the interviewing panel.[12]

And just how did a young man in search of a career in imperial service acquire his seemingly indispensable qualification of "having character"? The answer to that crucial question was, too, self-evident enough to excuse its asking: by playing games, of course, by having made, and best of all having led, the school eleven (cricket or soccer teams) or the college fifteen (rugby football team). Unquestioning (at least aloud: hence the unorthodox image of Rudyard Kipling's Stalky or the hero of Alec Waugh's *Loom of Youth*) participation in organized games was part of the public school lore and ethos, and captaincy became tantamount to a quasi-guarantee of instant authority and all-round approbation. To quote the judgment of the *Diction-*

ary of National Biography on Alfred Lyttelton, statesman, sportsman, and secretary of state for the colonies, "The fact that he was the first player of his time, of cricket, football, rackets and fives [handball], made him like a king in the school [Eton]."[13]

Yet the formula for success was more significant and more substantial than that Kipling's "flannelled fools at the wicket or the muddied oafs at the goals"[14] did, by definition, make first-rate colonial administrators. Britain's public schools set their sights higher than on training rulers of native races alone. They aimed to turn out *la crème de la crème* for the topmost home careers, too, from among those sons of the rising middle class to whom the professions were now rapidly becoming opened: church, law and the bureaucracy, the armed forces, the foreign service, and politics—gentlemen all. Even those who had nothing so common as a salaried career in mind, the sons of the old aristocracy and of the landed gentry, were still sent to a public school even if they did not invariably go on to the university. The qualification of being a good sportsman (always provided it was as an amateur; never a professional, with all the class nuances attaching to such a status) could be at once an integral product of the public school as well as a social open sesame and a professional entrée card. In general terms, from about 1850 certainly up to 1939, and frequently into the 1950s, success in sport at school and college furnished the common denominator between county gentry, city professions, and the colonial squirearchy. In the absence of unspeakable evidence to the contrary, indicating the "cad" or "bounder" against being a "good chap" or "sound feller," it furnished prima facie evidence of being a gentleman: one who could be relied on to play fair, to win with modesty, and to lose with good grace. And in careers in which specific attributes were at a premium—initiative, reliability, quick thinking, determination, leadership, all the elements of guts and go—it offered even more. Success at games came to be equated with the stamp of having character. "The public schools," notes Mark Girouard, author of a classic study of modern chivalric codes, *Return to Camelot,*

> looked for a code of conduct to inspire an elite which they deliberately saw themselves as producing. And one of the main codes of conduct that inspired them was the mediaeval code of chivalry which they really brought up to date for English public schoolboys and British Empire rulers.[15]

That such a line of argument reflects as much of Britain's social history as it does of its imperial administration is not denied. The accomplished but unambiguously amateur sportsman, the effortless and modest leader, the man who would at once be looked to and could unfailingly be relied on in moments of crisis, this idealized product of the public school was as welcome in manor and manse, in city, chambers, or club, as he was in bush and *boma* [upcountry post]. Borrowing from fiction for a moment, John Masters got it right for British society with his portrait of Guy Rowland, trans-mogrified from hero of Wellington's Bigside to Royal Flying Corps ace within a year of leaving school;[16] just as Somerset Maugham, with his vignette of Alban, the too-good-by-half tennis player who gave the impression that there was no one in the colony worth his while playing with,[17] and, more recently, William Boyd with his type-cast hero of the imperial scene, the ADC Wheech-Browning, who "could happily have condemned the accused to death and then gone out for a game of lawn tennis with the police inspector without a qualm,"[18] have kept it right for the imperial scene.

Insofar as it is possible to separate British society's pre-1939 respect for athletic attainment in its imperial from its domestic context, this chapter treats only of what one writer has somewhat sententiously called "Gentlemen of the Empire."[19] Accordingly, it concentrates on an examination of the conspicuous criterion of athleticism in Britain's recruitment of African administrators, what the selectors were looking for, and why they awarded it such consistently high marks. It goes on to ask how important the athletic imperative was, both to the colonial administrator once he was at his post and to those he administered, and in conclusion attempts to assess the legacy of his games mystique in independent Africa, by placing the athletic imperative in its proper perspective in imperial administration.

The Athletic Imperative and Colonial Service Recruitment

Nowhere in the structure of any of Britain's public professions, not even schoolmastering, is the link between athleticism and acceptability clearer than in the search for the model imperial administrator. Reduced to its simplest—yet not so simple as to be without a substantial measure of encouragement to the candidate and of approbation in the eyes of his sponsors and selectors—the reasoning seems to have run thus. The success of the district officer in Africa depends on his possessing "character"; character is tested, developed, and proved by participation in team games; team games are an important and integral part of the British public school system. Therefore, the best type of colonial administrator will be found among those with a recognized record of above-average athletic success at school or university. Lord Cromer had no hesitation in putting forward this kind of weighty argument when, at the turn of the century, he revealed his noble vision for the creation of an elite corps of British officers to staff the new territory of the Anglo-Egyptian Sudan, comprising "a cadre of active young men, endowed with good health, high character and fair abilities . . . not the mediocre by-products of our race but the flower of those who are turned out from our schools and colleges."[20] Here indeed was the rationalization of Kipling's stirring call to Britain to "send forth the best ye breed."[21]

Nevertheless, despite the respect paid to athleticism as an influential—or at least strongly predisposing—factor in the collective decision making of the imperial service selection process all the way from, as it were, Winchester and Wellington to Whitehall and West Africa, it would be misleading to suggest that this particular criterion of seeming eligibility was always operative during those sixty years or so when the Colonial Office was sending out the best men (or what they thought was the best) to exercise dominion over the proverbial palm and pine. Modification to the primacy of the athletic imperative in the selection of imperial administrators came from two principal sources. One was the need for change necessitated by colonial chronology. The kind of administrative cadet required or available for Africa in the pioneering years of the present century was very different from that on offer or in mind, fifty years later, for the closing decade of the empire. The second is the changing nature of the selection process, if not always the principles, over the years within the CO. Yet, as we shall see, in the final analysis the primacy of the athletic imperative in the selection of imperial administrators was characterized by as much continuity as change, at least up to the mid- or latter-day 1950s, when recruitment on permanent and pensionable career terms gave way to *ad hoc* contract appointments. Then, along with the change in need, went no less a change in the supply of personnel applying and the kind appointed.

Although the British Colonial Service reaches back to at least the 1830s, its real expansion came at the turn of the century with the acquisition of Britain's tropical African empire. To the commercially oriented West African settlements of Accra, Lagos, Freetown, and Bathurst, a whole series of crown colonies and protectorates were added within a matter of a few years either side of Queen Victoria's diamond jubilee (1897): Kenya, Nigeria, Nyasaland, Somaliland, Uganda, and the Condominium of the Anglo-Egyptian Sudan. At the end of World War I, Britain's colonial jurisdiction in Africa was increased by responsibility for the mandated territories of Tanganyika and parts of the Cameroons and Togoland and, only four years later, by the incorporation of the former BSA Chartered Company fief of Northern Rhodesia. Finally, in the 1930s, the Colonial Office began to help staff the High Commission Territories of Basutoland, Bechuanaland, and Swaziland. Africa was now Britain's predominant area for colonial administration, in fact and in the public mind. A separate Tropical African Service was created and quickly took the lion's share of Britain's imperial administrators, as the following figures show when recruitment for the colonial empire was at its zenith:

Regional Distribution of Colonial Administrative Service Posts				
Region	*1947*	*%*	*1957*	*%*
West Africa	690	38	728	31
East/Central Africa	700	39	1,054	44
Southeast Asia	264	15	350	15
Elsewhere	140	8	230	10
Totals	1,794	100	2,362	100

Source: A. H. M. Kirk-Greene, "The Thin White Line: The Size of the British Colonial Service in Africa," *African Affairs* 79, no. 314 (1980):25–44.

At the turn of the century, such a flood of new posts had meant temporary measures and staff improvisation until the recruitment process could catch up with demand. Fortunately, the new British empire in Africa was not totally without experienced resources. In Nigeria and British East Africa (later Kenya), two of the largest of the new territories, a number of old chartered company personnel could be transferred to the provincial administration, although, as Governor Girouard at the time and Richard Cashmore in retrospect have demonstrated,[22] the quality of some of these new commissioners was erratic and their behavior on occasion eccentric enough to be far removed from the more orthodox and uniform public school standards that were subsequently to dominate recruitment. In the Sudan, the largest territory of them all, the field administration in its early days was carried out by British officers seconded from the Egyptian army. Everywhere, too, there were would-be colonial administrators coming forward from among officers who had served in the Boer War, who had grown to like the "frontier" life in Africa and who believed they had acquired "a certain way with the natives."

The unarguable skills of that pioneer generation of African administrators often coincided with the needs of their apprenticeship. Conditions were rough and called for a high degree of rugged self-reliance in lonely and often dangerous circumstances. Administration was rudimentary, leaving much to initiative and off-the-cuff decision making. Domestic comfort and social amenities were scant; female companionship scarcer still. This was the era of "pacification," a time for action first and administrative philosophy a long way second. Its spirit is summed up, not too fancifully, in the archetypal Mr. Commissioner Sanders, Keeper of the King's Peace, a slim and dapper figure in spotless white, sitting "cross-legged on his canvas chair, chewing an unsmoked cigar and drawing little patterns with his ebony stick in the sand," with a Browning strapped to his hip, "its grip shiny with use," and a voice that "had the quality of an ice-cold razor" as he addressed the wrong-doer with his hard little smile:

> I am Sandi, who sits for [the] king on the Great River. I am a man quick to kill and no respecter of kings or chiefs. I have ploughed little kings into the ground and the crops of my people have flourished on the bones of princes.[23]

It was the moment, too, for the military officer to show his civilian competence. This he often did with credit and on occasion with distinction. There was even a school in African administration that argued that not only was the military man the principal available source for recruiting administrators in a hurry, he was also the best choice for that particular phase of empire. Seldom has the essentially male context of colonial service been more robustly and exclusively masculine than in that pioneering period.

The officer element also brought with it the characteristic regular army's love of sport. Africa proved something of a sportsman's paradise. Naturally, sport in the isolated European station life of up-country Africa about 1905 could not refer to those organized team games that had been the staple of school life. Rather were they the traditional pastimes of the imperial mess, manly and individualistic: riding, racing, polo, pig-sticking, and, above all, hunting and shooting wildlife. Speke's description of Uganda as "a shocking country for sport" referred to opportunities for game, not games, the kind of sport encapsulated in Samuel Baker's gory vision of "whole hecatombs of slaughter" and still met with by R. A. Snoxall on his first posting to colonial Uganda fifty years later: "Within a radius of 40 miles of Kampala I could find sporting interests in profusion. If not cricket or golf, there was sailing or rough shooting, duck, guinea-fowl, red-legged partridge or green pigeon."[24] The opportunities for and objectives of sport in Africa at this period were trophy hunting, not team-games participation, a fact unequivocally expressed in the typical memoirs of soldier-administrators such as Capt. B. R. M. Glossop's *Sporting Trips of a Subaltern* (1906), Lt. Col. W. T. Shorthose's *Spade and Sport in Pagan Land* (1934), Col. H. C. Lowther's *From Pillow to Post* (1911)—with its catalogue of ninety-two different types of game shot, from quail to elephant—Col. A. H. W. Haywood's *Sport and Service in Africa* (1926), Brig. J. Willcock's *The Romance of Soldiering and Sport* (1925), Lord Cranworth's *Profit and Sport in British East Africa* (1919) and Gen. E. A. Alderson's *Pink and Scarlet; or Hunting as a School for Soldiering* (1913).

Even as this period of African administration developed, a more formal method of appointing colonial administrators was coming into operation. This was the office of the patronage secretary (unestablished and unpaid).[25] Those who called on him, with a letter of introduction from some patron, in his office in Downing Street, had an undoubtedly better chance of making the necessary favorable impression on this key figure if they came from Eton, the Guards, or the home counties, where shooting, hunting, and fishing were an immediate index of "the right type," than the lad from Lancashire or Manchester Grammar School, who, regardless of the evidence of his intellect, was assumed not to know a right barrel from a left or which meal of the day was called "dinner"—in the unlikely event, that is, of his having applied to the Patronage Office in the first place. In the Edwardian era such attitudes were rarely questioned; did not the hymn reverently sung in church each Sunday describe the appointed social order of "The rich man in his castle, the poor man at his gate/God made them, high or lowly, and ordered their estate"?

But the new Tropical African and the Sudan Political services had to be made respectable so as to attract the same kind of applicants as the Indian Civil and the Eastern Cadet services were already successfully doing. In its search for the right type, Whitehall turned to the universities. Undergraduates were encouraged to think of Africa as well as the East for a career in imperial administration. By 1910 Oxford had provided its talent scouts, notably in the service of the Sudan; Cambridge had created a lectureship in a West African language; special training courses were arranged at London's Imperial Institute; and Edinburgh and Trinity College, Dublin, began their lifelong connection with the supply of able graduates for the African civil services. Family links and personal introduction still played their part. Sir Geoffrey Archer started his career as the unpaid private secretary to his uncle Sir Frederick Jackson, HM Commissioner in Uganda, and Sir Frederick Lugard appointed his own brother, Maj. Edward J. Lugard, as his; C. L. Temple's father had been governor of Bombay; Hubert and Mark Young, both future colonial governors, were sons of the lieutenant-governor of the Punjab. But at least there was competition now to get into a service with a growing reputation, and the "right" men were beginning to come in from the public schools and universities.

It was the Great War that changed the whole system of Colonial Service recruitment, as so many things besides. First, from 1919 qualifications were widened, so that having been an officer in the war was in itself something of a temporary token of eligibility. Indeed, there is evidence in the recruitment files to suggest that in the immediate postwar years the military service qualification replaced the athletic one. Secondly, by 1926 Oxford and Cambridge universities had agreed to organize one-year training courses for the Tropical African Service cadets selected by the Colonial Office, while London University's new School of Oriental and African Studies (SOAS) was ready to offer its unique resources to cadets. Thirdly, in the mid-1920s Britain decided to open up its hitherto exclusively British Colonial Service to selected men from the Dominions, first from Canada and later from the Antipodes and South Africa.[26] Fourthly, the patronage secretary was abolished in favor of an established personnel post in the CO, eventually styled director of recruitment. Finally, from 1930 onwards the Civil Service Commission was brought into the recruiting process and became associated with the final Colonial Service Appointments Board (CSAB). For almost forty years, from 1910 till his retirement in 1948, the key figure in the selection of colonial administrators by the Colonial Office was R. D. (later Sir Ralph) Furse. Along with, to a lesser extent, C. J. (later Sir Charles) Jeffries in charge of the new Personnel Division, these two CO officers rightly deserve to be called the father and uncle of the modern British Colonial Service.

Thus by the 1930s, and especially after the slump, supply began comfortably to exceed demand. Now the Colonial Office was not only able to take its pick but also to attract a number of outstanding graduates from Oxford and Cambridge, including many who would earlier have opted for the prestigious Indian Civil Service. Even when numbers left little margin, Furse insisted that he would rather leave a vacancy unfilled than accept an applicant who failed to measure up to his requirements. It was very much Furse's concept of what type of candidate would make a good DO and which would not that set the tone of Colonial Service recruiting throughout the interwar years and immediately afterward. Officially, the CO rubric called for "University men who have just taken a good degree and who possess, in addition to a high academic qualification, those personal qualities of leadership, adaptability and strength of character which are essential to the successful colonial administrator."[27]

Less officially, and other things being equal, Furse was on the lookout for "self-reliance, self-sufficiency in loneliness, foresight, imaginative sympathy," and went for the man with what he called the "imponderables" of character and personality—"not excluding physical presence and bearing."[28] More hostilely, the "third-class games buff" stereotype [a jock who just scrapes a low pass in his degree]—perhaps more wrong than right—set some student advisers against the Colonial Service. One such purist professor, significantly perhaps from London University, who was also an eminent member of the Inter-University Council, "disapproved of most male colonial administrators on the grounds that many had been through Oxbridge [Oxford or Cambridge] getting skills in boat propulsion or ball games rather than reaping intellectual fruits or in pursuit of scholarship."[29] It was the same distorting image that Edward Atiyah uses in his caricature of the Sudan's District Commissioners, when he comments on upper-class Britons' good fortune in having "an empire to provide them with careers which require 'character' and athletic skill more than intellect."[30] In summary, it was the young public-school man who could strengthen his attainment of a middle-of-the-road degree with an above-average record of achievement in school and college team games that became the CO cynosure. "I cannot see," mused the College Bursar to the Senior Tutor in one of C. P. Snow's Combination Room scenes, when the latter attempted to console his colleague on his son's likely poor showing in his Tripos results, "why our colonies should need third-class men with a capacity for organized sports."[31] It was a question that Furse would not have hesitated in answering. It was not the athletic capacity as such that mattered but all that this was felt to promise in the way of "character."

Even after the massive injection of men (and women) into the Colonial Service at the end of World War II, with 553 district officers recruited in 1946 and another 226 in 1947 compared with an average of about 80 a year between the wars, there was to be no slackening off in the 1950s. The sudden availability of Colonial Development and Welfare funds to help the territories improve their economic and social infrastructure as a prelude to further political liberalization and constitutional advance led to an influx of expatriate staff, a phenomenon deftly labeled as "the second colonial occupation."[32] It was not until the second half of the 1950s, by which time independence had become a reality in West Africa and a probability in East, that the CO switched from permanent and pensionable to contract terms for its overseas administrators. If this change marked the end of the primacy of the athletic imperative in its selection process, it was also the end of the demand as well as of the supply. By then perhaps such criteria no longer mattered, for colony or CO. The end of empire in Africa was imminent (the Gold Coast became independent in 1957, Tanganyika in 1961, Northern Rhodesia in 1964, and by 1966 the Colonial Office had closed down), and the kind of applicant who had for half a century been the exemplar of the DO "type" was now either not forthcoming or else was not what was wanted. The fact that to dismantle and hand over an empire called for attributes often very different from the ones cherished by those who had made and ruled it was a lesson many a senior colonial administrator, recruited in the 1920s, learned the hard way in the 1950s and 1960s, from new-look administrative cadets and impatient African politicians alike. The athletic imperative, and all the assumptions of "character" that went with it in the Fursian image, had "had a good innings." Now it was time "for stumps to be drawn" (to wind up the game).

We shall next examine how this conspicuous criterion in the selection of the British imperial administrator actually operated, first in the selection process and then in the field. This is most tellingly done by illustrations of the primacy of the athletic imperative in imperial administration drawn from Colonial Office papers and personal Colonial Service experience. Because of the sensitivity of personnel matters, not all of these sources are attributable.

The Athletic Imperative in Selection

The milestone Warren Fisher Committee on Colonial Service appointments laid down in 1930 that what the CO should be looking for in its administrative cadets was "vision, high ideals of service, fearless devotion to duty born of a sense of responsibility, tolerance, and above all the team spirit."[33] As we have seen, the person in whose hands they left the responsibility for identifying and securing such paragons was Ralph Furse. Educated at Eton and Balliol College, Oxford, his standards not unexpectedly reflected his own vision of what made the "right type." His image of the idealized English public schoolboy was never far from his "pukka plus" thinking. A senior colonial civil servant put it like this:

> I think that if Major Furse had been asked in the early twenties what kind of men he and his staff wanted for the Colonial Administrative Service, he would, having looked up at the ceiling and finding it empty of cherubim and seraphim or any angelic host, have settled for those qualities which the tough character-training of the boarding school and then the broad training of the mind provided by the older universities combined to foster. He wanted men who had been prefects and had come down from the university with at least a Second-class Honours Degree, preferably in Greats or the equivalent. He looked neither for brilliance—men with Firsts went into the Indian Civil Service anyway—nor for Blues, but he did want people who had learned at school the elements of leadership and to carry a little responsibility, and who had, at the university, learned to be sympathetic with the other man's point of view and yet to be detached and self-reliant. Especially he looked for men likely to have enough imagination to act on their own initiative and enough courage to carry the responsibility of doing so.[34]

In an unpublished memorandum, Furse had once enumerated a daunting list of attributes: "character, tact, a good manner and address, equanimity of temperament, a capacity for sympathy, and a healthy and active body."[35] In return, the attractions to the potential DO should, he believed, be essentially spiritual—and perhaps just a shade romantic, or at least idealistic:

> The challenge to adventure, the urge to prove oneself in the face of hardship and risk of health, of loneliness often and not infrequently danger; the chance of dedicating himself to the service of his fellow men, and of responsibility at an early age on a scale which life at home could scarcely ever offer; the pride of belonging to a great Service devoted to a mighty and beneficent task, the novelty of life in unfamiliar scenes and strange conditions.[36]

In a similar way, the Sudan Political Service's tradition of leaving the selection of its new entry to its own officials meant that they tended to look for a replica of themselves in the applicants.

Research into the qualifications of those who were successful at the final CSAB between, say, 1926 when the special TAS courses were initiated at Oxford and Cambridge, and 1956, when recruitment on permanent terms began to dry up as the opportunities for a full career overseas started to shrink, at once emphasizes the prominence attached to the athletic record of candidates. So overwhelming is the evidence that it might not be too fanciful to ascribe to the CO "recruiting sergeants" the belief that proven prominence in team games at school and university was a qualification in itself—not, of course, in isolation, but nonetheless as an indispensable attribute among the lot. For instance, the initial application form (P1), which every candidate was required to complete, included a separate section eliciting his athletic record. AB's Submission, or formal curriculum vitae presentation with interview notes, prepared for the CSAB may be taken as typical. Methodically it listed "Prefect, rugby fifteen, cricket eleven" against his preparatory school record, "House prefect, cricket eleven, rugby fifteen, senior fives [handball], senior diving, underofficer OTC" for his public-school achievements, and "Captain of rugger, vice-captain cricket, shooting eight" among his university activities.[37] It is pertinent to note how the assumed importance of these schoolboy athletic achievements was emphasized during a man's service; e.g., the Gold Coast annual confidential form for reporting on political officers in the 1930s contained the specific question "Is he fond of games or sports generally?" No less significant, perhaps, is the continuing belief in the virtue of these "qualifications" even after retirement; e.g., the list of school and college colors was frequently included as part of the standard curriculum vitae submitted by former colonial administrators in their application to their Resettlement Bureau for a "second career" job after early retirement.[38]

At the second stage, for those who were not weeded out by their application form alone, references were taken up. Here again the story is the same. Nearly always these included testimonials from housemasters, headmasters, and college tutors. Furse resolutely eschewed the kind of selection by examination that governed admission to the Diplomatic, Home and Indian Civil Services and (up to 1934) the Eastern Cadetship entry for Ceylon, Malaya, and Hong Kong. Instead, he relied on personal interviews and confidential references. Considerable weight was attached by the CO to this kind of assessment. In these recommendations no opportunity would be missed of citing athletic success, along with its underlying assumed proof of character and leadership, by a conscientious referee who from experience knew all about how to sponsor a winner to the Colonial Office. Some of the dons at Oxford and Cambridge developed a close and trusted liaison with Furse, acting as his talent spotters on the lookout for likely district officer material, just as Benjamin Jowett had done in so sterling a fashion at Balliol for the ICS in the second half of the nineteenth century. Some of Furse's "secret list" of recruiting confidants are today no longer on that list: reports from Claude Elliott of Jesus College, Cambridge, Humphrey Sumner of Balliol, and W. T. S. Stallybrass of Brasenose College were all way above suspicion. Those from P. A. Landon of Trinity, Oxford, and Sir John

Masterman of Christ Church (later provost of Worcester College) enjoyed the added importance of being written by distinguished scholars who had also been distinguished athletes: what is more, Landon was the son and grandson of Indian Civil Service officers. Robert Heussler includes a number of verbatim references in his admirable study of Oxford's contribution to the making of the British Colonial Service—"just the type of boy to occupy later on a position of responsibility"; "a good type of English public school man"; "would maintain the best traditions of English government over subject races", "he is a gentleman, a man of character."[39] That these are commonplace and in no way selective remarks is borne out by further files and CSAB submissions consulted by the present writer. Such a procedure of personal referees allowed a candidate for the Colonial and Sudan services to capitalize on any nonintellectual activity, notably success in sport, in a way denied to his peer competing for the Indian, Diplomatic, and Home Civil Service examination.

Candidates whose assembled dossier of personal record and references seemed worth continuing with would then proceed to the third stage. This was a face-to-face interview at the Colonial Office with one of Furse's experienced assistants, what he called his "corps of veterans." In exploring some of the entries the candidate had included in his form, and in eliciting explanations of why others had been omitted by him, once again at least as much attention was ritually given to games, recreations, and personal interests as to academic qualifications. "A good man to have in a tight spot"; "Looks you straight in the eyes"; "Sound"; "Made a good impression"; and "A very good athlete, brains I expect fair" reflect the tenor of these entries.[40] They also reveal what sort of qualities the interviewers were looking for behind and beyond the completed application form with its formal qualifications. One candidate has related how, aware of the penchant of the CO for games-minded candidates, he replied to the parting question of "And what are you going to do now, Mr. Dodd?" by saying he intended to spend the afternoon at Lord's cricket field. "Splendid," commented the interviewer, "I'll just get my hat and come along with you."[41] Fortunately, William Dodd genuinely was a cricketer at heart!

The same held true of the fourth stage, the final CO selection board. Besides Furse or his representative as its executive secretary, the CSAB would generally include a retired colonial governor, perhaps a captain of industry, a senior academic or headmaster, and on occasion a younger officer from the service on leave in the U.K., all brought together under the chairmanship of a regular member of the Civil Service Commission. The present writer, who had the good fortune to sit on both sides, as it were, of the final CSAB table, remembers not only having to answer but also being encouraged to put questions about team-games achievements: in his first incarnation, as a candidate, the question of his class of degree was ignored till he had been dismissed and had reached the door! The P1 form, the references, the Submissions, the interviewer's notes, and the questions put at the final board, speak volumes about the athletic imperative.[42] Another sidelight, minor but meaningful, on the importance attached to the athletic imperative lies in the fact that, at least up to the mid-1960s when the CO ceased recruiting, it was a standard social norm for those who had been awarded a Blue (i.e., those who had been chosen to represent Oxford or Cambridge university in a major sport) to wear, on this kind of formal occasion, a Hawks' or Vincent's Club tie (election to these respective Cambridge and Oxford clubs was more or less restricted to those who had played for their university at a major sport). Fortunate (and frequent) was the candidate who could encourage himself with a quick sartorial glance along the table as he entered the interview room and hope that he sensed a silent and sympathetic "Snap!" ("Me too!").

The registers of successful candidates maintained by the Colonial Office testify to a certain imbalance between the importance seemingly accorded to athletic achievement and academic attainment. The latter generally consisted of a single entry, "upper second" or "third" under class of degree. On the other hand, two or more lines were often taken up with details of school colors for this game, college captaincy of that team, a Blue for some sport and even a county trial or international cap. For example, out of the twenty candidates accepted for the Colonial Administrative Service at the CSAB of 1931, 30 percent are noted as having a Blue. The following year, out of the twenty-seven probationer DOs, ten have a note of superior athletic distinction beside their name. In the list for 1933, the school and university record is very detailed; e.g., "OTC, rowing Blue, captain Boat Club," "School prefect, head of house, school hockey eleven, college hockey eleven, Sergeant OTC," "Monitor, school rugger and soccer," "Scholar, school prefect, underofficer OTC, captain rugby fifteen, captain college cricket, Oxford University Occasionals [the university's second field-hockey team]."

Again, in Kuklick's anatomy of the cohorts in the Gold Coast administration recruited between 1900 and 1939, she found that for 1931–35 every cadet appointed was classified as a "sportsman" (defined for her purposes as fulfilling at school or college the Fursian criterion of being "good at games") and 95 percent of those accepted between 1936 and 1939, while over the whole decade 90 percent of the intake had held major school office.[43] Pat O'Dwyer, who was recruited for the Colonial Service in 1932 when, in the middle of the depression, vacancies were few and far between, writes "I only got a Third in the History Tripos, but I had boxed for Cambridge and captained the Jesus rugger fifteen, as I had done at school also, and I got some fairly decent character references from my former headmaster, H. H. Hardy, and my College tutor, C. A. Elliott, who went on to be headmaster of Eton"[44] (the last-named was, incidentally, one of Furse's most trusted referees). On hearing of his successful application for an appointment as a DO in 1929, Kenneth Blackburne's reaction was not untypical for a man of his talents: "My first thought at the time was delight that I would be sent back to Cambridge for a fourth year—at the expense of the Government— and with a remote chance of winning a Blue by rowing in the Boat Race."[45] Gann and Duignan are not to be faulted in their encapsulation of the men who ruled Africa: "the Colonial Office wanted the kind of cadet who had been prefects in British public schools, who had played cricket and made it into the rugby first Fifteen."[46] This portrait is accurately symbolized in the type of DC whom Beryl Steele remembers successfully encountering on her appointment as one of Tanganyika's first Women Administrative Assistants: "Within moments I felt I had established the necessary kind of rapport with this most English of middle-class Englishmen, an Oxford rowing Blue who liked to work and play hard."[47]

It was the separate Sudan Political Service that seems to have carried to the furthest this reliance on athletic achievement as the hallmark of character, initiative, and leadership in the selection of young Britons for service in the empire. While there has recently been made available enough statistical evidence to explain why the Sudan often enjoyed the sobriquet of "The Land of Blacks Ruled by Blues," the same source puts it beyond all carping doubt that this was not a case of zero-sum equation.[48] As the following figures, derived from an analysis of the athletic and academic record of every one of the 310 graduate district officers selected for the Sudan Political Service during its fifty-three years of expatriate recruitment demonstrate, in the case of the Sudan DOs more brawn in no way meant a corresponding shortfall in brains—i.e., it was not simply the civilian equivalent of Sir Evelyn Wood's notorious maxim on the cavalry's ordering of recruitment priorities, "It is better for a young officer to have a good seat than a good head." That point having been made, it is equally clear that in no other cadre of DOs recruited for Anglophone Africa does the athletic imperative in imperial administration achieve such awesome prominence. H. C. Jackson had good cause to wonder as he looked round his group of seven other district officers destined for the Sudan: one had captained Oxford, and then Scotland, at rugger; another had captained Cambridge at cricket; and there were a soccer Blue, a rowing trials man, a county cricket player and a country rugby cap. "I think," Jackson confided to his diary, "we had been chosen mainly because we were athletes."[49]

Out of the 310 direct graduate appointments made to the Sudan Political Service between the first in 1901 and the last in 1952 (the remaining 80 or so were army officers on transfer or secondment, mostly in the service's formative years), 30 percent had gained a Blue, or its equivalent outside Oxford and Cambridge, and represented their university in a major sport.

The distribution by chosen game is in itself of interest. It shows 21 Blues awarded for rugby football, 13 for cricket, 12 for athletics, 11 for rowing, 8 for hockey, 6 each for soccer and shooting, and a further 16 for other games. Displaying further athletic excellence yet, twelve of these gained a double Blue and one, the legendary R. K. Winter, won a triple Blue. Many of them had been selected to play for his team for each of his three years up at the university, while several had captained the various teams. N. S. Mitchell-Innes, for instance, was captain of both cricket and golf at Oxford, and had played cricket for England on the Marylebone Cricket Club's tour of New Zealand; P. Munro had captained Scotland at rugby football on top of his two Blues; and a number of other Blues were also internationals. The impression they must have made when appearing before the Sudan Agency selection board will be easily imagined by those who have followed the argument of this chapter!

In terms of earlier comment about the shrinking of the athletic imperative as a factor in the selection of imperial administrators after World War II, the periodization of the prominence of the Blue in the Sudan Service markedly confirms our assumption of such a trend. Whereas twenty-eight Blues were recruited between 1902 and 1918, and as many as fifty-eight over the following twenty-five years (and the total intake averaged less than a dozen a year between the wars), only seven Blues featured among the fifty-four DOs recruited for the Sudan between 1945 and 1952—a period that included the swollen postwar intake to compensate for the lean years of 1940–44. Little wonder that visitors to the Sudan, like O. Keun, were quickly struck by how many civil servants were Blues or well-known athletes, or that the impression made on a member of the incoming governor-general's private staff was almost palpably that "to a large extent the governing of the Sudan is in the hands of Old Blues . . . everywhere one went, the world of athletics was upheld."[50] H. A. MacMichael, on the other hand, influential civil secretary in Khartoum and with thirty years in the Sudan Service behind him, himself a public schools fencing champion and Cambridge boxing and fencing Blue as well as a First in classics, found nothing untoward in the importance so obviously attached to the athletic imperative by the selection boards. "We were proud of athletic distinctions," he admitted, "and did not regard them as altogether irrelevant."[51] What that relevance was sensed to be is well summed up in the conclusion of a leading (and outsider) interpreter of the Sudan Political Service, Robert O. Collins:

> The fact that most members played games and participated in sports gave them a similarity of outlook which was clearly reflected in their handling of administrative matters. The *esprit de corps* which bolstered the provincial polo team was equally applicable in organizing a road gang or supervising the construction of a bridge.[52]

Despite what might be called the dazzling cerulean brilliance of the Sudan experience, a word of caution is necessary in the interpretation of such sporting prowess among colonial administrators. It applies to the whole premise of the athletic imperative as advanced in this chapter. For all the emphasis undeniably attached to the games motif by selection boards, it was essentially the house, school, or college team captain that was the favorite of the selectors, not simply the brilliant Blue or the international cap. It was the very good rather than the excellent for excellence's sake that they had in mind. If they were offered both, in the shape of a Blue, naturally they took it, but it is in the widespread record of athleticism in school and college team among the majority of DOs recruited between the wars rather than in the scattering of Blues that the evidence of the athletic imperative in Britain's imperial administration is at its most telling. Above all, for the selection boards the potential high-flier was, other things being equal, thought to be the man who had captained his team, whether it was the university eleven, the college eight or the school fifteen. P. A. Landon of Trinity College, Oxford, explained the importance that he attached to captaincy of a college team by saying he wanted to know what the other members of the team thought about him.[53] Did he have judgment as well as a good eye for a ball? Was he followed because he was respected and liked, or only because he was a good athlete? It was in that captaincy, in what sociologists today call peer leadership, that the essence of district officer potential lay: initiative, determination, self-reliance, competence, integrity, decisiveness, quick thinking, and a sense of institutional loyalty. What counted was the ability to get on with colleagues, to command respect from juniors, and to lead without bossing. For public service as well as public school, that is what "good character" was mostly about.

But in the long run the Colonial Office, attracted as it undoubtedly was by public school-cum-Oxbridge as the ideal catchment area for the recruitment of colonial administrators, was interested in securing the best man for the job and not simply in acting as the exporter of those positive and pronounced British class values to the colonies for that class's sake alone—however similar the result may have been in the end. If the CO was right in setting store by the shibboleths of "character" and "leadership" in its search for the epitome of the imperial administrator, some way had to be found of assessing such intangible qualities. Too elusive to lend themselves to the mathematical rigor of formal examination results, they could, the CO felt, best be elicited through personal references and interviews. In such an evaluation, athletic excellence became the logarithm tables from which to calculate potential performance. It was a device widely used in interwar Britain, not in the Colonial Office or at the Sudan Agency alone, for identifying "character" and evaluating the chances of finding the "right type." That this was a widespread and accepted "home" as well as a "colonial" formula for success in the first half of the twentieth century in Britain is implied by the despairing complaint of Mrs. Damien about her shy son Leo in one of Ernest Raymond's novels: "Why isn't he out like Rob Ingram, shooting and fishing or playing cricket? *He'll have to go among men sometime.*"[54] If the vulnerability of the system lay in its penchant for intuition, its proof lay in its respectable level of success. Granted a middle-of-the-road intellectual capacity (the CO was satisfied with a good second-class degree) and the conventional standards of personal integrity and morality, the selection of the school and college games-player appeared to the CO a far safer bet for imperial service than searching for the "swot," or grind.

Up to the end of World War II, colonial administration was essentially upcountry administration. It was typically outdoor work, the open-spaces life, saddle and safari, not files and fine prose in the confines of an office at headquarters. Dangerously, the myth grew up that only rural administration was real administration and that secretariat pen-pushing was not what one had joined the Colonial Service for. Before 1939, the "Sanders of the River" syndrome was strong, and even in the 1950s most district officers (but not necessarily their wives) resented being transferred to headquarters, longing—and angling—for a reposting to district work. Young cadets were expected to spend at least three-quarters of each month out on tour, and district officers had to submit "Touring Returns" to headquarters and be ready to explain why they had spent so many days in station instead of out on trek. Thus the athletic imperative could be easily rationalized. In the Sudan the provincial governor of Kassala, R. E. H. Baily, who had played cricket for Harrow and Cambridge, used to circulate a leather-bound book among his staff every morning, in which they were expected to indicate against their names the particular form of exercise they would be taking that afternoon. He would then arrange the games accordingly.[55] "It was thought," explained another administrator, "that men who liked outdoor sports would not only be physically fitter than those accustomed to a more studious and sedentary existence, but would also be more inclined to lead an active life of riding or shooting."[56] A similar view was held by a colonial governor who had himself been a DO:

> For native administration the qualities in scholarship and academic attainment are not to be prized so highly as the leadership of men. . . . Brilliance in debate can hardly equal the initial advantage gained in youth by having led in the field a body of well trained and disciplined young men of similar age.[57]

Those may have been voices from before the Great War or the 1920s, but in diaries, letters, memoirs, and interviews from district officers posted to Africa right up to the latter-day 1950s, it is the descriptions of being on trek and the memories of safari or *ulendo* [trekking] that make the greatest impression on and give the deepest job-satisfaction to the colonial administrator. The schoolboy romance of the Sanders story was an unconscionable time a-dying.

The Athletic Imperative in Operation

With the prominence of the athletic imperative in the selection process for Britain's imperial administrators now firmly established, it is possible to advance the argument and consider the impact of the Selection Boards' chosen favorites in the field. Safely selected, what did the games-gifted district officer do with his prized skills once he got to Africa? Were they of direct advantage in the performance of his duties? Could he even utilize them? In short, what did the above-average capacity for organized games, which had assumed a palpable importance in the recruitment process, and which, as we have seen, so mystified C. P. Snow's College Bursar, really mean when the moment came for the colonial administrator to start the job for which he was held to be so well suited? After all, as a puzzled, desk-bound postcolonial African bureaucrat once said to the writer, "It is not as if your *mission civilisatrice* included the objective of turning us all into Olympic gold medalists—or, if it did, you made a pretty poor job of it!"

To an extent the answer to the question lies in the wider social context of pre-1950 Britain and not in Colonial Service circles alone. We have earlier noticed the public school code of "play up and play the game" and its postschool extension into "a games-player is more of a gentleman and more welcome than a prig or a poodlefaker" [philanderer]. These principles, applicable at home as much as in Britain abroad, were enshrined in Cromer's imperial dictum about his vision of the ideal African administrator and promoted in the lore that "playing games will make sure you do not play with yourself at school or with native women afterwards." Some of the same Victorian ethos underlies the perfectionist concept in Cecil Rhodes's will, with the prize going to those who could count among their talents athletic distinction as well as scholastic attainment and moral force. Such middle- and upper-middle class values were hugely reinforced on the Western Front in 1914–18. Thousands of their sons, transformed overnight from schoolboy to subaltern, met their deaths leading their men over the top with the same mixture of youthful panache, pride, and marginally controlled nerves as a few months earlier they had led their team onto the Close in the cock-house final, deaths followed by the razzmatazz of the games bloods ritualized in the Sunday evening sermons in chapel and on the war memorials in Big School, where, as the Marlburian epitaph saw it, "They leave behind them as they fall/A nobler fame than that of bat and ball." This, of course, was the essential reservoir from which the "Gentlemen of the Empire" had been overwhelmingly drawn, for right down to 1947 the non-public schoolboy remained a rarity in Britain's imperial and diplomatic services. Up to the eve of World War II, however, the link between public school and imperial service, between school prefect, college athlete, and colonial administrator, remained direct, conspicuous, and effective.

But what became of the captain of the fifteen? What did the rowing Blue and cricket cap do in Africa with these talents that they had put to such good use in their interview at the CO? Most exemplars of athletic excellence did not, I suspect, have all that great a chance to practice their athletic skills again after disembarking at Accra or Dar es Salaam (the deck sports, an integral part of social life on the boat journey out, presented a splendid opportunity to many a games buff for what was possibly his final athletic fling). The cumulative athletic experience of colonial administrators posted to one province alone over a period of some five years may serve as an illustration.

Bornu, in northeast Nigeria, was the province to which T. E. Letchworth, who had three times stroked the Cambridge boat (the rainfall was under ten inches) had been posted in the 1920s. He was promptly ordered to spend his first six months on horseback, among the sand dunes and black cotton soil quagmire! Thirty years later, D. G. Milne, a lacrosse Blue, on arrival in Bornu found that nobody in the Native Administration could even describe the game, let alone play it. J. G. Davies and J. E. A. Baker, both fives Blues, never played the game again because there was no court in Bornu and turned to social tennis like their peers (save that theirs was of a formidably higher standard). To the same province came another DO, whose passion for cricket had, in a one-man station, to be converted to the excitement of listening to the ball-by-ball Test Match commentary on the BBC World Service, while he meticulously kept the scorebook over after over. In Bornu, too, it took the present writer, who had enjoyed playing hockey at Cambridge, five years before he had the opportunity to pick up his stick again (other than to pursue a snake). Other Blues, too, had perforce to hide their colors under an unathletic bushel.

It was the inveterate team-games player, the apple of the CSAB eye and often earmarked by the CO as likely to make the best type of colonial administrator, who often came off worst up-country. "They can play cricket, I believe," mused one unathletic disbeliever as he surveyed the new entry to the Sudan Political Service, with their carefully ranked attainments of "the supreme distinction of a university Blue and possibly also the minor honour of a First . . . but that isn't much use in a country where there's no turf."[58] Individual games-players might fare a little better, for tennis (of a sort, as Somerset Maugham's DO, Alban, scornfully perceived) was often an integral part of the station club or residency grounds. Riding and hacking were commonly—though not ubiquitously—enjoyed, and in the emirates of northern Nigeria polo was possible: yet how starkly few of its administrators had played polo at school or for their university! W. R. Crocker saw in the game no more than an opportunity for old-style residents to bully and punish the uppity cadet entry.[59]

A few colonial administrators found themselves in a situation where they could not only continue to indulge in their favorite sports but might often improve on them. Where teams could be raised from the longer-established schools or from military or police barracks, soccer and hockey, frequently of a high standard, could be found. In capitals like Lagos and Accra, and even more so in Nairobi and Kampala with their sport-loving Asiatic populace, cricket and hockey became a way of life, and fortunate was the athletic DO posted there. B. Greatbatch, D. H. Lloyd-Morgan, J. E. A. Baker, H. G. Jelf, P. A. Grier, G. M. L. Blackburne-Kane, J. T. Combes, and V. L. Cornish were just half a dozen of many Blues who simultaneously served in the secretariats at Kaduna or Lagos and did their best to recapture their athletic prowess. Intercolonial matches were played regularly in West Africa, and the Twigas, Kobs, and Kongonis cricket clubs from the East African territories extended their rivalry to the cricket grounds of rural England whenever sufficient numbers of their members were on summer leave.[60] While African participation in these teams was often inconspicuous, some more individual games assumed a strong African dimension during the colonial period. In southern Nigeria, for instance, a game at the African tennis club was sometimes more rewarding in social (even political) than in athletic terms, while in northern Nigeria polo reached a very high standard, especially in Katsina, and right from the 1930s provided one of the few opportunities in the Muslim emirates for interracial mixing on the sports field. They were thus both examples of what the Collector in E. M. Forster's *A Passage to India* (1924) thought of as "a bridge game," as well as often a first-class sport among different races that could bring "the fire of good fellowship to their eyes"—and was it not his cocky subaltern's view that "any native who plays polo is all right"? The horse has a long and revered history in Africa. "The Sport of Kings" constituted as much a social as a sporting event in most colonies, but no governor can claim to have emulated the amateur jockey ("Mr. Rolly") reputation of the earl of Minto before he became viceroy of India ("Isn't that the gentleman who only jumps hedges?" was Curzon's remark on learning who was to succeed him in Calcutta). On the eve of independence two northern Nigeria DOs again distinguished themselves in the saddle: W. D. Wilson bravely rode a mount at the Lagos races and D. J. Muffett, for all his 230 pounds, came in a gallant third in the fifty-mile horse race between Gusau and Kaduna.

Yet even the brightest of Blues must fade with the passage of years, so that by the time the colonial administrator was senior enough to be posted substantively to the secretariat his athletic skill (and trim) might well have grown dull with desuetude or withered with the climate. All the more credit, then, to those superathletes who rose above the unathletic opportunities of their administrative routine, like P. Wyn-Harris, who while a DO in Kenya won a place on the 1933 and 1936 Everest expeditions; J. G. Wallace, who spent his leaves from the Nigerian plains climbing K2; J. Cornes, who could be seen running round the dozen-mile circumference of the Kano city walls so as to maintain his international reputation as an athlete; F. W. Carpenter, who, when Margery Perham encountered him in the lonely Cameroons in 1932, had on his previous tour been invalided and then "astonishingly, walked straight back to his old place in the England hockey team as centre-forward";[61] and, perhaps the most remarkable athletic performance of them all, the three serving DCs from the Sudan (J. H. T. Wilson, W. G. R. M. Laurie, and A. Gillan) who represented Great Britain at the Olympics, the first two winning the coxwainless pairs twelve years (and a war and a wound) after they had rowed for Cambridge.

Some did try to pass on their skills and communicate their athletic zeal—not always with success. The inimitable Bones, assistant to the legendary Sanders, decided to teach the Isisi and Akasara warriors how to play rugby football: fortunately "he discovered the little knife before the next scrum was formed," leaving the local chief to comment to his DO, "Lord, this game is like war without spears, what will be the end of it?" The present writer's "sporting memoirs" include the reprimand given to the young Muslim scribe who on school sports day cast aside his voluminous gown to accept a challenge to a hundred-yard race and, running to victory barechested and in shorts, found himself publicly reproved by the chief as a shameless infidel; the minister of education taking his guard, with *his* gown so successfully obscuring the stumps that his wicket remained inviolate to the best of Cambridge bowling throughout the innings, though his score remained at nought; and the local cheers (or were they jeers?) from the unbelieving crowd of folk down from the hills as "their" DO won the donkey race on Coronation·Day, 1953. At a later stage, thanks to the personal enthusiasm of the premier of northern Nigeria, Alhaji Sir Ahmadu Bello, the game of fives, which had been introduced by S. J. Hogben in the 1920s to Katsina Higher College, where most of the first generation of the north's political elite were educated, assumed a "mixing" role comparable to that of polo in the prewar north. The premier was regularly to be found playing Eton fives most evenings, often with his athletic permanent secretary (an Oxford soccer Blue).[62] The writer, having been educated at Rugby, where the game is played according to different rules than at Eton, remembers taking urgent lessons on how to play the other sort of fives from a member of the premier's entourage on learning of his posting to the capital! Incidentally, in Nigeria the game was played with a tennis ball, much to the initial consternation of the Eton team when they visited Kaduna in 1962. Golf never really caught on as an African game, so that President Kaunda and Chief Anthony Enahoro are doubly distinguished in their chosen recreation. As for track and field, the East Africans have established a reputation second to none in the Commonwealth Games for long-distance races, while West Africans seem to have excelled at field events. The latter have also reached international standard in boxing, and the first African tennis player qualified at Wimbledon in 1983. There is, alas, no cause to associate his achievement with any coaching or inspiration from some DO tennis Blue, for Nduka Odizor caught the eye of an American academic, Robert Wren, who took him back to Texas to improve his tennis as a student there.[63] The occupational risks (or exposure to insidious allegations of "brutality toward the natives," if nothing worse) of the boxing, fencing, judo, or shooting Blue were probably too great to encourage him to continue practicing his sport in Africa!

Individualistic games and pastimes are perhaps beyond the scope of this chapter, but it would be a pity to suppress the fact that some fine open-air table tennis can be found in the backstreets of Lagos. One Nigerian administrator, I. F Gunn, marked his many years with the publication of a little jewel of a memoir, *With a Rod in Four Continents* (1981); another, Capt. G. D. Money, tried to teach his African staff bridge; two more ensured that Scrabble, willy-nilly, earned a place in the memory of most of the first generation of northern Nigeria's own district officers; while yet another, better nameless, taught his European cadets mah-jongg and, so they anxiously believed, incorporated their scores into his assessment of their promise (or otherwise) in his confidential annual report on them.

A special place must be given to soccer. Its significance in Africa is already the subject of academic research. The introduction of the game has all the makings of an epoch-making event in the same way as the introduction of cocoa to the Gold Coast a century and more ago, save that whereas the name of Tetty Quashie has passed into history, nobody can yet identify the originator of soccer in colonial Africa. Even if those who believe that the game will one day be "proved" to have been an African invention, its colonial origins forgotten, turn out to be wrong, its standard in South America and its role in Africa suggest that it can only be a matter of time before a team from Africa wins the World Cup.

So much for the microview of the athletic imperative in operation among Africa's administrators. At the macrolevel, the parallel between the principles and practice of "indirect rule" on the one hand, that policy of ruling through rather than over the African emirs and chiefs—"the whisper behind the throne" syndrome—and on the other the ethos of public-school prefectship and team spirit, was at the time commonplace to anyone acquainted with the code of both institutions. Today its significance may elude the student of imperial or British social history who, less and less likely to have the earlier experience of finding oneself living next door to a retired Provincial Commissioner, is all the more mystified and fascinated by the transformation of prefect into proconsul and the transfer of values and virtues from, as it were, Eton to the emirates and Marlborough to Matabeleland. The public schools and their playing field ethos did more than help win the battle of Waterloo; they were to ensure the successful manning of an empire, too. As Furse once confided to an American scholar examining the making of the Colonial Service at Oxford, "We could not have run the show without them: in England, universities train the mind, the public schools train character and teach leadership."[64]

What all this amounted to in the long run by way of the administrators' impact upon the evolving colonial state and their influence on their successors need not detain us long. With the end of empire, the colonial administrator was replaced by the African bureaucrat; district officers made room for ministry officials; and the emphasis of government shifted away from the rural to the urban scene, from the local to the national forum, from the arena of the outstation to the focus of the capital. Now, for better or for worse, government was in the hands of men who had never stood up to a pace bowler in their lives, who did not know a leg-spinner from a yorker, and who had been stumped only by a parliamentary question. What remains here, then, is to assess what impact the games-playing presence of a colonial "athletocracy" had on its African successors. In doing so, we are not unaware of the fact that many a first-rate colonial administrator, too, could not distinguish a bumper from a boundary and had thankfully never scored a goal or cared to hit a ball since those miserable schooldays when he had been compelled to do so three times a week.

Among schools and institutions of higher learning in independent Africa, the athletic legacy has remained. While in the colonial period Empire Day (May 24) and school sports were inseparable, today only the latter has survived. Yet it is arguable that this survival is an aspect of the cultural legacy of colonialism, not the administrative one. In general, Africa can today provide few traces of the fact that once, infinitely less than a lifetime ago, Mr. Batt, double Blue, had been the DO here, or that Mr. Ball, county player, spent three years as PC in this riverain station or that hilltop *boma*. The relics are few: the weed-filled shell of a collapsed squash court, where half-Blue Boot had sweated pints in an effort to keep fit and had once (only) persuaded the modernizing chief scribe to join him in knocking hell out of a little black ball; the overgrown tennis court in the residency garden, where a county-colors district officer had judiciously allowed His exhausted Excellency to win 6–0, 6–1, for the sake of what he believed to be tact (but not for promotion: "clearly gone to seed" was the subsequent report in HE's touring notes); and half-disbelieved stories told under the tamarind tree by old men of how, as government messengers or policemen under the *Serikali* [colonial government], they had been placed in a huge semicircle and told to stop, with their bare shins, hard red balls hit at them by Bwana Innings, or else formed into platoons of fifteen to give chase to the European officers who had then run off with the football—in, believe it or not, their hands!

If the sporting heritage of the athletic administrator is far less than might be expected from such an input of talented games-players, there is one area in which the legacy remains prominent. This is in the sports vocabulary of the English language. Listening to an African politician or bureaucrat, or reading the editorial of an African newspaper, time and again one is struck by the persistence of sporting metaphors like "below the belt," "the ball is in your court," "stumped," "he's had a good innings," and "it's not really cricket."* Yet before the old Blue ex-district officer becomes too excited by the thought of the impact he must obviously have made after all, it is only fair to suggest that these are cultural rather than administrative artifacts, whose origins in bat and ball may be quite as unperceived as the parallel lexical hangovers derived from medieval sports such as jousting and falconry still extant in modern English.

Conclusion

In drawing attention to the conspicuous phenomenon of the athletic imperative in the selection of Britain's corps of colonial administrators in Africa, this chapter has done more than document and confirm its hitherto simply suspected existence. It has shown that, in the minds of those responsible for the recruitment of Africa's cadet entry, there was a professional rationalization of the linkage not only between public schoolboy and potential proconsul but also between athletic excellence and likely administrative success. Heussler has suggested that to Furse the best indication a candidate could give that he might make a good colonial administrator was the entry on his application form "School Prefect"; or, better still, "Head of School."[65] For this writer, it is no less plausible to claim, from a study of the CO personnel process, that at least an equal thrill of pleasure crept up the CSAB spine when it saw before it "Captain of School Eleven," "Captain of College Fifteen"; or, better still, "Rowing Blue and Captain of Boats." The qualities held to be indispensable in the making of the district officer included many of those proved to be inseparable from the making of the school prefect and captain of the college team. Because the Colonial Office resolutely eschewed selection through competitive examinations and placed its faith in personal

---

*However, in ex-colonial terms, both India and the West Indies present a very different cricketing face to that of Africa. India won [1983] the World Cup, over twenty-five years since independence, and in the same year Alan Ross published a biography of Ranjitsinhji, India's prince of cricketers, whose name was on every British schoolboy's lips in the first decade of this century when he played—for England. In the West Indies, W. L. Bell, C. M. G., M. B. E., formerly of the Ugandan provincial administration, used to direct his newly arrived Ministry of Overseas Development experts to spend a whole day watching a cricket match on one of the islands before they attempted to understand or advise on the local situation. (I have this on personal information.) What, one may legitimately wonder, will happen to the celebrated cricket matches played at Banjul now that the Gambia has confederated with noncricketing Senegal?

record, references, and interviews, the athletic performance of its candidates offered headmasters and university tutors—whose reports were often crucial—the most satisfactory way of assessing the apparently quintessential yet arguably least satisfactory qualities to define: those of "initiative," "determination," "decisiveness," "self-reliance," and "leadership," together subsumed under the elusive but prized attribute of "having character." Furthermore, athletic criteria allowed the Colonial Office selection boards a ready yardstick, and one commonly understood by interviewer and interviewed alike, in their ultimate responsibility of choosing the men most likely to succeed as district officers.

Under the creed of the interwar years, namely the paramountcy of bush administration and the belief that African service meant above all life up-country, the arguments for the athletic imperative came fully into their own. Colonial administration seemed both to require and reflect the initiative of the quarter-back, the quick thinking of the scrum-half, the dogged determination of the forward, the decision and on occasion the courage of the lone full-back. Games taught a young man how to look after himself, against the time when he would often be left to his own resources. They kept him healthy, against a land where even the simplest medical facilities could be two or three weeks' trek away. They made him manly, against the moment when, alone, he might have to face—and deter—a hostile crowd. They taught him the art of the blind pass and the concealed googly, against the whole colonial situation of "white man's bluff" in which confidence, not brute strength, was the key to success for the "thin white line." As captain of the eleven he had learned above all—or so the assumption concluded—how to lead by example, to generate cooperation without resentment, and to co-ordinate rather than command. In brief, in his role as colonial administrator, he was able to bring into play much of what he had learned and practiced as school prefect and team captain.

In explaining the importance attached to a capacity for organized team games in gaining admission into the "athletocracy" that appears to have characterized Britain's imperial administration in Africa between the wars, we have challenged its relevance to the actual job, apart from the generally accepted connection between sport and keeping fit in the tropics. We have also seen that, once posted to Africa, the work and the social and climatic conditions meant that the games-gifted DO rarely found much opportunity to indulge his enthusiasm for team sports, and it was the exception rather than the rule for him to continue in the athlete's limelight. Ironically, he probably had less chance to keep up his games than his counterpart in the city or the Home Civil Service, in whose selection athletic achievement had been largely ignored and had remained obdurately unassessed. At the same time, we have drawn attention to the remarkable analogy to be drawn between the prefectism of public-school life and the policy of indirect rule in

African administration, arguing that the District Officer often seemed to be the head boy of his house and the captain of his college team writ large: browner at the knees, broader in the waist, and with a solar topee instead of the eleven or fifteen cap on his head, but still recognizably the same determined and dedicated "leader" of his team.

Finally, we have noted that the link between athleticism and administration has not survived the colonial period. It did not take the postcolonial African bureaucrat long to reject the image of the captain of the eleven, all-rounder and amateur, as the ideal administrator, and opt for the trained specialist: a B.Sc. in economics or a B.A. in public administration was now to count far more than having scored a century (a hundred runs) at Lord's or being able to wear the Leander rowing-club blazer at Henley. Only the idiom of sport has persisted in the administrative cadre; and even this is used today to describe not sporting but work and social relationships. Which system turned out the "better" rulers, in terms of humanity and honesty as well as of dedication and competence, remains for later generations of the ruled to judge.

Within this summary examination of the rise and fall of the athletic imperative in imperial administration several caveats need to be entered in the interpretation of the evidence now amply adduced. It is important to warn against the oversimplification of the "Blacks ruled by Blues" image. First, many but by no means all colonial administrators were games buffs: some of the best in each cohort were athletic Philistines, butterfingers to the bone. Secondly, few of the athletically gifted DOs were actually Blues: the majority had played with success in their school and college teams rather than with distinction for the university. Thirdly, we may safely discount any assumed ideological motivation of the games-playing district officer: none felt that his contribution to the alleged *mission civilisatrice* (whatever that was or whenever he may fleetingly have thought about it) was to offer an extension of his athletic self by training, as it were, future W. G. Graces from The Gambia or tomorrow's Bjorn Borgs from Botswana. Where such sporting demigods have since arisen on the African scene, any seminal influence of the athletic DO is hard to trace. Athletic excellence in the colonial administrator was at the most a means to an end, never an end in itself. It was held to make the Briton a better administrator; it did not seek to make the African a better athlete.

Again, we must be aware of the insidious implication of the zero-sum game when applied to the attributes of the colonial administrator. More brawn was not necessarily to be paid for at the price of less brain. There is need for a modicum of the latter even when there is a surfeit of the former, and that was the kind of candidate the Colonial Office and the Sudan Agency warmed to, the captain of games with a sound degree. If they were offered more, so much the better: but more of both qualities, the First and the Blue, not the "Cap" and the dunce. We have already taken note of the above-average number of administrators recruited for the Sudan who had a first-class degree. Some of them had a Blue, too, and most had represented their college or captained their school team. The Colonial Service also numbered among its district officers more Firsts than common myth would have it, and the Hawks'/Vincent's badge of high athletic distinction was no rarity. It was the combination that counted, the competent all-rounder, and all the undertones that such a makeup conventionally implied in the esteem of contemporary British society.

It is this last assumption that introduces the final element for the promising candidate, beyond his record of athletic competence and a reasonable education. In the interwar years, when the public schools still provided the overwhelming majority of candidates for Britain's imperial administration, their products brought with them more or less a guarantee that they were, *ipso facto*, "gentlemen." Debatable as such a "qualification" may be today, in the period under review its rationale was virtually unquestioned—at least by those responsible for selection and by most of those selected.

In ninety-nine cases out of a hundred the public school underwrote three guarantees to its products for imperial service: some brain, some brawn, and lots of breeding. The balance between the first two was flexible, often tilted in favor of the second. As for the third, for good or bad, "class" was virtually a qualification in itself. Its self-bounded definition was "ex-public school." Like the other two attributes, it was not quite indispensable; but, like them again, near enough to make no difference. As A. C. Arden-Clarke, himself a champion boxer, wrote home to his parents in 1920, describing his delighted first encounter with a Colonial Service colleague: "he is a pukka sahib."[66] "We were mostly the younger sons of the professional middle class," declared K. G. Bradley, in one of his revealing contributions to Colonial Service history, "and had been given a Sound Old-Fashioned Liberal Education in the Humanities in preparatory and public schools, ending with a degree from one of the older universities."[67] None of the three qualifications—education, games, being a gentleman—was wanted in the potential colonial administrator without a modicum of the other two. Flashman was good at games and had been to a leading public school, too; but, predictably perhaps, he came to a sticky end, as George Macdonald Fraser has so brilliantly reconstructed.* Tom Brown probably suspected the Flashman flaw. Furse would have put his finger on it in, if you like, a flash. As one senior proconsul expressed it to the writer twenty-five years after his career had come to a close, "In our service, Brearley would have got in, but Boycott and Botham would never have passed the board." From one colonial administrator to another, no further gloss was needed.

---

*The reference is to a series of *Flashman* novels, so successful in the 1970s.

It could be argued that, for all the rigor of the athletic imperative, brilliance at games was not the first or the indispensable quality sought in imperial administrators. If, as we believe, athleticism did constitute a component in the Colonial Office epitome of the district officer, it was only one such element: along with the need for some brawn went an even greater need, as the years went by, for more brain. The exemplar of the good DO, of course, had a measure of both. And even when we have satisfactorily established the prominence of the athletic imperative in the selection of Britain's imperial administrators in Africa, however hedged it may have to be with modifications, we still cannot be certain what it all meant to Africa's "athletocracy" in the end. Perhaps the most acceptable argument is that it both contributed to and reflected an integral part of the ethos and esprit de corps of the interwar Colonial Service. That administrative service was itself very much a microcosm—almost a replica—of the public school and university context from which, between 1920 and 1950, the vast majority of the colonial cadets came.

In the end, the team-games motif, so sought and welcomed by selection boards as an estimable quality and as widespread among successful candidates as it undoubtedly was, was possibly more important in a colonial administrator's relations with his expatriate colleagues than with his African wards. In the final analysis, too, the athletic imperative was probably just as influential in helping him to *become* a district officer as to *be* one. It is thus perhaps by the code and the spirit in which the job was approached and in the application of the common attributes of the successful games-player, not in any direct relevance between sport and the art of colonial administration, that the continuing search for the athletic administrator can best be understood. It was not games but all that they subsumed, in the way of "character," that helped to project the successful team athlete into the image of the model young colonial administrator.

Notes

1. See in particular J. A. Mangan, *Athleticism in the Victorian and Edwardian Public School,* 1981; Patrick A. Dunae, *Gentlemen Emigrants: from the British Public Schools to the Canadian Frontier,* 1983; Rupert Wilkinson, *The Prefects: British Leadership and the Public School Tradition,* 1964, esp. chapter 9; H. B. Gray, *Public Schools and the Empire,* 1913; J. Gathorne-Hardy, *The Public School Phenomenon,* 1977; J. R. S. de Honey, *Tom Brown's Universe,* 1977; R. Lambert, *The Public School Ethos,* 1977; and J. A. Mangan, " 'Gentlemen Galore': Imperial Education for Tropical Africa— Lugard the Ideologist," *Immigrants and Minorities* 1, no. 2 (1982): 149–68; "Social Darwinism, Sport and English Upper Class Education," *Stadion* 6 (1982): 92–115; and "Christ and the Imperial Games Fields: Evangelic Athletes of the Empire," unpublished lecture, University of Alberta, April 1983.
2. George Santayana, *Soliloquies in England,* 1922. Italics added.
3. Odette Keun, *A Foreigner Looks at the British Sudan,* 1930, 49.

4.   From an abundant literature on indirect rule, a useful introduction is A. H. M. Kirk-Greene, *The Principles of Native Administration in Nigeria: Selected Documents 1900–1947*, 1965.

5.   Robert Heussler, *The British in Northern Nigeria*, 1969, 182.

6.   "The Sun Never Sets," BBC Kaleidoscope (Radio 4) program, 12 April 1982 (quoted by courtesy of the BBC).

7.   From Sir Henry Newbolt's poem "The Island Race: *Vitai Lampada*". On the eve of World War I, an anonymous piece of schoolboy doggerel that enjoyed a wide circulation was entitled "Ten Commandments of a Public School Boy." Among these were the following items of belief:

1.   *There is only one God; and the Captain of the XV is his Prophet . . .*

6.   *I must play Games with all my heart, all my soul and all my strength . . .*

8.   *Enthusiasm, except for Games, is bad form . . .*

8.   Sir Frederick Lugard, *The Dual Mandate in Tropical Africa*, 1922, 132.

9.   Margery Perham, *West African Passage*, 1983, 186.

10.   Quoted in *Daily Telegraph*, 19 December 1982.

11.   F. B. Nelson, *The Major Differences in Teaching in the United States and East Africa*, 1964.

12.   The writer was involved in the program directed by Prof. Robert Heussler (1961). I understand that Professor Heussler's second autobiographical memoir (forthcoming) contains many recollections of Furse and the CSAB input into the Maxwell School experiment of the early 1960s. For a perspective on the CSAB procedures, see Sir Ralph Furse, *Aucuparius*, 1962, chapter 10.

13.   *The Dictionary of National Biography, 1912–1921*, 1927, 349.

14.   From Rudyard Kipling's poem "The Islanders."

15.   BBC, "The Sun Never Sets." See also Philip Mason, *The English Gentleman: the Rise and Fall of an Ideal*, 1982.

16.   John Masters, *Now God be Thanked*, 1979.

17.   Somerset Maugham, "The Door of Opportunity," *The World Over: Collected Stories*, 1951. He makes a comparable point in his description of Elliot Templeton, at once accepted into society because he was "well-favoured, bright, a good dancer, a fair shot, and a fine tennis player"—*The Razor's Edge*, 1944, 5.

18.   William Boyd, *The Ice Cream War*, 1982, 28.

19.   J. McLaren, *Gentlemen of the Empire*, 1940.

20.   Lord Cromer, *Political and Literary Essays*, 1914, 4.

21.   From Rudyard Kipling's poem "The White Man's Burden."

22.   See Report, Girouard to Crewe, 26 May 1910, CO 533/74, quoted at length in G. H. Mungeam, *British Rule in Kenya, 1895–1912*, 1966, 215–17; and T. R. Cashmore, "Your Obedient Servants," unpublished Cambridge Ph.D. dissertation, 1966.

23.   See A. H. M. Kirk-Greene, "Sanders of the River," *New Society* (November 10 1977): 999.

24.   Manuscript contribution to Oxford Development Records Project (ODRP), "The Development of Education in Uganda," 1982, in Rhodes House Library, Oxford. The Speke and Baker quotations are both taken from Christopher Hibbert's excellent anthology, *Africa Explored: Europeans in the Dark Continent, 1769–1889*, 1982.

25. The ODRP has recently acquired for Rhodes House Library a number of the patronage secretary's desk diaries covering the first decade of the present century.

26. See my account of the Dominions Selection Scheme in the *Canadian Journal of African Studies* 15, no. 1 (1981): 33–54.

27. Quoted in C. J. Jeffries, *The Colonial Empire and its Civil Service,* 1938, 135.

28. Furse, 230, 228.

29. Quoted in Beryl Steele, manuscript contribution to Oxford Development Records Project, "Women Administrative Assistants," 1982.

30. Edward Atiyah, *Black Vanguard,* 1952, 96. Although Malaya is not within the jurisdiction of this chapter, its Colonial Service context may be held to justify the inclusion of the remark by one 'old Malayan hand': "The ship called in at Singapore and they played cricket against Singapore Cricket Club. My uncle made a hundred and the Governor said, 'You're the sort of man we want in the Malayan Service' " (so he joined the medical service there). Quoted in Charles Allen, *Tales from the South China Seas,* 1983, 18.

31. C. P. Snow, *The Masters,* 1941, 24.

32. The phrase is used in D. A. Low and J. M. Lonsdale, "Introduction," *History of East Africa,* III.

33. *Committee on the System of Appointment in the Colonial Service,* 1930, Cmd. 3554, 23.

34. K. G. Bradley, *Once a District Officer,* 1966, 28–29.

35. Quoted in Kirk-Greene, "Dominions Selection Scheme," 39.

36. Furse, 221.

37. Autobiographical memoir (unattributable) collected by ODRP, 1983.

38. Overseas Services Resettlement Bureau papers (unattributable), ODRP, 1981.

39. Robert Heussler, *Yesterday's Rulers,* 1963, 19–20, 74–76.

40. From unattributable Submissions and the manuscript diary of a senior member of the Colonial Office Personnel Division (not yet open to researchers). See also the confidential guide to Colonial Service interviews printed for use in the Colonial Office, *Appointments Handbook.* From its detailed, relaxed appendix on the art of interviewing, two quotations reinforce the argument of this chapter: (i) "It is a major and constant aim of your enquiry to discover character"; and (ii) "You will have noted the extent to which your candidate was a leader or organizer at school or university in games, clubs, societies and so on; for his role even in these youthful activities may indicate much. To be head of one's House, Captain of Boats or a cricket Blue is in the long run a fleeting distinction, yet it may be at once a test and a presage of character."

41. W. A. Dodd, manuscript contribution to ODRP, "The Development of Education in Tanzania," 1982. Illuminating anecdotes of the interview stage for the Sudan Political Service are to be found in Sir Gawain Bell's autobiography, *Shadows on the Sand,* 1983, chapter 1.

42. At the time of writing, I am carrying out further research into CSAB procedures by interviewing CO officials who worked with Furse and others who sat on the Selection Boards.

43. Henrika Kuklick, *The Imperial Bureaucrat: The Colonial Administrative Service in the Gold Coast, 1920–1939,* 1979, table 2.

44. Manuscript contribution to ODRP's "HMOCS Data Project," 1983.

45. Sir Kenneth Blackburne, *Lasting Legacy,* 1976, xiii.

46. L. H. Gann and Peter Duignan, *The Rulers of British Africa, 1870–1914,* 1978, 200.

47. Beryl Steele, ODRP contribution.

48. A. H. M. Kirk-Greene, "The Sudan Political Service: A Profile in the Sociology of Imperialism," *The International Journal of African Historical Studies* 15, no. 1 (1982): 21–48 (subsequently expanded and reprinted as *The Sudan Political Service: A Preliminary Profile,* Oxford, 1982). The Sudan statistics presented in the following pages are derived from this source.

49. H. C. Jackson, *Sudan Days and Ways,* 1954, 15.

50. Keun, *A Foreigner,* 49; Collie Knox, *It Might Have Been You,* 1983, 205.

51. H. M. MacMichael, "Introduction," *Sudan Political Service, 1899–1956,* n.d., 4.

52. R. O. Collins, "The Sudan Political Service: A Portrait of Imperialists," *African Affairs* 71 (1972): 297.

53. Quoted in Heussler's *Yesterday's Rulers,* 116.

54. Ernest Raymond, *Child of Norman's End,* 1934, 280. Italics added.

55. Bell, 30.

56. Jackson, 15.

57. Sir Geoffrey Archer, *Personal and Historical Memoirs of an East African Administrator,* 1963, 25.

58. Sir Sidney Low, *Egypt in Transition,* 1913, 89–91. A comparable thought of paradox lay behind the formation of the Royal Wajir Yacht Club in the desert province of Kenya's Northern Frontier District.

59. W. R. Crocker, *Nigeria: A Critique of British Colonial Administration,* 1936, 241.

60. Among the documentation collected by the ODRP are F K. Butler's pamphlet *Cricket in Nigera* (Lagos, 1946), the score card of the Nigeria vs. Gold Coast cricket match played at Lagos in March 1947, and the scorebooks of the Entebbe Cricket Club in the 1930s. On Lagos, see also Sylvia Leith-Ross, *Stepping-Stones,* 1983, 85.

61. Perham, 213.

62. See photographs xi(b) of fives and xi(a) of cricket, in Sir Ahmadu Bello's autobiography, *My Life,* 1962.

63. See "Wimbledon Bright Spots," *West Africa,* 1983, 1551. In a letter in the ODRP files there is an interesting recollection of the somewhat longer history of African participation in athletics in East Africa, under the patronage of the Administration (T. Colchester to A. Clayton, 2 December 1982).

64. Quoted in Heussler, *Yesterday's Rulers,* 1983, 82.

65. Heussler, 96.

66. Quoted in David Rooney, *Sir Charles Arden-Clarke,* 1982, 4.

67. K. G. Bradley, *Once a District Officer,* 1966, 4.

5

Sport and African Soldiers: The Military Diffusion of Western Sport throughout Sub-Saharan Africa

ANTHONY CLAYTON

Soldiers have generally attached a high importance to sport, especially those trained in the British tradition. A casual glance at any past (or present) British Army regimental journal will at once show the importance and honor belonging to the regiment's sporting achievements. Indeed the first recognized athletics meeting held in England was at the old Royal Military Academy, Woolwich, in 1849, a fact recorded by Woolwich's historian, Brig. Gen. Sir Gordon Guggisberg, the famous governor of the Gold Coast from 1919 to 1927.[1] There are a number of reasons for this importance attached to sport by soldiers; some obvious, some rather less so.*

The first reason was the simple one of physical fitness, with its essential link to overall well-being and robustness. Any military commander must have had, well up on his list of training priorities, that which kept a soldier fit for long and arduous marches carrying heavy loads, and then to remain awake and alert on duty at night all during a period of stress, privation, and perhaps extremes of climate. Sport was correctly seen as an important part of the personal development of the soldier for this; with fortune the soldier's power of initiative to deal with local minor difficulties and injury would also be increased. And closely related to individual robustness and self-respect (well summed up in a recent British Army recruitment slogan, "Walk Tall") was that of pride in the membership of a unit whose standards must not be betrayed. Success of unit sports teams, both from the prestige point of view

---

I am very grateful to Dr. Simon Baynham, Dr. Richard Holmes, and Mr. Hedley Willmott of the Royal Military Academy, Sandhurst; Dr. David Killingray of Goldsmiths' College, London University; and Mr. Bill Nasson of Cape Town University for a number of helpful comments and additions to this chapter.

*In the interests of space and relevance, this chapter will not be entering into theoretical debate on the nature of combative instincts—whether these represent a skewed or exaggerated competitive instinct or a more general human one for blood and violence. All this writer would say is that different continents produce varying manifestations of combative instincts essentially the same, and those who engage in that debate will find much rewarding material within the African military to develop either major line of argument.

and from the point of view of the working together of individuals as part of the unit's team, was therefore the next important factor. And at the national level, both the reputation of the armed forces and national self-respect as a whole were enhanced if the armed forces produced good athletes.*

Rather less obvious to outside observers but very important to those officering military units were the internal social benefits that team sport could bring. At its simplest, games were a chance to "let off steam,"[2] important in the closed societies of fit young men; tensions that arose in crowded barrackrooms were thereby released. Games were also an opportunity for the very mild saturnalia that a well-disciplined unit occasionally permitted (Christmas rituals in which officers waited on soldiers at table were another example). The captain of the team was not always the senior-ranking player; a soldier could beat an officer in a race or take a ball off him in a tackle, all very satisfying. Further, the glamour of uniform put aside, much of regimental soldiering was tedious and monotonous; training exercises of interest were often hamstrung by a lack of funds. Sports, at least in part, filled both gaps. Much of the day-to-day human-intercourse side of military life, too, was banter about, and intense interest in, trivia, small personal foibles of individuals, and minor unit achievements. Sports afternoons could fill the blanks on weekly training programs for which headquarters allocated no funds; they did so massively in the interwar years.

Further into the background were other uses and needs for sports and games. Soldiers, especially those in volunteer armies, were often outdoor extrovert personalities, but conformist by temperament and as such prepared to accept some distillation of instincts for violence into harmless channels. Soldiers, too, were going to be officered by men, who, with distinctive uniforms and insignia again put aside, would lead by techniques that included (one hoped) professional competence, a measure of personal regard, in some cases amounting to charisma—and often an element of theatre or bluff. Providing he was not a fool in professional terms, an officer's participation in games and sports would produce reactions from soldiers summed up in phrases such as "he is a good chap" and "yes, he is a bit of a character," and authority and discipline were thereby strengthened. The bluff element was of particular importance in units such as the white-officered King's African Rifles (KAR) and Royal West African Frontier Force (RWAFF) in which there might be only some twelve or fourteen white officers and two warrant officers at a time in the pre-1939 years.

In the nineteenth century especially, certain sports (often equestrian) were

---

*In the 1936 Berlin Olympics, for example, the British armed service officers athletics club, the Milocarian Athletic Club, produced four members of the British national team, a matter of great pride at the time.

seen as particularly useful for developing an officer's powers of command with especial reference to "eye for ground," care of men,[3] and also by a further and partly self-developed distillation of the instincts of violence, the prevention or control of excesses by soldiers on the battlefield. Such excesses might otherwise be mindlessly cruel or counterproductive; killing a prisoner was as caddish a thing to do as was shooting a fox. The perception was in fact more often a claim for sports designed to display a social ascendancy than any adequate military rationalization. But nevertheless this self-development was judged to be a character-forming self-discipline, and with value in dynamic problem solving—speedy response, effective action obtained while on the move.

Related to the ideas of self-control was a final ingredient noticeable in the British and other military systems, the association of sport with concepts of manliness. Sport was seen as one of the most important facets of that term of warm praise within the British Army, "he is a good all-rounder." This concept of manliness contained an element of Darwinism in that the fittest would survive the best, but it was far from being a crude assertion that "might is right." "Games all have rules, they teach you to observe rules"; "Play hard but be generous to losers"; "no foul play"; and other similar phrases all conveyed a belief in a moral worth of good games-playing, a belief that was the production (but by no means an exclusive production) of the British public (i.e., private) school system. "Manliness" in this pattern of sport was seen as a useful outlet and an energy-consuming substitute for young empire-builders in achieving this second character-forming muscular Christian self-discipline.[4] Both self-disciplines served to provide an officer with a sense of moral superiority.[5]

The British idea that sport might be useful as a means of containing soldiers' overexuberant sex lives seems also to have been taken to the colonial regiments, though specific documentation is, not surprisingly, absent on so sensitive a subject. An indicator, however, is the prevailing of mission influence over those who favored unit brothels, which, as a consequence, were officially only countenanced on active service away from home territory—and home missionaries. The point merits mention as French practice, to be noted later, appears to have been the reverse in all respects.

These, then, were the approaches taken by the British military, the enormous majority of whose regular officers were from public-school backgrounds, to the colonial empire and the colonially raised regiments of the first half of the twentieth century. These views, along with those on the merits of parliamentary democracy and neoclassical education, were to be donated to Africa as part of the colonial mission. They were brought to societies that had previously experienced little or nothing of the Hellenic concept of the individual athlete or nonfunctional sport-for-sport's sake Western team-game concepts. "Manliness" in precolonial Africa had been developed and displayed, both for military and frequently also for social and political purposes, in dance.

In "African Dance and the Warrior Tradition,"[6] Judith Hanna outlines the role and significance of dance, especially warrior dances, in those of pre-colonial Africa's societies that included—very varying—forms of military organization. The majority of the qualities that dance was perceived to offer will immediately strike a historian as familiar. Hanna records that "a principal function of dance has been to control and organize social interactions"; that dance is a three-dimensional exercise in space using force, mental energy, muscular strength, and gravity; that dance can convey the reconstruction or symbol of a battlefield with attacks, retreats, leadership styles, and manners of eliminating one's opponents; that dance offers actuality, "a warrior dancing as a warrior and treated as one"; and that African dancing involved discipline and teamwork in its correct performance and included for the benefit of spectators of the opposite sex "visible displays of manhood, health and liveliness." She continues to note that dance could have a religious or political connotation, especially if leaders participated, were present, or being praised, that dance expressed dangerous impulses in a relatively safe way even though occasional rival groups dancing could lead to fights among themselves or their supporters, and that rules existed to ensure below-the-belt safety. She quotes the Uganda writer Okot p'Bitek's citing of an unwritten constraint: "No one touches another's testicles." Among descriptions of warrior dances that she provides, of special interest are the Zulu competitive warrior dancing in which squads danced in drill units to a military tactical plan, and Kikuyu dances that firstly practiced dexterity in the holding of shields and spears and jumping while holding them, and secondly provided for affective-readying, or warming-up, exercises. The colonial African soldier, particularly in the very early years, may well have viewed team sports such as football (soccer) as a rather tepid white man's warrior dance, along with drill and other routines.

The earliest example of the impact of British Army sports appears in an area outside the main parameters of this chapter, the white South. The enormous British military presence at the time of the 1899–1902 war established football on a popular basis among the Colored population of the Western Cape. Teams still playing today bear names clearly showing their British county regimental origins: the Sussex Rovers, Devonshire Rovers, Argyll Spurs, and Wiltshire Rovers. British battalions recruited local mule-drivers, ox-drivers, scouts, and other minor auxiliaries. These learned football while serving along with the British infantrymen; on a few occasions British battalion teams even included Colored players of promise.

ANTHONY CLAYTON

Large crowds began to attend such football matches in several areas, particularly in the ports—East London, Port Elizabeth, and Cape Town—the interest of blacks as well as Coloreds so being awakened.[7]

At regimental level, within the RWAFF and the KAR association football teams were usually (but not always) encouraged from the early years, initially with mixed results. Col. R. Meinertzhagen noted in his diary for 26 June 1902:[8] "We tried some sports which were not a success as the winner had to fight the rest afterwards. I noted that the winner of a race 2¼ miles long did the course in exactly 14 minutes." An article in the *United Service Magazine* of 1914 describes early unit sports in northern Nigeria, though one game is rather more of the "it's a knockout" variety than a field sport:[9]

> The sports, in which the men of the regiment are encouraged to indulge, are mostly of British origin. They are very keen on wrestling and tug-of-war and greatly enjoy dipping for toros. A toro is a threepenny-bit. A large basin of flour, in which a number of toros have been buried, is placed on a table. At the side of the table is a pail of water. The competitors, stripped to the waist and with hands behind backs, one by one dips his face into the water and then plunges it in the flour, attempting to pick up a coin with the teeth. The crowd of sightseers at the public display I saw at Zungeru shouted with delighted amusement at the ludicrous appearance of each contestant as his features emerged from the flour.
>
> The favourite sport of the mounted infantry is wrestling on horseback. That itself is pretty exhilarating. A spice of added excitement is provided by the mounts, which enter into the spirit of the situation with zest by darting at and attempting to viciously bite one another.

Although some commanding officers offered little encouragement and sporting life was limited,[10] most battalions of both regiments were by the 1930s competing in army, and sometimes in West Africa national football and track-and-field championships;[11] in the early years track-and-field sports were the soldiers' preference. Particularly in the pre-1939 years, supervision was necessary to develop any rudimentary form of team consciousness. Basketball followed in the 1930s and 1940s. Differing views were held by commanding officers on the merits of rugby[12] and boxing, some units competing, others not. A medical danger, that of injury to a spleen swollen and weakened from malaria, was recognized. Football was of course for long played barefoot or in canvas shoes. Success by unit or subunit (i.e., company) teams slowly came to be regarded as important. Indeed fetishes or charms were often carried by players[13] or buried near a goal to help the goalkeeper, and vanquished teams would sometimes allege their failure was due to sorcery.* In addition to horseback wrestling and

---

*At the time of writing, November 1982, the manager of Birmingham City Football Club is enlisting the services of exorcists to try to obtain more fortunate results on the club's home ground.

118

toro, three other African games appear to have been played; white officers, who played in mixed teams for all British games,* joined in the first two but not the third. The first was *karamoja*, a KAR game in which teams composed of any number of players tried to carry a football to the opponent team's goal; when a player was touched by a member of the opposing team he had to drop the ball.[14] Gambia's company of the RWAFF had its own game in the 1930s, "a running game with teams of six—rather like baseball—only they used a tennis racket and ball."[15] Another game played by Africans only centered around the throwing of pebbles into prepared holes in the ground; this game was known as *chock* in the KAR[16] and was akin to the Swahili game of *bao*; a West African variant was known as *owerri* and was played by most RWAFF units. One British "officers' game," polo, merits mention in the core colonial African context; this was played by British military officers in north Nigeria from the early 1900s onward. It appealed to a number of leading north Nigerians, including a shehu of Bornu, an emir of Katsina, and one or two Nigerian school principals. Polo ponies were bred and teams formed.[17] The game was of significance, as at play the north Nigerian elite were meeting their colonial rulers on almost equal terms, another of the links between these two important groups. It was not, however, until the 1950s that Nigerians began to appear in military polo teams; this also applied to the Gold Coast.

With the exception of units raised in British Somaliland, British colonial African regiments were generally well disciplined. During World War II, however, prolonged campaigning and absence from home placed discipline under severe stress on two occasions. The first occurred after the victories won over the Italians in Ethiopia and Somalia in 1941. The British command, after the initial shock at finding African soldiers "on strike," reacted very sensibly, providing leave and rest facilities. But during the tense initial shock period, when responsible NCOs of proven loyalty and service were under arrest and appeared likely to face very severe disciplinary sentences, black-versus-white football matches were organized "to keep the temperature down,"[18] apparently all in very good humor, at least at surface level. Later in 1944 the East African Division experienced a second large-scale reluctance to continue campaigning in Burma. When, after a long and punishing fighting advance its units reached the Chindwin, a number refused to cross. Again the British command's reaction was one of intelligent recognition that men were being pushed too far, and units were returned to rest camp areas in India for recuperation in which organized team games and individual athletic events played the major part.[19]

---

*The Kaiser's officers did not play games with their soldiers, but from Weimar onward German officers joined in unit teams. Soviet-conscripted naval personnel watch all-ranks deck games on Her Majesty's ships with fascination and bewilderment.

While games and sports clearly played a role in the life of the colonial regiments (and also of course colonial police forces) a number of indicators suggest, however, that the role was nowhere as significant as in metropolitan British units. *Ngomas,* or other dances, continued, in a form only slightly restrained (British officers were expected to participate for ten minutes) and certainly were seen as more essentially "warrior" than games-playing by ordinary soldiers. Dances of course retained ethnic links, different ethnic groups performing in their own style. Games and sport also never seem to have figured in recruiting or reenlistment as pull factors, as they certainly did and do in the British Army. The language of sport does not seem to enter significantly into the normal expression of senior officers trained before independence. A study of two books by senior African officers, Col. (later Gen.) Akwasi A. Afrifa's *The Ghana Coup,* and Gen. Olesegun Obasanjo's *My Command,* contain no reference to sport nor any use of sporting analogies; a third work, Gen. Albert Ocran's *Politics of the Sword,* only notes "fair play" once and "cheats" twice in discussing politics and politicians.[20] This paucity and absence are all the more remarkable in Afrifa's book, as he devotes three pages to his stay at Sandhurst praising its camaraderie, military training, discipline, and food—even its academic work—but with no mention of sport, although he played several games. No mental relation of political or military events to successes or failures on the playing field seems therefore to have been transmitted. Officers with whom the writer has discussed successes or failures of African military regimes have not used sporting analogies, the most usual conceptual framework being military; "this matter was a command decision," "this was a failure in command," etc., "Col. Philip Effiong [the Biafran military commander] reporting for redeployment, sir." Lastly no mention of sport or reference to sport in analogy appears in any soldiers' songs that this writer has been able to collect,[21] although traditional warrior praise rituals, slightly modified, were sung.

Exceedingly little material is available in English, and only a limited amount in French, on the French colonial forces other than the over-publicized Foreign Legion. Such works as this writer has been able to consult suggest that French colonial regiments attached little importance to sport;[22] games at unit level only received, for the metropolitan army, official French military approval as late as 1927. This is not surprising. Such sports as were practiced for most of the colonial era were either viewed as part of soldiers' physical training programs or were so *ad hoc* as to amount to little more than knockabout evening football among off-duty soldiers. The Foreign Legion's formal training program evidently included boxing, wrestling, running, and fencing; there was on the legion's commemorative day an annual unit athletics meeting; the Spahis (Algerian cavalry) engaged in polo and tent-pegging. Off duty, some soldiers occasionally kicked a football about at the end of the day but the remark of the old Etonian, Adrian Liddell Hart, "Outside our instruction periods there was little or no organized recreation,"[23] appears to sum up the position not only in respect of the Legion, in which he served, but the whole colonial army.

There were a number of reasons for this. Overall French colonial philosophy saw colonial African soldiers much more in the terms of paid mercenaries and much less as individuals or members of a "regimental family" of the British tradition. By French thinking, initiative was less highly rated and individualism was discouraged; it might even have to be crushed. By British thinking, even within a white-officered colonial regiment an element of nurturing the individual survived and a little initiative was welcomed. French colonial units were often conscripted; they were also much more continuously on active service, frequently in areas where water was very scarce. "Manliness" seems to have centered on the marching performance of units; training time occupied by sports in a British unit's program would be filled by marching (eighteen miles a day average, with equipment in whatever heat would appear to have been the foundation of the program). No need to curb sexual exuberance by means of sport was seen—the very concept would have appeared both joyless and imprudent. The French military establishment, indeed, presided over an extensive military brothel service, the *Bordels Militaires de Campagne*, which supervised arrangements that extended over whole suburbs of the major garrison towns and on occasion took to the field in mobile form to support troops on active service, totally uninhibited by any religious considerations. A number of French officers and NCOs whose African service might be for their career, or if not, for very much longer periods than the short secondments of British regimental officers, formed semipermanent liaisons with African women,[24] *"mariage à la mode du pays,"* and evidently saw no necessity to sublimate sexual desires in sport. That such arrangements would (after the end of World War I, though not before) not have been permitted in British colonial Africa is at least in part due to the "play games and leave the native women alone" public-school ethos.

In the last colonial years, from 1945 to independence, the picture changes. Firstly within all British African colonies an ever-greater interest in European-style sports and games is to be seen. One reason for this was an already noted growing awareness of and pride in local or ethnic football teams that competed in the big cities to the interest, enjoyment, pride, or shame of the migrant urban workers. The sporting experience gained in wartime military service also played a part. Where big concentrations of African troops from all colonies were assembled, as in preparation for and in the aftermath of the Italian East Africa, Madagascar, and Burma campaigns, football and sporting teams were drawn from battalions (or in the case of the three British "High Commission" territories of southern Africa, pioneer labor units) recruited in one colony; they saw themselves as representatives of that territory in their interunit matches. The African Pioneer Corps from southern Africa, for example, organized a Representative International Challenge Cup competition during which, in a final at Ancona in Italy in July 1945, Swaziland beat Basutoland by three goals to one.[25] Further, in some territories football had in any case been specifically associated with protonationalism from prewar days.[26]

Another reason was the accelerating expansion of education services, most schools offering some form of sports and games, often watched by passersby. In some favored schools coaching was of a good standard. The military was able, therefore, to develop an interest in sports and games in a number of cases (but far from all) already aroused in soldiers' home areas. Many British officers, particularly in West Africa, found platoon or company spirit could be created more effectively when centered on interplatoon or -company football than intercompany training competitions.

The British saw an expanded role for the colonial African regiments after World War II, although it was realized that these could never replace the Indian Army as a reserve of manpower. The new role finally changed the status of the KAR and the RWAFF from that of internal security gendarmerie duties to that of nonmechanized infantry. This role required a much greater number of British officers (available following regimental amalgamations and through national service), and a higher physical fitness standard for serving soldiers. The War Office began to appoint specialist Army Physical Training Corps (APTC) instructors; these men of course had a special interest in sport. They in turn trained African instructors; by 1946, for example, over a hundred of these latter, supplemented by an even larger number of partly trained assistants, were serving in the units of the four West African colonies.

One of the APTC officers, Major Tomalin, serving in the Gold Coast in the middle 1940s, made a number of interesting observations on his work in an article in the corps magazine.[27] Tomalin noted the enthusiasm of African soldiers for physical training and games requiring skill or effort, but lamented some difficulty in coordination in physical training. He also, interestingly, wrote, "the African always likes to excite or stimulate himself before any form of exercise. To cater for this, all P.T. periods are preceded by an African dance which can take the part of informal activity and only lasts for a few minutes. The effect this has on the ensuing period is remarkable." Of actual proficiency in games Tomalin noted "above average" skill in football, especially ball control and kicking, although the game was still played barefoot. Hockey, cricket, and boxing were all being played by Gold Coast soldiers at the time, some of the boxers going on to compete in the national championships. It is clear from the article that the instructors' work was very popular; "Football creates great interest among the population and

A session of boxing instruction at the West African Army Physical Training Centre, Ibadan, 1942. Courtesy of Maj. L. Laxton, British Army Physical Training Corps. Photo in the possession of Dr. A. Clayton, The Royal Military Academy, Sandhurst.

all matches are well attended. The spectators are sensibly critical and always show a knowledge of the game." The conclusion of the article is especially interesting as it shows that not only did the army benefit from the increased games awareness and interest of the general public, but it was itself also contributing to that increasing awareness. Tomalin wrote:

> In conclusion I can say that the effect of Physical Training in the Army has been so marked as to make the civilian population request the educational authorities that Physical Training should play its part in the normal life of the West African citizen. Several A.P.T.C. Instructors have recently volunteered to assist at several youth centres in Accra in P.T., boxing and athletics.

An example of the spread of enthusiasm can be seen in an event in 1953 when the Second Gold Coast Regiment, posted to Tamale in northern Ghana, organized an athletics fixture in which teams from the army, police, Tamale Training College, and the United School, Tamale, all participated.[28]

In East Africa new games were also tried, the Fourth (Uganda) KAR for a while experimenting with rugby in which Idi Amin, at that time an NCO, proved a very able player.[29] When new barracks were built in either East or West Africa provision for a Physical Training Wing and for sports fields was included. The new-weaponry-and-tactics courses generally included sports afternoons, partly for recreation but also partly to train the NCOs in the organization of games as well as their unit specialization. Proficiency in sport, and therefore perhaps a demonstrated ability to captain a team, often facilitated an NCO's promotion prospects.[30] Some British generals also had

Inter-squad basketball competition in the bush, 1942. Courtesy of Maj. L. Laxton, British Army Physical Training Corps. Photo in the possession of Dr. A. Clayton, The Royal Military Academy, Sandhurst.

their own positive views on the importance of sport; one such was General Sir Lashmer Whistler, commander in the Sudan from 1948 to 1950 and in West Africa from 1951 to 1954. Other new activities, limited however to Nigeria only, included sailing, in which a few of the newly commissioned Nigerian officers joined in the army's sailing activities, hitherto "white only," and polo, in which a very few socially acceptable Fulani joined in polo teams of units serving in the north.

It is difficult to trace the individual military proselytizers of particular sports. So often these were junior or relatively junior officers or sergeants serving with an African battalion for two to three years only, initiating or just keeping going a unit athletic or sporting team. Officers sent to Africa were, apart from the specialist APTC staff, not selected with any reference to their sporting ability; very often (as in British units then and now) an officer would be told to take charge of a particular game within the unit even if it was not his preferred sport. Continuity in proselytizing can therefore be more clearly seen in police forces. To offer three examples, the work of Leslie Peach, Paddy Field, and David Henderson, all regular senior Uganda police officers, in developing the force's boxing, track, and field sportsmen led to members of the force appearing in international events of the highest standard, including Amateur Athletic Association championships in London, and Commonwealth Games in the case of the track-and-field athletes. Peach was himself a heavyweight boxer, and Field had been an RAF officer before joining the Uganda Police.[31]

Inevitably much difficulty still continued to attend upon the building up

124

of team spirit and on the decline, sometimes related, of morale within a team not enjoying a successful season. The only solution open to European instructors is described, in an example from the last months of the war, by an African Pioneer Corps officer:[32]

> Best of all the Swazis liked their game of football, and were never happier than when a match against an opposing team had been arranged. . . . But in spite of the many other fine qualities the Swazis possessed, they were in the beginning not good "sports" in the usual sense of the word, and were inclined to be sullen and morose in defeat.

> After much patient lecturing and schooling in the principles of "sportsmanship," however, they improved astonishingly, on all occasions latterly congratulating their opponents on any victory won.

A new spin-off benefit from sporting proficiency began to be perceived by both the British and the French in the last colonial years: the small but useful contribution that military sporting teams could make, when operational conditions so permitted, in internal security duties. These contributions were twofold. Firstly, military sporting, usually but not invariably football, teams competed against local civilian teams in the areas in which they were operating, so increasing military acceptability.[33] Equally important, when security forces might be of very mixed origins, i.e., British metropolitan troops, KAR, local regular and local reserve police forces, ethnic levies, or even as in the case of Malaya KAR and Fijian units operating amid total strangers, was the reinforcing of cohesion and mutual confidence in each other. The French experience of this, however, was to turn sour. French military football teams engaged in the Special Administrative Sections and psychological operations staff projects for improving relations by means of matches with local Algerian communities became an FLN target in the late 1950s. The usual result of an FLN bomb or small-arms attack on a game was a vengeful military overreaction that instantly undid much previous laborious repairing of relations. The Portuguese, toward the end of their colonial rule, appear also to have used football as a means of securing acceptability in internal security operations.[34]

Much preliminary work had therefore been accomplished by the time Africanization of the officer corps began, in the case of British and French West Africa in the early 1950s and in the case of East Africa in the last years of the decade. At all stages in both Britain and France, officer training included specific sports training. In France, this took place at the school for overseas officers at Fréjus and at St. Cyr-Coëtquidan, and also at the reserve officer training school at Cherchell in Algeria, which was used prior to 1962 by some African governments. In Britain it was conducted at the short-service-commission Officer Cadet Schools at Eaton Hall and Aldershot

(Mons OCS), at the Royal Naval College, Dartmouth, and the Royal Air Force College, Cranwell, and, perhaps most importantly, at the Royal Military Academy, Sandhurst. In West, and later East Africa locally organized commissioning courses followed a similar pattern.

In the 1950s the Sandhurst cadet course lasted eighteen months, later extended to two years (six terms), a system that lasted to 1972. Within this length of time cadets with potential for games or athletics could have that potential greatly developed; others could be introduced to games and sports. Time was available not only to train and play, but also to learn how to organize meetings and fixtures. Sandhurst additionally provided a well-balanced diet, which not all had enjoyed before their arrival there, and a very carefully planned general physical training program obligatory for everybody. African cadets generally kept to the games and sports of their acquaintance rather than embarking on new ones such as canoeing, cricket, or sailing. Almost everyone from all over the African continent played football. The East Africans, with occasional Zambians, figured in cross-country running, Tanzania producing several very fine runners. East Africans, Central Africans (Zaire and Zambia), and West Africans all contributed to academy athletics teams; in general terms, the East and Central Africans were notable for their performance in middle-distance track-and-hurdle events, with the West Africans distinguishing themselves in field events—high jump, long jump, triple jump, and occasionally pole vault. Some cadets from several regions of Africa played basketball well, a few Ghanaians appeared in boxing teams, and one or two Nigerians on the polo team.

The importance of Sandhurst lay, however, not only with academy team members, but also in internal competitions within the academy. Cadets were posted to one of twelve companies along with British cadets with whom they had to have at least working relationships, and often looked for and developed much more lasting and cordial ones. Competing for the company team was a vital step toward being accepted and gaining self-respect in this strange environment. Being captain of one of the company teams (with the organizing "leadership" experience that went with it) might lead to Sandhurst's mark of approval, appointment to the cadet hierarchy of government of underofficer and cadet NCOs in the final term. Participation, the "even if you are not very good, have a go" maxim was also all very much part of the Sandhurst ethos; cadets who avoided all games were poorly viewed by their fellows and instructors alike. Large numbers of cadets, therefore, were always involved; in an intercompany football match eight to ten African players on the field was usual in the 1960s. Some cadets even competed for the British Army, or other service teams; the young Yakubu Gowon, for example, joined the Milocarians. And even when the length of Sandhurst's course was reduced in the early 1970s, a change coinciding with a reducing demand for places from African countries, the overall ethos was continued. A number of the Sandhurst-trained athletes of the 1950s and 1960s were of first-class national or international standard; the most notable perhaps was Robert Kotei,* whose high-jump record of 2.06m is likely to remain on Sandhurst's record list for as long as the academy exists.† The big WEMCAM (West European Military Cadet Academy Meeting) athletics fixtures of the mid 1960s were remarkable experiences to watch as Ivory Coast, Senegalese, Niger and Volta cadets competing for St. Cyr encountered Ghanaian, Nigerian, Kenyan, Tanzanian, and Zairois cadets competing for Sandhurst. Some Zairois and Rwanda athletes also competed for the Belgian Royal Military College. The whole experience was one that in the years of the 1950s and early 1960s strengthened bonds between the former metropole and the new officers in a very close way.

The impact of all this, as evidence of the transmission of the colonial message, is to be seen in the vigor of sports life in postindependence African armies. As a first example, the Nigerian Army in 1964 may be examined.[35] The highlight, the Interservices Athletics Meeting, in which the army, navy, police, and prisons competed, was held in Ikeja; the head of state, President N. Azikiwe, was present, Mrs. Azikiwe presenting prizes and trophies. At unit level, the First and Second battalions of the Nigeria Regiment were in the U.N. Congo Force, but nevertheless both found time and teams to compete, with great success, in football, track and field, and basketball U.N. Command Sports competitions, and against certain local teams. In Nigeria major units (i.e., units of lieutenant colonel command size) usually held their own internal athletics and intercompany football, basketball, and track-and-field events; brigades held interbattalion fixtures, and in respect of athletics there was an interbrigade event. An army cross-country championship and interunit team fixtures were held, and there were interunit hockey, football, and basketball championships. The 1964 *Nigerian Army* magazine included an article by Capt. J. I. Chukueke, "The Value of Warming Up Exercises in Athletics," a subject that would make a special appeal to an officer reared in a society of dance tradition, and even a unit as small in size and preoccupied with shift work as the Lagos Military Hospital was able to field football, hockey, and basketball teams—and saw it as important to do so. The Nigerian Military School at Zaria (an army-run secondary school) and the Nigerian Military Training College both made good provision for sports and games in their programs. Reading accounts of

---

*Maj. Gen. R. E. A. Kotei, Ghanaian Army. Executed on the orders of the Armed Forces Revolutionary Committee, July 1979.

†At the time of writing the academy's 400m hurdles (Sumbeiywo, Kenya), high jump (Kotei, Ghana), long jump (Munene, Kenya) and triple jump (Muema, Zaire) records are still in the names of African former cadets. The 800m, 1500m, and 3,000m records had been African-held for a number of years.

these events gives an impression that particular pride was attached to performance in tugs-of-war, which has certain similarities with traditional dance, as an expression of manly and martial virtues at soldier level.

Material available on Ghana also offers another example. The major event was a football championship competition of five teams: First Brigade, Second Brigade, Support (i.e., logistic) Services, navy, and air force. Each had had its own internal competitions first. The army possessed its own physical training staff, some British-trained, at least one Soviet-trained; American military aid included sports equipment. Equestrian sports in the Ghanaian army were primarily soldier- rather than officer-oriented, as one squadron of the Reconnaissance Regiment was a mounted one. Swimming was unpopular; with the notable exception of Gambia, this attitude was common to many African armies where hinterland peoples had limited experience of water and coastal peoples had learned survival rather than competition swimming, and found change difficult. A Ghanaian Army football team was invited by General Amin to play against a Uganda Army team, as part of Amin's efforts to secure popularity in different areas of the continent; the team returned from Kampala with memories not only of football but of the hostesses provided for them after the match. Individual players were also selected on occasion to be members of general national teams. This practice was common in both Gambia and Sierra Leone, whose cricket teams were mainly military men, the game making little appeal beyond an Anglicized coastal elite.

In Zimbabwe military sport had an even more important function. At the close of hostilities in 1980 former Zimbabwe People's Revolutionary Army (ZIPRA) and Zimbabwe African National Liberation Army (ZANLA) insurgents were concentrated at assembly points with the intention that after suitable reconciliation and integration training, the new Zimbabwe National Army should be formed from both the two former insurgent forces and from personnel of the former Rhodesian Army, mostly, naturally from its African or mixed African-and-white units. The reconciliation arrangements, often sponsored by British Army personnel, generally began with introductions; these were followed by volleyball matches and the laying out and use of football fields. Games evidently played a very important part in breaking down the hostility that had existed between units in violent conflict with each other only a few weeks earlier.[36]

Evidence of the importance of sport in Francophone African armies since independence is difficult to obtain, but a Paris magazine, *Afrique Défense*, provides a certain amount of useful material. Various issues over the last four years have recorded arrangements that exist in several armies. Senegal's armed forces have an annual football championship competition in which the navy, military units, gendarmerie, and fire service teams compete.[37] There is also an annual cross-country championship event[38] (three veteran levels, ages thirty-five to forty-two covering 4.5 km; forty-three to forty-nine covering 4 km, and forty-nine and over covering 3 km, together with two under-thirty-five races, one of 4 km and one of 9 km) held at Dial Dop Camp; there are both individual and unit team winners. Both these events follow preliminary regional- and unit-level competitions, and are arranged by a body called the *Association Sportive des Forces Armées* (ASFA). In the Ivory Coast a similar body, the *Service Centrale du Sport Militaire*, organizes interunit football, handball and volleyball championships; boxing would appear also to be encouraged as the Félix Houphouët-Boigny national boxing championship was won by a serviceman in 1980.[39] The same pattern occurs in Gabon, where the *Ligue Militaire Omnisports* organizes competitions, football evidently being the most important, between army, air force, gendarmerie, firemen, and public-service teams. Cameroon's *Association Sportive des Forces Armées et Police* (ASFAP) was set up in 1978 to coordinate an already established program of interservice team competitions between the army, navy, air force, police, and gendarmerie. Football, hand-ball, volleyball, and basketball are the main games.[40] Congo (Brazzaville) held its first military football championship in 1980, the head of state being present at the cup final.[41] In Benin a military team won the national football championship competition in the 1980–81 season.[42] In Togo football is played by military teams. There is also an important annual national mili-tary athletics championship meeting. In 1979 teams for this event were sent from the Presidential Guard, the First Infantry Regiment, the Second Infan-try Regiment, the para-commando unit, the logistics regiment, the air squadron, the navy, and the gendarmerie; the winners, perhaps fortunately, were the Presidential Guard.[43] International military fixtures are also held. Francophone West African army teams whose countries are members of *Union des Fédérations Ouest-Africaines* (UFOA) compete in the Eyadama Cup football competition.[44] A West African military cross-country cham-pionship is held every two years in different countries. Senegal, Ivory Coast, Togo, Mali and Sierra Leone sent teams in 1976, 1978, and 1980; Ghana sent a team in 1976 and 1978 but not in 1980; and Guinea entered in 1980 for the first time.[45] Another organization, the *Conseil International des Sports Militaires*, arranges regional meetings. One such for boxing was held at Abidjan in 1981, Nigeria's boxers particularly distinguishing them-selves.[46]

Even from this necessarily very incomplete picture a few general themes emerge as noteworthy. Clearly sport, in this case military sport, is seen to have a nation-building role. The presence of senior commanders and on occasions heads of states at fixtures, and trophies bearing the names of heads of states, bear witness to this. It is also evident that as part of this role military sport becomes institutionalized, with European-patterned associa-tions, unions, and federations created to further sport; these bodies are state-sponsored financially. Finally one or two interesting political sidelights appear. Military sport crosses the Anglophone/Francophone divide, and Guinea's appearance in the 1980 cross-country event is another move in the overall pattern of that country's wish to end its former Soviet-sponsored isolation and return to more normal relationships with other West African countries. Another international dimension can be seen in the small-scale provision of training facilities for instructors, coaches, or equipment by Britain, the United States, and the Soviet Union.

Before considering questions of sport and elitism, perhaps one other claim may cautiously be advanced for sport in the colonial and postindependence era; its possible contribution to the erosion of witchcraft beliefs. Sport is a competition in a small arena, in which players know their opponents and their capacities. This knowledge, reinforced by clear evidence of the simple sporting proficiency and superiority of certain players, and the worthlessness of charms and fetishes as safeguards against these, have very likely served to diminish many individuals' beliefs in sorcery on a number of occasions. The sports team, too, has provided something of a new kinship network in which, perhaps for the first time for many members, the network has included members from other ethnic groups, even perhaps from groups hitherto particularly distrusted.

The main question, however, that must arise in the minds of political historians considering the role of sport in the African military is whether or not it has contributed to elitism, either officer-cadre elitism, or the perceptions of different armies of themselves as being an elite within the national society, both attitudes with heavy political implications and specific consequences in some countries. It is perhaps best to consider the question of elite within the nation first, leaving armies' own internal elites until later.

There is very little doubt that military sport has contributed to the overall self-perception of most African armies as special repositories of national honor, as exemplars of the virtues of self-discipline and true comradeship together with the eschewing of corruption and decadence. Armies, large or small, are discrete social systems that in Africa may or may not be stable. The command structure within armies and units, to use Luckham's terminology,[47] represents the "vertical dimension" of cohesion; sport is one of the "horizontal dimensions" along with smartness on parade, robustness on exercise or in operations, and contentment in the barrack rooms and NCOs' and officers' messes. Success in sporting events reinforces the horizontal dimension within units and effectively projects an army's view of itself as a custodian of virtues to the nation and public as a whole.[48] Success in the white man's sports has also satisfied those within as individuals or outside the Army as part of the public who felt a need to catch up with the white man, or who felt a continuing need to be reassured that they had caught up—attitudes evident to anyone who has ever instructed at a Western military academy. These reasons explain the developing military concern for, and use of, sports, the programs of fixtures, and the institutionalization noted earlier. The point is well summed up by the observation made by Colonel Koute of the Senegalese Army, who at an international sporting event in Togo declared that ASFA teams (i.e., those of Senegal's uniformed services) would always "worthily represent the country in the concert of nations."[49] A converse side must, however, also be noted: sporting defeats could very sharply lower the prestige of a unit, and perhaps also of its commander, in the eyes of others, with consequent interpersonal tensions and loss of morale.

Much more difficult to assess is the measure with which sport has contributed to officer elitism. It is perhaps first wise and useful to draw a distinction between fun and self-importance on the one hand, and elitism on the other. It is fun as a senior officer to arrive in a smart car with a flag on the hood amid a whirl of salutes and then graciously to present prizes at a sports fixture—fun, self-important, but not necessarily elitist. What should one look for? Such answers as can be provided to the following five questions seem to provide the best clues for this inquiry. What is the officer corps, what are the lines of communication within it, and has there been a significant sports-oriented input at any particular time? Have military sports served to strengthen officers' isolation from civilian life? If the military officer's profession has been generally rated lowly, has success in sport served to improve the profession's image? Was, or is, sporting prowess a factor in promotion, and if so, have any sports achieved this better than others? And related to the last, were or are there "officer sports"?

The nub of the answer to the first question, concerning the officer corps, is perhaps not one so much of size as the fact of the massive injection, in the late 1950s and early 1960s, of a very high percentage (at the time) of British- and French-trained products. These were young officers who had imbibed to the full the Western military athletic tradition and were able to set a pattern and a style in the crucially important immediate postindependence years.* Career mobility particularly at a time of turbulence caused by rapid Africanization together with interunit competition spread the gospel around the various units of the army whatever its size; the army's essential unity of a structure secured conformity.

Most Anglophone African officers' messes possess squash courts and tennis courts; some possess swimming pools and stables. At the Ghana Military Academy cricket (not to survive for long), squash, and tennis were played. Luckham's comment that "one of the Nigerian officers' role-images quite patently is the country-gentleman posture of British officers, and

---

*A comparison can be made with the enormously important group, as trend-setters for the Indian Army of the 1940s and later, of the Sandhurst-trained "King's Commission" Indian officers of the 1920s.

hence the continuing emphasis on field sports and the like"[50] lays the foundation for an answer to our second question, the role of sport in any isolation of officers from civilian life. Officers see themselves as a corporate brotherhood, isolated from civilian life with their personal lives (and those of their families) fused with their profession; sport strengthened this ethos in the early years and still continues to do so. Sport, one of the forces of integration within the army, emphasizes and underpins military patterns of behavior and routines, as it is one of the means by which the skills, rituals, and attitudes can be stamped upon a young officer in a way both painless and often agreeable.* Sport, with its good-winner, good-loser restraints upon excesses of behavior also strengthens the gentleman image and thereby that of officers' individual and collective senses of honor and moral superiority. In one respect only did the Anglophone officer break totally with this transmitted and fairground mirror view of the British Army officer ethos of the 1950s; no need for sexual restraint was seen by most young officers, nor therefore of sport serving any useful purpose in achieving this.

Turning to the third question, the general public view of the military and any role of sport in improving a lack-luster image, it must be said at the outset that the military profession was rated low in colonial and early postindependence Africa. Officers' defensive reaction to this popular view was to retreat further into isolation with periodic manifestations (the most political of which were coups but of course included the well-publicized and well-patronized military sporting events) of concepts of honor affronted by a decayed civilian life. Rhetoric also began to emphasize the virtues of the military as men of practical common sense rather than political theory in national administrative matters. Such practical common sense was learned, among other things, on the sports field, it was claimed. An element of anti-intellectualism, of brawn rather than brains, is obviously present. Some evidence suggests that a number of schoolboys began to view the physical and sporting side of army life as a deterrent, a view paradoxically likely to reinforce rather than diminish the military's perception of sport increasing the prestige of their profession—this increase being based on criteria of the officers' selection and approval rather than generally accepted views.

Evidence available for the answering of the fourth question, sport and career advancement, does not seem to add much weight to any general thesis that sporting prowess has automatically secured advancement. Promotion has depended upon a wide variety of factors: general personality and efficiency, ethnicity, who knows who, classmates, political interference from above, etc. In a few cases, especially in the absence of any class structure or a military families tradition and with therefore a consequential

---

*In this context sport can again justifiably be related to drill, the more terpsichorean manifestations of which convey the same impact, though not so painlessly.

greater openness of entry, sporting prowess does appear to have provided an advantage not open to sportsmen in some more traditionally structured armies. One example was General Kotei of the Ghanaian Army, whose high jumping took him to an Olympic Games but who was not otherwise a good officer. General Ankrah of Ghana and General Amin of Uganda, both (very different) heads of state, were army boxing champions. Other senior officers in the Ghanaian, Kenyan, Nigerian, and Tanzanian armies have had good athletics or football records, but they have been also efficient, well regarded, and politically acceptable at the time of their promotion—the postindependence African version of the "good all-rounder."*

The last question, are there "officer sports" within African armies and if so have they contributed to officer elitism, appears only relevant in the context of Nigeria, where social hierarchy divisions in the north facilitated entry into the army of a group of polo-playing officers; this group, Fulani or Fulani-controlled, appears to have secured the advancement of certain of their number.† Nigerian officers also played hockey occasionally, including skilled other ranks on their unit teams. Overall though, there are only a few indications that either general sporting or officer sporting proficiency have served markedly to increase officer elitism either specifically by facilitating promotion or by especially enhancing the status of the officer above that of the soldier.

But nevertheless, when sport is viewed in the context of each army as a whole, from answers to the first three questions it can be claimed that the colonial legacy of sport has made a significant contribution to the sense, within each army, of being the national elite, and has also made some contribution to the particular elitism of officers in some armies especially in Anglophone Africa, as the officer bearing part of that national elite. But this latter contribution is but one of a number that have made up officer elitism, and in no way the predominant one. Nor in the case of general army elitism has the "horizontal dimension" of sporting pride served to prevent the various breakdowns of discipline and authority that have occurred since independence. Indeed, an unpleasant reverse side of the coin, that prowess in sport has contributed to overall arrogance and on occasions brutality toward the civil populace, is only too likely. Fit men, confident of physical prowess, are prone to be overassertive, especially if a victory has been celebrated with alcohol.

In conclusion, it may be said that it is doubtful whether any area of the world in recorded history has had to undergo such upheaval in a hundred

---

*Several well-known officers may be named as examples: Brig. D. Asare (Ghana); Gen. H. Sarikikya and Col. G. Sayore (Tanzania); and Gen. I. D. Bisalla, D. Ejoor, and Y. Gowon (Nigeria).

†At the Nigerian Military Academy all cadets were at one time required to ride; the outstanding example of a successful polo-playing officer was Maj. Gen. H. Katsina.

years as black Africa from 1880 to 1980. Along with new political and economic orders and new loyalties extending beyond immediate kinsmen were introduced new smaller-scale horizons of community and family that extended even to personal pastimes. Military, and in the case of British territories, also police, proselytizing of these new pastimes have certainly played an important part in the acceptability of change at the smaller-scale, and a noteworthy if not great part at the level of the new nation itself.

Notes

1. Capt. F. G. Guggisberg, *"The Shop": The Story of the Royal Military Academy*, (London: Cassell, 1912), 209.

2. In a scholarly work, this useful phrase perhaps needs precision. Ruth Munroe's description (in the context of dance) is valuable: "provides a healthy fatigue or distraction which may abate a temporary rage crisis and thus allow more enduring personality patterns to regain ascendancy." Quoted by Judith Lynne Hanna in Ali A. Mazrui, ed., *The Warrior Tradition in Modern Africa* (Leiden: E. J. Brill, 1977), 121.

3. A quantity of military biography and memoirs develops this theme. One title summarizes adequately: *Pink and Scarlet Or Hunting As a School for Soldiering,* by Maj.-Gen. E. A. Alderson (London: Hodder and Stoughton, 1913). The superb original Lionel Edwards watercolors from this work, illustrating the theme were, until 1939, hung on a specially carved wall in the Royal Military College, Sandhurst, library for the inspiration of cadets.

4. This subject is alluded to only obliquely in written literature. H. B. Gray, *The Public Schools and the Empire* (London: Williams and Norgate, 1913), quotes from Dr. C. F. Watts's hymn: "finds some mischief still for idle hands to do" (191). Other important code phrases were "moral discipline of the school and field" and the teaching of "duty to the Empire" (195). At this writer's school a master phrased it more clearly: "If you play games you will leave the native women alone."

5. For a typical example in an article entitled "Leadership and the Commanding Officer" in the *British Army Review* 50 (August 1975): 44, Brig. H. C. Illing, a pre–World War II regular officer, wrote: "Self-discipline, based on sound moral principles and the belief in the rightness of our cause, must be our aim." Later in the same article, Brigadier Illing recalls his 1939 company commander's exhortations to soldiers, which included reading the section of King's Regulations concerning venereal disease and advising "Fear God, honour the King, shoot straight and keep clean."

6. Mazrui, 111–33.

7. I am most grateful to Mr. Bill Nasson of Cape Town University for this information, gathered during his research into black involvement in the war.

8. Col. R. Meinertzhagen, *Kenya Diary, 1902–1906,* (Edinburgh: Oliver and Boyd, 1957), 22–23.

9. John R. Raphael, "Unknown Mr Atkins, The Soldier of Northern Nigeria," *The United Service Magazine,* 1914: 638.

10. Even in a battalion as good as the Fourth (Uganda) KAR, no football was

played as late as 1936. Maj. Gen. H. Borradaile to the author, 9 December 1982. The First (Nyasaland) KAR played football at unit levels, but not beyond. Col. D. H. M. Bannister to the author, 13 January 1983.

11.   "District and Provincial Athletics started in the early years and were going quite well by 1932. Just as shouting for Kenya at the Nairobi Stadium in 1940 was probably the first glimmerings of a national emotion for some Luo railway gangers, so the first sense of tribal unity rather than dislike of people over the river came from District and Provincial athletic rivalries. . . . I had a leading part in selecting the Kenya team [football] which went to Kampala [in 1942] and brought back the Gossage cup after ten years' defeat by Uganda. I took the team there by train and it was a revelation how strong was identification of emotions with a territorial entity . . . it takes a good 24 hours right through the night from Tororo onwards, we were feted. I doubt if Nairobi station had till then seen a bigger crowd." Letter, T. C. Colchester, formerly Kenya Administration, to the author, 21 December 1982.

12.   A mid-1920s reference to KAR soldiers being taught rugby appears in the Earl of Lytton, *The Desert and the Green* (London: Macdonald, 1957), 242.

13.   "As late as 1937 the following warning was given to troops competing in the annual regimental sports in Nigeria and confirmed in print on the programmes: 'Any team or individual displaying a ju-ju, or anything purporting to be a ju-ju or charm, or claiming to possess a ju-ju will be disqualified.' " Maj. Gen. James Lunt, *Imperial Sunset, Frontier Soldiering in the 20th Century* (London: Macdonald, 1981), 183.

14.   The game is described in the Oxford Development Records Project (hereafter ODRP), KAR Collection, papers of Maj. T. R. King.

15.   ODRP, RWAFF Collection, papers of Lt. Col. T. N. Hawtin.

16.   ODRP, KAR Collection, papers of Maj. G. Whitworth.

17.   R. L. B. Maiden, "Polo and Ponies in Nigeria," *Corona* 8, no. 3 (March 1956): 93.

18.   ODRP, KAR Collection, papers of B. A. Young.

19.   ODRP, KAR Collection, papers of Maj. E. A. Swaine.

20.   A. K. Ocran, *The Politics of the Sword* (London: Rex Collings, 1971), 64, 66. When Prime Minister Attlee launched the National Coal Board in 1947 he remarked that it was going in to bat on a sticky wicket, but he hoped it would score a number of sixes. When President Kenyatta inaugurated a new constitution in 1964 he decreed national dance festivities.

However, at the end of the Nigerian civil war in 1970, among the placards carried by jubilant Lagos crowds were several saying "Gowon 12, Ojukwu 0," a reference to Gowon's twelve-state federal constitution and Ojukwu's defeat.

21.   These included some forty Ghanaian and a number of Nigerian and East African soldiers' songs. A selection appears in A. Clayton, *Communication for New Loyalties, African Soldiers' Songs* (Athens, Ohio: Ohio University Press, 1979).

22.   A major text, Gen. R. Hury, ed., *L'Armée d'Afrique, 1830–1962* (Paris: Lavauzelle, 1977), makes no mention of sporting achievements of or within units. Neither do Lt. Col. Burin des Roziers, *Le 1er Régiment de Chasseurs d'Afrique* (Paris: privately published, 1964), Erwan Bergot, *La Coloniale du Rif au Tchad, 1925–80*

(Paris: Presses de la Cité, 1982), nor Joel Tavaro, *Les Derniers Joyeux: "Bat d'Af"* 1960 (Montreuil: La Jeune Parque, 1968).

23. Adrian Liddell Hart, *Strange Company* (London: Weidenfeld and Nicholson, 1953), 68. The great mass of Foreign Legion literature has nothing to add to Liddell Hart's comment except that A. Perrott-White in *French Legionnaire,* (London: Caxton, 1953) notes the boxing, wrestling, running, and fencing within his unit's training program.

24. John Julius Norwich, *Sahara* (London: Longmans, 1968), 82–83 describes this system at work, noting that it received official encouragement.

25. F. P. van Oudtshoorn, "Swazi Regiments of the African Pioneer Corps in the War 1941–45," Public Records Office, DO 35/40 71.

26. For a Tanzanian example of this see A. Clayton, *The Zanzibar Revolution and its Aftermath* (London: C. Hurst, 1981), 16–17. Significantly, in Zanzibar dance groups were also so associated.

27. Maj. H. A. Tomalin, "Physical and Recreational Training in West Africa," *Mind, Body and Spirit, Journal of the Army Physical Training Corps* 21 (June 1946): 23.

28. *Gold Coast Police Magazine* 1, no. 4 (1953): 12.

29. ODRP, KAR. Collection, papers of Maj. C. E. Broomfield.

30. Judith Listowel, *Amin* (Dublin: IUP, 1973), 22–23, notes Amin's prowess both as a boxer—Amin had been Uganda's light-heavyweight champion for nine years—and as an athlete. It is clear that his achievements developed his authority in the barrackroom, and therefore his career.

31. I am indebted to M. J. Macoun, late commissioner and inspector-general of the Uganda Police, for this information, September 1983.

32. Van Oudtshoorn, DO 35/4701.

33. For example, see Gregory Blaxland, *The Final Historical Record of the Buffs, 1948–1967* (Canterbury: The Queen's Own Buffs, 1967), 95. Blaxland notes the regiment, during the campaign against the Mau Mau as "making friends with the Kikuyu by entertainment and competitions, such as archery, between natives and soldier hosts. Great crowds came to these affairs and they undoubtedly played an important part in building-up morale."

34. Al J. Ventner, *Munger Africana Library Notes 19: Report on Portugal's War in Guinea-Bissau* (Pasadena: Munger, 1973), 147 provides an example.

35. *The Nigerian Army Magazine* 2 (1964) provides the detail that follows.

36. Capt. J. B. A. Bailey, "Operation Agila-Rhodesia, 1979–80," *The British Army Review* 66 (December 1980): 19.

37. *Afrique Défense,* no. 30, September 1980: 8.

38. *Afrique Défense,* no. 13 (April 1979): 9; no. 40 (July 1981): 16.

39. *Afrique Défense,* no. 29 (August 1980): 12.

40. *Afrique Défense,* no. 9 (December 1978): 16.

41. *Afrique Défense,* no. 31 (October 1980): 17.

42. *Afrique Défense,* no. 43 (October 1981): 16.

43. *Afrique Défense,* no. 22 (January 1980): 16.

44. *Afrique Défense,* no. 13 (April 1979): 9.

45. *Afrique Défense,* no. 36 (March, 1981): 47. The event includes both a short-distance and a long-distance course competition.

46. *Afrique Défense,* no. 37 (April 1981): 20. Boxing is taught as part of

training for some cadres in the Nigerian Army. At the Physical Training Centre at Zaria selected personnel, notably military policemen, are taught boxing, judo, karate, and aikido in a special self-defense course. *Afrique Defense,* no 46 (January 1982): 13.

47.   Robin Luckham, *The Nigerian Military, 1960–1967* (Cambridge: Cambridge University Press, 1971), 85–86.

48.   See also, for example, Ocran, 64: "As one commentator once said, there is something in military uniform which reflects all that is best in a state, namely national pride, humility, patriotism, fair play and a feeling for the underdog. This may well be so."

49.   *Afrique Defense,* no. 13 (April 1979): 9.

50.   Luckham, 117.

6

Ethics and Ethnocentricity:
Imperial Education in British Tropical Africa

JAMES A. MANGAN

> Realise the importance of games. It's in football and cricket and rowing that Englishmen get that splendid moral training which no other nation gets. Germany and France overwork their boys, . . . nearly always they are stunted and weak. None of them get that magnificent sporting instinct which is the real foundation of our great Empire. So what I want to say to you boys is: "Play up and play the game." Be proud of your reputation for efficiency in games—it is the source of . . . higher imperial efficiency.[1]

This homily *From a Pedagogue's Sketchbook* of scenes from the Edwardian public (i.e., private) school describes a foolish, but perfectly serious, philosophy of education fashionable during the late Victorian and Edwardian eras—the heyday of the British Empire. And in empire it was a philosophy that frequently reflected the values and impulses of the expatriate educator, in part shaped the structure and organization of leading schools, and to an extent, affected the beliefs and behavior of the aborigine.

The Victorians believed that they had something to offer the world: "they were all missionaries in a sense, . . . bringing something which would 'improve the native.'"[2] Improvement took several forms, but it was essentially ethical. The morality of Africa and Africans was a constant concern of the Victorian, whose own moral values, if he was a product of the public-school system, were often shaped substantially by experiences on playing fields, depicted in metaphors and similes associated with team games, measured in terms of performance at the wicket or in the scrummage, and encapsulated in the famous admonitory exhortation, "play the game." It was precisely this state of affairs that led to the ambivalent motto observed by Julian Huxley at a school in Nairobi in the nineteen-twenties: "O God, help me win, but if in thy inscrutable wisdom thou willest me not to win, O God, make me a good loser."[3]

Largely as an outcome of the production of wealth and the growth of the middle classes resulting from the maturing of the industrial revolution, Britain experienced a huge expansion of private education in the second half of the nineteenth century. Schools were enlarged or created. The middle classes sought to enter or imitate the handful of partially reformed "Great Public Schools" of an earlier genesis—Eton, Harrow, Winchester, and Rugby. It is now a truism to assert that for a complex set of reasons, team games became the staple of existence in old and new schools respectively, that athletic boys were the symbols of excellence, and that athletic masters enthusiastically perpetuated the cult of "athleticism," as the rationalization for this obsession with games has come to be labeled.[4] The late Victorian era saw also, of course, the consolidation of a vast empire—the consequence of accident, intent, and miscalculation during the previous three hundred years. The fusion of these three elements—middle-class emulation, ideological enthusiasm, and imperial inheritance—resulted uniquely in the widespread dispersion of the supposedly character-forming attributes of public-school athleticism—the cultivation of a sense of duty, the development of courage, a knowledge of obedience and command, and feelings of loyal fellowship—over those proudly displayed and widely scattered crimson patches to be found in Foyle's *Modern School Atlas* during the decades before the Second World War.

Arising out of their preoccupation with games, the public schools in the latter half of Victoria's reign possessed a sure image of sound boyhood—the *beau idéal* of the system was exemplified in the person of Dan Legge, an unpretentious Haileyburian who fell in the Boer War at the age of twenty-four and who received the following obituary in the school magazine:

> "Dan" he was when he was turning gristle into muscle, and filling his lungs with good, clean English air about his home in the Derbyshire hills. "Dan" he was when he first set off to try and hammer into his hard English head the rudiments of a gentleman's education, with a dogged resolution which showed that he would do something big when the work at hand was more to his liking. "Dan" he was at Haileybury, when he plodded his way up the school and stormed his way into the XV, and left on the mind of every boy who was in form, set, team, or anything else with him, the impression firmly stamped that, after all, the best man of the lot is the man that means to fear God and speak the truth, and live a clean life, and do his level best at whatever turns up to be done, whether he likes it or whether he does not. "Dan" he was, up at Trinity College, Oxford, . . . where he plodded through his schools to his degree with the same steadfastness as of old, where he took a place in Oxford Athletics, which he left with the reputation of being about the lightest and best forward that ever played Rugby football for Oxford against Cambridge.[5]

"Dan" won this euphoric "valete" because he exemplified so admirably the rudiments of the Victorian gentleman's education: perseverance, endurance, honesty, godliness, purity, and courage. In short, he possessed in large measure the solid virtues of a decent character. The formation of character was the essential purpose of Victorian *elitist* education—at home and overseas. Technological skill and intellectual facility both ranked lower in educational priorities. Much as the imperial administrator, missionary, and schoolmaster occupied themselves with the issue of the technical and literary education of the native populations of the empire, the widely held view was that of Brig. Gen. Sir Gordon Guggisberg,[6] governor general of the Gold Coast, now Ghana, from 1919 to 1927: "Education is the keystone of Progress: mix the materials badly, omit the most important and the arch will collapse; omit character-training from education and progress will stop."[7]

In a booklet on colonial educational policy Guggisberg warmed to his analytical task: "No success will come," he warned the imperialist, "no matter how high our education or how perfect our trade training . . . if character is neglected." In pressing this point, he demonstrated an orthodox Anglo-Saxon upper-class view of intellectual ability: "Brain to a leader is of no use unless backed by force of character. Britain herself, mother of the greatest Empire the world has ever seen owes her position far more to the force of character of her sons than to their brain."[8] The training of character was only effective when it utilized metropolitan machinery, methods, and masters: boarding schools, the house system, games, the scout movement, and housemasters—instructors who had themselves had their characters developed in British public schools.

As Guggisberg illustrates, insular conviction and missionary enthusiasm demanded that character training was for export to the empire. To Africa and elsewhere throughout the later years of the nineteenth century and after traveled officials, officers, priests, and teachers from their privileged schools, taking with them a concern for the education of the "African"— both indigenous native and white settler[9]—and the motivation to create out of promising and unpromising material alike, black, brown, and white replicas of Dan Legge. Here we are concerned with those trainers of character, mostly from public school and ancient university, who used the games field as the medium of moral indoctrination.

This phenomenon is now a curiosity of history, but its legacy in the form of contemporary recreational games and sports is to be found all over modern Africa. In the beginning, however, these activities were part of the "cultural baggage" of the British imperialist,[10] carried from coast to hinterland in an effort to dispense the ideals of an upper-class education to "lesser breeds" greatly in need of them. As such, these activities constitute a neglected and fascinating study in pedagogic ethnocentricity, hegemony, and diffusion.

With amused acuity, the suggestion has been made that the great majority of colonial officials exuded the public-school values of their adolescence, with the result that the "old time district commissioner's office commonly suffused a faint air of the prefect's study."[11] Administrators like R. A.

Codrington, the same source has asserted, behaved like "schoolmasters" in control of large numbers of black "pupils":

> Robert Edward Codrington, charged with organizing a civil service for the British South Africa Company in northeastern Rhodesia, . . . specifically asked for young recruits from England with a middle-class background and good physique, giving special preference to university men with teaching experience, locally known as "bum switchers." Codrington himself, tall, with a commanding presence, sporting a neatly clipped mustache, and gruff of speech, was just the sort of man who would have made a stern but respected headmaster at a British public school, and it was in many ways the schoolmaster's outlook which he brought to Northern Rhodesia. White government, he argued, had to be based on prestige, for the amount of military force available was small. The "natives" were but children. He felt convinced, therefore, that officers who could produce testimonials certifying the ability to keep British schoolboys in order would do equally well as district officers in remote outstations.[12]

Sir Frederick Lugard, first governor-general of Nigeria, was another who demonstrated this pedagogic paternalism. In 1923 Lugard published his famous work *The Dual Mandate in British Tropical Africa.* It was a blueprint for colonial action and included two chapters on education. Lugard was both an idealist and a pragmatist. These chapters contained practical recommendations, a concern for vocational training, and some good sense, but idealism was uppermost in his mind. He sought, first and foremost, to remove the moral "mote" from the native eye. In his opinion, in the provision of education for the African the primary purpose of all schools was the formation of character rather than the mere acquisition of book-learning or technical skill.[13] This objective was to be achieved by means of government control over schools and by the careful internal organization of the schools themselves. Colonial governments should establish a code of practice that would embody "proper educational principles"; they should have control over unaided schools and be in continual close consultation with mission schools.

The "proper educational principles" he was seeking may be understood from his Nigerian regulations, which stated that government grants should be allocated in part for tone, discipline, manners, and character as exemplified by the virtues of loyalty, respect, and obedience. Within the schools, especially those for higher-ranking Africans, the means of implementing his basic objective included expatriate staff, residential accommodation, school prefects, and the encouragement of games. In short, Lugard advocated boarding schools for Africa, which, in his own words, "should approximate to the model of an English public school in its internal organisation—in regard to school-houses, dormitories, class and living

JAMES A. MANGAN

rooms, playgrounds, and the rules respecting school boundaries, roll-calls, 'exeats' (holidays), meals, and hygiene." In this kind of establishment, he argued piously, the African would learn to be "less self-centered," would take pride in the corporate body of which he was a member—the school, house, and games team—and begin to understand the meaning of "playing the game." Lugard made much of the value of games in developing the character of the African schoolboy. As he wrote with the most complete conviction: "It is in the play-fields and recreation hours more especially that the public school spirit can be evolved."[14] And he placed great store by the recruitment of the right type of schoolmaster: "The careful selection of British staff is a matter of supreme importance. They should join the boys in outdoor games."[15]

In *Education As Cultural Imperialism*, Martin Carnoy has remarked of Western colonialism that "the European powers used education to effect change, but only those changes that solidified their influence . . . the intended function of education was to help . . . transform the local economic and social structure in ways which strengthened European commercial and political control."[16] This was undoubtedly true of Lugard. What he espoused was education for obeisance. He was disturbed by independent minds, contrary values, and burgeoning nationalism. He demanded from the African the same conformity, fidelity, and deference that the Victorian public-school housemaster demanded of his charges. He was irritated by the educated native "out of touch with the people, imbued with theories of self-determination and half-understood catch-words of the political hustings, acutely sensitive to any fancied racial discrimination and rapidly drifting towards the goal of 'Indian unrest,' "[17] and he harbored the belief that "if moral discipline and standards of duty do not keep pace with material development, society will drift towards the rocks like a ship without ballast or rudder."[18] "Play fields" he thought especially effective, in the creation of moral discipline and standards of duty allegedly so lacking in the uneducated and educated native alike. Long after Lugard retired from Nigeria his concern with the transmission of public-school training to Africa remained acute. He returned continually to the subject of the need to place character training before intellectual training, and he remained anxious that the tradition of discipline typical of the English public-school system as well as its code of honor might be passed to African schoolboys in order that they become "efficient, loyal, reliable and contented: a race of self-respecting native gentlemen."[19]

It was not only distinguished administrators who concerned themselves with the ingredients of imperial education; the most distinguished of imperial soldiers could be equally interested. In November 1898 after Omdurman, Kitchener issued an appeal in Britain for funds to build a college to the memory of General Gordon. His motives were not wholly altruistic. Accusations of cruelty by the British press in his handling of the Mahdists after Omdurman "made him keen to establish a college which would not only prove his own personal goodness but also contribute to the progress of the people whom he had conquered."[20] In a little over a month £120,000 was donated, and in 1900 Kitchener returned to the Sudan to open the school, which he named the Gordon Memorial College. Britain was proud of its investment. Shortly after the Great War the college had no less a personage than the king as its patron, and among the trustees and executive committee could be counted Field Marshal Viscount Allenby, Earl Cromer, Gen. Sir Reginald Wingate, W. M. C. Norman, and Sir Henry Craik. It was "the center around which the educational system was built," and its creation "represented the most important event in the history of Sudan education." More significantly it remained the only secondary school in the Sudan until after the Second World War: "the government was obsessed with the fear of producing an educated, unemployed class who would prove to be politically dangerous."[21]

Lugard was by no means the only imperialist who was irked by the nationalist "political charlatan." Cromer, Kitchener, Wingate, and Currie, the architects of imperial Sudan, all subscribed to the same principles of training in limited vocationalism and cooperative loyalty in order to avoid the "process of manufacturing demagogues." The impact of Egyptian nationalism in the Sudan was a constant anxiety in the minds of these and later officials. Currie, who was appointed director of education in 1900, set out his educational aims as follows:

> The creation of a competent artisan class, which is entirely lacking at present.
>
> The diffusion among the masses of the people of education sufficient to enable them to understand the merest elements of the machinery of government, particularly with reference to the equable and impartial administration of justice.
>
> The creation of a small native administrative class who will ultimately fill many minor government posts.[22]

For his part, Wingate, who became governor-general in 1902, considered that the most important element of education lay in encouraging "moral and religious instruction which requires a sense of duty, unswerving integrity, and loyalty in the public and private relations in life."[23] Consequently educational ambitions for the Sudanese were similar to those for the Nigerian. The purpose of education at Gordon College was unashamedly to produce young men to fill the junior ranks of the government civil service, and to inculcate respect, docility, and fealty. Edward Atiyah, a Lebanese Oxford graduate who joined the staff of the school in 1926, remarked in his autobiography *An Arab Tells His Story*:

> It was a military not a human institution. It was a Government School in a country where the Government was an alien colonial government—the British tutors were members of the political service. They were there in the capacity of masters and rulers, and the second capacity over-shadowed the first. The pupils were expected to show them not the ordinary respect owed by pupils to their teachers, but the submissiveness demanded of a subject.[24]

"To all those with generous heart," stated an early historian of the Sudan, "who revere the memory of Gordon and honour the names of the noble, self-sacrificing redeemers of the Sudan—Kitchener, Cromer and Wingate—and desire to do their part in bearing the white man's burden this College must make an irresistible appeal."[25] It did. The British reached deep into their pockets to support "a mighty work . . . carrying light and civilisation into the heart of Africa and uplifting benighted peoples."[26] The process of elevation predictably followed well-tried and amply proven ways. Indeed, given the appetites and talents of the political service, whose members, mostly public-school and Oxbridge (Oxford or Cambridge) graduates, were frequently recruited on the basis of athletic ability,[27] it is not surprising that the school closely aped the English public school. Life was Spartan, discipline was harsh, and games were part and parcel of the boys' education. "Winchester by the Nile," one warden (headmaster) liked to call it. "This had no relation to reality," a housemaster at the college in the early thirties recalls, "except that the 'manly' and sporting was emphasized. The school was divided into seven Houses. . . . Football of the soccer variety was played a great deal. . . . Each house had its own team and there was an inter House competition. There was also a College 'eleven' and first team stockings were awarded with ceremony with the whole school assembled."[28] In reality, "the warden presided over an old-fashioned imitation of a second-class English Public school."[29] Its aims were limited but sure: "No science was taught within the college; no art; no foreign language other than English; and no extra-curricular activities were held," but games were an essential part of the curriculum.

After the Second World War with a growing commitment to the fashionable concept of trusteeship—the view that the nation was "held in trust" for the natives until they reached political maturity—the Sudan witnessed the gradual expansion of secondary schooling throughout the country. Its general nature has been described by W. M. Farquharson-Lang:

> Allowing for a fair margin of difference, there were similarities between the education in English public schools and secondary schools of the Sudan before 1955. Both were elitist and highly selective. Both were looked upon as training grounds for leadership. . . . They were largely exclusive, the boys being recruited mainly from the landowning classes (squires and sheikhs), in the country, a safe distance from urban temptations, and the

boys were brought up to regard the success of their house and school as a most commendable achievement in education.[30]

Old rivalries and excess of zeal, however, could on occasion distort the noblest of ideals. At the Nugent School, Loka, in the southern Sudan, intertribal football organized along house lines, "between pupils as different as Greeks and Icelanders," had to be abandoned for a time owing to the internecine ferocity of the encounters.[31]

For many years the scattered, heterogeneous and impecunious colonial territories possessed neither the revenues nor the personnel to develop education; the early initiative, therefore, was left to the missionary organizations. As a result, secondary schooling arose more often than not out of church endeavor. Invariably, it represented a combination of education in Christianity and leadership, the one to complement the other in the conversion of native Africa. And conversion was the outright objective. In the forthright words of Bishop Tucker of Uganda: "It cannot be too often or too strongly insisted upon that the *first work of a Christian Mission is to Christianise not simply to civilise.* Christianity can never be evolved out of civilisation. Civilisation, in its best sense, follows in the wake of Christianity."[32] Without Christian schools there would be no Christian leaders, argued J. H. Oldham, and with impeccable Hegelian logic, he concluded, "the maintenance of Christian schools is indispensable for the accomplishment of the missionary task."[33]

Access was predominantly for the privileged of black society. As after the Reformation, when the Jesuits intelligently set up schools for the nobility in order to influence the powerful, so the early twentieth-century missionaries established schools for the sons of chieftains with the same purpose. When Bishop Tucker, for example, encouraged a subordinate in his plans for a "public school" at Mengo, he did so because he believed that the children of the native aristocracy were neglected by parent and missionary alike, yet, "if the ruling classes of the country were to exercise in the days to come an influence for good upon their people, and have a sense of responsibility towards them, it was absolutely essential that something should be done . . . for the education of these neglected children."[34] Something was done. In each diocese in Uganda, high schools were established: boarding schools charging high fees and catering mostly for the sons (and daughters) of chiefs.[35]

Invariably the missionary set about his task in the spirit of Sir John Lawrence: "We are here by our own moral superiority, by the force of circumstance and by the will of Providence. These alone constitute our charter of government and in doing the best we can for the people, we are bound by our conscience and not theirs."[36] Yet, however certain of its

The school at Magila, British Central Africa. 1890. From Gertrude Wood, *Letters from East Africa, 1895–1897* (1898).

superiority, the missionary conscience, of course, was not uniform. The various religious organizations, each with their own dogmas and shibboleths, competed intensely for the souls of Africa; consequently, "there were almost as many kinds of education as there were kinds of missions."[37] The concern here is with the upper class missionaries of the Anglican church. Their pedagogic purpose was uncomplicated: to create in Africa "the spirit of the school at its best as . . . breathed . . . in England after generations of experiment—the spirit of the team, of discipline, of local patriotism."[38] No tradition has been more powerful in the development of secondary schools in East Africa, stated the educationist Eric Lucas,[39] than that of the English public school. This is probably true of British Africa as a whole. The responsibility for this rests with the upper-class missionaries of Anglican persuasion.

The role of these missionaries in "ludic diffusion"—the spread of British team games—has been badly underestimated.[40] It is time to set the record straight. It was wholly logical that the Anglican missionaries' concept of education mirrored the prevalent and fashionable metropolitan ideal of muscular Christianity as ostensibly upheld and implemented in the establishment schools of England. The desirable fusion of morality and manliness in the Anglican missionary mind is abundantly clear from the following statements of intent and recapitulation associated with two of the most famous secondary schools in East Africa: King's School, Buda, in Uganda and Alliance School in Kenya. A little after the creation of King's in 1904, the first headmaster, H. W. Weatherhead,[41] described its role in these committed words: "The school is . . . an attempt to raise the ideals and tone of the whole Christian community, in Uganda and the neighbouring countries, through careful training for three years in a Christian atmosphere by means of the wholesome discipline of a boarding school, organized on the

King's School, Buda, Uganda, ca. 1920. From Thomas Jesse Jones, *Education in East Africa* (n.d.).

lines of a public school . . . focussed on the all-important point of the strengthening of Christian character."[42] Four houses with imperial connotations were established: England, South Africa, Australia, and Canada. They were intended to contain twenty-three boys each for reasons, wrote Weatherhead, "obvious to anyone who knows about football"![43] Cricket was begun in 1915, permitting a later claim to the longest cricketing record among Uganda schools, and by 1923 football and track and field also flourished and there were interhouse competitions in tennis and swimming. The school also quickly established an "Old Boys'" club, which had a football team and weekly Bible reading session.[44]

At Alliance in Kenya, established in 1926, the second headmaster, Francis Carey, in his first annual report asserted that "Christianity and games were only a part of the life of the school but were indeed its most important elements,"[45] and his successor, Lawrence Campbell, on his appointment in 1963, briefly summarized the history of the school: "From the first, Alliance has set out to be a Christian family of boys and masters. The heart of everything is our primary loyalty to Jesus Christ. It means that all we do—class work, games, school life, personal relationships, as well as Chapel and the rest—should be seen as service we offer to our Master. Through all these we seek to serve him and help our boys to become strong, intelligent, Christian men."[46] This ambition to create strong, intelligent Christians resulted in a belief in games as deeply rooted at Alliance as it was at any English public school.[47] Carey and Campbell were the "Bahadurs" (admired leaders) of Christian Africa, captains in a militant team of late Victorian muscular missionaries who "hoped that in providing education they would also be able to form Christian character." Such missionary schoolmasters provided their boys with a complete way of life: table manners, cricket, church attendance, and Christian morality.[48] They looked to create Tom Brown in tropical Africa: brave, truthful, helpful, a gentleman and a Christian.[49]

Elsewhere in East Africa, if the religious aspect was sometimes less explicit, games were just as important to the process. At the Makerere College in Uganda in the twenties, "the general organisation . . . resembled an English boarding school, with dormitories or 'houses,' a school cap, prefects, occasional corporal punishment, and compulsory games and physical training."[50] The college motto attempted to live up to the effort— *Tugummikiri-zenga* (In all things let us be men).[51] About the same time at Tabora school for the sons of chieftains, "the Eton of Tanganyika," boys received "the standard educational grounding, as well as a taste for football, a good deal of discipline, and a real esprit de corps."[52] West African imperialists were not to be outdone. The Church Missionary Society Grammar School in Freetown, Sierra Leone, with four houses, Primus, Secundus, Tertius, and Quartus, was impressively unexceptional in style and purpose:

> The school was run on public-school lines, with its Boarding Department forming the backbone of its tradition. For uniform there was the school cap, the proudest possession of each boy. It was purple with white hoops and the badge featuring a book, a diagonally extended telescope, and the motto. On Sundays and other formal occasions the uniform was navy blue jacket, white trousers, straw boater and the school ribbon. The ribbon consisted of two purple bands separated by a white one. Fifth-form prefects and sixth-formers alone were entitled to wear the school badge attached to the hat ribbon. This badge was as precious as the colours to an Oxford or Cambridge Blue.
>
> Games were compulsory, each afternoon being reserved for a form or a group of forms. . . . We played cricket in the dry season, and football in the rainy season, under the supervision of the appropriate master. Our own form master, Mr. Hycy Willson, was Assistant Games Master.
>
> There were competitions for the house shields in cricket, football and athletics, including cross-country running.[53]

And the government school for the sons and nominees of chieftains situated at Bo in Sierra Leone "approximated to the model of an English public school in its internal organization, and every effort is made to inculcate the public school code of honour."[54]

The convictions and courage of the missionary took him to uncongenial places. Certainly one of the most uncongenial until well into the twentieth century was the west coast of Africa, but as we have seen, the malignity of its climate did not deter him from doing God's work. In Ghana, formerly the Gold Coast, the first missionary schoolmaster was Rev. Thomas

Thompson, fellow of Christ's College, Cambridge, a member of the Society for the Propagation of the Gospel, who set up as missionary and schoolmaster at Cape Coast Castle in 1752. Methodists, Catholics, and others followed. By the second decade of the twentieth century over five hundred schools, unevenly scattered throughout the country, catered to about 12 percent of the children of school age, most of them boys. Government support was pitiful—some 3 percent of total government expenditure—and it was not until 1927, arising out of the personal sponsorship of Governor Sir Frederick Gordon Guggisberg, that the elements of British upper-class education became an integral part of secondary schooling. Guggisberg's interest in education has already been touched upon. It was almost all-consuming. He was yet another schoolmaster manqué earning his bread as an administrator. R. E. Wraith, his biographer, has written with wry humor:

> Perhaps he should never have been a soldier or colonial governor, for he was a born headmaster. The annual Budget Sessions of the Gold Coast Legislative Council were in fact, from 1919 to 1927, Speech days in all but name, at which the Head, at inconsiderate length, spoke of the School's achievements in the preceding year, and commended the promising pupils, black and white, by name and form. The whole subject of education, both in practice and theory, became a passion to the point of obsession.[55]

This obsession assisted him in the ordering of his priorities. The worst feature of the Gold Coast, he stated emphatically in 1924, was the absence of a system for training African leaders. The solution, he declared with equal emphasis, lay in the creation of secondary schools where character training took pride of place in the curriculum. "Our first step," he announced in the same year, "in filling this gap will be taken this year in the building of Achimota College. This will be an institution at which the African youth will receive, first and foremost, character-training of such a nature as will fit him to be a good citizen."[56] His chosen instrument of inculcation was the Reverend A. C. Fraser, and it was in the persons of Guggisberg and Fraser that the various ideals of imperial soldier, administrator, and missionary blended most successfully.

Fraser was educated at Merchiston Castle School and Trinity College, Oxford. He had taught at the turn of the century in Uganda and had been principal of Trinity College, Kandy, Ceylon, from 1904 to 1924. His views on education for the African were like those of Guggisberg, in some respects radical and in some respects conventional. He held that indigenous arts, crafts, traditions, and languages should be promoted, but equally he maintained that character training was much the most important thing. It had a British patent: "It must come above all . . . from boys living in close relationship in field, dormitory and classroom. It will be forwarded greatly by responsibility in self-government given to the boys in increasing measure, till captains and prefects have a large share in the ruling of the school and college."[57] Throughout his time at the Prince of Wales College at Achimota, Fraser was engaged with a fierce single-mindedness in a cultural and spiritual hegemonic endeavor. He never for one moment doubted the efficacy of games in this action. Having placed considerable emphasis on them in both Uganda and Ceylon,[58] he was delighted with his first view of the site at Achimota: "It consists of four square miles of land," he wrote, "with a good slope for drainage; and beautiful playing fields are being planned; one cricket field in area and shape might well rouse the envy of the Surrey XI who only have the Oval."[59]

In the official opening of the college on 28 January 1927, Fraser said in his speech: "I am sure Africans do not desire to become Europeans or to become like them,"[60] yet the school song gave evidence of an intense desire on his part to mold the African to a large extent in an Occidental image:

> From Kumasi or Accra, from the Volta or the Prah
> We are brothers and our mother is the school.
> She will guide us all and each
> So to learn that we may teach,
> So to subjugate ourselves that we may rule,
> Play the game,
> Shout her name,
> Spread her name afar.
> She's ahead of all the host,
> She's the school of whom we boast,
> She's the glory of the Coast,
> ACCRA-A-A[61]

The staff was heavy with masters familiar with public-school mores and included more than a dozen graduates from Oxford and Cambridge. It comes as no surprise therefore to discover that the house system was carefully developed, that school routine followed metropolitan practice, and that whatever the fashionable theories in liberal colonial circles, no major concessions were made to indigenous tradition or inclination. The deliberate fostering of African music, arts, crafts, and dances in response to official and personal sympathy with the currently promoted concept of "adaptation" must be juxtaposed with the adherence to metropolitan institutional organization, timetable, and ideology:

Morning	5:30	Rising Bell
	6–6:20	Physical training
	6:20–6:50	Cleaning dormitories
	7–7:50	Breakfast
	8:00	Assembly and prayers
	8:15–12:00	Classes

Afternoon	12:15	Lunch
	2–3:30	Classes
	4–6:00	Exercise
	Monday	House games
	Tuesday	School games
	Wednesday	Gardening
	Thursday	House games
	Friday	Social service and free time[62]

And the pursuit of indigenous tradition itself, however well intentioned, was clearly circumscribed by unspoken assumptions. "Teaching . . . will be most of it based on a truly African foundation," argued an anonymous contributor to *Round Table* in 1925, and he continued in a vein of unconscious irony:

> One of the staff has, for instance, been studying Gold Coast music. He finds that its folksongs have strong musical resemblances to old folksongs in Britain and Europe. He proposes to teach the children to sing and to understand the music of their own songs. This done, he would give them similar folksongs from Europe. He would then bring them on—two out of every three of lessons should be critical—to understand the gradual development of European music. They would learn to appreciate the light tuneful music of the Renaissance, French and Italian, the Elizabethans, and so on through Handel and Mozart to Bach, who appeals to them as no other does.[63]

Another commentator, after announcing in the *Journal of Negro Education* in 1935 how special care was taken not to alienate the African from the praiseworthy features of his own tribal heritage, then concluded that the belief in training in the fundamentals of Christianity and the idea of "playing the game" permeated the whole atmosphere of the college.[64]

The essential Britishness of the educational experience is perhaps best gauged from the obituary of one of the school's first pupils, Yaw Gyamfi, nephew of Nana Prempeh, Kumasihene of the Ashanti:

> Yaw was tall and strong for his age [eleven years] and soon proved himself a leader not only in athletics but in class work. . . . Through no will of his own he was set on a pedestal by the other children, as one to be respected and copied but too high for intimacy. Instead of accepting the distinction he ignored it and won the love of his house by the whole-hearted way in which he entered into all their activities. He was accessible even to the youngest, and it was due to his rare modesty and eagerness to accept advice from his fellows, in his duties as captain of games, and head monitor in the children's boarding house, that he was saved from the isolation common to school heroes. In 1929 . . . Yaw entered into the junior boarding house for

those between the ages of twelve and sixteen. Though one of the young members of the house he was unanimously elected a dormitory monitor. His last year was one of purest joy. He made many close friends; his early promise as a scholar in the school was more than maintained in the College; he was the best boxer in the College; he was captain of house hockey and in all the other house teams, in the inter-house athletic meeting he was the strongest competitor from his house and won places in the junior events; he joined the Junior Orchestra and made a very encouraging start as a violinist. It seemed that he could turn his hand to anything and do well.[65]

Elsewhere in the Gold Coast it was the same story. The education provided at St. Nicholas's Grammar School, founded in 1910 at Cape Coast, by the nineteen-thirties was impeccably correct.

St. Nicholas's is run on the lines of an English public school. . . . The seed of our public school spirit has taken firm root in the warm soil of West Africa, and the plant is already well established and sturdy. Cricket and even Rugby football hold their honoured place, and in athletics, which are especially popular, the school stands at present first in the Colony and holds the coveted Aggrey Trophy. Less pressure from modern languages leaves more time for the study of English, Latin, and Greek. Last year, under the guidance of an African master, the boys produced the *Antigone* of Sophocles in their own Greek theatre, built in the open air, and rendered the odes in the original Greek. Evidence of a not unfamiliar spirit shows itself in the school slang, in which a detention is "tea," recreation "release," and a whipping "construction."[66]

In any record of the diffusion of games and the games ethic throughout Africa the oddity, the eccentric, and the nonconformist deserve a passing mention. They had their impact. For a variety of motives, missionaries took the game developed in the British public schools beyond the coastal fringe and deep into the heart of Africa. Not all the proselytizers were from public schools, nor did they all create "public schools," nor were they all men. Marion Stevenson (1871–1930), a Scot born in Forfar, played her small part in the diffusion of British games—in the interests of discipline and more importantly of purity. Her mission school at Tumutumu in Kenya was well stocked with a supply of tennis balls, and when lessons were over, the youngsters had a game that proved a great asset; exclusion from it was a useful punishment for irregular attendance. However, football was the favorite pastime and one she fully encouraged as a distraction from licentiousness and as a stimulus to self-denial. Her biographer wrote that "one might wax lyrical over the part that football has taken in attracting and educating the lads, and giving them an outlet for their energies, in place of fighting and bad dances,"[67] and further praised the value of the game in teaching esprit de corps and unselfishness to the apolaustic African!

Miss Stevenson was not alone in her attempt to create a restrained aesthetic. In her antipathy to suggestive rhythmical contortions, she had a strong affinity, for example, to the Reverend Geoffrey Twistleton-Wykeham-Fiennes, a teacher at St. Mark's College, Mapanze, in the Diocese of Northern Rhodesia, who introduced English dancing to his African boys—country dances, sword dances, and morris dances and thus brought to young Africa "a new experience of enjoyment," which was a far cry from "the dubious experiences of some African village dances."[68] The contributor to *Round Table* introduced earlier thought sexual excess in Africa a general condition. "What can be done?" he asked in exasperation. The teacher "finds a race of magnificent physique but subject throughout great tracts—both in wedlock and out of it—to the curse of sexual indulgence.[69] Some hope for a change, he conceded, lay in games. Such missionary repugnance at "uninhibited" native hedonism was widely felt.[70]

Another who used football as an early moral purgative and distraction was G. L. Pilkington, the Harrow schoolmaster, who joined the Church Missionary Society in 1889 and was killed in Uganda nine years later. Pilkington was a muscular missionary much admired by the church romancers of the period, who wrote in simple, eulogistic terms of imperial crusaders of his ilk. He created something of a reputation by cycling from Frere Town in Kenya to Kampala, the capital of Uganda. The physical endurance and capabilities of this Victorian knight-errant are worth recording. At Kikuyu his diary reads:

> From Kibwezi (from which I started a fortnight ago) to this place is about 330 miles, most of it country . . .
>
> *Sunday, 20th December.*—Kibwezi to Nzawi, 57½ miles, only half the road rideable; arrived at 5.30 pm.
>
> *Monday, 21st.*—Kilungu, 10 miles, fearful road.
>
> *Tuesday, 22nd.*—Machakos, 37 miles, fearful road.
>
> *Wednesday, 23rd.*—To Kikuyu, 47 miles, good road; 2½ hours delay owing to tyre; arrived at 6 pm.
>
> *Thursday, 24th.*—Rested.
>
> *Friday, 25th.*—To Naivasha, 47 miles; tyre broke down three times; should have been there 2 pm., got there 5.30 pm., having had to ride on deflated tyre, or should have been benighted; tyre spoiled . . .
>
> *Saturday, 26th.*—Rested; failed to mend tyre.
>
> *Sunday, 27th.*—Went on with mail men, shoving bike, to Kambi ya Mbaruk, 29 miles: hard work.
>
> *Monday, 28th.*—to Kambi ya moto, 30 miles through grass 5 ft. high; fearful day.
>
> *Tuesday, 29th.*—To Ravine, 25 miles; bad road. Here Mr. Jackson with infinite kindness put on rope and raw hide on hind wheel as substitute for tyre, and gave me provisions for the road.[71]

G. L. Pilkington, missionary in Uganda circa 1890, from Charles F. Harford-Battersby, *Pilkington of Uganda* (n.d.).

On arrival at Mengo in Uganda, he claimed a record for the time he took from London—seventy-four days, and after quickly settling in, lost no time in introducing Harrovian practice: "We have started football lately. I play most afternoons. It is great fun and good for the boys."[72] Later a fellow missionary wrote, "Archdeacon Walker has got a football out from England, and Pilkington has been diligently coaching the boys . . . he enters with great earnestness into it . . . I, with my boys and about ten others, stood Pilkington and another lot. We got two goals each. We play on a large grass field between Kampala and Rubaga."[73] Tragically, Pilkington's playing days were soon to be over. He was killed weeks later on 11 December 1898 in a mutiny by Sudanese troops.

Another keen missionary footballer was Arthur Douglas, who also died in tragic circumstances,* but not before he had successfully encouraged soccer in his missionary school on the shores of Lake Nyasa in British Central Africa in the face of irritating problems caused by the local terrain, which emerged in a letter to England describing a typical school day:

---

*He was shot by a Portuguese colonial official, apparently protecting an African girl from being raped.

. . . school 8.30–12; then their first meal—porridge, beans and salt; then school again 2.0 to 4.0 the last three-quarters of an hour being given to physical exercises, either dumbbell exercises, of which I have got a very complete scheme, or else hoeing the ground. Then at 4.0 o'clock they are free for football or anything else that is going. Alas! my football bladders have lately been bursting like fireworks. I sat up one night, trying to mend five holes with seccotine and patches from another bladder worse than itself. What a pathetic appeal!—especially to a man who once sent me two footballs, for which I didn't thank half as soon as I ought. Then a jolly good bathe in which I often join. . . . Then Evensong; then their second meal—porridge beans and salt; then three-quarters of an hour's school, followed by one hour in which to trot about; then prayers and to bed. . . . Doesn't that sound an ideal sort of life?—and certainly a well-filled day is the way to keep these lads happy and disciplined.[74]

Not all Christian missionaries, even of the most impeccable credentials, were of the view that Western physical activities were imbued with valuable moral qualities and useful antidotes. Arthur Shearly Cripps (1869–1952), who had been a superb athlete at Oxford, track-and-field man, rower, and boxer, considered these things of little pedagogical value when he went as a missionary to Rhodesia in 1900 under the auspices of the Society for the Propagation of the Gospel. Splendid physical properties stood him in good stead in the circumstances of missionary work: "He was to get some real jogging in weekly trips from Enkeldoom to Umvuma, thirty-two miles away where he took a service for the Africans in the morning and then by swift walking and jogging managed to get back to Enkeldoom for the evening service,"[75] but athletic effort was incidental to his real enthusiasms. Cripps became an admirer of the African and his culture, and was not in any way inclined to attach high value to the importation of Western cultural activities. In fact, he spent a considerable time opposing those less attractive ones of exploitation and racism. To the disgust of his fellow countrymen he had "gone native" in a curious sort of way and could always be counted on for an opinion biased in the African's favor.[76]

Cripps was wholly out of step not merely with his countrymen but with most Europeans in Africa. The imperial policies of France, Germany, and Britain in the period between the scramble for Africa and the retreat from colonialism had certain similarities. All three nations were concerned with the economic exploitation of the colonies and the best utilization of their resources—including human resources. The colonialist everywhere "desired native education in order to train human tools for his economic and administrative machine and make more efficient servants of the natives."[77] The German policy in Tanganyika before 1914 is quite explicit on this point:

Arthur Jeffrey Douglas, missionary in British Central Africa. From B. W. Randolph, *Arthur Douglas, Missionary on Lake Nyasa: The Story of His Life* (1912).

Association Football— beginnings: Likoma, Lake Nyasa, ca. 1906. From B. W. Randolph, *Arthur Douglas, Missionary on Lake Nyasa: The Story of His Life* (1912).

Association Football— consolidation: First Eleven, Masena School, Kenya, ca. 1920. From Thomas Jesse Jones, *Education in East Africa* (n.d.).

156

The native himself is the chief asset of the colonies. Only with his help can the rich resources of these territories be exploited. Thus development of the native's ability constituted the principal of German colonialisation. . . . The government official . . . needed office assistants who could read and write, and the presence, in important centres in the interior, of natives who understand German and could interpret government decrees to their fellow-countrymen simplified the task of the administration to an extraordinary degree. The State also needed artisans and other workers for its Stations.[78]

Some years later the French for their part, were equally candid:

Education has, as its first effect, a large increase in the value of colonial industrial output through multiplying the intellectual abilities and capacities among the masses of colonial workers . . . as skilled mechanics, foremen, inspectors, clerks to supplement the numerical insufficiency of Europeans and satisfy the growing demands of agriculture, industrial and commercial colonialisation enterprises . . . to train native-commissioned officers.[79]

The British were no different: secondary schools were essentially "conveyor-belts for the supply of clerks to commerce and government service."[80]

Dissimilarities between nations, it has been argued, were as pronounced as the similarities.[81] The French supposedly pursued a policy of "assimilation" based upon "a belief in the ultimate unity of mankind and the gradual absorption of the primitive races by the advanced European races"; the British in the later years of occupation supposedly made more of the policy of "adaptation" of education suited to the needs and traditions of the indigenous peoples. Remi Clignet sums up a general view:

It is often asserted that French authorities promoted the emergence of a class of "black Frenchmen," with values, aspirations, and cognitive styles analogous to those of European educational institutions. In contrast, the British have been viewed as repudiating such a notion in their system of indirect rule, which attempted accommodation with Africa and aimed at perpetuating African existing social organisations.[82]

The Portuguese, it was thought, had something in common with the French.[83] The Germans and the Belgians,[84] it would seem, were not greatly concerned with either perspective, but in any case the generalization regarding France and Britain was a gross oversimplification.

A fashion for stressing differences has prevailed in the study of African colonial history. The tendency has been "to seek and exaggerate differences rather than similarities between colonial policies."[85] The Whig interpretation of history has prevailed; conclusions have been the product of prior convictions and not the outcome of empiricism.[86] There was no simplistic

Girls drilling at the missionary church at Kota Kota, British Central Africa, ca. 1900. From B. W. Randolph, *Arthur Douglas, Missionary on Lake Nyasa: The Story of His Life* (1912).

dichotomy between "assimilation" and "adaptation" in the respective territories. The contrasts between the two systems have been exaggerated: "Both colonial powers wavered between 'assimilationist' and 'adjustive' policies."[87] Ideological assertions have been considered naively at face value while local reality and indigenous response have been ignored. In fact, at times the British were as keen on Anglicization as the French were on Gallicization; in reality the British colonies "produced a larger number of partially Europeanized Africans imbued to some extent with metropolitan values, than the supposedly assimilationist minded French."[88] Furthermore,

> British policy was probably more assimilationist than the French at the secondary school level, . . . Curricula tended to replicate metropolitan forms. Moreover, the secondary system was much less differentiated, consisting mainly of "academic" schools, in spite of earlier British efforts to develop secondary vocational and agricultural training.[89]

Cambridge Certificate Examinations, Christian worship, prefects, uniforms, houses, and games were mechanisms of initiation into British culture, symbolizing and actualizing enculturation and disassociation. These mechanisms constituted a psychological and cultural process of induction. The elements of *rites de passage*, we have been informed, are withdrawal from the family, isolation in "a marginal environment," a convinced and convincing preceptor able to promulgate new values and impose new norms, absorption of restricted information, didactic chastisement, and tests of fortitude.[90] And these were all explicit features of the British imperialist secondary school. Successful passage through the school denoted transfer from the status of childlike, primitive African to adult, civilized "European"![91] As tests of fortitude and more, games played their

Boys drilling at St. Peter's High School, Uganda, ca. 1920. From Thomas Jesse Jones, *Education in East Africa* (n.d.).

part in the deliberate deracination of the African. In this regard, of course, whatever the French and British similarities, the British *were* idio-syncratically different. Games as part of the curriculum were a distinguishing feature of the secondary school both in the empire and Britain. French, German, Belgian, and Portuguese educationists were essentially indifferent to the potential for moral instruction inherent in team games and passed up the ethical hegemonic opportunities offered on playing fields. The European games of twentieth-century Africa were the gift of the British imperialist and were provided not so much for pleasurable relaxation as for moral improvement.

The "educated" African, we are informed, was profoundly unsympathetic to certain characteristics of colonialism: rationalizations that "explained" political subordination and economic restriction, and promotional structures defended in terms of white adequacy and black inadequacy.[92] Consequently, antithesis, paradox, and contradiction were base elements of African reaction to Western education. The school in early twentieth-century Africa was the means of dramatic social change, "the main agent of modernization," but not in ways the colonial educator wholly intended. The motives of many Africans interposed between imperial intention and fulfillment:

> It is one thing to indicate the formal differences between French and British policies; it is another thing to demonstrate that these policies had different implications so far as the diffusion of education is concerned. Actually, both systems have had very similar consequences. The functions of an educational system are after all, as much determined by its societal context as they are by the educational structure or policies pursued. In this light,

The Boys Brigade, Kikuyu, Kenya, ca. 1920. From Thomas Jesse Jones, *Education in East Africa* (n.d.).

Boy scouts and cubs of the First Zanzibar Troop ca. 1920. From Thomas Jesse Jones, *Education in East Africa* (n.d.).

differences between French and British educational systems may be of less moment than similarities or divergencies between the traditional social structures into which the schools were transplanted.[93]

In truth, the extent of African accommodation was as significant as the British attempt at assimilation. Black "refractory" reservations were influential.[94]

In an effort to analyze African reaction to modern education, six chronological stages have been postulated: outright conservatism, selective acceptance of modernity, partial reinstatement of tradition, and extensive reinstatement of tradition.[95] It is a tidy but unsubtle classification. In particular, total acceptance of modernity constitutes a crude depiction of reality. Tom Brown, for example, was an ideal seldom actualized in motherland or colony.[96] The eudaemonic zeal of his advocates was poorly rewarded. The pupil culture in both locations proved dominant. Physical and intellectual Darwinism respectively ensured a general rejection of the fictional ideal. In Africa an indigenous form of "adaptation" prevailed over metropolitan concepts of both "assimilation" and "adaptation."

The unlooked-for consequences of the hegemonic process can be seen in Musgrove's analysis of an Ugandan boarding school in the 1950s.[97] He posed the question as to how far the character and quality of its work were shaped respectively by tribal experience and by metropolitan influence. In his view British values resulted in an institutional structure that negated tribal association, placing a new emphasis on the novel associations formed around dramatic society, literary club, and cricket team: "Loyalties unknown outside the school are now felt—to the class, the team, the informal group, the House (which stirs strong feelings of rivalry in the inter-house sports and games) and to the school."[98] These groupings, he argued, reduced distinctions significant in the wider society; thus Babito aristocrats lived in apparent harmony and equality with Bunyoro commoners. Alien cultural ideas and values were, in turn, transmitted to the villages, where the boy gained high status by virtue of his privileged knowledge, consequently "at home on holiday [he] is usually treated as an honoured guest: no work is expected of him . . . and he is welcomed home as a decoration to the family entourage."[99] The school, claimed Musgrove, despite its inability to meet indigenous needs, was an institution in which a new ideal type of man was shaped, the "educated man," and he continued, "It may be that this ideal had a counterpart in the ideal of the great hunter or the great warrior of former days, and if so, the new ideal has effectively replaced it."

But here is the paradox. Ironically this ideal had little in common with the robust English public schoolboy of the Victorian and Edwardian eras promulgated so enthusiastically by the imperial schoolmaster and allegedly cast in the mold of Tom Brown but in reality as frequently shaped in the image of the fanfaron, Flashman. It was much more akin to the "swot" (grind) so despised by the public school "blood" (athletic hero):[100] "The most cogent criticism of a boy and encouragement to different behaviour," remarked Musgrove, "is to point out that his present conduct is not that of an *educated man*. The exhortation to be "good," manly, loyal, Christian, or even courageous meets with far less response. The boys judge Europeans by their educational status: they count a man's degree and diplomas and by them measure his worth."[101] The nature and potency of the ideal of the "educated man," stated Musgrove, was fundamental to an understanding of education in Uganda. It stemmed from the assumed power of literacy invested in the early imperialist.

All over Africa firmly enunciated principle and generally incomplete implementation was the norm. Whatever the ambitions of the Christian missionary, the main function of the school for the African was to offer the means of realizing an ideal of self conversant with an image of high status, social success, and occupational security. There was frequently tension between the motives of the European and those of the African.[102] In effect, they moved along different motivational trajectories. Western education to the African was a symbol of potential power. "Schools grew up like mushrooms," Ngugi wa Thiong'o wrote of the Kenyan Gikuya territory, "and there they stood, symbols of people's thirst for the white man's secret magic and power. Few wanted to live the white man's way, but all wanted the magic."[103] To the European education was the means at one and at the same time of ensuring subservience and bringing about improvement—economic subservience and moral improvement. Given that "all colonial societies were caste structures composed of a subordinate indigenous caste and a superimposed endogamous colonial elite," it followed that to the European, education for the black was often in reality an attempted instrument of social stasis, while to the African it was a utilized instrument of social advancement; and so Africa demanded and accepted "the public school" package, but for its own ends.[104] The metaphors of both Western theology and sport were often seen as mere rhetoric. What Phillip Foster noted of the Ghanaian was equally true elsewhere in British Africa:

> In viewing the development of education in terms of the expectations of Africans and the purpose it served for them, rather than from the viewpoint of the colonial power, African pressures for academic forms of education and particularly for academic secondary education are readily understandable. In practice the African clientele of the schools received very much the kind of education that they so reasonably desired. During the nineteenth century most British educationists on the coast had espoused the cause of technical and agricultural education as a key to eco-

nomic development. African parents, however, like those elsewhere, did not send their children to school to meet the need for economic growth: they sent them there to maximise their children's opportunities within the emergent occupational and prestige structure created by colonial rule.[105]

To claim this of African parents as an eventual generality is not to overlook variation in response to, and in the timing of the development of, Western education in different parts of British Africa—among other things, the product of longevity of contact, the early nature of this contact, the struggles between the imperial powers, and the strength and self-confidence of local cultures—but to reflect the views of many African and European commentators.[106]

It was the academic aspect of British education that the African embraced most avidly for sensible secular reasons:

> . . . entry to white collar employment and . . . technical and professional training was determined by competitive examinations which were based on a literary curriculum. Young Africans compared unfavourably the comforts of the missionary bungalow and the luxury of an administrator's motor car with the drudgery and hardship of tilling the land: They contrasted, however inarticulately, a world of illiterate, custom-bound subsistence agriculture in the village with a world of towns, clerks, salaries, machines—the "modern" world. Agriculture came to stand for backwardness and "bush"; progress started with book-learning in the schools.[107]

Such was the extent of African rejection of education "adapted"[108] to the traditional way of life and advocated so strenuously by the "enlightened" imperialist in the twenties in celebrated reports like *Educational Policy in British Tropical Africa*, that the Beecher Committee's Inquiry in 1949 into the scope, content, and methods of African education in Kenya found that the technical and practical emphasis had virtually disappeared.[109] The Alliance school, for example, had abandoned its vocational training in favor of a concentration on the Cambridge Certificate as early as the start of the Second World War! A commonsensical selective process was at work in the mind of the African, for good reason:

> When schooling is the route to salaried employment, and Governments recognise the paper qualifications of examination results as the test of schooling, is it surprising that the learning of examinable information becomes all-important? that curricular activities not easily examinable should seem irrelevant? that the whole process of character-training appears to lack any necessary connection with Western schooling? or that the principle of adaptation to environment should be suspect from the start? All such principles can so easily appear as devices designed by the ruling

power to keep the African back, at the very time when he is beginning to surge forward.[110]

Paradoxically, therefore, the African view was frequently more assimilationist than that of the British and French administrator.[111] Paradoxically, again, it was the truly progressive official who after the Great War advocated parity of educational experience. There can be little doubt that this assertive selectivity was further stimulated by an unhappy contradiction between Western precept and practice. In the sharp words of one Nigerian:

> In giving moral instruction, Western education often ran counter to the example given by other agents and agencies which were popularizing the Western way of life among the natives. It was . . . unrealistic to expect the public school code of honour to take root in the social confusion resulting from colonialism. More often than not, the attempt to introduce this code of honour led to no more than the adoption of the outward trapping of the English gentleman.[112]

There is yet a further point to be considered. Christianity and education in Africa have been closely associated; the former has been the means to the latter. Consequently, native reaction to the missionary cannot be viewed simply as a religious response to a religious message.[113] The reality was more complicated. Missionary idealism (and bigotry) were often tolerated for material ends. Religion was frequently used by the African as a secular tool. As the uncle of the hero in Onuora Nzekwu's *Blade among the Boys* advised his young nephew, whipped by the missionary for idolatry, the ransom for education must be paid: "You must go to school. Suffer in silence and when you finally leave school choose and live by your own standards."[114]

"Everywhere," wrote S. G. Williamson of Africa, "the Church and the School nestle side by side,"[115] but the disproportionate emphasis on education of the literary type had not led to a fusion of Christian ideals and indigenous culture. A scholar with a split mind had been produced—leaning toward Western culture yet rooted in traditional life. The influence of the church had been disappointing for four reasons: sectarian rivalry, the inappropriateness of the message of docility to the nationalist determined to fight for freedom, the nationalist's demand for the subservience of religion to the state, and the apostasy of Christian schoolteachers.

The Africans' redefinition of educational priorities was clearly a manifestation of anti-imperial self-assertion. The rejection of the central significance of the games ethic in the educational process was an act at one and the same time of pragmatism and principle; it represented materialism and nationalism. Academic qualifications, not "playing the game" (in both senses), were the ways to personal fulfillment through the realization of prosperity and autonomy. There was no currency, occupational or political, in kicking footballs and swinging cricket bats. In a situation of "backwardness" that held the promise of advancement through the classroom, there was little inclination to indulge in "play" and considerable preoccupation with the rewards of "intellectual" credentials. In the late nineteenth and early twentieth centuries the English public schoolboy escaped from the classroom; the Africa "public" schoolboy escaped into it. His *toga virilis* (gown of manhood) was not the football strip but the graduate gown.

The novels of Chinua Achebe, W. Conton, J. W. Abruquah, Onuora Nzekwu, and Ngugi wa Thiong'o provide collectively a clear-eyed African view on the native lust for learning and the certain rewards of the school certificate.[116] Africa's schoolboys celebrated the attractions of pen and slate rather than the pleasures of bat and ball.

> Father, mother
> Provide me with pen and slate
> Land is gone
> Cattle and sheep are not there
> Not there any more
> What's left?
> Learning, learning.[117]

By and large, the African was unimpressed with the imported concepts of Tom Brown, assimilation, and adaptation. Character mattered less than accreditation, and husbandry was less attractive than professionalism.

Of course, games were not rejected out of hand. The imperialists comprised an elite that set standards over a range of behavior. English gentlemen played games; aspiring African gentlemen could do no less. And there were notable exceptions to the rule of academic bias; Kwame Nkrumah was not wholly immune to the athletic attractions of a public school education. An early student at Achimota, he later wrote of his college days: "Although I was desperately keen on learning . . . I never became a swot or a bookworm . . . I discovered that sportsmanship was a vital part of a man's character, and this led me to realise the importance of encouraging sport in the development of a nation."[118] In general, however, these games were far less significant to the black pupil than they were to the white master. They held far fewer moral connotations. In taking this stance, unknowingly the twentieth-century African "public" schoolboy was keeping step with the twentieth-century British public schoolboy, whose own earlier priorities, athletic rather than religious, were being transformed against his will by political reform, state scholars, technology, and public examinations.[119] In both places as the century progressed it was the muscular Christian schoolmaster with his facile metaphors and similes of the playing fields who was increasingly out of step.

Notes

1. Francis Duckworth, *From a Pedagogue's Sketch Book* (London: Chatto and Windus, 1912), 68.

2. Phillip Mason, "Cold Baths, Prudery and Empire," *New Society,* 4 February 1971: 201.

3. Julian Huxley, *Africa View* (London: Chatto and Windus, 1931), 152.

4. See J. A. Mangan, *Athleticism in the Victorian and Edwardian Public School* (Cambridge: Cambridge University Press, 1981), passim.

5. *Haileyburian,* 6 February 1901: 83–84.

6. Frederick Gordon Guggisberg (1869–1930) was born in Toronto. He attended the Royal Military Academy, Woolwich, and joined the Royal Engineers in 1889. From 1902 to 1914 he surveyed the Gold Coast, Ashanti, and Nigeria for the Colonial Office. He was surveyor-general of Nigeria from 1910 to 1914. He had a distinguished military career during the Great War, becoming assistant inspector-general of training, G.H.Q., France, in 1916. (*Who Was Who 1929–1940,* 565). Guggisberg was a lifelong lover of cricket—a playing member of the Marylebone Cricket Club, the Free Foresters, and other fashionable cricket clubs. As director of the Gold Coast survey, he thought his workmen "deserved to be taught cricket," presumably "a powerful weapon with which to keep the *Pax Britannica.*" R. E. Wraith, *Guggisberg* (London: Oxford University Press, 1967), 40.

7. Brig. Gen. Sir Gordon Guggisberg, *The Keystone* (London: Simpkin, Marshall, Hamilton, Kent, 1924), cover quotation.

8. Ibid., 13.

9. The emphasis in this chapter is on black Africa. For a consideration of the diffusion of the public-school games ethic among white settlers in South Africa see J. R. de S. Honey, *Tom Brown in South Africa* (Grahamstown: Rhodes University Press, 1972), 3–28.

10. For a discussion of this point see Brian Stoddart, "Sports as Cultural Imperialism: Exploratory Thoughts on the British Case," unpublished paper.

11. L. H. Gann and Peter Duignan, *Burden of Empire* (London: Pall Mall Press, 1968), 208.

12. Ibid., 210.

13. Sir Frederick Lugard, *The Dual Mandate in British Tropical Africa* (London: Blackwood, 1922), 431–32.

14. Ibid., 431.

15. Sir Frederick Lugard, *Political Memorandum No. 4: Education,* 134.

16. Martin Carnoy, *Education as Cultural Imperialism* (New York: McKay, 1974), 82.

17. Lugard, *Dual Mandate,* 424.

18. Sir Frederick Lugard, "Education in Tropical Africa,' *Edinburgh Review* (July 1925); 493.

19. Lugard, *Dual Mandate,* 426.

20. Mohamed Omer Beshir, *Educational Development in the Sudan 1898–1956* (Oxford: Oxford University Press, 1969), 26.

21. A. Theobald and W. M. Farquharson-Lang, "Higher Education under Condominium Government," *Durham Sudan Historical Records Conference,* 1983, 4.

22. Sir James Currie, "Educational Experiment in the Anglo-Egyptian Sudan 1900–33," *Journal of the African Society* 33 (1934): 357.

23. Beshir, 46.

24. Edward Atiyah, *An Arab Tells His Story* (London: Murray, 1946), 23.

25. Percy Martin, *The Sudan in Evolution* (London: Constable, 1921), 162–63.

26. Ibid., 163.

27. See J. A. Mangan, "Education of an Elite Administration: The Sudan Political Service and the British Public School System," *International Journal of African Historical Studies* 4 (1982): 671–99; and A. H. M. Kirk-Greene, "The Sudan Political Service: A Profile in the Sociology of Imperialism," *International Journal of African Historical Studies* 3 (1982): 21–48.

28. Letter from Alan Theobald to the author dated 16 October 1983. Dr. Theobald served in the Sudan Educational Department from 1929 to 1959. From 1929 to 1936 he was a tutor and housemaster at Gordon Memorial College.

29. Theobald, letter to author.

30. Theobald and Farquharson-Lang, 5.

31. G. F. Earl, "A School's Opportunity in the Southern Sudan," *Church Missionary Outlook* (July 1937): 154.

32. A. R. Tucker, *Eighteen Years in Uganda and East Africa* (London: Arnold, 1908), I, 108. Some of the earliest references to school cricket and soccer on the African continent occur in the early publications of the Universities Mission to Central Africa, of which Tucker was a member. See for example, Henry Rowley, *Twenty Years in Central Africa,* 2d ed. (London: Wells Gardner, 1881), 181; Gertrude Ward, *Letters from East Africa,* 2d ed. (London: Universities Mission to Central Africa, 1901), 147; and Gertrude Ward, ed., *Letters of Bishop Tozer* (London: Universities Mission to Central Africa, 1902), 134, and 144. For a later statement equally as zealous as that of Bishop Tucker, Phyllis C. Garlick, *School Paths in Africa* (London: Highway Press, 1933); and Mabel Shaw, "Educating Africa: New Loyalties for Old," *The Listener* (25 September 1935): 530–31.

33. J. H. Oldham, "Christian Education in Africa," *Church Missionary Review* 75 (June 1925): 307.

34. G. P. McGregor, *King's College, Budo: The First Sixty Years* (Nairobi: Oxford University Press, 1967), 6.

35. H. T. C. Weatherhead, "Educational Experiments in Uganda," *The East and West* 15 (1917): 214–15.

36. Quoted in Sir Christopher Cox, "The Impact of British Education on the Indigenous Peoples of Overseas Territories," *The Advancement of Science 13* (September 1956): 126.

37. Victor Turner, ed., *Colonialism in Africa* (Cambridge: Cambridge University Press, 1971), III, 321.

38. Weatherhead, 217.

39. Eric Lucas, *English Traditions in East African Education* (London: Oxford University Press, 1959), 4, 14.

40. Allen Guttmann, "The Diffusion of Sports and the Problem of Cultural Imperialism," unpublished paper, 1983, 9.

41. H. W. Weatherhead, graduate of Trinity College, Cambridge, was an Anglican priest who went to Uganda in 1896 as a C.M.S. missionary. He was

headmaster of Budo during the first six years. In 1906 he was joined by his young brother H. T. C. Weatherhead. He had been educated at Emmanuel, Cambridge, and in 1900 had joined fellow C.M.S. missionaries in central Africa. He was equally committed. For an example of his impassioned Christianity, see his article "The View-Point of a Muganda Boy," *Church Missionary Review* 24 (March 1911): 156–60.

42. H. W. Weatherhead, "The Educational Value of Industrial Work as illustrated in King's School, Budo, Uganda," *International Review of Missions* 3 (April 1914): 344–45.

43. McGregor, 11.

44. Weatherhead, "Educational Experiments in Uganda," 217.

45. Earnest Stabler, *Education since Uhuru: The Schools of Kenya* (Middletown, Conn.: Wesleyan University Press, 1969), 10.

46. Ibid., 112.

47. Ibid., 106.

48. Turner, 327.

49. Thomas Hughes, *Tom Brown's Schooldays* (Harmondsworth: Penguin, 1971), 66.

50. J. E. Goldthorpe, *Makerere College Students 1922–1960* (Nairobi: Oxford University Press, 1965), 9.

51. Margaret MacPherson, *They Built for the Future: A Chronicle of Makerere University College 1922–1962* (Cambridge: Cambridge University Press, 1964), 15.

52. Huxley, 96.

53. Robert Wellesley Cole, *Kossah Town Boy* (Cambridge: Cambridge University Press, 1969), 187.

54. "A School for Paramount Chiefs in West Africa," *Overseas Education* Z (January 1934): 55. Further details of the 130 schools within the fuller context of the evolution of West African education are to be found in F H. Hilliard, *A Short History of Education in British West Africa* (London: Nelson, 1957).

55. Wraith, 5.

56. G. E. Metcalfe, *Great Britain and Ghana: Documents of Ghana History 1807–1957* (London: Nelson, 1964), 598.

57. C. Kingsley Williams, *Achimota: The Early Years 1924–1948* (Accra: Longmans, 1955), 11.

58. W. E. F Ward, *Fraser of Trinity and Achimota* (Accra: Ghana Universities Press, 1965), 17, 162.

59. Williams, 19.

60. Williams, 23. Fraser made much of the avoidance of denationalization. See, for example, "Aims of African Education: Avoidance of Denationalization," *International Review of Missions* 14 (March 1925): 514–22; "Denationalization," *Gold Coast Review* 1 (September 1925): 71–73; and a further short article entitled, "The Real Function of the Prince of Wales College, Achimota," in *Elders West African Review* (August 1931): 100–103.

61. Williams, 25.

62. Williams, 45–46. See also *Achimota College: Report of the Committee Appointed in 1932 by the Governor of the Gold Coast Colony to Inspect the Prince of Wales College and School, Achimota* (London: Crown Agent for the Colonies, 1932), 36–37.

63. "Education at the Prince of Wales College at Achimota," *Round Table* (May 1925): 86.

64. T. Walter Wallbank, "Achimota College and Educational Objectives in Africa," *Journal of Negro Education* 4 (July 1935): 230–45.

65. Williams, 47.

66. H. Drake, "Self-Help in West Africa," *Overseas Education* 7 (March 1935): 21.

67. Mrs. H. E. Sott, *A Saint in Kenya* (London: Hodder and Stoughton, 1932), 112–13.

68. Geoffrey I. F. Twistleton-Wykeham-Fiennes, "St. Mark's College, Mapanza in Northern Rhodesia," in A. G. Blood, *The Fortunate Few* (London: Universities Mission to Central Africa, 1954), 92–93.

69. "Education at the Prince of Wales College," 90.

70. See Geoffrey Gorer, *African Dances* (London: Lehmann, 1949), 175–76.

71. C. F. Harford-Battersby, *Pilkington of Uganda* (London: Marshall, 1898), 305.

72. Ibid., 320.

73. Ibid.

74. B. W. Randolph, *Arthur Douglas: Missionary on Lake Nyasa: The Story of His Life* (London: Universities Mission to Central Africa, 1912), 206.

75. Douglas V. Steere, *God's Irregular: Arthur Shearly Cripps: A Rhodesian Epic* (London: SPCK, 1973), 31.

76. Ibid., 83.

77. *The Year Book of Education 1935* (London: Evans, 1935), 817.

78. Quoted in W. Bryant Mumford, "A Description of German (Pre-War Period), British, French and Dutch Policies in Selected Dependencies," *Year Book of Education*, 1935, 822, from "Education in the German Colonies before the Great War," *Columbia Educational Year Book*, 1931, 603–4.

79. Mumford, 831, from "Education in the French Colonies," *Columbia Educational Year Book*, 1931, 272.

80. David Mitchell, "Light in the Darkness: Missionaries and the Empire," in *The British Empire* (Nederland: Time-Life International, 1972), 354.

81. Remi Clignet, "Inadequacies of the Notion of Assimilation in African Education," *The Journal of Modern African Studies* 3 (April 1970): 426. See also B. Ipaye, "Philosophies of Education in Colonial West Africa: A Comparative Study of the British and French Systems," *West African Journal of Education* (June 1969): 93–97.

82. Clignet, 426.

83. For full details of the colonial policies of both countries, see Jean Suret-Canale, *French Colonialism in Tropical Africa 1900–1945*, Till Gotheimer, trans. (New York: Pica Press, 1968); and James Duffy, *Portugal in Africa* (Cambridge: Harvard University Press, 1962).

84. For discussions of German colonial policy, see John Lliffe, *Tanganyika under German Rule, 1905–1912* (Cambridge: Cambridge University Press, 1969); Harris R. Harris, "Education in East Central Africa: The German System Outlined," *The Empire Review* 117 (October 1910): 185–90; and Hans Vischer, "Native Education in German Africa," *Journal of the African Society* 14 (January 1915): 123–

42. For discussions of the Belgian colonial policy, see Georges Brausch, *Belgian Administration in the Congo* (London: Oxford University Press, 1961). For an interesting comparison of British, French, Belgian, and Portuguese policies, see L. J. Lewis, "Education in Africa," *The Year Book of Education 1949* (London: Evans, 1949), 312–27.

85. M. Semakula Kiwanuka, "Colonial Policies and Administrations in Africa: the Myths of the Contrasts," *African Historical Studies* 2 (March 1970): 295.

86. Ibid., 314.

87. Remi P. Clignet and Phillip J. Foster, "French and British Colonial Education in Africa," *Comparative Education Review* (October 1964): 191; and Clignet, 425.

88. Gann and Duighan, 279.

89. Clignet and Foster, 195.

90. W. J. Ong, "Latin Language Study As a Renaissance Puberty Rite," in P. W. Musgrove, *Sociology, History and Education* (London, 1970), 234–35.

91. See Christina Bolt, *Victorian Attitudes to Race* (London: RKP, 1971.)

92. Immanuel Wallerstein, *Social Change: The Colonial Situation* (New York: Wiley, 1966), 38.

93. Clignet and Foster, 195.

94. See for example, D. W. Furley and T. Watson, "Education in Tanganyika between the Wars: Attempts to Blend Two Cultures," *The South Atlantic Quarterly* 65 (Autumn 1966): 470–71; W. M. MacMillan, "The Importance of the Educated African," *Journal of the African Society* 33 (April 1934): 137–42; and Victor A. Murray, "Education under Indirect Rule," *Journal of the Royal African Society* 34 (July 1935): 227–68.

95. Margaret Read, "Cultural Contacts in Education," *The Advancement of Science* 8 (March 1952): 366–68.

96. For a discussion of the point in a British context see J. A. Mangan, "Darwinism, Sport and Upper Class Education," *Stadion* 6 (Autumn 1982): 92–115.

97. F. Musgrove, "A Uganda Secondary School as a Field of Culture Change," *Africa* 22 (June 1952): 234–49.

98. Ibid., 235.

99. Ibid., 240.

100. See Mangan, *Athleticism,* 171–77.

101. F. Musgrove, 243.

102. For a strongly expressed view on this point, see Ako Adjei, "Imperialism and Spiritual Freedom," *American Journal of Sociology* 50 (November 1944): 189–98. For a different perspective on the issue of religious tension, see David B. Barrett, *Schism and Renewal in Africa* (Nairobi: Oxford University Press, 1968).

103. Ngugi wa Thiong'o, *The River Between* (London: Heinemann, 1965), 68.

104. A. R. Thompson, *Education and Development in Africa* (New York: St. Martin's Press, 1962), 43.

105. Phillip Foster, *Education and Social Change in Ghana* (London: RKP, 1968), 105–6.

106. For a general statement on this divergence see Margaret Read, *Africans and their Schools* (London: LG, 1953), 9–12. For a specific example see Sheldon G. Weeks, *Divergence in Educational Development: The Case of Kenya and Uganda* (New

York: Teachers College Press, 1967). For an illustration of indigenous resistance, see G. B. Lawrence, "Apathy: An Example from the British Cameroons," *The Year Book of Education* (London: Evans, 1956), 87–94. For a further discussion of the issue of resistance, see Otto F. Raum, "Resistance Factors and the Transformation of African Society," *The Year Book of Education* (London: Evans, 1954), 215–21.

107. Stabler, 11.

108. For examples of arguments in favor of "adaptation" to "African needs," however variously defined, see Bronislaw Malinowski, "The Pan African Problem of Culture Contact," *American Journal of Sociology* 48 (May 1943): 649–65; W. Bryant Mumford, "Educational and Social Adjustment of the Primitive Peoples of Africa to European Culture," *Africa* 2 (April 1929): 138–61; and James W. C. Dougall, "School Education and Native Life," *Africa* 3 (January 1930): 49–57.

109. Stabler, 10.

110. Cox, 131.

111. Remi Clignet and Phillip Foster, *The Fortunate Few: A Study of Secondary Schools and Students in the Ivory Coast* (Evanston: North Western University Press, 1966), 8.

112. Ontonti Nduka, *Western Education and the Nigerian Cultural Background* (Ibadan: Oxford University Press, 1964), 105, quoted in J. A. Mangan, "Imperial Education for Tropical Africa: Lugard the Ideologist," *Immigrants and Minorities* 2 (July 1982): 163. See also Wallerstein, 19; and Georges Balandier, *The Sociology of Black Africa: Social Dynamics in Central Africa,* Douglas German, trans. (London: Deutsch, 1970), 45.

113. For interesting discussions of this point see F. B. Welbourn, *East African Rebels* (London: SCM Press, 1967), 177–78; and T. O. Ranger, "African Attempts to Control Education in East and Central Africa 1900–1939," *Past and Present* 32 (December 1965); 57–85.

114. Onuora Nzekwu, *Blade among The Boys* (London: Hutchinson, 1962), 87. For a wider discussion of this issue see Edward H. Berman, *African Reactions to Missionary Education* (New York: Teachers College Press, 1978).

115. S. G. Williamson, "Missions and Education in the Gold Coast," *International Review of Missions* 41 (July 1952): 365.

116. John Povey, "Education through the Eyes of African Writers," *Educational Forum* (November 1966): 95–102.

117. Thiong'o, 93.

118. Kwame Nkrumah, *The Autobiography of Kwame Nkrumah* (London: Nelson, 1957), 16.

119. Mangan, *Athleticism,* epilogue.

7

Hunting in Eastern and Central Africa in the Late Nineteenth Century, with Special Reference to Zimbabwe*

JOHN M. MACKENZIE

Great hunters and their hunting exploits figure strongly in the myths of origin of many peoples in East and central Africa. They figure even more strongly in the European myth of nineteenth-century conquest. It is surprising, therefore, that hunting as a vital point of contact and conflict between white and black in nineteenth-century Africa has received so little scholarly attention. This essay is concerned to explore the significance of hunting in the precolonial African economy, the role of European hunters as an advance guard to the coming of the flag (often providing a significant subsidy to many other European activities), and the manner in which, in the 1890s, African access to the animal resources of the region was briefly enhanced by the European presence, and then completely denied. Game meat ceased to be a significant factor in the African diet, an important source of protein, a hedge against famine. Through the operation of game and gun laws Europeans alone were permitted access to game resources, which by the end of the century had in any case been drastically depleted by the combined ravages of overhunting and rinderpest. Indeed, the near-extinction of the great herds of buffalo and antelope of all sorts that had occurred by the early years of the twentieth century represented little short of an ecological disaster attendant on the imposition of white rule.

This is not the place to consider the role of hunters and hunting in African myth, except to observe that hunters invariably derived great prestige from stories of ancestral hunting prowess, a fact that Europeans were able to capitalize upon. From a practical point of view, hunting constituted a significant, and little-noticed, sector of the precolonial economies of many agricultural peoples. It is difficult to generalize over a wide area of Africa,

---

*In the pre-colonial period, Mashonaland and Matabeleland will be used for Zimbabwe's respective provinces; for the colonial period Rhodesia, Southern Rhodesia, and Zimbabwe will be used according to context.

containing a great variety of peoples and economies. The purely pastoral Masai, for example, did not hunt, and it may be that the Kikuyu hunted more for skins than for meat,[1] but hunting of one sort or another was pursued by most other peoples in the region. Such hunting can, perhaps, be divided into three types: hunting for export (mainly ivory), defensive hunting to protect growing crops, and hunting as a domestic resource, a supplier of meat and skins. These were not of course exclusive categories: they merely represent the prime objective of each hunt. The elephant hunt produced the important by-product of vast quantities of meat, sufficient to reward the participants in large-scale hunts, while the leading hunters or the chiefs took the ivory. Game that attacked crops would invariably also be good to eat. Skins were a vital resource to many peoples, as clothing, sleeping karosses, hut furnishings, shields, and vessels. Indeed, the extensive use of skins gave rise to sumptuary laws. In Zimbabwe, and no doubt elsewhere, the finest cat skins, like the leopard, were reserved for the powerful.[2] Among the Ndebele, more sumptuous karosses were made from the finer skins extracted as tribute from subordinate peoples. Horns also had a variety of uses. Some Africans blew them as musical instruments, as signal clarions in both war and the hunt. Smaller horns were used as receptacles for gunpowder or gold dust.

It has been suggested that the Shona people turned to hunting only in times of famine.[3] No doubt hunting did become a more pressing need at such times, but it would also have become a more difficult operation since lack of water would cause game to withdraw to the few remaining running rivers. In fact, oral evidence suggests that precolonial hunting was an annual activity, led by specialist hunters who were able to marshal the labor of others in exchange for meat.[4] Protecting the gardens was a most important function of the hunter and the chief, but "offensive" as well as "defensive" hunting was also the norm. Africans in the region were constantly concerned to find a protein supplement to their basic carbohydrate diet of millet or maize porridge. Beans and monkey nuts, chickens, goats, and sheep partly supplied this need. But in areas where fish were unavailable, game meat offered the best alternative protein source. Cattle-keeping peoples in mixed economies seldom butchered cattle for meat, since cattle represented a complex religious, cultural, and economic system, a repository of wealth, a system of exchange and investment, and a prime source of ritual and taboo.[5] Certainly, the Ndebele, the neighbors and overlords of the Shona, regarded hunting as a most important part of their economy.[6] Ndebele hunting parties varied from large organized groups sent out by the king or his indunas* to small family groups, and almost every animal from the

---

*Chiefs who combined political, economic, and military authority.

small buck to the elephant as well as game birds was hunted. So highly regarded was the hunt that expert hunters could rise rapidly in royal favor.

There is ample evidence of a great variety of hunting techniques in use throughout East and central Africa on the eve of the European conquest. Traps and snares of great ingenuity were used almost universally to secure small mammals and even at times larger animals when placed around gardens. Among the Shona, the use of such snares constituted an important part of boyhood training.[7] On one of his East African expeditions, Frederick Lugard found that his porters set traps every afternoon to enhance their diet on the march.[8] Another technique used throughout the region was game pits, large trenches dug into game paths, sometimes fitted with sharpened stakes at the bottom, and covered by boughs and leaves.[9] These were designed to catch large game of all sorts and were sufficiently disguised to constitute a considerable hazard to European travelers and hunters, who often used game paths as convenient routes across difficult country. There are many stories of Europeans falling into such traps.[10] The traps were sometimes used in conjunction with beating techniques, the animals being driven between long lines of converging hedges formed by cut branches and bushes, often as much as a mile long, into an enormous trap where they could be speared. The missionary Thomas Morgan Thomas saw rhinoceros, eland, wildebeest, zebra, tsessebe, and reedbuck all caught in this way.[11] The Shona had nets called *mambure*, made of long strips of bark, which were also used in conjunction with large numbers of beaters. Karl Mauch saw the Shona of the Chibi district forming a great semicircular ring of nets as much as three miles long encircling and trapping the game.[12] Fish were taken from most rivers, although fishing was never as important south of the Zambezi as it was to the north, where it constituted an important part of the economies of both the Bemba and the Lozi peoples. The Lozi also hunted hippos from canoes, trapping them in an ever-decreasing area of shallows near the riverbank where they could be attacked by large numbers of spear carriers.[13] Moreover, in an extraordinary form of auxiliary hunting, many people were prepared to drive off beasts of prey in order to secure their kill from them.[14]

Some of these techniques, which must have been exceptionally hazardous, required the participation of large numbers of people. The ordering and control of such hunts enhanced the power of chiefs and of the principal hunters, who were often members of the chiefly family. This was particularly true as the use of firearms became more widespread and chiefs were able not only to control the distribution of guns, but also arrogate to themselves the most recent and effective models. Hunting elephants had for long been both the most lucrative and the most dangerous form of hunting. Africans used a variety of techniques to kill elephants, including game pits, beating and spearing from trees, hamstringing the elephants' Achilles tendons with hunting axes, and shooting with crude firearms like tower muskets, which were the only guns available to Africans until the late nineteenth century. The insatiable demand for ivory in the Western world in the nineteenth century and the buoyant prices maintained by ivory throughout the century ensured that elephant hunting, significant in Africa for centuries, reached a great peak in this period. In Barotseland, in western Zambia, the king commanded a great annual hunt, involving hundreds of participants, in which elephants were trapped in the angle of the Chobe and Zambezi rivers and as many dispatched as possible. In 1875, the hunt was led by King Sepopa, and took place in late October.[15] The elephants were driven by fire and by beaters to the trapping point, where they were caught between two hundred canoes and over a thousand hunters on foot. Two thousand men were said to have participated in all. The 1875 hunt was a comparative failure, but in another year no fewer than ninety elephants were killed.[16]

Sepopa's successor, Lewanika, similarly took command of the hunt. Indeed through the hunt he elaborated his position at the ritual center of the state. In 1889 he gave a Martini-Henry rifle to his son, Letia, and the prince's first kills were met with a shower of congratulations from around the kingdom.[17] The hunt had become a chiefly rite of passage. Lewanika reserved a particular hunting area for his own use, and had a hunting lodge built for himself.[18] As well as the annual elephant hunt, there were also great hunts for meat and skins. Hundreds of animals penned on an island by the Zambezi floods were attacked by fleets of canoes. In 1887 the floods on the Zambezi were low and many of the animals escaped.[19] This failure was regarded as a considerable disaster. Under the influence of Europeans, Lewanika seems to have increased the scale and frequency of the hunts as well as elaborating the ritual associated with them. In 1895 three great hunting expeditions took place. The king commanded the hunt from an anthill, where he waited while the animals were surrounded and beaten toward him by hundreds of men. He insisted on making the first kill and piercing the animal with his own hand. "Alas!" wrote the missionary François Coillard, "the pretensions of royalty multiply in an alarming manner; ceremonies are becoming more and more complicated."[20] The last great Barotse hunt took place in 1913.[21]

The kings of the Ndebele, Mzilikazi and Lobengula, also commanded large numbers of men in the hunt. T. M. Thomas suggested that hunting was a means of using up the surplus energies of Ndebele warriors when not fighting and raiding.[22] Thousands of them hunted by driving the game forward in an immense circle many miles in circumference. The animals so enclosed were speared when trying to break through or when finally trapped in the ever-reducing circle of beaters and hunters. The resulting meat, Thomas suggested, was all taken to the king and disposed of by him.

JOHN M. MACKENZIE

Lobengula, like Lewanika, set aside his own hunting ground. He too was influenced by the whites, whom he tried to control. The great elephant hunters Westbeech and Phillips traveled and hunted with him in 1868.[23] Just as Lewanika's hunting exploits were stepped up with the growing influence of Europeans and modern arms, so too were those of the Ndebele. Travelers repeatedly met well-armed hunting parties of varying size, and many suggested that both the Ndebele and the Shona regarded the hunt as a source of sport and excitement, as well as of profit for some and protein for all.[24]

It was in fact through contact with European elephant hunters that African rulers first began to ride the tiger of the European advance. White hunters appeared in central Africa from the 1850s, and by the 1870s and 1880s they had become very nearly a flood. Both Mzilikazi and Lobengula attempted to control the entry of white hunters into their kingdom, but with limited success. At the beginning of his reign in 1870 Lobengula issued hunting regulations restricting white hunters to enter by a particular route, charging a license fee of a gun (to the value of fifteen pounds) and ammunition to hunt.[25] He permitted whites to hunt only in the outer regions of his kingdom and attempted to ensure that Ndebele hunters did not suffer from unfair competition from the whites.[26] Both Lobengula and Sepopa of the Lozi attempted to use white hunters to their own ends,[27] in diplomacy and in exploiting their ivory resources. Favored hunters and traders became convenient conduits for the flow of ivory from their territories and a useful source of firearms and ammunition. Sepopa formed a close relationship with George Westbeech, who spent almost eighteen years in Lozi country hunting and trading,[28] after several years' hunting south of the Zambezi. Westbeech was able to survive the upheavals of the Lozi state and maintained his influence under Lewanika. Thomas Baines, G. A. Phillips, and F. C. Selous all, at different times, exercised influence at Lobengula's court.[29]

The figures for the export of ivory and the consequent destruction of elephants in this period are staggering. The hunter William Finaughty, active between 1864 and 1875, shot 95 elephants in 1868 yielding five thousand pounds of ivory.[30] Henry Hartley killed between 1,000 and 1,200 elephants in his career.[31] Boer hunters were even more successful. In 1867 Jan Viljoen shot 210 elephants in one trip, and Petrus Jacobs was alleged to have achieved yet more prodigious feats with the gun.[32] Karl Mauch's bag for one season in 1867 was 91 elephants yielding four thousand pounds of ivory.[33] All of these hunters hunted from horseback, but with the slaughter of the 1860s, elephants retreated to the "fly" country and north of the Zambezi, where they could only be hunted on foot. It was at this point that G. A. Phillips and George Westbeech hit upon a system that maximized ivory exports while minimizing risks to themselves. They operatd as ivory entrepreneurs employing large numbers of African hunters (as many as fifty at times), supervised by young Boer and mixed-race hunters. It was by this technique that Westbeech sent out no less than ten to fifteen tons of ivory each year he was hunting and trading in Barotseland between 1871 and 1888.[34] Mauch's average was forty-four pounds per animal; Finaughty's fifty-two pounds. Westbeech's annual figure represents the destruction of 420 to 630 elephants each year. In 1876, forty thousand pounds of ivory were traded on the Zambezi in one season, representing about 850 elephants.[35] In the following year, the figure declined to twenty-five thousand pounds, illustrating the increasing difficulties of finding elephants. By 1886, Lewanika was lamenting that the riches of his kingdom in ivory were almost all spent.[36] By the time F. C. Selous arrived in central Africa in 1872, the elephant was already retreating to the remoter areas, and he devoted the later part of his career to the largely unsuccessful search for a new elephant hunting ground.[37] His repeated attempts to penetrate the area that is now eastern Zambia were thwarted by African resistance.

The ivory hunters did a great deal to prepare the way for subsequent imperial advance. Indeed, the decline of ivory resources reduced the black kings' bargaining power. Westbeech succeeded in reorienting the Lozi country's trade away from the Ovimbundu traders of Angola and therefore away from the Portuguese coastal sphere.[38] Westbeech did much more to ensure the acceptance of missionaries like François Coillard at the Lozi court. Elephant hunters helped the concession hunters of the 1880s to achieve their ends, and Selous played a crucial role in guiding the British South Africa Company's (BSAC) pioneer column into Mashonaland in 1890.

Moreover, ivory acted as an important subsidy to the second level of the imperial advance. If the great hunters and traders were only interested in the personal fortune that could be secured from ivory, others were concerned to use it to finance other objectives. The London Missionary Society (LMS) missionary, Thomas Morgan Thomas, who arrived at Inyati in northern Matabeleland in 1859, hunted and traded to finance his mission.[39] In 1870 he was expelled from the LMS for these activities, but he returned to found an independent mission, which he subsidized from his hunting exploits between 1874 and 1884. The Moir brothers, who founded the evangelical trading concern, the African Lakes Company (ALC) to pursue Livingstone's favored combination of Christianity and commerce, used ivory as a means of furthering their ambitions. As F. L. M. Moir put it in his memoirs, the large sums realized from ivory kept the company going, "and so enabled it to carry on the work for which it had been founded."[40] Soon the great missionary Robert Laws was lamenting the fact that the herds of elephant Livingstone had seen in the Shire and Nyasa areas had all disappeared.[41] Both Karl Mauch and Thomas Baines funded their prospecting expeditions on the proceeds of ivory sales.[42] To this end, Baines and Mauch (on different trips) joined forces with the great elephant hunter, Henry Hartley, who had first noticed the gold workings while hunting. Those who sought real gold financed their mineralogical expeditions on the basis of "white gold." Many publicists for the hunting trips into the interior designed to bag all kinds of game as trophies, as well as see famous sights like the Victoria Falls, pointed out that such trips could be financed by the shooting of a few good elephants. One hunter advertised in *The Field* that he would lead such expeditions into central Africa.[43]

The exploits of Frederick Lugard illustrate the manner in which hunters, campaigners, and administrators fused in the years just before and after the establishment of white rule. When Lugard arrived in Africa as a penniless adventurer in 1888 he was taken on by the ALC as a combined elephant hunter and leader of campaigns against the Arab/Swahili traders on Lake Nyasa.[44] Similarly, in Uganda in the early 1890s Lugard mixed his campaigns with elephant hunting and partly financed the former from the latter, a highly advantageous arrangement for the impecunious Imperial British East Africa Company.[45] The looters of African wildlife became the conquistadores of African peoples. Sir Geoffrey Archer who later became governor of Somaliland, of Uganda, and of the Sudan, announced in his memoirs that he very nearly became a professional elephant hunter, under the influence of the great hunter Neumann, whom he met in Kenya.[46] Instead, he became district commissioner of Kenya's Northern Frontier District,[47] and there he augmented his salary by annual elephant hunting. Sir Alfred Sharpe, an early governor of Nyasaland, had been an elephant hunter, as had Robert Coryndon, who became a BSAC administrator in Northern Rhodesia and later governor of Uganda and Kenya. All the company administrators of northwestern Rhodesia were eager hunters who encouraged Lewanika's developing taste for the hunt.[48] During the First World War, Sharpe made an extended journey through central and East Africa, and again partly financed his expedition by elephant hunting.[49]

Because ivory was such an important export from East and central Africa in the nineteenth century, elephant hunting has received a measure of attention from historians. The hunting of buffalo, antelope, and other forms of game has, however, been almost entirely ignored. Yet there are certain significant similarities between this form of hunting and elephant hunting. The hunt for ivory led to a rapidly retreating elephant frontier. The hunting of other forms of game likewise led to rapid depletion. In southern Africa, the early hunters and travelers wrote of the plains of the Orange Free State and the Transvaal as being covered in game.[50] By the 1870s Boer and other hunters had largely destroyed the game resources of the region. Hunting opportunities in the west, in what are now Botswana and eastern Namibia as well as in the interior, provided a not insignificant lure to Boer trekkers. The Boers even moved up into Angola by the end of the century and shot out vast quantities of game before they were ejected by the Portuguese in the 1920s.[51] The retreating elephant frontier left a wide game zone behind it, which was to be exploited ruthlessly during the last two decades of the century by professional hunters, sportsmen, and the pioneers of the new imperialism.

Commercial pressures were an important part of this exploitation. The game was able to satisfy a number of late Victorian tastes. Hunting had become the supreme expression of Victorian manliness, an activity with an ideology closely identified with contemporary militarism and imperialism. Hunters in the late nineteenth century were greatly influenced by the classics of southern African hunting by Cornwallis Harris, Gordon Cumming, and W. C. Baldwin,[52] who had traveled and hunted at a time when the teeming herds of game and the hunting frontier were considerably further south in southern Africa. But the hunting ideology had a much deeper penetration than those able to afford to be its practitioners. Popular writers of the period, notably R. M. Ballantyne, W. H. Kingston, G. A. Henty, Mayne Reid, and many others glorified the hunt.[53] Children's journals, school magazines and travelers' tales were filled with stories of hunting. Imperial officers like Baden-Powell and Alderson were concerned to point out the connections between the hunt and war.[54] Baden-Powell's experience of spooring and observation were incorporated into his scouting stories and codes and linger on in *Scouting for Boys* to this day.[55] Inevitably, such a powerful hunting ideology led to dramatic forms of display. Hunters sought to fill their homes with skins and trophies, and the taste rubbed off on those who did not hunt. Skins and horns became a feature of most middle-class homes, as stay-at-homes attempted to bask in the reflected glory of the hunt. One dealer in Kroonstad in the Orange Free State was reported to have handled two million skins from the interior between 1878 and 1880.[56] Hunters in Rhodesia after the arrival of Rhodes's pioneer column in 1890 found a ready market for skins and trophies when all other forms of economic activity failed.

The other great Victorian taste that was to encourage the activities of hunters in central Africa was the craze for natural history. The discovery and classification of species (often an artificial subdivision of regional variants) was a great prize for any explorer or traveler. Even a railway engineer could have two forms of small antelope named after him.[57] This proliferation of species led to natural history collecting on a large scale. The Natural History Museum in South Kensington, the Smithsonian Institution in Washington, and a host of other museums and private collections employed hunters to supply examples of every conceivable species and subspecies. All this activity could actually place species at risk, just as the contemporary craze for birds' egg and butterfly collecting seriously reduced the numbers of some

179

rarities. Selous perfectly combined all these activities. He was a commercial hunter who turned to specimen collecting for museums in the 1880s and built up large personal collections, including an enormous collection of butterflies. The hunter and administrator Robert Coryndon shot what were then thought to be the last two white rhinoceros in Mashonaland in 1893.[58] They were carefully mounted and sold, one to the Rothschild Collection, no doubt at a suitably inflated price for its rarity value. The other went to the Cape Town Museum.

But game hunting provided an even more significant function in the white advance. Just as ivory provided, and continued to provide, a subsidy to other concerns, missionary and commercial, exploratory and administrative, so did game constitute a vital support system for the often exiguous survival of European pioneers. All the precolonial hunters, prospectors, traders, explorers, and missionaries did of course live off the land. That represented no mean subsidy when large numbers of porters, beaters, and servants had to be fed. In June 1886, for example, George Westbeech found himself feeding a party of hunters and carriers numbering eighty-six in all.[59] Given the necessity of human transportation throughout eastern and central Africa, such parties were common as late as the First World War, when Sir Alfred Sharpe's expedition required at least one hundred porters.[60] Many hunters and travelers discovered that they could "sweeten" local peoples by supplying them with meat. David Livingstone himself had done this,[61] and hunters like Westbeech did it on a grand scale.[62] Missionaries found that they were welcome less for the Gospel than for the gun. T. M. Thomas relates how at the end of a sermon to a large company of Africans in the 1860s his listeners sought their reward for patience by demanding that he shoot some animals for them.[63] On a journey to the Zambezi, Thomas was subjected to constant demands from his followers that he should shoot game for them.[64] Another missionary reported that the delight of a people on hearing he was to establish a mission on their territory seemed to be primarily related to the fact that he would hunt for them.[65] The successful missionary in Africa had also to be a successful hunter, as a reading of the works of Coillard, Arnot, Donald Fraser, and others amply demonstrates.[66]

But for missionaries, as for other pioneers, hunting was to become a much more significant operation than merely a "sweetener" of the local populace. All the memoirs and works of exploration of the period repeatedly allude to the insatiable demand of Africans for meat.[67] Explorers, missionaries, pioneers, and administrators all testified to this, and one is left wondering whether it demonstrates the importance of hunting in the precolonial economy and in the African diet or reflects the comparative failure of the precolonial hunter. Certainly European success was often now based upon African tracking expertise and precise knowledge of the environment.

Most of the European hunters were dependent on African auxiliaries, bush-men trackers (in southern Africa), or the advice of local people eager to secure meat for themselves. And Europeans were able to capitalize on this craving for protein by shooting game in staggering quantities in order to supply camp followers, laborers, and potential or actual converts. Ivory had acted as a subsidy when sold on a buoyant market. Meat by contrast was a concealed subsidy, but a no less important one for that. Bishop Knight-Bruce was said to be able to keep Africans happy on his mission lands in Manica by keeping them well supplied with food and meat, despite paying them very little.[68] Donald Fraser was under constant pressure to supply his mission with meat, and found that he could keep all his followers in food—including a school of some seventy catechists—by trading meat for other foodstuffs to the surrounding populace.[69] Isaac Shimmin, the leading Methodist missionary in Mashonaland in the 1890s, prided himself on his hunting and was prepared to pit himself against local lay hunters.[70]

Shooting meat and trading it for grain was a vital survival technique of all earlier travelers. Even the very grand expedition of Lord Randolph Churchill indulged in such trade.[71] The archaeologist J. Theodore Bent also subsidized his studies by hunting and trade.[72] When Bent and his wife traveled to Rhodesia to excavate the Zimbabwe ruins in 1891, they employed a young hunter called Harrington to keep their party supplied with meat.[73]

In 1890 the haphazard intrusions of hunters, prospectors, traders, and missionaries into central Africa were replaced by the systematic intrusion of the British South Africa Company. The chartered company dispatched a pioneer column and a protecting police force that was notable for the public-school, superior social class of many of its members.[74] Not a few of them were lured northward by the complex myth of central Africa, incorporating gold, adventure, and the hunt. Several proclaimed themselves influenced by the popular literature of the period, especially the works of Rider Haggard and the hunting books of Selous.[75] When the pioneers fanned out from Salisbury to stake their gold claims in late 1890, few of them wished to be settlers. Their prime desire was to get rich quick on the alleged gold reserves of the new colony and return home as soon as possible. In persuading Africans to take them to the many gold shafts excavated by medieval miners, they were free in distributing arms as rewards (arms that were subsequently used against them in the 1896–97 revolt). They also hunted almost daily to feed such labor as they could secure, to trade for grain with the locals, and, possibly to subsidize their prospecting from the sale of skins and trophies. There are several instances of Africans working solely for meat.[76] One missionary was said to have built his church by this technique.[77]

Although the pioneers were also allowed farms, few (except the Boers among them) desired to be farmers. One transport rider remarked that he had yet to meet a Rhodesian farmer who actually grew anything.[78] Nevertheless, they staked out their putative farms, hoping to secure labor from the Africans resident upon them, and find profit in a process of asset-stripping combined with the hope that the land would rapidly accrue in value. This asset-stripping involved the removal of all timber for sale to the townships, to such few mines as did develop, and later to the railways.[79] It also involved the shooting-out of all game anywhere near the wagon routes across the country or on alienated land. As the Hudson's Bay Company had discovered in western Canada, hunting and settlement were incompatible. Randolph Churchill, on his famous visit to Mashonaland in 1891, noted that same incompatibility in central Africa, and he urged that the BSAC's territories should be seen as a happy hunting ground for commercial killer and gentleman sportsman and not as a field for settlement.[80]

The building of the railways further contributed to the massive assault upon game. There is ample evidence that railway engineers had, like missionaries, to be good shots in order to keep their laborers and staff in meat.[81] Supplying meat to large numbers of laborers was a vital subsidy in both calorific and financial terms to the tight financing of railway lines like the Beira-Mashonaland railway, or its counterpart to Victoria Falls and beyond into Northern Rhodesia, all of which passed through game-rich regions. H. F Varian, one of the most distinguished of the railway engineers, was himself the son of a hunter (who had helped the Prince of Wales, later Edward VII, to bag his first elephant in Ceylon). Varian was an excellent shot and seems to have kept his men well supplied. Once the lines were built, they brought in a fresh flood of rather less intrepid hunters, some of whom were known, in the early days of the railway, to shoot at the rich game resources of the Pungwe Flats in Mozambique from the windows of railway carriages.[82] The tourist hunter's field of operation was greatly extended by the arrival of regular shipping services, the railway lines, and comfortable hotels. The Union-Castle Line guides to East and southern Africa from the 1890s devoted a great deal of attention to African fauna, hunting, and game laws.[83]

If the rich game resources of central Africa were to prove to be a significant subsidy to peaceable occupations like prospecting, missionary work, and "farming," they were also to prove an essential supply element in time of war. In both the war against the Ndebele in 1893 and the revolt of the Shona and the Ndebele in 1896–97, the provisioning of troops and settlers was a desperate problem. But this was a period when officers, not to mention the gentlemanly troopers of the local forces, were as proficient in the hunt as they were in the prosecution of war. Indeed the two military accounts of the revolt, by Baden-Powell and Lieutenant Colonel Alderson, make it clear that the authors saw little difference between the hunt and

African warfare.[84] Hunting stories abound in their books, and hunting metaphors were seldom far from their pens. This led Baden-Powell in particular to elide the hunting of animals with the hunting down of Africans. "The work," he wrote, "involved in the military operations was sufficiently sporting in itself to fill a good measure of enjoyment . . . coupled with the excitement incidental to contending against wild beasts of the human kind."[85] Elsewhere he remarked that "the longest march seems short when one is hunting game . . . lion or leopard, boar or buck, nigger or nothing."[86] Baden-Powell and Alderson encouraged their men and the local volunteers who joined them to see these campaigns as little more than sporting expeditions.[87] However, it was mainly the officers who made sport with the game, which could not shoot back, while troopers took on Africans, who could. Baden-Powell describes several columns as being saved by the shooting of game when other supplies were running short.[88] After the Ndebele revolt had been resolved in 1896, Gen. Sir Frederick Carrington, Baden-Powell, and Earl Grey, the new administrator, proceeded to Mashonaland enjoying a most successful hunting trip en route.[89] Shortly after their arrival in the capital, Fort Salisbury, they led the opening meet of the Salisbury hounds.

The supply difficulties of the 1896–97 revolt had been massively exacerbated by the rinderpest epidemic that broke out in early 1896, destroying hundreds of oxen in transport spans throughout the country, as well as entire cattle herds before proceeding like a bushfire through Bechuanaland and the South African territories, reaching Cape Town by the end of the year. Rinderpest had been introducd into the Horn of Africa, probably by infected cattle from India, in 1889.[90] From there it had spread, seemingly growing in virulence as it went, throughout East Africa. Lugard encountered it in Uganda in 1890.[91] The Zambezi seems to have briefly held it up, but once across that natural barrier in February or March of 1896, its progress south was unimpeded. Studies of rinderpest have generally concentrated on its effects on cattle, but it was no less devastating in its onslaught on the game of the region. Elephant, hippo, and rhinoceros were immune, but entire buffalo herds were destroyed. The large antelope like kudu and eland seem to have been particularly susceptible, although none of the buck were free of the scourge. At one stage it was thought that zebra had escaped, but they too soon succumbed.

As the rinderpest spread southward, hunters, warriors, and settlers commented with alarm upon this dramatic destruction of the game. Baden-Powell saw the ravages of rinderpest among the oxen of Bechuanaland as making the task of destroying the revolts in Matabeleland and Mashonaland in 1896 much more difficult than it otherwise would have been.[92] "The scourge of rinderpest" also reduced the quantities of game available to his troops, and no doubt it was partly for this reason that all game laws were suspended for the duration of the revolts.[93] H. F. Varian noted that in the rinderpest's "full toll of game throughout South-East Africa, buffalo were especially hard hit."[94] But for Varian, "the unnecessary and undesirable slaughter" of the game was the main evil, the success of a shooting trip being primarily judged by the numbers of animals killed, bags of three hundred being achieved in trips of less than three months. Sir Alfred Sharpe had seen vast herds of buffalo on the Congo–Northern Rhodesia frontier in 1890.[95] After the rinderpest had struck the area in 1892 there were none. Selous's biographer, J. G. Millais, claimed that in 1896, nine-tenths of kudu, eland, and buffalo were carried off by the rinderpest in the Pungwe district of Mozambique, and similar effects occurred in Rhodesia.[96]

By the time that rinderpest struck, however, the game frontier, like the elephant before it, was in rapid retreat. The game had long since departed from the high veld plains of the Orange Free State and the Transvaal. The decline in the numbers of game had already been noted in the last decades of the independent Ndebele kingdom. King Lobengula had indeed attempted to introduce conservationist measures, forbidding hunters, white or black, to take cow elephants or ostrich eggs.[97] In 1883, he fined the hunters Selous and Martin and others for shooting hippo against his wishes.[98] Ndebele hunters found that they had to move farther and farther from the heartland of their state in order to secure game of any sort. Traditional African hunting had been relatively inefficient, but their acquisition of modern guns had changed all that. Lobengula's efforts to control hunting can well be understood in the light of the scale of the bags of the well-known hunters. Selous, in *A Hunter's Wanderings*, proudly listed his kills. Between 1877 and 1880 he shot 548 head, of which only twenty were elephants.[99] With high-velocity magazine rifles, Europeans were to become even more devastatingly competent. Wherever game was disturbed by hunters, it lost its innocence and its curiosity. No longer did the herds graze near wagon tracks or railway lines. They steadily retreated from all lines of communication and from all the settlements of the white invaders.

When the pioneer column assembled at Macloutsie in British Bechuanaland, the presence of so many men soon ensured that no game was to be had anywhere in the vicinity.[100] As Hugh Marshall Hole put it, "The entry of the Pioneer column with its long train of waggons, its search-light and other military paraphernalia, probably gave the big game animals of Mashonaland a scare from which they never fully recovered."[101] Once the column arrived at Fort Salisbury, the professional hunter and natural history collector, William Harvey Brown, was sent out to secure meat for the new settlement. He described his wonder at finding great herds of game on the Gwibi Flats little more than ten miles from Salisbury.[102] By the following year, Lord Randolph Churchill's party proceeded to exactly the same area and found no game at all.[103] Churchill traveled with a famous hunter, Hans Lee (who was aided, as several other southern African hunters had been, by a bushman tracker), and it is clear that the expedition, which was supposed to be primarily an investigation of the economic potential of Rhodesia, was in fact almost entirely taken up with virtually daily hunting exploits. Churchill's book on his journey certainly spends more time on hunting than on economics. He describes the manner in which, when an area rich in game was found, the party would settle there for several days until the game had been driven off by the daily depredations of the hunt.[104] Everywhere Africans emerged to take advantage of the meat abandoned in trophy hunting. Churchill's party followed in the traditions of Selous and others in indulging in a veritable orgy of killing as the size of their daily bags frequently illustrated. As they traveled they often heard the shots of other hunting parties nearby. It is not surprising that others should soon have been lamenting the lack of game on all the main routes.

The BSAC introduced game laws at an early date. But they followed the pattern of the Cape Colony, where game laws were passed only when very little game survived. The Rhodesian ordinances were closely modeled on those of the Cape, establishing close seasons and imposing limits on the numbers of each species that could be killed in each year.[105] But all observers testify that in the years before the First World War the game laws were almost impossible to enforce. As we have seen in the case of the revolts, they were promptly suspended in times of difficulty. Even the animals that were proclaimed royal game continued to be hunted vigorously. In 1899–1900, the transport rider Stanley Portal Hyatt shot hippos because they produced the best leather for reins, thongs, whips and other items associated with transport riding.[106] He manufactured these items on the road and did a very profitable business in them in Bulawayo. When questioned about the hippos he always asserted that they had been shot in Portuguese territory, where there were no game laws. Hyatt suggested that one or two of the native commissioners did attempt to enforce the game laws while entirely ignoring them themselves.[107] The Union-Castle guides to South and East Africa annually encouraged hunters with the remark that game laws were very difficult to enforce, particularly in the remoter districts.[108] Some sectors of the Rhodesian pioneer community refused to observe them. When a herd of elephants (like the hippo, royal game) appeared in the Lomagundi District of Rhodesia in 1908, the local Afrikaans farmers shot them all out, and little could be done about it.[109] The same was true elsewhere in East Africa. Sir Charles Eliot commented on the impossibility of enforcing game laws in East Africa, particularly among settlers.[110] The missionary Donald Fraser was told by his local district commissioner not to worry about game laws, as they were suspended because of the advance of the tsetse.[111]

If game laws did little to hinder the white onslaught upon game, they were largely irrelevant to Africans. African access to game was denied primarily through the operation of gun laws.[112] Large numbers of antiquated guns had always circulated in Africa, but African ownership of guns grew enormously in the years immediately preceding and just after the imposition of white rule. Martini-Henry rifles were traded for ivory; rifles were also given in exchange for concessions. Europeans gave out rifles, including advanced designs like the Lee-Metford, in exchange for being shown old gold workings.[113] The Ndebele were not disarmed after the war of 1893, and in the revolts of 1896–97 Europeans were constantly surprised by the numbers and quality of the arms used against them. Until the revolts, these arms were of course primarily used for hunting. In 1893, one pioneer on a journey from the Tokwe to Bulawayo met at nearly every river "either a party of Matabele hunters with guns who were returning with hides or meat or I found their lately deserted camps."[114] When the revolts were crushed, the military and civilian authorities were determined to flush out African arms, and the first duty of the native commissioners throughout the country was to take in an extensive arsenal. Afterward a few chiefs were permitted to keep old tower muskets as symbols of status and as a means of protecting their gardens.[115] It was only for this "defensive" purpose that Africans were ever again permitted to bear arms except when enlisted to fight in European wars. As part of the same regulations, spears, assegais, and bows and arrows were also handed in, and the traditional iron-smelting industry collapsed.[116]

When Africans were resettled on reserves in the remoter areas of the country, it was now the administrators who became the greatest and indeed often the sole hunters. They protected African gardens, were called upon by villagers to shoot man-eating animals like crocodiles and lions, and continued to hunt whenever they could to supply their followers with meat and themselves with trophies and yarns to regale their guests and the readers of their memoirs. The connection between the prestige of the ruler and his prowess in the hunt had now been firmly transferred to the white administrators. Earl Grey hunted his way into Rhodesia in 1896 despite the scourges of war, rinderpest, failed rains, and famine that afflicted the country. His predecessor, Dr. Jameson, frequently indicated that he was more interested in hunting than in administration. On a visit to Fontesvilla on the Beira-Mashonaland Railway, the railway engineer found himself being questioned much more closely about the local hunting prospects than about the railway.[117] Similarly, on a trip to Victoria Falls in 1904 when he was premier of the Cape, Jameson delayed his train at the falls to sightsee and to hunt, and cut short his visit to the Wankie Colliery, which apparently bored him.[118]

All the early native commissioners were hunters and the first chief native commissioner, Brabant, seems to have been appointed largely on his hunting and veld-craft capacity, since he was subsequently discovered to be barely literate.[119] In later years the native commissioner H. N. Hemans refused promotion and always insisted on being sent to the remote Gokwe District because it was one of the few areas where the hunting remained good.[120] There it was a special treat for one of his assistants to be sent out on a tax-gathering safari because of the hunting that could be enjoyed en route.[121] The thin dividing line between big-game hunters and governors, like Robert Coryndon, Alfred Sharpe, Frederick Lugard, and Geoffrey Archer, has already been commented upon. When Winston Churchill, as parliamentary undersecretary of state for the colonies, visited East Africa to inspect the newly completed Uganda Railway in 1907, like his father he seems to have spent more time on sport than on business.[122] His private carriage was repeatedly detached and left in sidings at railway stations all across Kenya. His was a particularly sybaritic form of the chase, sometimes hunting from a railway trolley, which also carried victuals, champagne, and ice to refresh the distinguished Nimrod during the day. Great was his delight when he received a telegram announcing that the sitting of Parliament had been postponed by two weeks, enabling him to indulge himself further in East Africa.

Churchill hunted, as his father had done, for reasons of sport and prestige rather than for economic benefit. Hunting had been, at the very least, a valuable addition to the African diet, particularly in times of famine. It became a vital support system in the early years of the European encroachment upon Africa, in providing profits through ivory, and a not inconsiderable concealed meat subsidy to prospecting, farming, railway contracts, and administrative costs. By the First World War, by which time game had already been driven into the remoter corners of central Africa, hunting for sport had become virtually the norm. Overshooting had ensured that game had retreated well away from areas of white settlement and from lines of communication into remote river valleys, where reserves and controlled hunting areas could be established. In Zimbabwe, the concentration of the African peoples into reserves that soon became overpopulated and overstocked ensured that human settlement and the survival of game were incompatible in those areas too. Native commissioners shot out game not only to protect African crops, but also to protect white farmers and their stock. Game harbored the tsetse fly, which conveyed trypanosomiasis to cattle, horses, and humans. Tsetse control meant game control, and as the herds of buffalo and antelope recovered from the devastation wrought by hunting and rinderpest, they were subjected to repeated government-organized culls through the interwar years and into the 1950s.[123]

When famine struck in Southern Rhodesia in 1922, game meat was no longer available as a hedge against starvation. In this and all subsequent periods of failed rains, Africans had neither the opportunity nor the means to turn to the extraordinary protein bounty with which Africa had endowed their forefathers. One rare African source, the history of Manyika written by an employee of the Methodist Episcopal Mission Press in Umtali, Jason Machiwanyika (undated, but he died in 1922), lamented the removal of meat from the African diet:

> Europeans took all guns from Africans and refused to let them shoot game. But Europeans shoot game. Africans have to eat relish [the accompaniment to their maize-meal porridge] only with vegetables. If an African shoots an animal with a gun, the African is arrested and the gun is confiscated.[124]

When elderly Africans were asked in an oral research project about the changes to the landscape in the previous seventy or eighty years, all reflected on the compression of African peoples upon the land, the removal of trees from the landscape, and the disappearance of the animals with which they had formerly contested control of the African environment.[125] Despite the ravages of animals in the past, most seemed to think that the meat more than compensated for the danger to crops.

Helge Kjekshus has argued that in Tanzania, African hunting methods succeeded in keeping game away from settlement areas, and that Africans had in consequence created a successful ecological balance betwen humans and animals.[126] This balance was supposedly destroyed by European con- servationist measures, which led to the growth of animal stocks, the spread of the tsetse, and the allocation of land to game reserves which had formerly supported human settlement. Such a view can find little support in this study of central Africa. African hunting methods were relatively inefficient. They had little effect on game stocks until, with the distribution of ad- vanced firearms in the late nineteenth century, Africans were able to tip the balance against wildlife. Elephants were rapidly shot out and game became scarcer, a development that, as we have seen, caused alarm both to Lewanika and to Lobengula. The arrival of Europeans massively speeded up this process. Europeans briefly created a hunting bonanza for Africans, but over- hunting, rinderpest, revolt, and gun laws soon changed all that. The only access Africans were allowed to the hunt was the limited permission to protect their crops.

The hunt had been to Africans a significant route into the international economy through ivory, a source of meat and skins, and, if it had been a means for the enhancement of chiefly power and privilege, it had also acted as a route to meritocratic advance for the able hunter, particularly in the decades just before the establishment of white rule. For whites, the hunt had provided an irresistible lure to the interior, a means of establishing the social tone of settlement, a convenient subsidy to other white activities during the difficult years of the white advance, a source of pride, power, prestige, and popularity to the early administrators, and finally a rich man's diversion in the remoter corners of Africa.

By the time Europeans developed a conscience about animals in Africa, the damage had largely been done. Yet the reaction was quick to set in. The BSAC native commissioner and poet, Cullen Gouldsbury, declined to hunt.[127] Sir Charles Eliot, one of the first commissioners of the East Africa Protectorate, was a rare administrator who deprecated the hunt and asserted that only reserves, not the unenforceable game laws, could preserve African wildlife.[128] The missionary Donald Fraser became, according to his wife, increasingly sickened by the hunt, but found himself compelled to go on hunting to supply the needs of his mission.[129] The keen hunter, Sir Geoffrey Archer, when livening up an address to the Royal Geographical Society with some hunting stories, found himself tartly admonished by the president that gentlemen should restrict themselves to the camera rather than to the gun.[130] Sir Kenneth Bradley, a district officer in Northern Rhodesia and later director of the Commonwealth Institute, began his career as a fervent hunter, like so many of his colleagues. By the 1930s he described himself as tired and disillusioned with the chase, and carefully and unusually omitted hunting references from his memoirs.[131] It will be recalled that George Orwell reacted against the hunting obligations placed upon him when serving in Burma.[132] Distaste for the hunt had come to be a distinguishing characteristic both of the new type of administrator and of the anti-imperialist in the twentieth century, just as wholehearted espousal of it had been the mark of the true nineteenth-century adventurer and imperialist.

But game would never again appear in the great quantities and over the vast areas in which it had presented itself to early travelers in Africa. The reserves policy turned game into a spectacle for tourists and a source of sport to the privileged few. African hunters became "poachers," and the danger to wildlife was pinned upon people whose often puny efforts pale into insignificance when compared with the great devastation of the late nineteenth century.

Notes

1. F. Lugard, *The Rise of Our East African Empire* (London, 1893), I, 340. However, Lugard remarked that after the loss of their cattle through rinderpest, the Masai did indeed turn to game. See also Sir C. Eliot, *The East Africa Protectorate* (London, 1905), 138, 144.

2. T. M. Thomas, *Eleven Years in Central South Africa* (London, 1873), 97; Lionel Decle, *Three Years in Savage Africa* (London, 1900), 180; and H. N. Hemans, *The Log of a Native Commissioner* (London, 1935), 132–33.

3. D. N. Beach, "The Shona Economy," in R. Palmer and R. Parsons, *The Roots of Rural Poverty* (London, 1977), 39–40.

4. Some eighty interviews, which included questions on hunting, were

conducted by the present author in the Chibi, Gutu, Wedza, Mrewa, Mtoko, Godhlwayo, and Matobo districts of Zimbabwe in 1973–4. They are now deposited in the oral evidence collections of the Department of History of the University of Zimbabwe.

5.   However, some modification of the "cattle complex" idea is necessary. The meat of cattle was extensively eaten by the early Shona; Beach, 40. See also M. C. Steele, "The Economic Function of African-owned Cattle in Colonial Zimbabwe," *Zambezia* 9, no. 1 (1981): 29–48.

6.   J. R. D. Cobbing, "The Ndebele under the Khumalos, 1820–1896," unpublished Ph.D. thesis, University of Lancaster, 1976, 174–75.

7.   C. Bullock, *The Mashona and the Matabele* (Cape Town, 1950), 40–41.

8.   Lugard, 251.

9.   W. H. Brown, *On the South African Frontier* (London, 1899), 105. Similar techniques were used in precolonial Tanzania. See Helge Kjekshus, *Ecology Control and Economic Development in East African History* (London, 1977), 71; and Thomas, 115.

10.   E. C. Tabler, *Trade and Travel in Early Barotseland* (London, 1963), 98; Thomas Baines, *Explorations in South-West Africa,* (London, 1864), 509; Lugard, 323; and J. Johnston, *Reality Versus Romance in South Central Africa* (London, 1893), 43. The frequency of these stories implies a very widespread use of game pits.

11.   Thomas, 116–17.

12.   E. E. Burke, ed., *The Journals of Karl Mauch* (Salisbury National Archives of Rhodesia, 1869), 159–61; and F. O. Bernhard, ed., *Karl Mauch* (Cape Town, 1971), 220.

13.   F. Coillard, *On the Threshold of Central Africa* (London, 1897), 600; and Tabler, 43.

14.   Brown, 172.

15.   Tabler, 110.

16.   E. C. Tabler, *To the Victoria Falls Via Matabeleland: The Diary of Major Henry Stabb, 1875* (Cape Town, 1867), 173.

17.   Coillard, 365.

18.   Tabler, *Trade and Travel*, 67; and Coillard, 598. Lewanika's hunting lodge was surrounded by piles of heads, horns, and animal vertebrae. A picture of the hunting "box" appeared in Cassell's *Story of Africa*, II, 206.

19.   Coillard, 287. See also Gervas Clay, *Your Friend Lewanika* (London, 1968), 22.

20.   Coillard, 591. Cf. the contemporary proliferation of ritual in Europe and colonial Africa. See E. Hobsbawm and T. O. Ranger, *The Invention of Tradition* (London, 1983).

21.   Clay, 151.

22.   Thomas, 117.

23.   Tabler, *Trade and Travel*, 5.

24.   Bernhard, 163, 170; Cobbing, 175; Thomas, 193; Brown, 234; and Lord Randolph Churchill, *Men, Mines, and Animals in South Africa* (London, 1893), 225.

25.   J. P. R. Wallis, ed., *The Northern Goldfields Diaries of Thomas Baines*, 3 vols. (London, 1946), 325, 805.

26.   Cobbing, 175; Wallis, 299–300.

27.   When Norman MacLeod visited Lozi country, Sepopa used him and his party for the king's own ends, directing them where to hunt, confiscating their ivory, etc. Tabler, *Trade and Travel,* 109.

28.   Sepopa even moved his capital to Sesheke on the advice of Westbeech in order to be nearer the elephant hunting grounds. L. Gann, *A History of Northern Rhodesia* (London, 1964), 44.

29.   Wallis, passim. Other hunters, like John Lee, were also active there. F. C. Selous, *Travel and Adventure in South-East Africa* (London, 1893), passim. Phillips introduced Selous to Lobengula in 1872, by which time Phillips had already been hunting and trading in Matabeleland for eight years. F. C. Selous, *A Hunter's Wanderings in Africa* (London, 1881), 29. Not all elephant hunter diplomacy was successful. Lobengula refused to accept Henry Hartley as an emissary of the Transvaal Boers, and when Sir Bartle Frere sent the elephant hunter Patterson to Lobengula's capital in 1878, Patterson was murdered on receiving permission to hunt to the north.

30.   William Finaughty, *The Recollections of William Finaughty,* ed. G. L. Harrison (Philadelphia, 1916). In one five-month period, Finaughty shot fifty-three elephants, yielding three thousand pounds of ivory, an average of fifty-six pounds per animal.

31.   Selous, *Hunter's Wanderings* (Bulawayo, 1970), publisher's introduction to new edition.

32.   J. G. Millais, *The Life of F. C. Selous* (London, 1918), 74–75.

33.   Bernhard, 24.

34.   Tabler, *Trade and Travel,* 7. Westbeech realized £12,000 for the ivory he collected and received from Sepopa between 1872 and 1874. Clay, 16.

35.   Millais, 112.

36.   C. W. Mackintosh, *Coillard of the Zambezi* (London, 1908), 328.

37.   Millais, 120, 130, 158. It is an ironic fact that, alone in Africa, Zimbabwe's elephant herds have grown to such an extent that they had to be culled in 1983. Six thousand of Zimbabwe's forty-nine thousand elephants were to be shot. *The Observer,* 26 June 1983: 6.

38.   Gann, 41.

39.   Thomas, passim. See publisher's introduction to new edition (Bulawayo, 1970).

40.   F. L. M. Moir, *After Livingstone: An African Trade Romance,* (London, n.d.), 110, 99. Moir also commented upon the meat subsidy supplied by game, 116–18.

41.   R. Laws, *Reminiscences of Livingstonia* (London, 1934), 212.

42.   T. Baines, *The Gold Regions of South-East Africa* (London, 1877), 41; Wallis, passim; and Bernhard, passim.

43.   The hunter was Harry Ware; he led parties north in the late 1880s. Tabler, *Trade and Travel,* 29.

44.   Lugard, 12; and M. Perham, *Lugard, The Years of Adventure* (London, 1956), 70. Lugard had learned his hunting skills in India. Perham, 47–48.

45.   The value of ivory sent by Lugard to the coast averaged £5,300 per annum. Lugard, 428. Lugard remarked that Emin Pasha was able to collect enough ivory in the Equatorial Provinces to pay the costs of his administration. Elsewhere,

Lugard noted the decline of ivory imports into London during the previous thirty years. In the first half of the period, imports into London averaged 580 tons per annum; in the second half, 484 tons. Lugard, 505. For a longer perspective on the ivory trade of East Africa, see E. A. Alpers, *Ivory and Slaves in East Central Africa* (London, 1975). And for the importance of ivory in nineteenth-century trade, see J. Forbes Munro, *Africa and the International Economy* (London, 1976).

46. G. Archer, *Personal and Historical Memoirs of an East African Administrator* (Edinburgh, 1963), 10, 15–17. Archer remarked that Emin Pasha was none too happy about being rescued by H. M. Stanley in 1887–88 because of the great hordes of ivory he had amassed in the Equatorial Provinces.

47. Ibid., 45.

48. Colin Harding, *Far Bugles* (London, 1933). Both Coryndon and Codrington, BSAC administrators in Northern Rhodesia, had been members of the Bechuanaland Border Police and were keen hunters.

49. Sir Alfred Sharpe, *The Backbone of Africa* (London, 1921), 178–98.

50. R. G. G. Cumming, *Five Years of a Hunter's Life in the Far Interior of South Africa* (London, 1850); W. C. Harris, *The Wild Sports of Southern Africa* (London, 1852); and W. C. Baldwin, *African Hunting from Natal to the Zambezi from 1852–1860* (London, 1863). See also Nancy Rouillard, ed., *Matabele Thompson: An Autobiography* (London, 1936), 19–22, 235–36. Thompson's father went to South Africa to hunt in 1850, on inheriting £7,000.

51. H. F. Varian, *Some African Milestones* (London, 1953), 150.

52. Millais, 65.

53. Ibid., 228; and J. S. Bratton, *The Impact of Victorian Children's Fiction* (London, 1981).

54. R. S. S. Baden-Powell, *Sport in War* (London, 1900). Lt. Col. E. A. H. Alderson, *Pink and Scarlet, or Hunting as a School for Soldiering* (London, 1900).

55. R. S. S. Baden-Powell, *Scouting for Boys* (London, 1908), 82–96. Material on big-game hunting survives in recent editions; see that of 1981, 119–21.

56. Millais, 139–40.

57. Varian.

58. H. F. Hole, *Old Rhodesian Days* (London, 1928), 83.

59. Tabler, *Trade and Travel*, 56.

60. Sharpe, 33–34.

61. Horace Waller, ed., *The Last Journals of David Livingstone* (London, 1880), I, 145.

62. Tabler, *Trade and Travel*, 57, 81.

63. Thomas, 104.

64. Thomas, 365.

65. *Central Africa, A Monthly Record of the Work of the Universities Mission to Central Africa* 24 (1916): 147.

66. F. S. Arnot, *Missionary Travels in Central Africa* (Bath, 1914), 64. His men were always pressing him to secure more meat. F. S. Arnot, *Garenganze, Mission Work in Central Africa* (London, 1889), 188. He shot zebras to pay porters. Donald Fraser, *Winning a Primitive People* (London, 1914).

67. G. W. H. Knight-Bruce, *Memories of Mashonaland* (London, 1895), 41; Thomas, 386–88; Hemans, 40; S. P. Hyatt, *The Old Transport Road* (London, 1914),

176–77; and J. T. Bent, *The Ruined Cities of Mashonaland* (London, 1892), 33–34, and many other references.

68.   R. Blennerhasset and L. Sleeman, *Adventures in Mashonaland* (London, 1893), 180.

69.   Agnes Fraser, *Donald Fraser* (London, 1934), 239.

70.   Brown, 223. Shimmin was a close friend and admirer of Selous. See Shimmin's tribute in Millais, 369–73.

71.   Churchill, 254.

72.   Bent, 33. Bent employed large numbers of Africans on the excavations at Zimbabwe, presenting considerable commissariat problems.

73.   National Archives of Zimbabwe Historical Manuscripts Collection (NAZ Hist. MSS. Coll.), the papers of Hubert Tyler Harrington, HA5/1/1. Also reminiscences of L. C. Meredith (uncatalogued), who thought little of Harrington's hunting capacities.

74.   C. E. Finlason, *A Nobody in Mashonaland* (London, 1893), 99–100. Public-school networks soon established themselves. Selous was at Rugby. Baden-Powell, who wrote of "the freemasonry of the hunt," also pursued a public-school freemasonry. In Rhodesia he looked up all fellow Carthusians (alumni of the Charterhouse School, London) of any influence. Both Hyatt and Hemans were at Dulwich College. See also, NAZ Hist. MSS Coll., correspondence of Henry John Borrow, Borrow to mother, 26 May 1891, BO11/1/1—"various young sprigs of the nobility," "nondescript public schools types," etc.

75.   NAZ Hist. MSS Coll., Miscellaneous DR2, papers of W. I. S. Driver. Also Borrow papers, BO 11/1/1, Borrow to father, 24 September 1891.

76.   NAZ Hist. MSS. Coll., papers of J. J. F. Darling, DA 6/3/2; and Brown, 128, 147, 279.

77.   NAZ Hist. MSS Coll., reminiscences of William Edwards, ED 6/1/1.

78.   Hyatt, 173.

79.   Brown, 304, 305, 307. NAZ Hist. MSS Coll. Misc. DR2. W. I. S. Driver, who was the native commissioner at Selukwe, also made money out of timber-cutting contracts.

80.   Churchill, 199, 212, 330.

81.   Varian, 80, 83, 123, 166; and George Pauling, *Chronicles of a Contractor* (London, 1926), 135, 207.

82.   E. A. H. Alderson, *With the Mounted Infantry and the Mashonaland Field Force* (London, 1898), 52.

83.   *The Guide to South Africa for the Use of Tourists, Sportsmen, Invalids, and Settlers,* 1st. ed., (Castle Mail Packets Company, 1892–93). Over thirty pages were devoted to game, hunting, and game laws, material that remained largely unchanged until the 1930s in successive editions.

84.   Alderson, *Mounted Infantry;* and R. S. S. Baden-Powell, *The Matabele Campaign* (London, 1897).

85.   Baden-Powell, *Sport in War,* 17–18.

86.   Baden-Powell, *Matabele Campaign,* 417.

87.   Alderson maintained the metaphor of the fox hunt throughout his account of the Mashonaland campaign. *Mounted Infantry,* 45, 56. At different times he compared hunting the Shona to rabbiting from bolt holes (93), shooting snipe (110),

and scaring rooks (114). On one accasion he told his men to treat an attack as an August bank holiday outing (83). When the acting administrator of Mashonaland, Judge Vintcent, joined Alderson's column, Alderson described him as being "like a schoolboy out hunting in the holidays at the idea of having a go at the Mashonas" (117).

88.   Baden-Powell, *Matabele Campaign,* 308, 338, 403–4. The white laager at Enkeldoorn survived on game shot every day by the (mainly Boer) menfolk (420).

89.   Baden-Powell, *Matabele Campaign,* 436, 445.

90.   C. van Onselen, "Reactions to Rinderpest in South Africa 1896–97," *Journal of African History* 13, no. 3 (1972): 473. Kjekshus, 126–32.

91.   Lugard, 356. "Through all this great plain we passed carcases of buffalo; and the vast herds of which I had heard and which I hoped would feed my hungry men, were gone!" "The breath of the pestilence had destroyed them as utterly as the Winchesters of Buffalo Bill and his crew . . . have destroyed the bison of America" (359). See also 527–28, where Lugard recounts the different effects of rinderpest on the various game animals.

92.   Baden-Powell, *Matabele Campaign,* 15. In one area, he despaired of shooting game for his men when he found carcases of kudu dead from rinderpest (327).

93.   Baden-Powell, *Matabele Campaign,* 22.

94.   Varian, 77.

95.   Sharpe, 74.

96.   Millais, 183, 209.

97.   Cobbing, 175.

98.   Selous was fined £60 and always regarded the imposition as unjust. Fifty hippos had been shot because the trader Martin wished to send sjamboks to Cape Colony, where they were much in demand. Selous, *Travel and Adventure,* 135–38.

99.   Selous, *Hunter's Wanderings,* 444–48.

100.   A. G. Leonard, *How We Made Rhodesia* (London, 1896), 25.

101.   Hole, 82.

102.   Brown, 113–19.

103.   Churchill, 211.

104.   Ibid., 170–73.

105.   The Game Law Amendment Ordinance of 1886, Cape Colony: game licenses were stipulated in the BSAC Charter of 1889, and the regulations were extended in the Game Law Amendment Ordinance no. 7 of 1893, Ordinance no. 6 of 1894, regulations 198 and 199 of 1898, and a long series of regulations in 1899, the Statute Laws of Southern Rhodesia. I am grateful to Rhodes House, Oxford, and the Bodleian Law Library, Oxford, for researching these ordinances and supplying photocopies to me.

106.   Hyatt, 182–83, 271–74.

107.   Hyatt, 174–75.

108.   *Castle Guide* (later *Union-Castle Guide) to South Africa,* 1899–1900 edition, 218. In any case, owners of land could shoot all animals on their land; and prospectors, farmers, and travelers could shoot what they required for food, over ten miles from townships. One early writer on Rhodesia described the town-dwellers as spending their weekends hunting in the bush. Percy F. Hone, *Southern Rhodesia* (London, 1909), 21.

109. Hole, 84.

110. Eliot, 277–78.

111. D. Fraser, 294.

112. The Possession of Arms by Natives and Asiatics Restricting Regulations, 1897; The Delivery of Arms to Natives and Asiatics Restricting Regulations 1897; and the Rifle and Ball Ammunition Ordinance of 1902.

113. The African police also took Lee-Metfords with them when they deserted. Baden-Powell, *Matabele Campaign*, 35.

114. NAZ Hist. MSS Coll., correspondence and other papers of J. W. Colenbrander, 1881–1917, Vavasseur to Colenbrander, 6 May 1893, quoted in Cobbing, 175.

115. The author was shown Chief Vhondo of Gutu's tower musket in 1974 and was told that it had been used the week before to chase baboons from growing crops. By the Possession of Arms by Natives for Self-Protection Act, 1932, native commissioners were permitted to issue a rifle and no more than ten rounds of ammunition for the purpose of protecting crops against wild animals. I am grateful to Dr. M. C. Steele for this and several other points relating to the later period.

116. J. M. MacKenzie, "A Pre-Colonial Industry, the Njanja and the Iron Trade," *NADA* 11, no. 2 (1975).

117. Varian, 66.

118. NAZ Hist. MSS Coll., papers of Herbert Percy Hale, HA4/1/1.

119. NAZ Hist. MSS Coll., papers of Mansel Edge Weale, WE 3/2/5.

120. Hemans, 5.

121. Hemans, 48, 153. Hemans emphasized the importance of hunting to the administrator's prestige, 83. Lugard also wrote that hunting was a vital part of his expeditions both to enhance his prestige with his followers and to keep his men happy. Lugard, 279.

122. W. S. Churchill, *My African Journey* (London, 1908).

123. I am grateful to Dr. M. C. Steele for this point.

124, NAZ Hist. MSS Coll., Jason Machiwanyika, MA 4/1/2.

125. Interviews collected by the author. See footnote 4 above.

126. Kjekshus, 69–79.

127. Cullen Gouldsbury, *Rhodesian Rhymes* (Bulawayo, 1932), publisher's introduction to new edition (1969), 5.

128. Eliot, 275–76.

129. A. Fraser, 148.

130. Archer, 15.

131. Kenneth Bradley, *Diary of a District Officer* (London, 1943), 56. Despite the fact that he took "little pleasure in killing," the appetites of his "30 weary carriers" on tour demanded that he shoot. Kenneth Bradley, *Once a District Officer* (London, 1966).

132. George Orwell, *Shooting an Elephant and Other Essays* (London, 1950).

8

Pugilism and Pathology:
African Boxing and the Black Urban Experience in Southern Rhodesia

TERENCE RANGER

Introduction

In December 1938 Southern Rhodesia's chief native commissioner and secretary for native affairs, Charles Bullock, received a letter from the secretary general of the British Social Hygiene Council, Inc. The letter announced that one of the sessions at the Ninth Imperial Congress to be held in London in July 1939 would be devoted to "Labour and Leisure Overseas." It asked that Bullock should attend and present a paper on African recreation in Southern Rhodesia.

> We are most anxious to present to the Congress at that session some account of the measures being taken in various parts of the Empire to promote leisure occupations and recreation in Native Locations and among organised bodies of native labour.[1]

It came as no surprise to Bullock that an imperial congress should concern itself with recreation in the African townships of Southern Rhodesia. The subject had been one of his own main anxieties for the past two or three years, and he had brought it before the Rhodesian prime minister, Godfrey Huggins, for an authoritative ruling. Nor did it surprise him that sport in the townships should be seen as a matter of social hygiene; his own concern had been precisely to balance the interests of social hygiene with those of social control.

Sport in Southern Rhodesia had always been more than play. Sport for whites—especially cricket—had been a symbol of racial and national qualities; a ritual of affirmation at which Africans were at first mere spectators or adjuncts. In November 1895, for example, the Anglican missionary, Douglas Pelly, came together with the local native commissioner and a couple of white traders for a game of cricket in the Makoni District of eastern Rhodesia. "To bat and bowl with heaps of boys to field," he told his parents. "A highly satisfactory way of playing, all fun and no fag."[2] Soon, however, African pupils at the Anglican mission schools were themselves playing football (soccer) as part of the process of inculcating the virtues of

196

discipline and teamwork. The complex process of instructing Africans in European games while at the same time denying them the prestige that athletic skills generated was thus initiated in Southern Rhodesia.

This process has not so far been much studied by historians of Zimbabwe. But the history of African sport has developed as one of the strands within the impressive new South African historiography of black working-class culture. Belinda Bozzoli has recently summed up the paradox of black South African football history:

> Economic, political and military domination were accompanied often by indirect, or in some cases directly manipulative, attempts at cultural influence and control over the leisure-time of blacks. Some success was achieved amongst blacks who "thought it was good for them which they copied from a civilised nation who were the ruling element." There were reported reductions in crime, drunkenness, gambling and other "objectionable practices" as a result of the spread of football. But the connections of soccer with movements of protest and resistance grew to at least the same proportions as those with missionaries and do-gooders, as this cultural activity associated with colonial conquest was seized upon, and made their own by ordinary players, spectators and officials, as well as nationalists and populists, against the background of a growing capitalist system, whose hunger for markets and commodities ultimately encroached upon the game and transformed it.[3]

Urban social history in general is by comparison underdeveloped in Zimbabwe.[4] This chapter is no more than a footnote to a future Zimbabwean historiography of urban sport and social control, drawing as it does on a handful of files relating to only one topic out of all those that need investigation. Yet it so happens that this topic—black boxing bouts in Salisbury during 1938—is interesting both in itself and also more widely because it was taken as a test case by Chief Native Commissioner Bullock. Bullock, who was internationally recognized as an expert on the "traditional" and rural cultures of the Shona and Ndebele, believed that nobody fully understood what happened to men who came out of those cultures into the towns. In particular, he believed that the municipal officials responsible for the African locations did not understand what they were doing. He instanced their mishandling of African boxing as a major demonstration of this incomprehension. And he used the question of boxing both to press for more effective measures of urban social control and also to initiate the first "scientific" study of urban Africans in Southern Rhodesia. The story of black pugilism in Salisbury in 1938 is illuminating, therefore, as an instance of African appropriation of European forms to their own ends; as the occasion for an argument over social control; and as the context for the enunciation of the first systematic propositions about "urbanization" in Rhodesia.

Recreation in Salisbury Location in the 1930s

At the end of 1930 the Native Affairs Commission, Salisbury Municipal Location, took evidence on conditions there. Among its terms of reference was the "provision for the welfare and general advancement of the Native inhabitants of the Location," and the commissioners were instructed to look at "sports grounds and Hall and general provision for recreation."[5] The Salisbury Location had become, so the commission reported, "an important Native township . . . no longer, as it was twenty-three years ago, a housing place for temporary labourers." It had a population of over three thousand Africans, though "four-fifths of the Natives in the Location are, we think, practically inarticulate."[6] Evidence to the commission was therefore given only by municipal officials, missionaries, and mission-educated elite Africans.

Albert Edward Horne, the location superintendent, told the commission what provision was currently made: "There are two football grounds and there is room for more. . . . Each tribe in the Location have their allotted piece of ground set aside for dancing, and each tribe sticks to its own ground."[7] Thereafter missionaries and elite Africans appearing before the commission pressed for more facilities under greater control. "Provision should be made to fill up the natives' spare time," said Rev. Frank Noble. "These Sunday dances (which now cover the whole location and turn the place into pandemonium) should only be allowed on the set Sports ground," testified Lt. Col. Soul of the Salvation Army. "Organised sports would help to check vices and fill the time of the young bloods more profitably."[8] Elite Africans were even more emphatic. John Muketsi, a Sotho member of the Southern Rhodesia Native Association, complained that the location was dominated by immoral women:

> The only form of amusement at present is dancing of an undesirable type. I am fully in agreement with encouraging natives in sport. It keeps them occupied and diverts their attention from other things. Unfortunately they cannot organise themselves. I would suggest a scheme to be controlled by a European. When the scheme has been properly established a responsible native might be put in charge.[9]

An official delegation from the Native Association endorsed these notions of sport as social hygiene: "Sport would distract natives from forms of vice."[10]

But the Salisbury Municipality was at this stage unready to accept formal responsibility for the controlled provision of sports. As the town clerk told the commission,

> The Council feels that it has no responsibility. . . . With regard to the suggestion that there should be someone to organise native games, we have felt that a Committee should be formed from voluntary workers in the city

to undertake this work, but I do not consider that it is a question for the Council.[11]

Whatever the municipality's reservations on grounds of cost, recreation facilities did expand through the 1930s and so too did white consciousness of the need for control. By the beginning of 1937 there were "two football fields, tennis courts, cycle and athletic grounds available for recreation. A cricket ground is at present under construction. The grounds adjoin the Municipal compound. The most popular game is association football; cricket is in its infancy, so far as the local Bantu are concerned."[12] In October 1937 the Salisbury City Council, "assisted by the Government of Southern Rhodesia," appointed a European native welfare officer, "a new departure in the administration of the City." By January 1938 it was reported that "the organization of choirs, dance, athletic, cycling and cricket clubs is well advanced, and a physical training class for juveniles in which keen interest has been shown, has been started."[13]

In all this, the Southern Rhodesian cities were following South African examples of a decade or more earlier. As Paul la Hausse tells us in his study of Durban, a native welfare officer had been appointed there in 1930 in order to "establish some kind of hegemony over 'dangerously' autonomous sporting bodies such as the Durban and District African Football Association. Extensive attention was devoted towards the control of dances and dance halls." "Ruling classes," writes la Hausse, "have an unambiguous stake in the forms of popular culture and thus popular culture becomes a crucial area of struggle between the dominant and dominated classes."[14] By 1938 in Salisbury most forms of African recreation had likewise been brought under control. But there remained one worrying exception—African boxing, an autonomous activity, which had sprung up and become enormously popular without any direct European instigation, patronage, or influence at all. In May 1938 the new Salisbury welfare officer, Cordell, wrote to municipalities throughout South Africa and also to large industrial concerns, to ask them what their attitude was toward the control of boxing.

The town clerk of Durban replied that boxing was as much under control there as any other African recreation:

> The City Council provided a raised boxing ring at one of the Native Locations with a view to encouraging this healthy form of sport, among others, as a desirable outlet for their superfluous energy and to tutor them in the art of scientific boxing. . . . This form of sport is becoming very popular. . . . [There is] a proper boxing club with a European trainer.[15]

Similar replies came from Johannesburg, which claimed the credit for having initiated the policy of "cultivating and encouraging physical exercises (including boxing)." In Johannesburg African boxing clubs enjoyed the patronage of leading members of the European political establishment; the City Council donated several cups for prizes, and big tournaments were staged. An association was "formed for the control of amateur boxing among natives in this city. . . . The European community is desirous of encouraging boxing among the Bantu with a view to teaching them methods of self-defence without resorting to the use of a knife or other lethal weapon."[16]

It was true that the one Southern Rhodesian reply, from the chief compound manager at Wankie Colliery, reported that no boxing was allowed there: "I feel that the Native 'Sporting Instinct' is not sufficiently developed for this type of sport."[17] But the general tenor of the responses encouraged the Salisbury native welfare officer to proceed in his attempt "to formulate recommendations which will result in effective control of boxing among natives and a removal of the existing highly dangerous conditions attending their unorganised gatherings."[18] In June 1938 the Outdoor Sports Subcommittee of the Native Welfare Society, under Cordell's chairmanship, was asked to submit recommendations on the matter. And on June 30 Cordell met with the native commissioner, Salisbury, and three high-ranking officers of the British South Africa Police to hammer out a policy. They had before them a report from the chief superintendent of police in Bulawayo, which recommended a policy of control rather than one of banning. Cordell argued that

> the time was not ripe for legislation. He referred to boxing at Avondale and Corven's brickfields and was of opinion that boxing should be confined . . . to the Location where proper facilities would be provided; he was confident if organized boxing was approved that unauthorised boxing would disappear. . . . Control should be undertaken by himself and his committee and . . . the assistance of the Police should only be asked for as a last resort. . . . It was generally agreed that proper organisation would result in control being effective as in the case of Football matches.

Those present agreed that "to leave it as it is" was "the least desirable" course; to "wash it out altogether" was "most difficult, if not impossible"; and that to "permit it if controlled" was the "most expedient."[19]

Through the months of August and September 1938 an experiment in controlled boxing was carried out. By October the City Council was prepared to add pugilism to its range of activities:

> The Council at its Meeting yesterday [wrote the town clerk on 27 October] resolved that the European Native Welfare Officer be authorised to allow native boxing in the Location to continue, subject to such boxing being properly organised and controlled, any disturbance threat to be reported to the Commonage, Gardens and Aerodrome Committee.

A sum of twenty pounds had been voted to build an "adequate fence around the boxing ring."[20]

Chief Native Commissioner Bullock and Boxing As a Special Case

One might have expected that Chief Native Commissioner Bullock, who had often voiced his anxiety over urban crime and disorder, would have been pleased at this steady regularization of African recreation in Salisbury. But in fact it was precisely Cordell's determination to control and hence to recognize boxing that most worried him. On 23 July 1938 the chief native commissioner wrote to the prime minister's office to express his anxiety. In previous reports he had

> foreshadowed the need of specialised research and thought with a view to effecting adjustments in the conditions of life in urban areas; and recent correspondence as to so-called boxing contests which has been shown to the Prime Minister indicates that in one sphere at any rate the need is now becoming immediate.

The native welfare officers in Salisbury and Bulawayo were "very useful practical men," but "with the best of intentions they may lead us into dangerous situations." Bullock thought that what was needed was "the services of a trained sociologist from South Africa for a period of six months or one year."[21]

Why did the proposal to control boxing so alarm Bullock and thus become the occasion for a sociological inquiry? It was not that Bullock was hostile to the whole idea of urban Africans engaging in European sport. In August 1939, indeed, he was to greet warmly a request from the Bulawayo Native Football Association that a trophy be donated: "I would be very glad to buy a cup from my private purse . . . I am anxious that I should provide a cup, or give some other encouragement to Native recreation in this my final year of office."[22] But boxing seemed to him, as to many other Europeans, to constitute a special case.

African boxing had long been regarded by missionaries and their leading converts as particularly undignified and disruptive. In November 1927 the Methodist Stanlake Magorimbo had protested to the *Bantu Mirror*: "It is a great shame today to see African girls and boys shouting and jumping and wrestling in the town streets and compounds. . . . Even in our homes our ancestors never practised such things."[23] In 1931 the American Methodist Episcopal Church commented that:

> the Location in Salisbury offers attractions and temptations which are ruining the lives of tremendous numbers of the rural people who go there. . . . In many cases the people themselves go into sin and when they

come back to their homes they start dancing, boxing matches and other
amusements that almost break up Christian work at their stations.[24]

All this was in sharp contrast to the heroic and prestigious exertions of
Methodist boarding school football teams at the same period.

Another group of critics of boxing took further Magorimbo's assertion
that "our ancestors never practised such things." Throughout the late 1920s
and the 1930s there was a resolute attempt by the advocates of constructive
segregation to foster "traditional" African games and dances rather than
"proletarian" sports. The director for native education stressed that schools
must be rooted in local life: it was vital that "recreation, to include Native
games and approved rhythmic dances, receive adequate recognition. . . . In
place of the individualism and competitive spirit engendered by most cur-
ricula, we should endeavour to foster social activities, co-operation, mutual
service."[25] The leading advocate of this view was the musicologist Hugh
Tracey. Throughout the 1930s Tracey sought to attain social control by
reviving "traditional" art, music, and dances rather than by controlling the
new sports. In June 1930 he urged that an attempt be made to preserve
African music "in its original purity" by forming a choir under his own
"continual supervision."

> The nature of their music is such that no really useful results would accrue
> by approaching individual natives separately for it is essentially choral. . . .
> The fact that the raison d'etre of this enterprise is to demonstrate and
> record pure Bantu music would . . . be an additional and imperative reason
> for their very careful segregation.[26]

In October 1931 Tracey was planning an exhibition of native arts and crafts,

> to awaken in the present generation a national consciousness (as opposed to
> subconsciousness) in their art . . . to help combat thereby the evils of social
> disintegration and denationalisation that have arisen from European influ-
> ence in the country, and that are evident, possibly, in a certain loss of
> manhood and social responsibility.[27]

In 1942 Tracey was arguing that "we need in Africa the equivalent of a Cecil
Sharp research school" into African folk music and dance:

> The deliberate destruction of African art forms by Europeans . . . must be
> deplored by all who comprehend the social importance of art. . . . From
> such a school and within the immediate future the whole of the problem of
> social entertainment . . . would be rationalised upon a sound foundation,
> having due regard to European contact . . . and greatly reinforce the
> happier side of social segregation which our presence in Africa demands.[28]

For Tracey, boxing was a particularly objectionable activity, at once pro-
letarianizing and also endangering the fitness of the urban work force.

Instead of approved boxing, he argued in 1940, the municipalities should foster tribal dancing competitions, which would link workers to their rural communities and foster a proper sense of tribe.[29]

The white urban residents in general had yet another dislike of African boxing, quite apart from its "immorality" or "proletarian character." They feared that boxing would make urban Africans aggressive; and they especially disliked its popularity among domestic servants. The sociologist commissioned by Bullock commented on these features in his report of 29 June 1939. Boxing, he noted, had begun "amongst the youngsters attached to the Police Camp about 1915 but only attained to any significant dimensions about 1930/1. . . . Not only the prestige of the European form but also that attaching to the Police must therefore be noted as a powerful factor in the diffusion of boxing." Boxing became "the private pre-occupation of countless house-boys. . . . The Natives have taught themselves and pursued the sport in any secluded grove of trees or distant space that offered— some of these places being well recognised and the inevitable rendezvous for all those houseboys living near." These developments had alarmed employers. "Boxing had rapidly assumed the nature of a serious social problem." Yet "control of boxing was confused with the teaching of boxing and on the grounds of the undesirability of teaching the Natives to box the sport was left to spread its enthusiasm in a chaotic and wildly iresponsible manner. . . . As far back as 1935 all suggestions as to recognising boxing and running it properly were turned down":

> The most formidable argument used against boxing [remarked the report] was based on a fear of potential inter-racial trouble arising out of the increased ability of the Native to use his fists . . . and of the growth of a truculent spirit among them.[30]

Chief Native Commissioner Bullock did not share all of these reasons for hostility toward African boxing. Far from wanting to foster urban tribal identifications, he was himself most worried by the far-ranging tribal networks that underlay the boxing factions of Salisbury. (Boxing constituted "the nucleus of a wide and intricate system of tribal organizations," reported the sociologist in June 1939). Bullock believed that African boxing brought together three highly undesirable elements—individual African initiative in adapting European forms to their own ends; wider multitribal boxing associations, which could be mobilized for other purposes; and constant clashes between boxers who represented these multitribal associations, clashes that could precipitate large-scale fighting. Bullock believed that the notorious "faction" fights in Bulawayo over Christmas 1929 had been provoked by boxing rivalries. He thought the welfare officers gullible in regarding participants in boxing as precisely similar to keen footballers, since this overlooked the much wider and more autonomously African aspects of the boxing groups. So in July 1938 Bullock told the commissioner of police in Salisbury that while he did not feel justified in overruling the general consensus that boxing should be legitimated and controlled, he wished nevertheless to draw attention to the following dangerous features:

(1) The boxing is between champions of different tribes and the spectators are so grouped.

(2) Stone throwing by these groups has already begun.

(3) Weapons are brought to the Meetings.[31]

"My own feeling is that the situation is potentially dangerous," he told the superintendent of natives in Salisbury.[32] And as late as November, after the Salisbury City Council had definitely embarked upon the new policy of recognition and control, Bullock was writing to the staff office of police to warn of the prospect of "serious disturbance." In his view "bouts should be arranged between Natives of the same tribes; or at any rate not between tribes, groups or clubs between which any bad feeling is known to exist. Watch should be kept on the attitudes of groups of boxers associated elsewhere than at their sport."[33] These anxieties reveal plainly the ambiguities of urban social control. "Urban tribalism" had served many purposes for whites in the cities, offering them a crude ranking of jobs by presumed ethnic capacities and allowing them to divide and rule their work forces. But now Bullock had come to see it as constituting a dangerous principle of combination, fundamentally subversive of the social order.

The Dynamic of African Boxing in Salisbury

Because of the debate between Bullock and the proponents of control in 1938 there have been preserved for those months a series of detailed descriptions of boxing encounters in Salisbury. In default of direct evidence from African participants, which I do not possess, these reports can be used to provide a fuller understanding than the official debate over social control can offer. They can also be used to show how social control of African sports operated in practice.

Boxing contests took place just outside the Salisbury Location at the intersection of Ardbennie and Beatrice roads. They attracted crowds of two thousand or more and caused great excitement. European observers found them very puzzling since each contest was so short, so few blows were exchanged, no one was ever knocked out, and no points were awarded. This lack of structure struck them as being primitive; on the other hand they were disturbed by the lack of violence in the bouts themselves. The boxing on 10 July 1938, for example, was witnessed by the superintendent of police of Salisbury Town. As he reported:

The method of arranging the contests was not clear, nor how finality was reached in each bout. It appeared that various officers of the numerous boxing clubs arranged the fights, these same persons intervening when they thought the bout had gone far enough. The bouts lasted but a few minutes each, no apparent finality was reached in any of them. There were no definite rounds but short cessations occurred by mutual agreement. . . . If one "gave up" for a few seconds, through fatigue, his opponent was pleased to entertain the crowd by strutting around the ring in the fashion of a native dancer while his adversary recovered.

The superintendent noted the "entire absence of any ill-feeling" among the contestants. He also noticed that "certain bouts caused much more excitement among the crowd than others," but he could not tell whether this was because of tribal feeling or "appreciation of the skill, or lack of it."[34]

Other reports emphasized the "tribal" basis of the contests:

On my arrival [reported Constable Cowling on the boxing on June 26] there were about 200 Natives gathered in a rough circle, no boxing had as yet taken place. A short time afterwards, a procession of natives arrived, these I was given to understand were Mkorakore [*sic*] and Alien tribes, they formed half the ring while on the other side the Mzezuru and Makoni tribes stood. Then one of these tribes sent forth a challenger into the boxing ring who putting on the boxing gloves, walked around the ring challenging any native from the opposing side to fight him. Then one would come forth and a fight would begin, which never lasted more than three or four minutes.[35]

On 3 July the two factions were dressed variously in "red and black" or in "blue uniform," the former being "Alien natives" and the latter "indigenous natives":

The Blues . . . occupied one side of the arena and the Reds the other side. One member of the Red party entered the ring. He wrapped his fists with pieces of rag and the remains of an old pair of boxing gloves. One of the Blue party did likewise. After dancing round the ring and exchanging several blows, both parties retired. A repetition of this occurred several times.[36]

However much the police observers disliked what they felt to be parodies of European boxing, there was nothing in what the boxers actually did that could be construed as a threat to law and order. Two other aspects of the contests were, however, more disturbing. One was that the boxers wore *Mangoromera,* "heavy leather arm-bands often embellished with brass studs" and containing medicines for success. "The Mangoromera arm-bands (which incidentally impede hand-cuffing) are significant of an undesirable attitude," wrote the chief native commissioner. Native Commissioner

Spicer thought these "under any organised boxing . . . must be the first thing to disappear. I can think of no surer way of dispelling the 'Mangoromera' illusion than, in course of time, engineering one or two 'real good hidings' of 'Mangoromera' believers at the hands of Non-Mangoromera boxers. I refer, of course, to defeats in the ring.'[37]

The other alarming feature was that bouts often gave rise to fighting among the competing factions. Thus on 26 June 'the native Constables became rather worried, as the Mkori Kori [sic] were getting very troublesome, and would not keep their places, but wished to enter into the ring and go over to the opposing side and fight them.' When the police ordered the crowd to disperse they refused to do so and instead began to stone the opposing faction. On 3 July 'an extra hard blow' being struck in the ring, "both sides [Blues and Reds] then rushed into the ring armed with knives, whips, and sticks and gave battle." Constable Cochrane thought that the boxing was "just an excuse for the Aliens and Indigenous natives to fight."[38]

Taking "control" of African boxing meant a number of different things in the minds of Cordell and the police. First, it meant controlling the bouts themselves. There had to be regular rounds with a bell to mark their end; there had to be a referee and a result; there had to be recognized rules of combat. In this way African boxing would be disciplined. Secondly it meant separating off the boxers from the audience. There must be a raised ring; then there must be a fence around the ring keeping the audience away from it. The whole ground must be cleared of stones and spectators must enter it by way of a gate, at which they could be searched for weapons. The boxing clubs must be made formally responsible for the behavior of their supporters. Gradually these changes were introduced.

The process began on 3 July. Native Commissioner Spicer arrived after the fighting of that day:

> I took the opportunity of addressing the crowd. I told them it was obvious that a very large number of natives were interested in boxing either as participants or spectators, that there are many people who are anxious that forms of entertainment appreciated by natives should be promoted and that it was possible that some facilities for boxing might be provided in the near future. . . . If such facilities were provided . . . boxing bouts would be conducted only on proper lines and that contestants and spectators would have to submit to discipline.

Spicer then showed them "the new boxing gloves" but told them that "owing to their behaviour earlier in the afternoon they would be withheld." The crowd responded exactly as Cordell had hoped. They applauded the idea of a raised ring and "the display of the new set of gloves was met with cheers of delight but the people accepted the disappointment at the temporary withdrawal without demur." The Nyasaland labor officer con-

cluded by addressing "the Nyasaland natives" among the crowd, "con-
demning any part they have taken in the week-end affrays."[39]

The new boxing gloves featured as an agent of social control in themselves at the next boxing on 10 July. Boxing began when "Mr Cordell
supplied the gloves" and when there was a danger of the crowd becoming
too excited, Cordell "removed the gloves," and boxing ended for the day.[40]
By 24 July a ring had been erected at the Welfare Sports ground; there were
referees; bouts lasted two minutes each; and a hand bell was rung at the end
of each round. Cordell acted as referee himself for the first two fights and
then handed over to one Jailos, a Zezuru employed at Kingsway Butchery.
Unhappily for Cordell these new disciplines backfired, and conduct that
was within the rules of boxing nevertheless outraged the crowd.

> In the last bout, after which I had intended to take the gloves away, one
> native boxer struck another several times, quite fairly, while his opponent
> stood with his back to him making no attempt to hit back. Boos came
> from the crowd and a movement started towards the ring.

"At least," wrote Cordell unhappily, "there was no danger to buildings . . .
nor to Location residents who were not interested in boxing."[41]

So the process went on through August. On 26 August the native
commissioner "met Boxing Club at Cordell's office and drew up rules"; on
9 September a member of the Salisbury European Boxing Association came
to act as referee. Gradually crowd incidents fell away. By the end of November the only difficulty being reported was the "excitability" or "truculence"
of the leader of the Nyasaland boxers, one Duri, "an enthusiast for the
sport, but temperamentally too excitable."[42]

Pugilism and Pathology: Boxing and Sociological Analysis

As we have seen, Chief Native Commissioner Bullock remained uncon-
vinced. While Cordell and Native Commissioner Spicer were putting
Salisbury boxing under control, Bullock was pressing ahead with his plan
for a sociological inquiry. It was thought too expensive to procure a South
African expert, but as the chief native commissioner told the town clerks of
Salisbury and Bulawayo on 24 August, "we have in this Department an
official who has been specially trained as a sociologist." Bullock suggested
that the municipalities might bear half the cost of an inquiry.[43] Bulawayo
turned the suggestion down. Salisbury approved and on 27 October 1938
the town clerk wrote to tell Bullock that his "suggestion to station a trained
sociologist in the Native Location has been approved."[44] There thus began a
"scientific" inquiry into African boxing.

The Native Department's sociologist was Roger Howman, who in August 1938 was stationed at the Mount Darwin District in the far northeast,
about as far from an urban Location as it was possible to be. Howman had

studied "anthropology, psychology, ethnic history, native languages and other related subjects" for an external degree at the University of South Africa.[45] Thereafter he had spent time both at the London School of Economics, where he sat in at Malinowski's famous seminar with Jomo Kenyatta, Audrey Richards, and the rest, and also at universities in America. Out at Mount Darwin, Howman was consciously in waiting for this training to be called on. He was delighted and astonished to receive Bullock's telephone call summoning him to carry out research in Salisbury.

What is fascinating about Howman's pioneer exercise in urbanization theory is the way in which the end result seems to have been shaped by Bullock's required concentration on boxing. Howman's initial response, written from Mount Darwin on 28 August, presented a remarkably modern approach to the study of urban Africans. It is worth citing at some length:

> I am afraid Sociology is very young, very uncertain and very ill-equipped for so unique a task and the magic of its name may lead "practical" standards to expect the impossible. It is by no means an applied science. . . . The main aspect is that I shall have to evolve my own procedure and methods of study, for anthropology has avoided such problems and sociology, while better equipped, in my opinion, to tackle them has tended to allocate them to anthropology. A combination of the two sciences seems to me to be inevitable and it was this development that I found in America. London has remained dominated by Malinowski; South African sociology is far behind; America is a fertile field of thought facing problems such as ours on an enormous and lavish scale.

Drawing on this American influence, Howman emphasized that "in such fluid conditions as those in our towns and in periods of social change we cannot study such undifferentiated mass ideas such as 'The Native' or 'The Location.' We have to disentangle that social unit which alone seems to preserve a certain measure of identitiy, that is, the family. The broad generalised study that takes in a large group is quite inadequate. . . . This means more intensive, more difficult and more prolonged research. To get at that subjective side of culture, the clash of norms, values and beliefs as they meet within the individual personality, the 'life history' and 'case method' is essential."[46]

It is tantalizing to speculate what might have been the fruits if this focus on the family, this insistence on the "life history"—both so characteristic of African social historiography today—had been applied to the towns of Southern Rhodesia in the 1930s.[47] In the event they never were. Perhaps it was the focus on boxing—with its supratribal clubs, its apparently "irrational" and magical elements—that turned Howman away from the individual and the family and toward resonant generalizations on "The Native" and "The Location." At any rate his conclusions on African boxing, when he presented them to Bullock in June 1939, constituted the most extreme statement of urbanization as pathological disruption rather than a pioneering study of individual adaptation.

Howman began with what he called the Tribal Primary Group as it existed in rural areas, "personal, warm, face to face," and the resulting Primary Group Mentality. "In its disintegration . . . lies the explanation of the social and personal disintegration which is so acute in our towns." In the town, "impersonal, superficial, touch-and-go contacts come to predominate . . . rational intercourse with others, calculation and coldness." Coming to town demanded "a suppression of the emotional life of the Native," who was making a passage from "the thousand little emotional and social ties that bind the Native in his tribe, the community of tradition, feeling, belief and action that lay behind social cohesion" to impersonality and "The Social Void." This transition was reflected in the towns by

> the increase of mental breakdowns, the fears, delusions, manias and psychopathic states, alcoholism, drugs, crime and suicide. . . . All the ingredients for the Social Void are here present in their most virulent form. The Native in his emotional disintegration is left helpless in the face of environment, the prey of random impulse and hooligan self-expression.

The town is the empire of measured time; the African becomes "an automaton, a passive receiver of instructions": "Contrast this with the fullness of his tribal life, the wealth of meaning and emotion he derives from each beast in the herd, each kopje with its legend . . . the numerous games, the hunting, singing and dancing."

What, then, was to be done? The answer did not lie in "more and stricter regimentation, more laws," in falling back on "the oldest and clumsiest device of social control, that of 'Ordering' and 'Forbidding.'" What was needed instead was "a practical planning," among other things, of recreation: "By specifically catering for emotional needs recreation can become a powerful mechanism of social control. . . . The recreational group is a primary group." Here Howman came to African boxing. In its present state African boxing was an example of mere "hooligan self-expression." But properly reordered it could go far to meet African urban emotional needs.

It was important, thought Howman, to teach Africans new games at once appropriate to their lives in the towns and also capable of acting as modes of association. The precise *form* of each European game was crucially necessary to convey, for it was the peg on which to hang "attitudes, rules, leadership, team-work, community feeling, self-imposed discipline and organisational and emotional associations." In order that the new games carried all these implications "careful and ample supervision is absolutely necessary" because "the sociology of the game will not diffuse to the Native without the most careful, deliberate and constant instruction." Boxing in Salisbury, as it had grown up, was an "example of diffusion," but because it had grown up in a purely African social context "boxing, as Form, has been deprived of Function and Meaning and simply got out of social control." There had been no diffusion of essential, "etiquette, code, control."

And yet, thought Howman, African boxing *did* offer some hope, and it did so precisely because of the tribal connections that Bullock so much deplored:

> Rather than condemning and stamping on tribalism we should endeavour to use the unifying influences and associations it spontaneously offers us, using them as the raw materials on which to work. Uniforms, badges, minor subscriptions, even separate tribal boxing rings . . . might be encouraged.

So, Howman concluded, we must build the rules of the European game upon the basis of "the old unity as it meets new conditions."[48] Howman thus lent the weight of his scientific authority to the policy of recognition and control of African boxing, leaving Bullock to vent his irritation by scribbling increasingly caustic marginalia on the edges of Howman's report.

Conclusion

Howman's conclusions can hardly satisfy us any more than they did Bullock, though for different reasons. It is hard to see in the dancing and strutting boxers of Salisbury the lineaments of fear, delusion, mania, and pathological trauma. It seems much more convincing to take up a half sentence of Howman's, which remains undeveloped in his report, namely, an admission that with boxing, as with much else, "the receiving Native culture attaches its own Meaning and Function to the new Form." Our evidence suggests that not only Howman but also the white policemen who watched African boxing found these new meanings and functions impossible to digest and all too easy to reprehend. Moreover, Howman's report does not allow adequately for the fact that the urban "tribalism" that formed the context for boxing was in itself an old form given new meaning and function. Thus Howman interpreted a boxing alliance between the so-called WaKorekore, MaBlantyre and WaManyika in "traditional terms": "I later found out from Mr Blake Thompson that there is a long historical and totemic affinity between the WaKorekore, the Nyasaland people and the WaManyika."[49] This was in fact a mere fantasy: the urban collaboration of these groups was based upon no ancient totemic affinity but rather on the fact that they all traveled along the northeastern route to Salisbury.

What seems to have been going on with the emergence of African boxing was an exercise of adaptive creativity on the part of urban Africans. The whole story is one that illustrates not only the many different senses in which the idea of social control could be developed, but also the impossibility of imposing total social control in any of these senses. As Frederick Cooper writes in his splendid introduction to *Struggle for the City:*

> Colonial officials, mining companies, and railway administrators built their cities, mines and workshops, but not as they would have liked. The kind of society that emerged was not a natural derivative of a social category known as urban. . . . What the planners had to face was not merely the mobilization of labor power, but the control of human beings, of people living in societies and immersed in cultures. As workers sought to shape their lives as individuals and as members of collectivities, they too shaped the life of the city.[50]

The African boxers of Salisbury can be linked with Cooper's female brewers of illicit beer, and with their customers, as shapers of "an urban culture that was antithetical to hard work, that accepted forms of conduct that the state defined as criminal, and whose very cultural separateness made it at least a potential base for political organization."

Notes

1. Secretary-General, British Social Hygiene Council, to Secretary for Native Affairs, Salisbury, 23 December 1938, file S.1542.S.12, 1936–1939, National Archives, Harare, Zimbabwe (hereafter NAZ).

2. Douglas Pelly to his parents, 8 November 1895, file PE 3/1/1, NAZ.

3. Belinda Bozzoli, "Introduction: History, Experience and Culture," in *Town and Countryside in the Transvaal* (Johannesburg, 1983), pp. 21–22. Bozzoli cites a chapter in this book by Tim Couzens, "An Introduction to the History of Football in South Africa." She also cites an earlier paper by Couzens, "Moralising Leisure-Time: The Transatlantic Connection and Black Johannesburg, 1918–36," in S. Marks and R. Rathbone, eds., *Industrialisation and Social Change in South Africa: African Class, Culture and Consciousness, 1870–1930* (London, 1982).

For other treatments of the social history of sport in South Africa see: Paul la Hausse, "The Struggle for the City: Alcohol, the Ematshini and Popular Culture in Durban, 1902–1936," History Workshop, University of the Witwatersrand, January–February 1984; and Robert Archer and Antoine Bouillon, *The South African Game* (London, 1982).

4. The most striking published exception, which also makes some very interesting remarks about African boxing, is Charles van Onselen and Ian Phimister, "The Political Economy of Tribal Animosity: A Case Study of the 1929 Bulawayo 'Faction Fight,'" *Journal of Southern African Studies* (October 1979). Stephen Thornton's work on the history of the African population of Bulawayo, when completed and published, will provide an essential context for studies of sport in that city. A doctoral dissertation is now under way on the history of Salisbury.

5. Terms of reference, Native Affairs Commission, Salisbury Municipal Location, file S.85, NAZ.

6. Report of Native Affairs Commission, Salisbury Municipal Location, file S.86, NAZ.

211

7. Evidence of A. E. Horne, 5 December 1930, S.85, NAZ.

8. Evidence of F. Noble, 5 December 1930 and C. N. Soul, 8 December 1930, S.85, NAZ.

9. Evidence of J. R.Muketsi, 6 December 1930, S.85, NAZ.

10. Evidence of Southern Rhodesia Native Association, 11 December 1930. The members of the delegation were B. Zata, Walter Chipwayo, I. T. Baminingo, C. Philip, Rusaro, and Amos Jakata.

11. Evidence of Town Clerk, 8 December 1930, S.85, NAZ.

12. Secretary, Native Affairs, Salisbury, to Secretary, United Council of Social Agencies, Durban, 3 January 1937, file S.1542.S.12, 1936–1939, NAZ.

13. Report by A. J. W. Wilkins, Medical Officer of Health, 12 January 1938, enclosed in Acting Town Clerk to Secretary, Native Affairs, 13 January 1938, ibid. A similar development took place at the same time in Bulawayo, where the new Welfare Officer taught part songs, table tennis, and checkers.

14. La Hausse, 4, 29.

15. Town Clerk, Durban to Native Welfare Officer, Salisbury, 19 May 1938, file S.1542.S.12, 1936–1939.

16. Acting Town Clerk, Benoni, to Native Welfare Officer, Salisbury, 30 May 1938; G. Ballenden, Non-European Housing and Native Administration Department, Johannesburg, to N.W.O., Salisbury, n.d., ibid.

17. Chief Compound Manager, Wankie, to Native Welfare Officer, Salisbury, 21 May 1938, ibid.

18. E. A. Cordell to Chief Native Commissioner, 13 June 1938, ibid.

19. Minutes of a Meeting Held at Office of Assistant Commissioner, British South Africa Police, 30 June 1938, ibid.

20. Town Clerk, Salisbury, to Hon. Secretary, Mashonaland Native Welfare Society, 27 October 1938, file LG 47/90, NAZ.

21. Chief Native Commissioner to Secretary, Premier, 23 July 1938, file S.1542.S.12, 1936–1939, NAZ.

22. Chief Native Commissioner to Hon. Secretary, Native Welfare Society of Matabeleland, 15 August 1939, ibid.

23. Letter from Stanlake Magorimbo, *Bantu Mirror,* 29 November 1927: 7, cited in Griff Foley, "Education and Social Change in Zimbabwe, 1890 to 1962," Ph.D. dissertation, University of Sydney, 1984, 330.

24. American Methodist Episcopal Church, *Official Journal* (1931): 32.

25. *Director of Native Education's Report,* 1928, 33, cited in Foley, 243.

26. Hugh Tracey to Chief Native Commissioner, 24 June 1930, file S.138.10, 1929–1930, NAZ.

27. Hugh Tracey's circular letter, 12 October 1931, file S.138.10, 1930–1933, NAZ. Tracey thought it necessary to "consciously dissociate" the decoration of a pot from the business of pot-making so as to create a distinct African aesthetic. The chief native commissioner backed Tracey's exhibition, asking all native commissioners to acquire objects to display.

28. Hugh Tracey, "African Music—A Modern View," *NADA* 19 (1942).

29. Hugh Tracey, "Native Dancing—A Wasted Asset," *NADA* 17 (1940).

30. Roger Howman to Secretary, Native Affairs, 29 June 1939, file S.1542.S.12, 1936–1939, NAZ.

31. Chief Native Commissioner to Commissioner of Police, Salisbury, 15 July 1938, ibid.

32. C. N. C. to Superintendent of Natives, Salisbury, 22 July 1938, ibid.

33. C. N. C. to Staff Officer, British South Africa Police, Salisbury, 17 November 1938, ibid.

34. Superintendent, BSAP, Salisbury Town, to Chief Superintendent, BSAP, Salisbury, 13 July 1938, ibid.

35. Constable B. S. Cowling to Sergeant, BSAP, Salisbury Town, 29 June 1938, ibid.

36. Constable G. P. Cochrane to Inspector in Charge, Salisbury Town, 3 July 1938, ibid.

37. Native Commissioner, Salisbury to C. N. C., 6 July 1938, ibid.

38. Reports by Cowling and Cochrane, 29 June and 3 July 1938, ibid.

39. Native Commissioner, Salisbury to C. N. C., 6 July 1938, ibid.

40. Superintendent, BSAP, Salisbury Town to Chief Superintendent, Salisbury, 13 July 1938, ibid.

41. E. A. Cordell, Report, 25 July 1938, ibid.

42. Native Commissioner, Salisbury to C. N. C., 15 November 1938, ibid.

43. Secretary, Native Affairs to Town Clerks, Bulawayo and Salisbury, 24 August 1938, ibid.

44. Town Clerk, Salisbury to Secretary, Native Affairs, 27 October 1938, file LG 47/90, NAZ.

45. Joy Maclean, *The Guardians* (Bulawayo, 1974), 243.

46. Roger Howman to C. N. C., 28 August 1938, S.1542.S.12, 1936–1939.

47. Ibid. In view of the current preeminence of students of the School of Oriental and African Studies in London in the historiography of the black working class in South Africa it is interesting to note that Howman found "no hint that the School had any practical use to us here; highly academic and mainly linguistic."

48. Roger Howman to C. N. C., 29 June 1939, ibid.

49. For Blake Thompson's unreliable speculations see Terence Ranger, "The Mobilisation of Labour and the Production of Knowledge: The Antiquarian Tradition in Rhodesia," *Journal of African History* 20 (1979): 507–24.

50. Frederick Cooper, "Introduction," *Struggle for The City: Migrant Labor, Capital and the State in Urban Africa* (London, 1983), 7–8.

PART THREE

CONTEMPORARY TRENDS

9

Africa's Triple Heritage of Play: Reflections on the Gender Gap

ALI A. MAZRUI

Sport is always linked to broader cultural and sociological forces. In Africa the links are to indigenous culture on the one hand, and to imported culture on the other. Race, class, and religion have all influenced African sport. So have sex and gender. But underlying all these factors is Africa's triple heritage of cultures. Indigenous traditions, Islamic ways, and Western practices have worked in tandem to shape the history of sport in Africa.

The Arabs once served to transmit the civilization of ancient Greece to medieval Europe. The works of scholars were translated into Arabic and studied in the academies of the Muslim world—from Damascus to Timbuktu, from the courts of the Moghul emperors in India to Al-Azhar University in Cairo, from Baghdad in Iraq to Al-Hambra in Spain. The rest of Europe paid some attention and learned about Plato and Socrates from Arab scholars. One aspect of ancient Greece that the Arabs did little to promote or transmit, however, was the field of sports and athletics—the legacy of the Olympic games.

Islamic civilization was too earnest to incorporate a subculture of leisure. The arts of relaxation and entertainment have survived in spite of Islam rather than because of it. In the Arab world, love songs and romantic music are barely tolerated. Moreover, the stringent Islamic rules of dress even for men, let alone for women, have hampered the development of athletics in much of the Muslim world. Exposed knees are considered a form of nakedness, and wearing shorts in a public arena is a violation of the moral code of dress. The code for female attire is even stricter, making the training of sportswomen or female athletes exceptionally difficult in much of the Muslim world.

Another Islamic factor that has militated against the development of sports is opposition to *maysir*, or games of chance. The commercialization of sports in Islam has been hindered by the *Shari'a*'s discouragement of profit-making on the basis of chance and speculation. At first the *Shari'a* (Islamic law) outlawed betting on races and other sports traditionally associated with gambling. But even less obvious forms of "speculation" such as rewarding a victor in a boxing bout have been frowned upon by Islamic law. This has slowed down the expansion of sports by curtailing their commercialization and has reduced the resources available for training, promotion, attraction of new talent, and general enhancement of sports as a social activity. Even the winning of prizes in a game can come close to being *maysir*.

Another debilitating factor is the nature of Islamic education, which in most Muslim societies refrains from mixing athletic training with organized leisure. The idea of school or college sports programs does not sit comfortably with the concept of a Qur'anic (Koranic) school or Muslim academy. Muslim children attending Islamic institutions have to regard the school as something entirely different from leisure. Muslim schools are centers for the promotion of morality, versatility in reciting the *Qur'an,* and general competence in religious studies. School sports are part of the Western tradition, not of the Qur'anic legacy.

The fast of Ramadan is yet another feature of Islam working against systematic training in sports. On the one hand, the fast is a discipline in consumption—an abstinence from food, liquid, smoking, and sex from before dawn until sunset each day during the whole month of Ramadan—that makes for fitness as well as restraint. In terms of weight management, most Muslims emerge slimmer from Ramadan than when they entered the fast, potentially more fit for sporting effectiveness. What is dysfunctional is its debilitating impact while it is actually going on. With neither water or food, many Muslims feel drained and short of energy during the whole of Ramadan. *"Leo saumu ni kali kweli kweli"* ("Today the fast is truly ferocious"). This is a common topic of conversation during Ramadan in the Swahili world. How draining is today's fast as compared with yesterday's! While general productivity declines, tempers usually run short.

Fatigue and irritability engendered by the fast are debilitating factors in competitive sports. Moreover, as Islamic believers are required to spend more time in mosques during Ramadan, and to avoid "frivolous" pastimes during the day, there is a basic incompatibility between the demands of the fast and the requirements of sporting effectiveness. As a result, most daytime sports cease during Ramadan.

Yet some minor nighttime games do flourish in parts of Muslim Africa during the fasting month. Certain games of cards prosper along the East African coast from about 10:00 P.M. to midnight. The games are played in teams, with no betting allowed. *Maysir* is more taboo than ever during Ramadan. Competitive card-playing is therefore purely for pleasure and not for gain—to kill time while believers await the last meal of the night after midnight following the last prayer during Ramadan, *taraweh*. The card games along the East African coast are a triple heritage par excellence. The cards are the usual imported Western packs. The games are primarily indigenous to the East African coast. The season for these particular games is almost exclusively the Islamic fasting month of Ramadan in the evening.

In the rest of the Muslim calendar there are more substantive sports, which Islam has helped to foster in Africa. The most colorful are connected with animals. In northern Nigeria the horse is used not only as a beast of burden but also as a sporting animal. Polo is a highly developed sport among the Islamic emirates of the north. In the Horn of Africa the camel is used not only for milk and transportation but also for some kinds of entertainment, including informal camel races. In summary, however, the Islamic impact on sport has often been negative, ambiguous at best.

Nor has the Western impact on African sport and play been homogeneous or monolithic. Some games are specific to particular colonial powers. Cricket, for example, is almost exclusively associated with countries once ruled by Great Britain. What is more, Africa's cricket is also race-specific. It has failed to capture the imagination of black Africans, while immigrant Asians as well as immigrant whites have embraced it as one of their favorite sports. Also race-specific is the game of hockey in Africa. Where it is played at all, it tends to be dominated by citizens of southern Asian ancestry (the Indian subcontinent).

Some games are class-specific. Lawn tennis and golf are monopolized by the new middle classes of Africa, regardless of race. But class in Africa is sometimes culturally rather than economically defined. Immersion into the new conquering culture of the West can change a person's status and class affiliation. Some imported sports are *culture-intensive*. One has to be substantially Westernized before one can be attracted to the sport of lawn tennis, for example. Soccer, on the other hand, is largely *culture-neutral*. The majority of African soccer players are minimally or not at all Westernized. Rugby seems to demand much greater Westernization than soccer.

Some colonial powers emphasized acculturation more than others. France especially pursued policies of intensive assimilation of colonial subjects. In the French-speaking part of Cameroon the elite is more attracted to culture-intensive games than in English-speaking Cameroon.

Sports generally have a more institutionalized place in British-style educational establishments than they have in French-style schools. One possible result is the greater Anglophone African success in the Olympic games, particularly when compared to Francophone Africans from south of the Sahara. The great African Olympic heroes have come disproportionately from countries like Kenya, Tanzania, Nigeria, and (only partially Anglophone) Ethiopia. The 1984 Olympic Games in Los Angeles produced less impressive African results than in the past, but even at Los Angeles it was primarily to Anglophone Africans that the black continent looked anxiously for one or two triumphs.

Linked to this issue of comparative colonial legacies in sport is the fact that the Francophone world has no real equivalent of the Commonwealth Games, those large-scale gatherings in which countries previously ruled by Britain test out each others' athletic skills. The Commonwealth Games are often a kind of rehearsal for the Olympic Games. Unfortunately, from this point of view, the French Empire was not as large or diverse as the British Empire. Francophone Africans are therefore not afforded a comparable preparation for the Olympics, although all independent African countries do participate in the inter-African games.

French-speaking Africans north of the Sahara have a different history, uniquely affected by both Islam and the Mediterranean world across the centuries. Morocco even managed to produce a woman gold medal winner in Los Angeles in 1984, despite the normally inhibiting effect of Islam on public performance by women.

In Africa as a whole, women are underrepresented both in culture-intensive imported sports such as lawn tennis and golf and in culture-neutral sports such as sprinting, long-distance running, and high jumping. The reasons for female underrepresentation in the two types of activities overlap but are not identical. The culture-intensive imported sports are elite-specific. Some African women are Westernized, of course, but in general the level of Westernization is still more pronounced among African males than among females. Culture-neutral games, on the other hand, are affected by the comparative degrees of competitiveness among African men and women. In order to explain these differences—and to consider the larger question of why African women have been almost as underrepresented in public sporting activities as have their Muslim counterparts elsewhere in the world—we need to look first at the relationship between sports and work, then at sports and sexuality, and finally at sports and war.

There is an assumption that the chivalry that protects women from heavy physical labor also prevents them from developing sporting physical skills. This assumption may make some sense in the Muslim world where, comparatively speaking, women are both spared physical labor and denied physical skills. But in much of black Africa this is simply not true. Black African women often do more physical work than their men. In some African societies women walk longer distances, carry heavier loads, and have to learn a greater variety of balancing skills than their men. So if the culture of work does indeed help to condition the culture of sports, and if African women can be so "physical" in their economic activities on the land, then why have they been so slow in excelling in the physical world of sports?

One reason may be that decision makers in Africa have been encouraging the wrong kind of sports. Perhaps more attention should be paid to the possibility of promoting marathon walks as a major sporting activity in

Africa. Children begin to walk long distances to school quite early, and women have been walking longer and longer distances for diminishing supplies of firewood and water. The whole tradition of long-distance walking could be used to detect talent and to structure new patterns of competitive sports. The very chores of collecting firewood could be given a new enthusiasm and liveliness as they are purposefully linked to training young girls for competitive walking.

Weight lifting could also be more systematically promoted among African women as well as men. In rural Africa one continues to be astonished by the enormous bundles of firewood on the backs of women walking long distances. Huge baskets of farm produce may be balanced on their heads at the same time. Such women are, of course, too busy to enter into sports. But rural culture would find new levels of animation if these simple chores were given greater value—and prizes were awarded to young men and women who excel in purposeful weight lifting and graceful carriage.

Indeed, graceful carriage and balancing skills could be developed into more than one sport. Familiar is the sight of an African woman with a sleeping baby tied securely on her back, a big basinful of water balanced on her head, and both hands busy elsewhere carrying baskets of fruit or cassava. She walks toward home with a deceptive sense of ease. Again those skills could be rewarded in leisure as well as exploited in labor, thus to be developed and integrated within a sporting culture.

But the purpose of this integration of work culture and sport culture could not simply be to give women greater access to new competitive games. The purpose should also be to encourage men to share the chores that were previously reserved exclusively for women. Skills of collecting, bundling, lifting, and carrying firewood gracefully should be cultivated among young men as well as young women. Turning these skills into proud competitive feats of triumph and honor would help to give them greater respectability as forms of work as well as forms of play. These new games of weight lifting, purposeful and balanced carriage, and long-distance walking could simultaneously turn women into proud champions and lead men into honorable chores.[1]

As for the linkage between work culture and sporting culture, it could itself become an honorable form of professionalization. The Olympic movement has long resisted—perhaps understandably—the idea of turning sports into a profession. The proposed new rural games for Africa are, in a sense, intended to turn rural professions into sports—an inversion of this position. The rural necessities of farming, herding, collecting firewood, and long-distance walking for pasture or water are all potential material for imaginative minds to help relieve the tedium of labor and to androgynize the heritage of sports. While the Olympic movement continues to frown upon the idea of turning sports into a livelihood, what is recommended here is the inverse process of turning work into sport—and narrowing the gender gap in both work and play as a result.

In addition to work, the aesthetics of sexuality relates to the question of African women in sports. What makes a woman physically attractive to men in Africa? If the measure of sexual attractiveness is fatness and the measure of fitness is slimness, then we have a wide *sexercise gap*. The sexercise gap is the gulf between criteria of sexual beauty and criteria of sporting competence.

In most traditional African societies, the sexercise gap for women was wide. Putting on weight was part of the process of acquiring elegance and poise. For example, among the Fante of southeastern Ghana and among the people of the Rivers State of Nigeria, an institution called the "fattening ceremony" has traditionally been specifically designed to enlarge the female's hips and behind. Paul Crispin reminds us of the issue in the past tense, but in fact these aesthetics are still very much alive. Says Crispin:

> Body adornment in Africa has gained varying emphasis depending on the ethnic symbols or aesthetic dimensions of the people. . . . It is particularly fascinating that the muscular development of the whole body is a sign of health and wealth. . . . Many years ago, before it became the fashion to trim down to scientific streamlining like 36-26-36 or 25-20-25, it used to be the pride of a man in the village to exhibit his "fat" stately, elegant wife who responded to the admiration of visitors by gorgeous royal slow steps delicately shifting the behind rhythmically from left to right with supple, well-nourished hands flexibly swaying from side to side to complete the picture of "the wife of a well to do man."[2]

In spite of his own claim that "those times have virtually passed," Crispin goes on to tell us about the "fattening ceremony" still practiced by the people of Calabar in eastern Nigeria. There the fattening process occurs in December or January and can last for a whole year or a year and a half. The ceremony is for adolescent girls between fifteen and eighteen years of age. Apart from getting a special diet, they are also taught traditional etiquette, manners, and the sex roles of the society.

In addition to these fattening ceremonies before marriage, Crispin tells us about a special type of fattening for girls who are regarded as "sickly or feeble." This ceremony is called the *Nkuho-Eket*. The girl's peers, fellow female teenagers, serve her certain foods in her special secluded room under the supervision of an elderly woman. The feebleness is supposedly conquered when the girl shows signs of responding positively to the "fattening process."[3]

The principle of big buttocks as a sexual asset for a woman is more widespread than just in Calabar. It is a standard preference in most parts of black Africa. In Nigerian humor, the term *bottom power* refers to the sexual tricks that a woman can play to get her own way. Sometimes the idea of bottom power is virtually the equivalent of a woman's sex appeal.

The demands of athletic prowess require a trimming down of bottom power and a more commensurate balance between weight and height. The athletics of weight are in conflict with the aesthetics of sex, and the resulting *sexercise ratio* is wide.

Islam has had a similar effect on the sexercise ratio, but less directly. By separating women from hard physical labor and confining most of them to the home, conservative versions of Islam have encouraged de facto fattening of women from an early age. Although bottom power might not be an aspect of Islamic aesthetics per se, the limited exposure of conservative Muslim women to either physical exercise or physical labor has resulted in declining standards of fitness among them.

Only in the third—Western—legacy of our triple heritage is the sexercise gap narrowed. In the Western tradition, slimness is a measure of both sexual appeal and physical fitness. The struggle to be athletically fit does not contradict the struggle to be sexually attractive. Athletics and aesthetics are fused; the vital statistics of the Olympiad are compatible with those of Venus.

In reality Westernized African women are less likely to be involved in hard physical labor than women in traditional indigenous roles. Traditional women are more likely to walk long distances for water and firewood and are more likely to be involved in digging and tilling. Yet Westernized women watch their weight a little more closely and are more likely to mix with Westernized men, whose aesthetics of sex have been modified by European values of slimness. Traditional rural women are probably more fit in terms of daily exercise than are their urbanized sisters, but rural folk are less informed about hygiene and have less access to modern medicine than do the Westernized sophisticates.

So the contradictions of the triple heritage continue to play havoc with both aesthetic standards and athletic measurements, with the lure of beauty and the temptations of sporting achievement, with the dialectic between the gold medal of sports and the gold bangle of adornment. In Africa these contradictions have tended largely to exclude women from competitive sports.

Even more fundamental in the marginalization of women in African sports is the divorce between women and both the warrior tradition of indigenous Africa and the *jihad* tradition of Islam. Perhaps more brilliantly than anyone else, the Dutch historian and philologist Johan Huizinga linked play with warfare in human history and regarded the play element as the dominant force in human culture. Like most theorists who focus on a dominant theme as an explanation of the direction of world history, Huizinga exposed himself to the inevitable charge of reductionism. In that, he was in the company of Karl Marx with his focus on economics, Jeremy Bentham with his avoidance-of-pain principle, and Sigmund Freud with his emphasis on sex. But like his fellow reductionists, Huizinga put his finger on an important factor in human behavior. There is indeed a significant historical and cultural link between play, warfare, and civilization itself.[4]

According to Huizinga, civilization has advanced through struggle, and that struggle has had to be subjected, in time, to certain "rules of the game." The history of the duel in Western culture and of the samurai in Japanese culture might be closely linked both to the history of boxing in twentieth-century sports and to the Geneva Convention's code concerning the treatment of prisoners of war:

> Most of the tales we hear of noble battles in beautiful styles are based . . . [on] heroic and romantic fiction. . . . Nevertheless, it would be wrong to conclude that this ennobling of war by viewing it in the light of ethics and aesthetics is but a "fair seeming," or cruelty in disguise. Even if it were no more than fiction, these fancies of war as a noble game of honour and virtue have still played an important part in developing civilization, for it is from them that the idea of chivalry became one of the great stimulants of medieval civilization, and however constantly the ideal was belied in reality, it served as the basis for international law, which is one of the indispensable safeguards for the community of mankind.[5]

But the rules of war quite early began to treat women as fundamentally different from men. Indeed, medieval chivalry in Europe idealized the woman as an object for gallant protection and honorable defense. The origins of sexism in culture go back farther than the days of European knights in armor, but the fundamental cause of sexism may still be linked to the division of labor, which armed men and turned women into objects for gallant protection by them. Huizinga detected a partially equalizing trend in the history of war and in the evolution of the rules of combat:

> We can only speak of war as a cultural function so long as it is waged within a sphere whose members regard each other as equals or antagonists with equal rights; in other words, its cultural function depends on its play-quality. This condition changes as soon as war is waged outside the sphere of equals, against groups not recognized as human beings and thus deprived of human rights—barbarians, devils, heathens, heretics and "lesser breeds without the law."[6]

Huizinga was correct as far as he went. European colonization of India, Algeria, or Swaziland was not regarded as "aggression"—but Hitler's invasion of Poland was. As the great Victorian liberal, John Stuart Mill, once put it, there is a great difference between the case in which nations concerned are of the same, or something like the same, degree of civilization, and that in which one of the parties to the situation is of a high, and the other of a very low, grade of social improvement. . . . To characterize any conduct towards the barbarous people as a violation of the Law of Nations only shows that he who speaks has never considered the subject.[7]

War and its rules did indeed create a measure of egalitarianism among European members of the community of nations, but the equality did not extend to the "barbarians" of Asia and Africa. What Huizinga, and to some extent Mill, considered inadequately was the disequalizing tendency of war in male-female relations even within European societies themselves. The ethos of armed men and protected women was the most persistent and most primordial of all forms of stratification. Women became marginalized not because they lost control of the means of production but because they were excluded from the means of destruction. Nothing in human history has been more responsible for the political subordination of women than their demilitarization.

In Africa and the Muslim world, that demilitarization took the form of exclusion from the warrior and *jihad* traditions. In one society after another, the fighters were the sons—and almost never the daughters. Given the link between sports and warfare, and given the separation of women from warfare, it stood to reason that women should also be excluded from the more demanding sporting endeavors. The absence of women on the battlefield meant the absence of women in the gladiator's arena, resulting in the diminution of womanhood as sporting material generally. The taxing physical exertions of war were supposed to be partially reproduced in the physical exertions of sporting combat. If women were ineligible for the former, why should they be fit for the latter? In Britain, such calculations led to the exclusion of women from rugby, soccer, and even cricket. In the United States, it kept women out of football as well as baseball.

Similar trends have been present throughout African history. Apart from occasional exceptions such as precolonial Dahomey with its Brigade of Amazons, the warrior tradition in Africa has been heavily masculine. Young boys have been initiated into warrior virtues of valor and endurance. In many cultures initiation into manhood and initiation into warrior status have been indistinguishable. The cultures that practice male circumcision have linked at times the symbolism of sexual prowess with the symbolism of the burning spear. The sexual virility of the male has been part of his armory of martial valor.

It is against this background of the masculinity of the warrior and *jihad* traditions that we have to understand the masculinity of the game of polo among the Hausa-Fulani in northern Nigeria, the masculinity of the bullfight on Pemba Island off the coast of Tanzania, and the masculinity of *tigil*, the Ethiopian form of wrestling. Says one account:

> In the countryside, the young males are paired off more or less according to age and strength; sometimes within a village, but more often one village against another. . . . Fights are usually held near a village after the harvest and the stacking of the grain, but before the threshing and winnowing. . . . The contestants are clothed in white breeches and tunics, with bare feet.[8]

Even more colorful are Ethiopian games involving horse riding. Horses may have been imported into Ethiopia by the "Oromo tribes." Oromo successes eventually convinced highland Ethiopians of the military value of horses. In time horses in Ethiopia were used mainly for battle and more rarely as beasts of burden. Donkeys and mules served the latter purpose. The third major use of horses (after carriage and combat) was for sport and entertainment. Particularly colorful is the *Feres Gugs* game:

> The game of gugs is based on warfare, but where a cavalryman carried two spears, a light one for throwing, and a heavier job for infighting, the gouks [gugs] player uses only light wood wands. The object is for members of one team to gallop off followed by the others who are supposed to hit them with their wands, either by hurling at them or by catching up and hitting them. Those being pursued are protected with traditional circular shields in hippo or rhinoceros hide, some covered with coloured velvet and decorated with gold and silver. As they tear away across the plain, they may dodge, hang off the horse or ward off with the shield. The riders are often in traditional costume, or at any rate the cloak and gold-fringed lion or baboon headdress!![9]

Horse-riding games and skilled horsemanship in Ethiopia are forms of sport that carry heavy martial associations. Precisely because of that, they are also games of high masculine profile.

It is one of the more curious gaps in African sport that archery has not evolved into a major form of entertainment. One reason may be that bows and arrows are still part of the technology of hunting and defense in parts of Africa, and people are self-conscious about converting them into skills of entertainment. The African Westernized elites are often embarrassed by the bow and arrow as an illustration of Africa's "primitive" technology. These elites frequently decide which sports should be promoted in their countries. Archery—though an activity in which Africans could excel internationally—is therefore carefully relegated to oblivion by the urban sophisticates.

Spear throwing, on the other hand, has managed to survive as a form of entertainment in countries like Zaire and Uganda. The competition in spear throwing is not usually based on aim and marksmanship but on strength, velocity and distance of throw. The game is still highly localized and has yet to become pan-Africanized. Indeed, the chances of its becoming an international sport between African countries are slim. In any case, such games exude masculine exclusivity, partly because they are based on the metaphor of war.

Wrestling is a more institutionalized and more widespread game in Africa. Among Ethiopians and the Nubians of upper Egypt and the Sudan, the arts of wrestling are centuries old. More recently, wrestling has acquired a new value in the Gambia and Senegal, partly in response to tourist curiosity. But what has persisted throughout history and throughout much of Africa, with few exceptions, is the obstinate masculinity of wrestling.

Boxing came to Africa with colonization, linking with indigenous culture through the tradition of wrestling. Once again, since boxing was a *fight*, it was implicitly a bridge between the culture of war and the culture of play. No African has symbolized this connection better than Idi Amin. Long before he became Uganda's president, Amin reigned for nine years as the nation's heavyweight boxing champion. In his simultaneous rise to pugilistic fame and to prominence within the Kings' African Rifles under British rule, he certainly combined the skills of play with martial qualities. In the words of David Martin,

> . . . he was the type of material the British officer liked in the ranks—physically large at six feet four inches and uneducated. The theory was that material of this type responded better to orders and were braver in battle. He endeared himself to his commanders by becoming the Ugandan heavyweight boxing champion . . . and by taking up rugby, where even if his skills were limited, his weight as a second row forward was a valuable contribution.[10]

Boxing has remained at once an arena of triumph for black people and an area of exclusion for all women. By helping blacks to achieve wealth and admiration, boxing has been a weapon against racism. But by being also the most masculine and one of the most financially lucrative of all sports, boxing has been a brutal symbol of sexism. The cause of racial equality has gained through black triumphs in the ring, but the cause of sexual equality has lost through the masculine orientation of this combative sport.

Recently, women have argued that much of their relative inferiority in sports is, as with other handicaps sustained by them, an outcome of conditioning over a long period of time. If black people excel in athletics and boxing partly because they have been socially underprivileged, women have rarely performed in athletics and perhaps never in boxing. The black man has asserted superiority in select areas of athletic performance in response to handicaps in other domains; the woman has exhibited inferiority in some of those same areas partly out of a broader closure imposed by society on women's participation in those fields.

While the *jihad* legacy reinforces the warrior tradition of indigenous Africa, the continent's triple heritage of cultures works dialectically to improve the prospects of African sportswomen. Islam and African culture sometimes fuse and sometimes recoil from each other, only to turn around and confront the powerful sporting forces of the Western world in which women athletes are increasingly encouraged and honored. The whistle has sounded. The match between cultures has begun.

Notes

1. The literature on women in Africa is now diverse and wide-ranging. Some of the more interesting works include Christine Obbo, *African Women* (London: Zed Press, 1980); Christine Oppong, ed., *Female and Male in West Africa* (London: George Allen and Unwin, 1983); Marjorie Hall and Bakhita Amin Ismail, *Sisters under the Sun: The Story of Sudanese Women* (Harlow, England: Longman, 1981); Stephanie Urdang, *Fighting Two Colonialisms: Women in Guinea-Bissau* (New York: Monthly Review Press, 1979); Nina Emma Mba, *Nigerian Women Mobilized: Women's Political Activity in Southern Nigeria, 1900–1965* (Berkeley, Cal.: University of California Institute of International Studies, 1982); H. J. Simons, *African Women* (London: C. Hurst, 1968); Nici Nelson, eds., *African Women in the Development Process* (London: Franc Cass, 1981); J. Goodwin, *Cry Amandla: South African Women and the Question of Power* (New York: Africana Publishing, 1984); Organization of Angolan Women, *Angolan Women: Building from National Liberation to Women's Emancipation* (London: Zed Press, 1984); A. Richards, *Chisungu: A Girl's Initiation Ceremony among the Bemba of Zambia* (London: Tavistock, 1982); Cherryl Walker, *Women and Resistance in South Africa* (London: Onyx Press, 1982); C. C. Robertson, *Sharing the Same Bowl: A Socioeconomic History of Women and Class in Accra, Ghana* (Bloomington: Indiana University Press, 1984); and Margaret Strobel, *Muslim Women in Mombasa, 1890–1975* (New Haven: Yale University Press, 1979).

2. Paul Crispin, "The Essence of Fattening," *The Democrat Weekly,* Lagos, Nigeria, 29 July 1984.

3. Ibid., 3.

4. Johan Huizinga, *Homo Ludens: A Study of the Play Element in Culture* (1949; reprint London: Granada Publishing Ltd., 1971).

5. Ibid., 117.

6. Ibid., 110–11.

7. J. S. Mill, "A Few Words on Non-Intervention," in *Dissertations and Discussions,* (London, 1967), III, 153–58.

8. *Ethiopian Festivals* (Addis Ababa: Ethiopian Tourism Commission, 1982), 15.

9. Ibid., 8. This author was a member of a BBC television team that filmed *Feres Gugs* in Addis Ababa early in 1984.

10. David Martin, *General Amin* (London: Faber and Faber, 1974), 15.

10

An Exceptional Case:
Politics and Sport in South Africa's Townships

ROBERT ARCHER

Sport in South Africa is distinctively politicized, to a degree rare in Africa or in other societies. For this, the laws and ideology of apartheid and the long tradition of social segregation in the country are largely responsible. Destined originally to preserve white control in the political and economic spheres, by gradual extension they have come to define, in essentially political terms, under what circumstances men and women may play sport with each other or engage in other social activities. The general rule is that interracial relations are discouraged, or are even illegal, except under specific and defined circumstances. The policy of apartheid, or "separate development," is based upon racial criteria. Members of South African society are defined at birth, by administrative decision, as "White," "African," "Colored," or "Indian." The administration distinguishes several categories of "African" according to the tribes to which they are held to belong. Under the laws of apartheid, Africans are required to reside permanently in tribal reserves (called Bantustans). The legislation does not take account of where individuals have been brought up or born. Workers employed in urban areas under white administration must seek permission to remain in them and require a special pass if they wish to travel from one town to another or from the tribal reserve to which they have been allocated to any other part of South Africa. In recent years, some of the "reserves" have been granted "independence" within South Africa's borders: this is true of Venda, the Transkei, and Bophuthatswana. Some 70 percent of South Africans are African. Some 80 percent of South African territory has been allocated by the South African government to the white minority.

The Indian and Colored minorities are in a rather different position under the law. They are not required to carry passes and may travel in many (but not all) parts of the territory. They also have residence rights in urban areas that the South African government has attributed to whites. This is because it is implausible to describe either minority as a "nation." Indians and Coloreds may own private property in white areas. They have also been subject to relocation, however, on a scale only less massive than Africans.

Whole communities have been moved from one part to another of South African cities.

Since 1948, South Africa has been governed by the National Party, which is committed to a policy of separate development. The white minority enjoys complete political power and is divided broadly equally between English speakers descended from British colonial settlers and Afrikaans speakers, descended from Dutch emigrants who began to settle from the latter half of the seventeenth century. South Africa became a republic when it left the British Commonwealth in 1961. In recent years, the government has encouraged white emigrants from many countries to settle in the country.

The white minority has a similar monopoly of control over the economy. Black South Africans* are not permitted to hold jobs above certain levels of responsibility. In most cases, their opportunities are restricted to unskilled labor and clerical work. A plethora of laws governs the access of black South Africans to housing, transport, education, sports facilities, lavatories, hospitals, and playing fields.[1]

In one way or another, each of these laws hinders black sportsmen and -women, and Africans in particular, from playing with South Africans belonging to a different racial category. Thus Africans may not use white facilities without permission, may not travel to matches on the same buses as whites, Coloreds, or Indians, sometimes may not shower or change in the same rooms as others, and may not travel far at all without permission. In most instances, they also live very far away from the other communities. Indians, Coloreds, and whites, in contrast, are not permitted to travel into African townships without permission, and all four groups require permits of one kind or another if they wish to play together or watch matches together at public stadiums.[2]

The official declaration governing sports policy in South Africa is quoted below. It goes by the name of the "multinational policy," a term that suggests a degree of integration in sport (sometimes, in fact, government spokesmen have used it interchangeably with the terms "interracial" or "multiracial") while it also respects the principles of "separate development" that require that each racial category recognized by the government should play sport separately.

> The federal council accept that, taking into account the applicable legisla-
> tion and regulations, the interests of South Africa and all its people in
> respect of sport can best be served in terms of the following policy:

---

*In this chapter, the term *black* will refer to all those South Africans classified by the South African government as "African," "Colored," or "Indian." These and the term *white* are used because the organiza- tion and practice of sport in South Africa cannot be understood without reference to them.

1. That white, Coloured, Indian and black sportsmen and women should all belong to their own clubs and that each should control, arrange and manage its own sporting fixtures;

2. That wherever possible, practical and desirable, the committees or councils of the different race groups should consult together or have such contact as would advance the interests of the sport concerned;

3. That intergroup competition in respect of individual types of sport be allowed at all levels, should the controlling bodies so decide;

4. That in respect of team sports, the councils or committees of each racial group should arrange their own leagues or programmes within the racial group;

5. That where mutually agreed, councils or committees may, in consultation with the Minister of Sport, arrange leagues or matches enabling teams from different racial groups to compete;

6. That each racial group should arrange its own sporting relationships with other countries or sporting bodies in accordance with its own wishes and that each should award its own badges and colours;

7. That if and when invited or agreed, teams comprising players from all racial groups can represent South Africa, irrespective of whether the type of sport is an Olympic sport or not, and that such participants can be awarded badges or colours which, if so desired, can incorporate the national flag or its colours;

8. That attendance at sporting fixtures be arranged by the controlling bodies.[3]

The wording of the statement is instructive: it emphasizes the autonomy of sports organizations vis-à-vis the government. Such autonomy is in practice difficult to imagine. The government's commitment to apartheid means that it could be tolerated only among those organizations that share the same basic political outlook. What the language reflects and recognizes is that the issue of discrimination in sport is such that it restrains the government and official sports associations from acting as they have done in other areas like trade union rights, marital relations, etc. Sport is not, and cannot be, outside political life. At the same time, the egalitarian ideology of international sport, its preeminent role in the social life of white South Africans, and the effectiveness of the campaign to isolate South Africa's official sports federations because of their racial discrimination have together forced the government to modify the rigor of its policies and have obliged official sports federations to claim that they support multiracial, fully integrated organized sport. Under these circumstances, it has not been politically advisable for the South African government to ban nonracial unofficial sports associations that are publicly opposed to the ideology of separate development: unlike antiapartheid political parties these organizations have been able to organize and campaign publicly for the right to multiracial sport since the 1950s.

The reason for this is relatively simple and due to the fact that the constitutions of numerous international sports federations, including the International Olympic Committee, forbid discrimination on grounds of race, belief, or religion. Since apartheid is constructed around a racialist principle, it has been relatively easy for critics of apartheid to prove that official South African affiliates are in breach of their constitutional commitments, and should therefore be expelled or suspended from the international sporting associations to which they belong. The success of the campaign to isolate South African sport is largely attributable to the fact that international sport is constitutional and hierarchically centralized.[4]

The exclusion of South Africa from international competition in most of the major popular sports has presented a sensitive political problem for the South African government, because sport has such a central role in South African social life. On the one hand, the white electorate has objected to the curtailment of international sporting contacts and blamed government interference for the boycotts. On the other hand, real integration of sport would certainly have provoked an electoral backlash.[5] Organized adult sport in South Africa has traditionally centered around segregated urban and country clubs, which are social gathering places and centers of recreation as much as foci of strictly sporting activities; integration of these clubs would have far-reaching social and sexual implications, and this is one of the most important reasons why whites have been so resistant to "multinationalism" below the competitive level. (Thus the policy is careful to say that integration at club level will be left entirely to the discretion of club members, while mixed school sport is pointedly said to be undesirable.)

The nonracial federations are today grouped within the South African Council on Sport (SACOS), which adheres to the principles of the Olympic Charter and probably represents the majority of black sportsmen and -women in several major sports. Against them, the official sports associations recognized by government claim that under multinational rules, they no longer practice discrimination and, being independent of government control, are eligible to rejoin their international bodies. Both thus claim to be fighting for multiracial sport in South Africa. Both are in competition for the loyalty of black, particularly African, sportsmen and -women, who constitute the vast majority of the population. This political competition, itself made possible by the space for dissent created by the international boycott and the adherence of both sides to international principles, defines the ways in which black sportsmen and -women perceive and practice their sport.

Sport requires facilities: fields, courses, pools, tracks. Equally important, to be played successfully, sports require continuous collective practice and training. In South Africa, as elsewhere, organized sport has developed around and within organized social life. For the white minority, in these three areas—facilities, education, and social context—modern sport has had a relatively uninterrupted history of growth. Brought over by British settlers, by the end of the century most of the major games had established themselves, were played widely (though they did not all have the same popularity among British and Afrikaners), and had seeded clubs and provincial or national associations.[6] Modern sports rapidly generated their own histories and planted themselves deeply in the social consciousness and habits of the white minority: cricket particularly during the nineteenth century among all classes, rugby among Afrikaners, soccer in the working class. In 1980, 19.7 percent of the white minority regularly played competitive or recreative sport, which has broadly the same kinds of structures as in European society, including sizable commercial sponsorship, a sporting press, and a professional elite.[7]

This continuity cannot be found in the history of black sport, which, like black history in general during the twentieth century, can be written as one of relocation—the physical removal of Africans, and more generally black South Africans, from urban areas claimed by the white minority to undeveloped areas distant from the urban centers. Whereas white clubs, schools, and the communities they serve are today several generations old, very many of the sports facilities created by black sportsmen and -women over time have been physically alienated, while very few have received the constant injection of new resources over time that generates competitive skills and permits clubs to achieve high standards at all levels. It is of course true that, in general, athletes in developing countries rarely have access to the same training facilities as those in economically developed countries. It must be remembered, however, that in South Africa, the density of excellent facilities available to whites, the high competitive standards attained by white athletes, and above all the passion for sport that is a feature of South African society as a whole, have made blacks in the country particularly conscious of their lack of opportunities. South Africa is the only country that officially denies equality of opportunity to its citizens on grounds of race and is unique in applying this ideology in the field of sport.

People from all three black groups began playing modern sports soon after they were introduced into the country. Cricket began to be played during the first half of the nineteenth century, football (soccer) and rugby and most of the other major sports between 1880 and the turn of the century. Black provincial, and then national, federations in both cricket and rugby had been founded by the turn of the century.[8]

During the interwar period, and particularly from the 1930s, in the mining areas of the Witwatersrand football was adopted en masse. It replaced cricket as the most popular sport, and began to supplant tribal dancing as the most prominent form of organized physical expression in the

ROBERT ARCHER

mines. Both cricket—seen as an English game after the Imperial Cricket Conference was formed in 1901—and rugby, which Afrikaners came to see as their "national" game—had colonial connotations by this time. Football, in contrast, became the sport of both the white and black working class during the interwar years—one of the few real contacts between them. Henceforward, it dominated South African sport numerically.[9]

For obvious reasons, sports were originally disseminated through the schools and in urban areas where blacks came most directly into contact with the white way of life. For the small black elite, in fact, sport became a criterion of integration within the colonial world.[10] At the foundation of Fort Hare, one of the few educational institutions that offered Africans a university-level education, almost the first initiative taken by the students was to make a field for themselves,[11] and the mission colleges, like the mission schools at that period, attached some importance to the moral and social values inculcated by sport.

Because the Indian and Colored minorities were city communities, and because few Africans were in a position to acquire a good education or urban employment, Indian and Colored sportsmen and -women were disproportionately represented. This remains the case today. It would be wrong, however, to conclude that Africans were not interested in sport. The evidence is that wherever educated urban communities formed, sports associations soon followed and played a considerable role in social life. Within the sports clubs that flourished around Kimberley at the turn of the century, for example, African players and clubs competed with Colored teams within regional competitions,[12] and a reading of Mweli Scota's *Who's Who*—a compendium of the leisure interests and achievements of prominent Africans—reveals how many of South Africa's African elite of the 1920s measured social standing in terms of the practice of sport or membership of sports clubs.[13]

Among the working class, grouped around the mining areas, organized sport emerged rather later and was encouraged by the mining houses and churches. The mines on the Witwatersrand, and also the major state employers like the railways, promoted football and cricket teams and provided some facilities for use by their employees.[14]

The gradual solidification of segregation between the wars caused splits to occur within some of the associations that had a multiracial membership[15] and increasingly nullified the few attempts that were made by white liberal opinion to encourage mixed sport. However, by the 1940s, Inter-Race Boards had been created in a number of the major sports, which promoted interracial competition between African, Colored, and Indian teams, each organized separately within their respective national or regional associations. Sport was quite widely taught in black schools, and standards were in some instances remarkably high.[16] Predictably, little organized sport seems to have been played in the rural areas. If anything, the number of occasions on which white and black athletes competed against one another was diminishing, though it had never been common. The extensive research into African social life that was carried out by urban sociologists during the 1950s[17] showed that the adoption of sport at this time correlated rather clearly with the adoption of an urban way of life and served in many cases as a criterion of settlement for urban Africans. Teams were perceived to represent urban or alternatively rural or semirural groups, and nomination to office (as in many other countries!) often reflected social standing in the urban community rather than eminence as an athlete.[18] In general, even in the passing attention they give to sports associatons, these studies bring to life the variety and vigor of sporting activity in the townships during this period.[19]

In particular, they show that in spite of the crippling lack of equipment and the evident shortage of facilities,[20] participation and membership of clubs was extraordinarily high in areas where the opportunity to play organized sport existed. In 1955, nearly half the African men aged between fifteen and thirty years old who were questioned in one survey claimed to belong to the Gompo Rugby Football Union (African), and in Cape Town the proportion of urban residents who had some connection with sporting clubs in 1954 was only exceeded by membership of the churches.[21]

The intensity of interest and participation is the more remarkable in view of the shortages of facilities and the restrictions imposed on access to them. In the absence of a complete public survey, it is difficult to quantify the shortfall in facilities with any objectivity. Many fields are unofficial and have been created by occupying and leveling waste ground. Others, like some of those used by the nonracial associations, are not recognized by the administration. Moreover, the quality of the facilities is generally very low, and many of them are in multiple use. As an indication of the need, 1,180 amateur soccer teams in Soweto were reported to have had fewer than eighty grounds to play on, while in Langa in the Cape thirty-six football teams shared one enclosed stadium without floodlights or seats.[22]

The figures given for individual membership of clubs and participation of the different racial groups are similarly inadequate in that they do not include those in non-racial associations, or unregistered, "unofficial" sports, which are, of course, widespread in the African townships. The official figures for membership of sports associations in 1982 underestimate real participation, considerable in some sports.[23] A Human Sciences Research Council report in 1982 estimated that 3.4 percent of African men took part in organized, competitive sport, compared with 9.6 percent of Indians and 4.2 percent of Colored men; all three groups were much less involved than white males, 19.7 percent of whom played sport. This figure does not allow for the fact that black sport is concentrated in the towns and remains weak in the rural areas; or that many blacks play recreational sport. The report underlined the inequalities in the provision of facilities and found that white schools owned 72 percent of all school facilities in South Africa, while 23 percent of schools had no facilities whatsoever. Whites owned 73 percent of all tracks, 83 percent of swimming pools, and 82 percent of rugby pitches. Their facilities were also superior to the facilities in black areas.[24]

The intensity of use of many of the facilities is described below for a Colored area near Johannesburg in the 1960s. It is a description that could apply to many African townships:

> They had five football fields, four sand and one grass pitch, all of which had been cleared by the community. The matches would begin at 7 am with the Under-7's. An older child would referee and then he would play in his own team later on in the morning—and so it went on until late at night, when the top teams would have quite a large crowd supporting them. By that time the matches were floodlit. It was much the same in Soweto. The teams were organised by the children themselves who would ask an older man to train them—they organised themselves into leagues all the way up.[25]

Such intensive use degrades the facilities, which is a very serious problem, particularly in sports such as cricket, which require a fine surface.

From at least the 1930s, black sports associations began "squatting" land they needed for pitches to play football, rugby, golf, and other sports that can be played on rough terrain.[26] Other facilities were provided by the municipalities, by employers, and, in the Colored and Indian communities, which have had the right, unlike Africans, to own land in white areas, by private clubs.

This last restriction, making it illegal for Africans to own land in most of South Africa, and the laws preventing Africans from residing permanently in urban areas, have been major factors restricting the spread of sport among Africans compared to Indians and Coloreds. More specifically, the law has often been used at different times to reduce contacts between African sportsmen and -women and the nonracial associations.

In the process of resettlement, African clubs have frequently lost facilities they have developed. They have rarely been well compensated or offered alternative facilities on these occasions. As a result, it has been extremely difficult for African clubs and associations to invest in and improve their facilities over time. Frequent cases might be cited. The experience of the Durban and District (African) Football Association, which was one of the most solidly organized African associations of the period, offers one example:

> [It] would clear and prepare land and prepare grounds, only to be moved out again into the bush. A white official of the Native Recruiting Corpora-

tion, donating a trophy to the [D. and D.A.F] Association, commented
that the Native footballers had been booted out by the Durban Corpora-
tion from one football ground to another, from Western Vlei to Lord
Ground and from there to the Eastern Vlei, and that each time this
happened, Europeans or Indians followed to occupy the ground.[27]

A more recent example involved the well-known nonracial rugby club in
Port Elizabeth, which had great difficulty legalizing its occupation and
development of a site in New Brighton.[28]

Secondly, the law has meant that Africans have been dependent upon the
goodwill of the municipal authorities (or their employers in some cases) for
access to any fixed sports facilities. In contrast, Indian and Colored sports
associations have been able to maintain some autonomy and have been able,
to a much greater extent, to purchase and improve their facilities. Indeed,
the survival of the nonracial movement can be attributed partly to the ability
of the Indian and Colored associations to control their own facilities. This
fact also helps to explain why the nonracial movement is concentrated in the
Cape and Natal provinces.*

Conversely, in certain sports the dependence of Africans upon public
facilities has given them a competitive advantage. This is notably the case in
athletics. In recent years, the mine authorities have opened their outstanding
sports facilities to the best athletes among their black employees, and a
string of top-class African runners has emerged—all of whom are affiliated
with the official South African Amateur Athletics Union recognized by the
government. No top-class Colored or Indian athletes have emerged in
recent years: most belong to the nonracial South African Amateur Athletics
Board, which does not have access to or own good running facilities. Nor
does the nonracial body have access to the miners, almost all of whom are
African and physically separated from the wider urban communities in the
mining compounds. In other sports, such as rugby, the majority of Africans
who play at a competitive level also belong to mining, police, or army
clubs, or are employed by the administration. The nonracial associations are
denied access to the facilities of these organizations, which forbid their
employees to play for nonracial clubs.[29]

On several occasions, official sports federations have used the municipal
authorities' control over facilities in African areas to prevent African, Colored, and Indian sports associations from combining effectively in multiracial competitions. The tactic was used to greatest effect in the early 1960s,
at a time when the first nonracial federations were being created. During the
1950s, black sportsmen and -women were organized in separate national
associations for African, Colored and Indian teams, which competed with

*The great majority of Coloreds live in Cape Province and the great majority of Indians in Natal.

each other within Inter-Race Boards. Not all the racially titled black organizations were in practice racially exclusive. Some, like the Durban & District African Football Association or the Indian Weightlifting Association, took action against any discrimination among members.[30] From 1951, the Nationalist government began positive discrimination against visits by black athletes to South Africa, and in 1956 defined publicly for the first time how its apartheid policy was to be applied in sport.[31]

Soon afterward, led by the footballers, weight lifters and table tennis players, the black associations took steps to form a national association to represent them—the South African Sports Association (SASA, 1958)—and to form national associations in each discipline. As a further step, in 1963 SASA associations formed a subcommittee; the South African Non-Racial Olympic Committee (SAN-ROC), to lobby internationally for the expulsion of South African affiliates from their respective international sports authorities.[32]

The political implications of taking these steps become apparent when it is recalled that the period 1956–63 was among the most intense in South Africa's recent political history and saw the heights of passive resistance, the Sharpeville massacre, the pass-burning movement, the banning of South Africa's most representative black parties, the formation of an underground armed resistance, and the arrest of Nelson Mandela and other leaders of the African National Congress. By 1963, sport had become a political issue, and most of the officials within the nonracial movement had been harassed or forced into exile.[33]

The formation of national multiracial federations opposed to apartheid threatened not only the position of the official (at this time all-white) federations, but also South Africa's reputation abroad. Moreover, it was always possible that the nonracial federations would attract the support of all black players, thereby making the position of the white federations internationally untenable. In both tennis and football, for example, the nonracial federations at first included the majority of organized African as well as Indian and Colored players.

The white official federations, supported by the municipalities, responded by closing all public facilities to African players who played with Coloreds and Indians. As a result, the nonracial federations in both tennis and football split, and a majority of the African players—supported by the official white federation—broke off to form a new racial body, leaving the Indian and Colored clubs, whose facilities were at some distance from the African townships, to continue on their own.[34] Throughout the 1960s, as they do today, official bodies claimed that the nonracial movement was unrepresentative of African (or white) opinion, even though this sort of pressure, as well as the effects of apartheid, have made it impossible to obtain any objective assessment of how African sportsmen and -women would react if the latter controlled their own facilities and were free to choose how to use them.

In the early 1970s, the same tactic was used again, this time against teams affiliated to the nonracial South African Rugby Union (SARU); but interestingly, with far less success. After 1973, nonracial federations formed a new national association to represent them, the South African Council on Sport. The government had also formulated its own "multinational policy," and the official South African Rugby Board began organizing individual matches for African and for Colored sides against visiting touring teams. Partly under the influence of the Black Consciousness Movement, however, many African clubs that had been playing in the official African South African Rugby Association began crossing over to the SARU after 1970. South African Rugby Board officials, members of the government, and also some Bantustan authorities began withdrawing facilities from African players and teams that played in the nonracial league. Pressure of this kind continues against African affiliates of the nonracial associations, particularly in the Bantustans.[35]

SARU affiliates responded, however, by competing instead on makeshift fields. The SARU 1975 challenge cup final, for example, was played on waste ground before an estimated crowd of some twenty thousand spectators.[36]

Education played a most important role in the inculcation of sport, which, since the colonial period, has been emphasized in white schools. After the Nationalist party came to power, however, almost all the private and mission schools that had catered to African education were taken over by the state. Between 1953 and 1971 the number of mission schools fell from about 5,000 to 438, and finally, by 1977 to 132, a fall of 97 percent.[37] The new curriculum introduced by the government devalued African (and also Indian and Colored) education in the interests of separate development, which required Africans to be unskilled. It also removed most of the elements of organized sport and physical education.[38] As a result, few African children, and certainly not those in the Bantustans and rural areas, came into contact with sport at school.

The Colored and Indian experience differs again from the African in this respect. The Indian and Colored communities have retained the right to administer private schools, albeit under the close surveillance of the authorities. The curriculum has continued to include sport, with the result that many more Indian and Colored children acquire sporting skills at a young age than do Africans. Under these circumstances it is not surprising to find that Africans have excelled in sports that rely the least upon acquired skills and expensive technical aids. They dominate football, play good rugby, and one or two golfers and several track-and-field athletes of distinction have emerged; in contrast, there are virtually no top-class African cricketers and no competitive swimmers.

In the new high-technology sports, black sportsmen and -women are at a general disadvantage. It is interesting that in very many cases, the sports in which South Africa has organized recent international championships have been technically inaccessible to black South Africans—all-white for economic rather than explicitly racial reasons: model boating (1976), power boating (1976), tug-of-war (1976), surf riding (1978), model yachting (1978), radio-controlled model aerobatics (1979), etc.[39]

In general, it is remarkable that, given their handicaps, so many good black athletes have appeared in South Africa. Those who have achieved international recognition include Precious McKenzie (weight lifting), Jake Ntuli (boxing), Basil d'Oliveira (cricket), Moshwarateu and Sydney Maree (track and field), Papwa Sewgolum, Vincent Tshabalala (golf) and Errol Tobias (rugby). In general, their careers can be grouped into two periods, before and after 1961, when South Africa left the Commonwealth. Until 1961, it was possible for black South Africans to compete abroad as Commonwealth champions. After that date, they no longer had this alternative and were effectively prevented from competing internationally unless they agreed to do so under the auspices of the officially recognized South African association. Between 1961 and introduction of the "multinational policy," in fact, black athletes had no opportunity to compete at all, since they were not eligible to represent South Africa. Thus McKenzie, Ntuli, d'Oliveira, and a number of others only competed on a representative level abroad, within the structure of the Commonwealth Games or for another country, whereas Tshabalala, Tobias, and other modern athletes either accept the terms set by the official federation or do not travel at all.

The nonracial movement did much during the 1950s and 1960s to unite black sportsmen and -women around international sporting principles and within single national associations. This economized on expense, increased the quality and variety of competition, and maximized the use of very rare resources and facilities. To some degree, this process also helped to depersonalize sports administration, which often suffered from competition for high-ranking positions.[40]

The policies of the government since the 1960s and under "multinationalism" have tended the other way and have increased the number of different associations which, in one way or another, are responsible for the administration of sport.[41] The creation of numerous small, unrepresentative racial bodies has also often increased the influence of particular individuals. Current government policy has the effect of promoting professional and competitive black sport and the "stars" who play in it, at the expense of amateur and school sport, which remains segregated, underfunded, and ignored. The Human Sciences Research Council's report on sport in 1982 underlined many of these deficiencies.

At the same time, the presence within South Africa of a viable alternative sports structure, represented by the nonracial associations, and the pressure from abroad of international disapproval, have led the government and the official sports organizations to invest more resources in black sport than in the past, and to offer more opportunities to African athletes in particular. New programs were introduced during the 1970s funding coaching courses for young African players and increasing their opportunities to play in occasional multiracial events. Thus Colored and African teams have been permitted to send a team to play in the Craven schools rugby week (a decision that caused a crisis among the white schools)[42] while the official South African Cricket Union has begun a coaching program for young African cricketers in the townships. In 1982 the government claimed it was spending ten million rand on black facilities and was involved in building 84 all-weather tennis courts, 82 tracks, 106 soccer fields, 147 netball* courts, and 73 rugby fields as well as modernizing stadiums and providing some indoor facilities.[43] It can plausibly be argued, in fact, that the official federations are attempting to buy the affiliation of black and particularly African athletes, and that this is a strong argument for promoting the international boycott and supporting the existence of an independent non-racial movement. Certainly black sport was never funded by government to the extent it is now that the status of official sport is threatened.

The emphasis being placed upon the development of African sport is understandable. It is first of all justified: by every criterion, African sports-men and -women are markedly disadvantaged, in relation to Indians and Coloreds, and even more in relation to whites. There is clearly, however, also a central political interest. If the official federations can recruit African players in sufficient numbers, by funding and rewarding those who accept official policy and by isolating and punishing those who do not, then they can hope to claim that they represent all sportsmen and -women in South Africa whether or not they represent the majority of Colored and Indian players. The latter, after all, are an even smaller minority than the white population.

The official federations and government bodies claim that SACOS only represents 13.8 percent of South Africans.[44] In reply, the nonracial federa-tions argue that they express the aspirations of most South African sports-men and -women, the great majority of South Africans who are opposed to apartheid. Yet apartheid, of course, effectively silences Africans from speak-

---

*English sport similar to basketball.

ing their minds. Moreover, except in football, they exert a comparatively small influence on sport. There is no way for the nonracial associations to prove they have African support. They are therefore not in a position to affirm that they are a representative organization.

In fact, the "multinational" sports policy and the incentives offered to African athletes and associations within it may be seen as an attempt, not just to weaken the international boycott of sport, but to divide the African majority from the nonracial sports movement, which, though it offers the silent majority a voice, an alternative vision of sport, cannot offer material assistance or even easy access to mixed competition.

The official federations have succeeded in organizing several international tours on the strength of the "multinational" reforms, and several visiting sports officials have declared that some sports have been effectively "integrated."[45] On the other hand, it is very unlikely, particularly in view of the general thrust of events in South Africa, that the official federations have won anything but the most limited collaboration in any sport from the African population. The nonracial movement has also had some success: in 1981, for example, the African tennis affiliate of the official tennis body merged with the nonracial association to create a new nonracial tennis association, TASA, which represents the great majority of black players. In February 1982, similarly, the nonracial swimming association SAASwiF merged with the South African National Amateur Swimming Association, based in Soweto, to create a new nonracial Amateur Swimming Association of South Africa, to which most black swimmers are affiliated.

Nevertheless, for the nonracial sports associations, the central challenge is unity with African sportsmen and -women. As we have seen, apartheid makes intimate cooperation almost impossible: pass laws restrict Africans' movements, Colored and Indian players may not travel freely into African townships, permits must be sought for mixed matches, mixed sport in schools is very carefully monitored, and municipal and Bantustan authorities are empowered to withdraw facilities from African clubs that do not respect government policy.

To the problems created directly by law must be added those, equally important, that are created by the relative inequality in living standards that exists between the Indian and Colored minorities as a whole (and the African elite) and the majority of urban and rural Africans. This gap is exacerbated in the field of sport. While it is true that, as elsewhere in the world, sport is relatively free of political sectarianism, it is nevertheless enjoyed and practiced by (in South African terms) middle-class people—the moderately prosperous black South Africans who live in the cities, have access to education, and enough wealth to invest some time and money in organized leisure. The nonracial movement in South Africa has been remarkably nonsectarian in political terms: it counts among its members people who belong to the African National Congress, PAC, Unity Movement, Black Consciousness Movement, Coloured Labour party, and of course members of churches and people from all professions and backgrounds, including a small minority of white sportsmen and -women. Nevertheless, there are relatively few working-class Africans involved. This is partly due to the careful way in which Africans have been segregated from contact with the nonracial sports movement; and partly due to the fact that the majority of Africans, who are the majority of the poor, have been physically removed from the cities, where access to organized sporting facilities and activities is possible.

The associations belonging to the nonracial movement themselves recognize that they are not representative of the majority of South African sportsmen. Before 1963, when SAN-ROC was formed, they called for equality with white athletes; for a period they asked to be recognized by international federations in place of the official (then exclusively white) federations. This is no longer their position. As nonracial organizations committed to the principles of the Olympic Charter and opposed to apartheid, they claim to speak for the future of South African sport. They do not claim, however, to be representative—since they do not represent white opinion, nor do they have the proven support of the majority of Africans. For this reason, they argue that *no* South African sports organizaton can at present claim to be representative of South African opinion.

Secondly, they claim that, if the official organizations practice discrimination by choice, even nonracial associations are obliged to make concessions to apartheid and fall short of true nonracialism. Indeed, the nonracial associations affiliated to the South African Council on Sport have had considerable difficulty in defining how they should judge whether the conduct of affiliates is acceptably nonracial, particularly since the introduction of the "multinational" sports policy has permitted clubs that adhere to government policy to organize regular or occasional mixed matches. Quite serious disputes have occurred within the nonracial movement recently when administrators or clubs have disagreed about what constituted acceptable concessions to apartheid. Should players agree to seek permits to travel into African townships for matches, for example? Should teams accept sponsorship from companies that support government policy? Should players go abroad to train?[46]

The nonracial movement is united nevertheless in its oppositoin to foreign tours, on the grounds that international sporting associations have correctly banned South Africa from competition because athletes in South Africa suffer racial discrimination. The laws and ideology of apartheid confirm that discrimination in every respect, and while those laws exist the nonracial movement argues that no sporting activity can be truly nonracial. Even those organizations that stand by nonracial principles and are opposed to apartheid should, under these circumstances, withdraw from international competition until the conditions under which sport can be played without discrimination are restored.[47]

In fact, neither side can claim to represent all South African sportsmen and -women (though official affiliates do make this claim) because neither is in a position to win the loyalty of the African majority. Both the nonracial sports associations and the official "multinational" associations claim to be imperfectly multiracial for the same reasons—the laws of apartheid and government policy. The "multinational" associations even claim that today they are independent of government. As a result, the two sides have been drawn into an increasingly acrimonious public competition for credibility as the more nonracial organization, a competition that naturally expresses itself most logically in attempts to win over or control the support of African sports federations, players, or spectators.

Powerless under the law, possessing few facilities and relatively undeveloped sports organizations, and with different interests as a social group from the white associations and indeed from many of the members of the nonracial associations, the future of South African sport nevertheless lies with the African majority—as it does in other areas. This is why African sports associations are courted by the official associations; without African support they cannot expect to reenter world competition.[48]

During the 1970s, football provided a dramatic example of this competiton, the more interesting because it is one of the rare sports Africans dominate. Until the middle 1950s, there were four identifiable football associations, representing respectively white, Colored, Indian, and African footballers. Some teams among the last three groups played together within Inter-Race Boards. After 1958, the three black federations united with the South African Soccer Federation (SASF), which in 1959 formed the first professional league in South Africa (SASF-PL). Soon afterward, the white South African Football Association formed its own professional league and also encouraged and sponsored the reemergence of separate African, Indian, and Colored associations, among which only the African association (later called SANFA, the South African National Football Association) had any numerical importance.[49]

By the early 1970s, in fact, there were no fewer than eight different administrations representing South African professional or amateur footballers. Six of these were under the control of the South African Football Association, which represented white footballers, including SANFA, for which most Africans played, while most Indian and Colored players belonged to the nonracial SASF The policy of withdrawing facilities from African teams that refused to play segregated football had much to do with this division, which was facilitated by the geographical concentration of

African clubs on the Witwatersrand and Colored and Indian clubs in the Cape and Natal.

The introduction of multiracialism in the early 1970s further complicated the structures of football, for another tier was added to the official structure: the Football Council of South Africa, responsible for coordinating the relations between the different racial associations affiliated to it. It was headed by the president of SANFA, George Thabe, who represented half a million African players. Thabe, a businessman employed also by South African Breweries, was reputedly close to Piet Koornhof, then minister of sport and the man who introduced the new sports policy.

"Multinationalism" led to a dramatic reorganization of the sport by releasing forces that had been held in check by the artificial dominance of the South African Football Association. In the first place, the rise of Thabe represented the eclipse of officials of the white association who were generally believed to be close to the (white) opposition South Africa party; at the same time the National party put itself in a position to control what is undoubtedly the most strategic sport politically.

In making it possible to play mixed professional football, however, the policy also increased the power of professional clubs, which were henceforth permitted to compete for the support of a huge African following. "Multinationalism" also gave black professional players an opportunity for the first time to compete on equal terms with whites, and they argued successfully for equal player status. The result was integrated professional football.

The erosion of segregation in professional football caused professional clubs to push for greater autonomy from their respective amateur parent bodies. It also sparked off competition between the official and nonracial professional leagues, which began poaching players and clubs from each other. This led rapidly to the bankruptcy of the white professional league affiliated to the South African Football Association, and eventually to the near collapse of the nonracial SASF-PL, since both were much smaller than the African league and commanded the support of far fewer spectators. By the end of the decade, the professional league affiliated to SANFA dominated professional football. Moreover, the crisis had led to a major difference of view between the nonracial South African Council on Sport and the South African Soccer Federation, which was suspended from the nonracial movement between 1978 and 1982.

In 1979, when George Thabe reasserted SANFA's control over the professional league clubs by intervening to stop a strike against discriminatory practices,[50] the government could claim that football was led by a black South African, that its "multinational" policy was working, and that the nonracial association was not numerically competitive. In fact, the changes demonstrated the penetration of commercialized spectator sport rather than a real transformation in the social organisation of football: in amateur football, played by the vast majority, segregation remained almost complete.[51]

If evidence was needed to show that the "multinational" policy had not won African hearts and minds, however, it was provided very quickly by the collapse of a short football tour organized unofficially in 1982, shortly after the World Cup. The tour involved several British professional players and had been prepared for some time in such secrecy that even Thabe, ostensibly in charge of South African football, claimed that he had known nothing about it! It was very effectively boycotted by both professional clubs affiliated to SANFA and by spectators, and was swiftly curtailed, at considerable cost to the organizers.[52] The professional clubs refused to play against a visiting side that they claimed was of inferior standard, while the spectators simply stayed away—continuing a long tradition dating back to the 1950s when black spectators began booing the Springboks and cheering visiting touring sides to express their disapproval of apartheid policies.[53]

Until the 1950s, the history of black sport in South Africa was a slow journey toward increased cooperation, leading eventually to integration at the end of the 1950s. The principal handicaps to the development of forms of sport in which large numbers of black South Africans could participate were the lack of resources, the thin spread of education, and the extent of social segregation. At present, sport is dominated by the political struggle between two ideologies, one segregationist and antiegalitarian, the other egalitarian and antiracial, which underpins the evolution of South African society as a whole. Sport is one of the few areas where this conflict, which is of course fundamental to South Africa's political future, can be engaged publicly. The prospects for the future hang upon the capacity of the nonracial movement to attract and keep the loyalty of black athletes, and African sportsmen and -women in particular. In a society as politicized as South Africa, sport cannot be exempt from general political pressures. Sport is, and will inevitably remain, a marginal political issue: the evolution and survival of nonracial sports organizations is not strategic to the future of the country as, for example, the growth of trade unionism might be. Moreover, even in sporting terms, the capacity of the nonracial sports movement to acquire greater authority and to be more representative depends upon change in other areas of society. In the final resort, as apartheid is at present constituted, the nonracial associations cannot cooperate intimately with the African majority, and with African sportsmen and -women. Apartheid similarly prevents African sports associations from organizing themselves effectively to play nonracially. While apartheid and social segregation in South Africa continue to entrench the poverty and racial inequalities that condition South African sport, sport without discrimination—of the kind that is taken for granted in other countries—is not possible, and sportsmen and -women will have to live with the promises of the future that the present nonracial movement holds out to them. As one black South African described the situation:

> When you look at our sport, you see a wall. You're playing, when you reach that wall you know there's no way out. . . . There's no incentive— like you might represent your country or go to the Olympic Games. Our sportsmen work to a certain point and thereafter they drop dead, hence there's not much enthusiasm for the youngsters or encouragement or some praise: when you're young, you see someone playing, you want to be in competition with them. But they are dying because their heroes don't go up anywhere, they come down.[54]

Notes

1. For factual information throughout the period from the 1950s until the present time, refer to the South African Institute of Race Relations (SAIRR) *Survey of Race Relations in South Africa,* Johannesburg.

2. Sam Ramsamy, *Apartheid, the Real Hurdle: Sport in South Africa and the International Boycott* (London: International Defence and Aid Fund, 1982), 19–23; also Robert Archer, and Antoine Bouillon, *The South African Game: Sport and Racism* (London: Zed Press, 1982), 45.

3. Announcement made on 23 September 1976.

4. Works describing this campaign include: Ramsamy; Archer and Bouillon; Joan Brickhill, *Race against Race: South Africa's "Multinational" Sport Fraud,* (London: International Defence and Aid Fund, 1976); Richard E. Lapchick, *The Politics of Race and International Sport: The Case of South Africa* (Connecticut and London: Greenwood Press, 1975); Peter Hain, *Don't Play with Apartheid: The Background to the Stop The Seventy Tour Campaign* (London: George Allen & Unwin, 1971); and Chris de Broglio, *South Africa: Racism and Sport* (London, International Defence and Aid Fund, 1970).

5. Archer and Bouillon, 206–27.

6. For a survey, see Archer and Bouillon, chapters 1–3.

7. Human Sciences Research Council, *Sport in the Republic of South Africa,* 1982.

8. Brian Willan, *An African in Kimberley: Sol T. Plaatje 1894–98,* mimeo, n.d.; André Odendaal, *Cricket in Isolation: The Politics of Race and Cricket in South Africa* (Cape Town, self-published, 1977), 307; and Archer and Bouillon, 317–18.

9. Ray Phillips, *The Bantu in the City: A Study of Cultural Adjustment on the Witwatersrand* (Lovedale: Lovedale Press, 1936), 308; E. Jokl, "Physical Education, Sport and Recreation" in Hellman, ed., *Handbook on Race Relations in South Africa* (Cape Town, London, New York: SAIRR and Oxford University Press, 1949), 457.

10. Willan.

11. A. Kerr, *Fort Hare 1915–1948: The Evolution of an African College* (London: C. Hurst & Co., 1968), 247–48.

12. Willan.

13. T. D. Mweli Skota, *The African Yearly Register, Being an Illustrated National*

Biographical Dictionary (Who's Who) of Black Folks in Africa (Johannesburg: Esson & Co. Ltd., 1932).

  14. For a survey, see Archer and Bouillon, 118–24, 133–34. In more detail, see: Baruch Hirson, *Tuskagee: The Joint Councils and the All-Africa Convention* (London: Institute of Commonwealth Studies, London University, 1978, mimeo); Tim Couzens, "Moralizing Leisure Time; The Transnational Connection and Black Johannesburg, 1918–1936," unpublished paper, Centre for International and Area Studies, University of London; *Report of the National Euro-Bantu Conference, Cape Town, February 6–9 1929* (Lovedale, Lovedale Press, 1929); Phillips, *The Bantu Are Coming* (London: Student Christian Movement Press, 1930); and Odendaal.

  15. Odendaal.

  16. Jokl, 450.

  17. The following should be mentioned: Monica Wilson and Archie Mafeje, *Langa: A Study of Social Groups in an African Township* (London, New York, Cape Town: Oxford University Press, 1963); B. A. Pauw, "The Second Generation" in Mayer, ed., *Xhosa in Town: Studies of the Bantu-speaking Population of East London, Cape Province,* III (Cape Town: Oxford University Press, 1963); P. Mayer, *Townsmen and Tribesmen,* vol. 2 of Mayer, ibid., 1961; Leo Kuper, *The African Bourgeoisie* (New Haven, Conn.: Yale University Press, 1965); and Sheila Patterson, *Colour and Culture in South Africa: A Study of the Status of the Cape Coloured People within the Social Structure of the Union of South Africa* (London: Routledge & Kegan Paul, 1953).

  18. Wilson and Mafeje, 177.

  19. For a survey, see Archer and Bouillon, 141–55.

  20. Wilson and Mafeje, 177; Jokl, and in *Report of the South African National Conference on the Post-War Planning of Social Welfare Work, 25–29 September 1944* (Johannesburg: University of Witwatersrand, 1944), 237; SAIRR *Survey of Race Relations, 1944–55;* Joyce Sikakane, *A Window on Soweto* (London: International Defence and Aid Fund, 1977), 53; Brickhill, 70; and Jane Norman, *Sporting and Other Recreational Facilities Available in Coloured and Indian Townships along the Reef* (Johannesburg; SAIRR, 1974).

  21. Wilson and Mafeje, 113–14, 125; and D. H. Reader, quoted in Mayer (1961), 220–21.

  22. See, for example, SAIRR *Survey* (1982), 355.

  23. Ramsamy, quotes official figures for 1980, 100–102.

  24. Human Sciences Research Council, quoted in SAIRR *Survey* (1982), 586–87.

  25. Private interview with South African living abroad, London, 1980.

  26. See, for example, Phillips (1939), 309.

  27. Kuper, 458.

  28. British Sports Council, *Sport in South Africa: Report of the Sports Council's Fact-finding Delegation* (London, 1980, mimeo), 52.

  29. Archer and Bouillon, 269.

  30. Pauw (1963), 173; Kuper, 357.

  31. Archer and Bouillon, 46.

  32. De Broglio, 3–4.

  33. Lapchick, 50; Archer and Bouillon, 27–28.

34. Mary Draper, *Sport and Race in South Africa* (Johannesburg: SAIRR, 1963), 40–67.

35. *Black Review, 1974–75* (Durban: Black Community Programmes), 181–83, 205.

36. Ibid.

37. Freda Troup, *Forbidden Pastures* (London: SAIRR, 1976).

38. UNESCO, *L'Apartheid, ses effets sur l'éducation, la science, la culture et l'information* (Paris, 1972), 63–64.

39. *Annual Reports of the Department for Sport and Recreation*, Pretoria, South African government.

40. See, for example, Kuper, 317; and Wilson and Mafeje, 121.

41. Archer and Bouillon, 250–88.

42. SAIRR, *Survey of Race Relations in South Africa, 1982* (Johannesburg, 1983), 588.

43. Ibid., 355.

44. Human Sciences Research Council, quoted in *Rand Daily Mail*, 7 September 1982.

45. For a survey of visits in 1982, see SAIRR, *Survey of Race Relations in South Africa, 1982*, 590–98; Ramsamy, 50–55, 61–67; see also British Sports Council.

46. Archer and Bouillon, 233–37; South African Council on Sport, *Reports and Minutes of Conferences,* Durban.

47. For the position of the Non-Racial Sports Movement in South Africa, see SACOS, *Reports and Minutes of Conferences,* Durban; for a survey, Archer and Bouillon, 228–44, 331.

48. See SAIRR, *Surveys;* and Archer and Bouillon, 245–88.

49. Draper, 40–67.

50. Archer and Bouillon, 255.

51. SAIRR, *Surveys;* and Archer and Bouillon, 252–59.

52. SAIRR, *Survey of Race Relations in South Africa, 1982*, 591; Ramsamy, 65–67.

53. Wilson and Mafeje, 123.

54. Private interview with South African living abroad, London 1980.

11

Sport as an Instrument of Political Expansion: The Soviet Union in Africa

BARUCH A. HAZAN

Soviet sport's relations with Africa (and for that matter, with any other country throughout the world) cannot be fully understood without comprehending first the essential characteristics of Soviet sport and its special ideological, educational, and diplomatic applications. It is these specific characteristics and applications that determine the extraordinary nature of Soviet sport and its important place in the comprehensive conduct of Soviet foreign policy.

Soviet sport is essentially a state enterprise of considerable political importance. Despite occasional assertions that "sport has nothing to do with politics" (as suggested often during the 1980 campaign against the boycott of the Moscow Olympic Games), Communist sports officials more frequently stress sport's political nature:

> We look at things realistically. Sport always has been, and is, a political matter—just as other spheres of social superstructures are. . . . It is the reflection of a class-divided world, but it plays a humane and progressive role, leading young people—regardless of their nationality, race, religion and political conviction—to acquire mutual knowledge.
>
> The highly ideological content and form of sports activities have a double mission under our conditions. First we want to educate our members to become conscious patriots and builders of socialism; apart from that we want to make use of ideological motivation for enhancing the standards of all forms of physical education. Experience teaches that it is impossible to master increasingly higher demands of sports training and to achieve maximum performance without understanding the main development trends of the present world . . . without a positive attitude to the workers' class and the results of its work.[1]

Being an enterprise of substantial political value, Soviet sport is the concern of state authorities. It is subject to, and supervised by, several party and state organs whose sole function is its direction and control. Furthermore, while the Soviet sports structure is topped by the Committee on Sport at the USSR Council of Ministers, it is not unusual for leading party and state organs to discuss Soviet sport's role, achievements and character, and to issue appropriate decisions, decrees, and resolutions.

This pattern was established early in the evolution of Soviet communism. Only several months after the October 1917 Revolution, on 22 April 1918, the All-Russian Central Executive Committee of the Soviets of Workers, Soldiers, and Peasants issued a decree that touched upon the special role of Soviet sport and physical culture. In December 1920 Lenin signed a decree creating the Soviet Institute of Physical Education. Numerous subsequent decrees and resolutions consolidated the character of Soviet sport as a state enterprise of political importance and provided the legal and authoritative basis of the party and state control and supervision of sport.[2]

Thus sports achievements in the USSR are not ends in themselves but are rather effective means of attaining political goals. These goals, mostly concerned with ideological principles, propagation, and penetration, make Soviet sport an integral part of the Soviet political and ideological apparatus and an asset of Soviet diplomatic strategy. As in the case of party control, the specific diplomatic functions of Soviet sport frequently feature in official statements:

> Article 62 of the new draft constitution applies to our athletes. They act abroad as ambassadors. Thousands and thousands of people who have never been in our country, judge everything related to our country and our people by them.
>
> When competing abroad the sports workers, members of the teams and coaches are obligated to use in their conversations with their foreign colleagues serious arguments about the great advantage of our system.[3]

Statements of African athletes like Nakole Tchalare, a basketball player from Togo who says he received political posters, books, and other material from Soviet athletes during the Mexico Universiade,[4] testify to the fact that the Soviet athletes act upon the advice and instructions of the party machine.

This function of facilitating the implementation of Soviet diplomacy is frequently expressed in more operational terms, such as "strengthening friendship and cooperation,"[5] "promoting understanding and confirming detente,"[6] "establishing friendly international relations and supporting the struggle for peace and democracy, and against imperialism and the new warmongers,"[7] and, finally, "facilitating the implementation of the Leninist peace policy, expanding international cooperation, strengthening peaceful coexistence, and unmasking the 'Cold War' forces' ideological subversion in sport and sports assistance."[8]

Of course, Russian athletes are not merely harbingers of propaganda and peace. They are symbols of political supremacy, their victories supposedly serving as vivid examples of the Soviet political system's superiority. According to the *Sovetskiy Sport* daily, "In the socialist society the successes of the athletes belong not only to them, but first of all to the society of the country which has sent them. This is the duty of the sportsmen to their society."[9] The logic of this assertion is simple: athletes are a product of their political and social system, and their superiority is an inevitable proof of the superiority of this system. In short, the victories of Soviet athletes serve Soviet society—demonstrating the advantages of communism.

Formal relations between the USSR and the African countries do not have a very long history. Soviet diplomatic relations with Egypt and Ethiopia were established only during World War II, and between the USSR and Liberia even later—in the postwar period.[10] These were the only sovereign black states in Africa until the early 1950s. The other African countries, subjected to colonial rule, were unable to establish continuous and meaningful contact with the USSR, and thus did not afford Moscow many political openings. Nevertheless, between 1920 and the early 1950s there were several Soviet attempts to play a part in developments on the African continent. When the First Congress of the Peoples of the East took place in Baku in 1920, an Egyptian delegation was invited to participate in its work. Unsurprisingly, the congress issued an appeal for struggling against colonialism and for the liberation of the African colonies,[11] and when the Rif Republic was established in 1921 on a part of the territory of Morocco, Moscow, unable to render any serious assistance, made various declarations of support, one of which was issued by the Fourteenth Party Congress in December 1925.[12] Some forty years later Ali Yata, secretary-general of the Moroccan Communist party, stated: "Although the country of the October Revolution was then unable to render any material aid to the Rif uprising, it gave the Rifs a great moral support."[13] Still, the fact remains that in the 1920s and the 1930s no black leader of any stature became firmly attached to the USSR, and only three Communist vanguard organizations—the parties of Egypt, the Sudan, and South Africa—came into existence prior to the 1950s. In fact, several black leaders once ardently pro-Soviet, such as George Padmore, one of those who most influenced the formation of Dr. Kwame Nkrumah's pan-African ideals, turned strongly against Moscow. Some of them became Trotskyite Fourth Internationalists; others simply became anti-Communists. Furthermore, several future African leaders who sought support from the Russian or European communist parties, for example Jomo Kenyatta and Félix Houphouët-Boigny of the Ivory Coast, grew disillusioned with Moscow even before they won power. They found communism incompatible with their sense of nationalism and their preference for a system of private enterprise.[14]

The real expansion of Soviet-African relations, then, dates back only to the mid-1950s. It was closely connected with the 1955 Bandung Conference of African and Asian States—the first serious indication of the growing political importance of the newly established African and Asian states, and with Moscow's realization that it had erred in regarding the passage of lands from colonial status to political independence in the post-World War II era as formalistic and essentially meaningless. The major reconstruction of the world political scene afforded unprecedented possibilities, whose "world-historic significance" was noted by Nikita Khrushchev at the Twentieth Communist Party of the Soviet Union (CPSU) Congress.[15]

Following the new importance acquired by Africa in Moscow's eyes, the USSR adopted a specific strategy based on an attempt to encourage the newly independent African states to embark on the Socialist path of development and thus consolidate their political independence. It cited the Soviet achievements as evidence that socialism constituted the inevitable future and held out the inducement of concrete economic aid to the states that chose such a course.[16] In the words of an official Soviet source:

> The new and independent African states consider the USSR as a powerful support of peace and social progress throughout the world, and an inspiring example of struggle. Our experience in socialist transformation facilitates the attempts of the progressive forces in Africa to solve the basic problems of their countries in the interest of the working people and the entire people. The purposeful and active foreign policy of the CPSU and the Soviet state significantly strengthened the positions of the national liberation movement in its struggle against imperialism.[17]

Thus since the mid- and late 1950s an intensified Soviet attempt to develop relations with the African states is evident. It aims to spread the political and economic influence of the Soviet Union in a manner consonant with its role as world power, to diminish or eliminate Western control and influence, and to promote the strategic-military and political goals of the USSR, especially those affecting the capacity of the Soviet navy. A vital precondition of achieving these goals is the creation and development of attitudes of goodwill and admiration toward the Soviet successes in every area of human existence, and all means of promoting such attitudes in African states and statesmen are assiduously cultivated. It is in this context that the USSR's sports relations with Africa have their importance for the Soviet state.

Soviet sources are somewhat unclear as to when the sports relations between the USSR and Africa gained momentum, various dates as far apart as 1954[18] and 1961[19] being occasionally mentioned. Even if there is some vagueness in this point, there can be no doubt about the turning point marking the intensification of the USSR-African sports relations. In 1961 at the fifty-ninth International Olympic Committee (IOC) session the Soviet Olympic Committee proposed a resolution to help developing amateur sport in Africa, Asia, and Latin America.[20] The resolution called for the consolidation of the Olympic committees of the developing countries, for the training of leading cadres and coaches, and for the provision of material aid for developing sport. All this was to be done by the national Olympic committees and the sports organizations of the countries with well-developed sports facilities and provisions.[21]

The IOC elected to adopt only a recommendation to found an Olympic Aid Fund, which was short of what the USSR and the Socialist countries envisaged.[22] The result was that the Soviet Union, independently from the IOC, intensified its aid for the developing (mostly African) nations and increased the number of experts and coaches to these countries. Simultaneously the Socialist countries continued to apply pressure on the IOC to embrace the original "Olympic Solidarity" program, which was eventually adopted at the 1973 Varna Olympic Congress, and a special commission was established to implement it.[23] The goals of the "Olympic Solidarity" program were defined by official Soviet sources in purely political terms. They included "coordinating the activity of the National Olympic Committees, propagating the Olympic ideas, promoting the alliance and unity of action of national and international sports organizations, which are participating in the Olympic movement, consolidating world peace and struggling against all forms of discrimination."[24] The "Olympic Solidarity" program is financed by the IOC, which allocates it one-third of its revenues from selling the rights to televise the Olympic Games. In 1977 alone the program awarded 1,359 stipends to students from the developing countries specializing in various areas related to sport. Some 553 stipends were given to African students.[25]

Despite the fact that the "Olympic Solidarity" program was initiated by the Soviet Union, it is essentially an IOC program, utilizing IOC funds. Nevertheless, the Soviet Union does not allow the African countries to forget who initiated the program and often speaks of it as if it were a Soviet enterprise. This, of course, does not prevent the USSR from criticizing the IOC for allocating "insufficient" funds to the African states. Furthermore, it seems that the USSR is not satisfied with these assertions. On several occasions, when the Soviet Union itself was allocated funds by the IOC under the auspices of the "Olympic Solidarity" program, the USSR transferred the money to African states "which needed the money."[26]

During the 1960s and the 1970s the USSR systematically developed sports relations with more than thirty African countries.[27] These relations are characterized by overt political-ideological overtones, typical of the entire Soviet approach to sport, and expected "to pave the way to cooperation and international exchange in all fields."[28] In this context the Soviet

Union attributes great importance to written contracts, treaties, and communiqués. Relations with the African countries are based on detailed written agreements and protocols with the African state and sports officials. These agreements specify the scope of the contacts, the areas of material aid, the exact number of Soviet experts to be sent to the relevant state and the duration of their work there, the number of stipends for students from the relevant African state allowed to study in the USSR at one of the physical culture institutes, and so forth. These agreements usually include political declarations on the importance of peace and friendship, and the obligatory condemnation of apartheid. They provide the USSR with a formal record of commitment on the part of the relevant African state, and with written proof of its support of the African cause. Their content is published by the Soviet press in foreign languages and announced on Radio Moscow's broadcasts to the African countries, and thus used as additional propaganda ammunition in Moscow's permanent worldwide propaganda campaign.

Soviet involvement in African sport encompasses the following areas: (1) competing against African athletes in national and international sports competitions; (2) sending Soviet specialists, experts, coaches, doctors, and sports administrators to the African countries; (3) training African cadres (athletes, coaches, and specialists) in the USSR; (4) providing African countries with financial aid and sports equipment; (5) exchanging sports delegations; (6) and pro-Soviet political statements and declarations concerning the struggle against apartheid.

The scope of the Soviet sports relations with other countries is impressive, especially when one considers the fact that they actually developed only in the last twenty to twenty-five years. In 1959 only 29 Soviet sports delegations traveled abroad.[29] Some twelve years later, in 1971, about thirty thousand Soviet athletes took part in competitions against foreign athletes, visiting some sixty-seven states.[30] During 1976 1,350 Soviet delegations went abroad, and about 1,500 came to the USSR. Some 32 percent of the Soviet cultural exchange involves sports contacts. Soviet representatives took part in 2,825 international sports events.[31] Today the USSR maintains sports contacts with virtually every country in the world.

Against this impressive background, the paucity of sports competitions between Soviet and African athletes is noteworthy. Such competitions are infrequent and usually have a pronounced unofficial and demonstrative character. Thus in 1971 only two thousand Soviet athletes took part in competitions against teams and athletes from the developing countries.[32] Since, as we have seen, more than thirty thousand Soviet athletes competed internationally during the same year, it is obvious that sports competitions against African athletes are uncommon events. Aware of this unpalatable fact, the USSR meticulously avoids any inclusion of numerical data on the number of athletes to compete against Africans, or the actual number of sports competitions, in its otherwise so fastidiously detailed sports coopera-tion agreements with the African countries. The truth is that when sports competitions between Soviet and African athletes do take place, they are usually organized as a part of celebrations marking the national holiday of some African country or the anniversary of the October Revolution. Thus when the sixtieth anniversary of the October 1917 Revolution was marked in Mozambique, Tunisia, Morocco, Benin, and other African countries, Soviet football (soccer) teams took part in the official celebrations and had several friendly matches against the local teams.[33] In 1977 Soviet athletes took part in competitions marking the national holidays of Zambia and Angola.[34] In 1981 a Soviet volleyball team visited Zambia on the same occasion, while an army basketball team took part in competitions in Algeria for the benefit of the victims of an earthquake.[35]

When Soviet athletes do travel to Africa, or African sportsmen visit the USSR, they do not necessarily compete there. Frequently, they just train together. In 1980 Ethiopian boxers, track-and-field athletes, and weight lifters, as well as Guinean basketball teams and Algerian wrestlers, bicycle riders, and track-and-field athletes came to the USSR for joint training with Soviet sportsmen.[36] Occasionally, Soviet teams combine training and friendly matches in Africa. This usually takes place during the winter (in the USSR) and involves football teams. In February 1982 the USSR national youth football team trained and played in Algeria and Morocco,[37] and Dynamo Tbilisi did the same in Tunisia in January 1979. Nevertheless, such events are rare.

Even when the USSR hosts major international sports events, African athletes seldom figure among the participants. Some twenty countries took part in the 1976 *Moscow News* gymnastics competition in Moscow, but only Algeria and Morocco represented Africa.[38] Although gymnasts from thirty-two countries took part in the March 1983 Moscow *Novosti* gymnastics competition, Algeria, Tunisia, and Morocco were the only African coun-tries that participated in the event.[39]

The 1979 Seventh Spartakiade of the USSR was a major exception. It served as the dress rehearsal for the Moscow Olympic Games, and appar-ently the Soviet sports authorities were interested in mass participation. Athletes from twenty-two African countries were flown cost-free to Moscow to take part in the competitions.[40] Incidentally, some of them excelled. The Ethiopian long-distance runner Mirus Yifter won the gold medals in the five thousand and ten thousand meters, as he did one year later at the 1980 Moscow Olympic Games.[41] These games were another case that involved mass participation of African athletes. During the months preced-ing the games the Soviet authorities sent several delegations to Africa to urge the African states to resist the Olympic boycott and take part in the games. They had some success. The delegation led by I. Rudoi, which visited Ghana, Liberia, Senegal, the Ivory Coast, and Sierra Leone, reported upon returning to the USSR that "the African leaders promised us that they see the Moscow Games as their own,"[42] while the delegation led by I. Novikov initiated a resolution on the part of the African Supreme Sports Council "to guarantee the extensive and representative participation of African athletes in the Moscow Olympic Games."[43] Eventually some twenty-two African states participated in the Moscow Olympic Games.[44] Perhaps this figure was disappointing when one considers the fact that Moscow maintains sports contacts with more than thirty African states.[45]

The reason for the infrequent sports competitions between Soviet and African athletes is twofold. First of all, Soviet athletes focus their attention on various European and world championships in which African athletes participate scarcely or not at all. Moreover, many sports in which Soviet athletes excel are relatively undeveloped in Africa, and thus no real competition is feasible. In truth, with the possible exception of some track-and-field events, African sportsmen cannot compete successfully against the Soviet athletes. Severe and frequent defeats would hardly contribute to implementing the various political and ideological goals of Soviet sport in Africa. Consequently, it is only sensible that aside from the Olympic Games, some official world championships, and a very limited number of international sports events, actual sports competitions between Soviet and African athletes are infrequent affairs. Even when such competitions do take place, they usually have the character of an amiable exhibition of the Soviet athletes' ability, which is helpful grounds in providing a practical point.

Some African sports officials, such as Louis Guirandou-N'Diaye from the Ivory Coast, contend that "lack of funds" is a major reason behind the scarce African participation in international sports events.[46] This reason cannot explain or justify the paucity of real sports competitions between Soviet and African athletes, because, as the cases of the Seventh Spartakiade and the Moscow Olympic Games showed, when Moscow is interested in competing against African athletes, funds play no role at all. All expenses are generously covered by the Soviet sports officials.

Sending Soviet experts and coaches to African countries is the major area of Soviet-African sports contacts. While the total number of Soviet experts in Africa is not very impressive,* most of the Soviet coaches and experts working abroad are stationed there. Numerical data provided by Soviet sources often prove vague and contradictory on the exact number of Soviet sports specialists working in the African continent. Even when supposedly precise information on the number of Soviet experts in Africa is disclosed (usually involving a single country), there are major discrepancies. Two

---

Moscow News no. 25, 19 June 1983, reports that in 1983 there were 120 Soviet coaches and sports experts in Africa.

different Soviet sources in 1982 discussing the Soviet-Algerian sports relations put the number of Soviet sports experts in Algeria respectively as seventy[47] and forty-six.[48] But whatever the exact figures, the USSR stresses its involvement. In 1982 Soviet sources reported that "200 Soviet sports specialists are working in more than 30 countries."[49] Pointing out that the specialists are being sent cost-free, within the framework of the Soviet aid to the developing countries, another Soviet source maintains that "dozens of Soviet specialists are working now in Africa."[50] While refraining from providing precise information on the number of Soviet specialists working in Africa, Soviet sources never fail to point out that their presence in Africa is a "handshake across oceans and continents, a manifestation of the Soviet striving toward peace, understanding and friendship among nations."[51]

The ideological terminology is used not only to explain the presence of Soviet experts in Africa in Marxist terms, but also to justify some difficulties caused in the Soviet higher physical culture institutes by the increasing number of Soviet specialists in Africa. Interviewed by *Sovetskiy Sport,* A. Shepilov, a high Soviet sports official, admitted that the activity of the Soviet sports institutes has been affected by the substantial number of Soviet experts working abroad, but pointed out that "the principles of internationalism take precedence in this matter."[52]

Many of the Soviet specialists working in Africa are former top athletes such as A. Sergeyev (wrestling, Algeria);[53] Robert Shavalkadze (track and field, Congo); Eduard Makarov (football, Algeria); Vasiliy Romanov, (boxing, Nigeria), and so forth.[54] They obviously are highly qualified, and what turns them even more attractive for the African states is that their services are provided cost-free. Soviet sources, resorting again to Marxist slang, describe this fact as a "selfless assistance," based on "contracts profoundly different from the very concept of 'contract,' used in the capitalist world."[55] The same sources describe the Soviet experts working in Africa as "people with broad horizons, familiar with the development aspects of sport in the relevant country, and not confined by the frames of their specific profession . . . who are to be found at the stadium or at the gym, and not on the beach or in a bar."[56]

Training individual African athletes and teams is only a part of the activity of the Soviet sports experts in Africa. Occasionally, their activity has purely administrative character; for example, helping in developing the organizational framework of African sport.[57] In other cases, Soviet specialists found and develop institutes of higher physical education. Thus, the Algerian Institute of Sports Science and Technology was established exclusively by Soviet experts in 1979.[58] During the first years of its existence, the entire teaching faculty was composed of Soviet experts,[59] who proved instrumental in training local cadres. Subsequently, it seems that the general task of the Soviet specialists in Africa is to transplant the Soviet sports system to the

African continent, including its training methods, administrative structure, theoretical postulates, and organizational framework.

The work of the Soviet sports specialists in Africa has been acknowledged and praised not only by various African sports officials, but also by many African leaders. Madagascan and Algerian ministers, among others, have praised the work of Soviet sports experts in their countries, while the Congolese government awarded the Soviet track-and-field coach Revaz Trapiadze a high state order for his contribution to developing sport in the Republic of Congo.[60] There can be little doubt that the successful activity of the Soviet experts in Africa contributes to enhancing Soviet prestige in that part of the world and to developing goodwill toward and admiration for the USSR. Furthermore, using invariably pure ideological concepts, the USSR ties its sports relations with Africa to the Soviet foreign policy activity, frequently stressing the "selfless" nature of the Soviet sports assistance, and occasionally indicating that the same kind of assistance can be provided in many other areas. In this context Soviet sport clearly acts as a political agent, facilitating Soviet penetration in Africa and serving as an example for and a bridge toward developing other kinds of cooperation.

Training of African athletic cadres and students in the USSR is another important aspect of the USSR-African sports relations. The precise number of African students studying the Soviet sports and physical culture institutes cannot be established. Soviet sources have reported that in 1981 some forty-nine specialists from thirty-two developing countries studied in the Moscow State Higher Institute of Physical Education;[61] that during the 1979–80 academic year there were three hundred students from the developing countries studying in the same school;[62] and that in 1980 more than eighty students "from Tanzania, Jordan, Tunisia, and other countries" graduated from the Moscow, Leningrad, and Kiev higher physical education institutes.[63] On the basis of this incomplete information it is impossible to establish the total number of African students studying at the Soviet higher physical education establishments. However, while being secretive about numbers (as usual), the Russians frequently stress that all African students receive scholarships, which cover the cost of studies and board.[64]

There is one very interesting aspect related to the studies of African students in the USSR. Their curriculum includes not only the general subject of pedagogy, psychology, anatomy, and various sports disciplines, but also certain additional subjects. In the words of Hedi Zghal, Tunisia's minister of sport: "The Soviet friends teach our students in Moscow not only how to break records, but also afford them an all-round education and teach them Russian—the language of friendship."[65] The political connotations of this statement are unmistakable. In an obvious attempt to influence the views of the African athletes and students studying in the USSR, Moscow subjects them to "extracurricular" Soviet propaganda. This improves Moscow's chances of using them later as "ambassadors of good will," or even more specifically as active members of their respective countries' societies for friendship with the USSR. Thus the Soviet effort to use sports relations as a bridge toward developing relations in other areas is evident.

While the admission of African students to Soviet physical education schools is an issue usually stipulated in the inevitable sports cooperation agreements,[66] sometimes African students enroll under different circumstances. Thus, according to a Soviet source, "many" of the African athletes who were flown cost-free to Moscow to take part in the 1979 Spartakiade "remained for training and study in the higher physical culture schools."[67] After completing their study in the USSR many of the African students acquire high posts in their respective countries' sports administration. Tunisian Mohamed Muldi Dahmank, for example, became the coach of the national swimming team after graduating from the Kiev Higher Physical Culture Institute.[68]

The USSR maintains close relations with African physical education students, graduates of the Soviet establishments, after they return to their countries. Occasionally Moscow brings them back to the USSR as participants in special sports courses and seminars for African sportsmen and sports experts and officials. Such events usually take place under the auspices of UNESCO and are subject to specific agreements, such as the one signed by the USSR Sports Committee and IOC President Samaranch in 1982, which stipulated the organization of a seminar for African hockey, swimming, wrestling, handball, and basketball coaches.[69] A typical seminar was organized in Moscow in January 1983. Some 112 sports specialists from thirty-eight developing countries took part. The participants studied anatomy, psychology, theory of physical education, organization and planning of sports activities, pedagogy, and the most recent Soviet achievements in these areas. As usual, the USSR authorities spared no expense in their effort to create a favorable impression among the participants. After the seminar ended Erasto Zambi, secretary-general of the Tanzanian Olympic Committee, said: "Recently I participated in a similar seminar in Great Britain. I must say that the level of the Moscow seminar was immeasurably higher. I was able to see not only the superb conditions and material basis of sport in the USSR, but also to witness the sincere willingness of the Soviet specialists to selflessly convey their experience."[70] Incidentally, Moscow seems to be very fond of this statement. During 1983 it appeared in several Soviet publications in foreign languages, *Moscow News* being one of them.[71] Similar self-praising statements, published by the Soviet media, include concepts and elements ("sincere willingness to help," "selfless assistance," and so forth), invariably used by virtually all Soviet propaganda statements on political and economic aid to the developing countries. Regardless whether Erasto Zambi (and many other African sports officials quoted by Soviet media) had really talked about the aforementioned concept (or even made such statements), it is a fact that such remarks turn into component parts of the Soviet propaganda effort, and thus serve specific USSR political goals.

The Moscow Higher Physical Culture Institute frequently organizes six-month courses for sports officials from the African continent. In 1983 it was reported that "in keeping with the 'Olympic Solidarity' program the courses in Moscow have already trained 200 people from 21 African countries."[72] These courses deal predominantly with the organizational aspects of sport. Sometimes special courses and training camps are arranged for specialists in one specific activity. Typical examples include the October 1982 Moscow seminar for African basketball coaches, organized under UNESCO auspices, the January 1979 Moscow seminar for African gymnasts, and the November 1982 special course for Algerian gymnasts at the Moscow Higher Physical Culture Institute.[73] In all these cases Soviet media published statements of participants, expressing their admiration for the USSR in general, and their positive impressions of Soviet training. Thus after the October 1982 seminar for basketball coaches Yusuf Duif (Senegal) said: "Our Soviet lecturers had no secrets. I will apply everything I learned here." Salahadin Garbi (Tunisia) said: "The Soviet methodology of training sportsmen is the most modern in the world. I shall try to train the Tunisian basketball players in the same way."[74]

Soviet sources make no secret of Moscow's attempt to turn African sports students and officials into pro-Soviet propagandists. On the contrary, when such results are achieved, they proudly report them. Thus, according to *Sovetskiy Sport,* after completing his studies in sports medicine in Moscow, the Mauritian Channu Intradut "became a propagandist of the new Soviet methods of healing traumas." Subsequently, Intradut became chairman of the Mauritian-Soviet Friendship Society, and frequently visited the USSR.[75]

Incidentally, publicizing the (invariably favorable) statements of African athletes and sports officials through the Soviet mass media and the foreign language programs of Radio Moscow and Radio Peace and Progress apparently does not entirely satisfy the Soviet authorities. They regularly inform the IOC on the development of the Soviet sports relations with African countries.[76] In this way new recruits are contacted, and the "selfless character of the Soviet assistance" stressed once again and pointed out as an example to other countries. Thus the indirect use of sport for propaganda purposes is expanded and enhanced.

Another aspect of the Soviet-African sports relations involves provision of material aid (for purposes of sports development) to the African countries, sending sports equipment and literature, and organizing related exhibitions and similar events. The Soviet Union provides substantial material aid to African countries for their sports development. In 1981 the USSR informed UNESCO that during the two previous years it had spent 2.5 million rubles for sports aid to the developing countries. Some seventeen African countries received Soviet aid for their sports development.[77]

The material aid takes several forms. Some, such as covering the expenses of African teams and students in the USSR, have already been discussed. Another is the provision of sports equipment to the African countries. Provision is usually stipulated in the various sports cooperation agreements and protocols. The 1982 sports cooperation agreement with Angola is a typical example.[78] Sometimes, however, sports equipment is handed over in the form of an unexpected gift. When the Kharkov football team Metallist visited Madagascar in 1977, "they presented their African friends with football uniforms and sports equipment."[79] Soviet sports officials visiting Africa regularly present equipment to their hosts. In 1980 the I. Rudoi-led delegation, which visited Liberia (among other countries), presented the Liberian sports officials with a "set of complete boxing equipment."[80] When a sports delegation led by Sergey Pavlov visited Ethiopia in 1982 it handed the Ethiopian hosts sports goods on behalf of the USSR Sports Committee.[81] The USSR also assists the African countries in constructing new sports projects[82] or in equipping new sports facilities. In 1982 the USSR equipped a newly constructed gym in an Algerian school.[83] The USSR Sports Committee also sends the African countries sports films and slides[84] and literature.[85] Sports exhibitions and photo displays are also frequently organized. They usually take place during the visits of USSR sports delegations,[86] although especially organized sports exhibitions are not uncommon.[87] As in the case of the courses and seminars for African students and sports experts, and for the same purposes, the provision of Soviet material aid is extensively publicized by the Soviet media, particularly by the Soviet radio broadcasts to African countries, and frequently reported to various international organs such as UNESCO, and IOC, and the Supreme Council for Sports in Africa.[88]

All aspects of the USSR-African sports relations have clear political overtones. However, no other aspect demonstrates this more clearly than the exchange of delegations and the publication of cooperation protocols and agreements.

Exchanging delegations is one of the cornerstones of the Soviet cultural exchange. Over 700 foreign sports delegations and teams travel annually to the USSR,[89] and many of them come from Africa. In 1973 the USSR and Africa exchanged 32 sports delegations, 116 in 1976, and 141 in 1977.[90] In 1979 more than 100 sports delegations from the developing countries visited the USSR and 140 Soviet sports delegations visited the same countries.[91] Delegations of Soviet sports officials usually visit Africa on special events. Both the Eighth General Assembly of the Supreme Council for Sports in Africa

(Algeria, 1978)[92] and the Ninth General Assembly of the Council (Cameroon, 1980)[93] were attended by Soviet delegations led by I. Novikov. In addition, major sports events in Africa, such as the African Games, are also attended by Soviet delegations. In 1979, during the period preceding the Olympic boycott, the number of Soviet delegations visiting Africa sharply increased. At that time Moscow repeatedly expressed concern that "reactionary forces will try to inflict a blow on the Olympic movement by staging a situation similar to the 1976 Montreal Olympic Games, which were boycotted by African states in protest against the participation of New Zealand, which had previously competed against racists."[94] Clearly, the main goal of the Soviet sports officials visiting Africa was to forestall a boycott. They usually met with African sports leaders, explained what they called "the USSR's constant struggle for the isolation of apartheid countries in the international sports arena"; "the USSR's intention to struggle against racism and apartheid;"[95] and Moscow's intention "to facilitate the expulsion of Rhodesia and South Africa from the world sports community."[96] In each country they visited, the Soviet delegations were anxious to obtain assurances of participation in the games. They left no stone unturned. The Soviet delegation to the Ninth General Assembly of the Supreme Council for Sports in Africa in Yaoundé, Cameroon, reported glowingly on the preparations for the games and expressed satisfaction with the Soviet efforts to create the best possible conditions for the participation of African athletes in the Moscow Olympic Games and the efforts of the Olympic Organizational Committee to guarantee the extensive and representative participation of African athletes in the games (meaning that Moscow would cover all expenses of the African delegations). Hope was expressed that the games would contribute to the increasing isolation of apartheid in the international arena.[97]

African delegations visiting the USSR are of a different nature. Their visits supply the Soviet propaganda machine with additional ammunition and provide another visible proof of the respective countries' relations with Moscow. Subsequently, such delegations usually tour the USSR's main cities and review their sports facilities, meet several Soviet sports officials, express gratitude for the Soviet sports assistance, and—most importantly—sign a sports cooperation agreement, thus satisfying Moscow's appetite for tangible proof of commitment (in any area) to the USSR.

The Soviet penchant for written agreements of any kind, including agreements and protocols on cooperation in sport, borders on the absurd. There is no other country with so many and so detailed agreements and protocols on sports cooperation. In 1979 such agreements were signed with twenty-five developing countries.[98] Agreements on principles of cooperation were signed with Angola, Algeria, Benin, Gambia, Zambia, Libya, Morocco, Tunisia, and Ethiopia, and actual protocols were signed with Angola,

Zambia, Libya, Morocco, Guinea-Bissau, Cape Verde, and Tunisia.[99] Most of these agreements covered a period of one or two years only, requiring constant renewal. In 1982, for example, a cooperation protocol for the period of 1983–84 signed with Ethiopia was acknowledged as "the fifth such protocol."[100] It seems that a periodical renewal of their commitment to Moscow is required from the African countries as a precondition of continuing sports cooperation with them. It also seems that it is not the success of the African athletes trained by Soviet coaches, but the number of cooperation agreements with the African countries, that serves Moscow as evidence of its successful sports cooperation with Africa.

The agreements and protocols are usually signed by the sports minister of the relevant African country and the chairman of the USSR Committee on Sport. The 1977 protocol with Algeria was signed by A. Fahdel, Algerian minister of youth and sport, and by Sergey Pavlov, chairman of the USSR Committee on Sport until 1983.[101] Additional examples are the 1982 USSR-Mozambican agreement on sports cooperation and protocol on exchanging sports delegations, signed by João Carlos de Conseia, national director for physical culture and sport, and V. Zakhavin, first deputy chairman of the USSR Committee on Sport;[102] the 1979 Tunisian-USSR agreement signed by Hedi Zghal, minister of sport and youth, and by Sergey Pavlov;[103] and the 1983 renewal of the same document, signed by the new Tunisian minister of sport and youth, Mohammed Kraiem, and by the new chairman of the USSR Committee on Sport, M. Gramov.[104] The agreements and protocols were very detailed. They describe every area of Soviet assistance, point out the specific teams that are to be coached by Soviet coaches,[105] and the number of delegations to be exchanged and athletes to be sent to each country.[106] During the 1979 Spartakiade similar agreements were signed with almost all participating African countries.

Occasionally, the USSR signs sports cooperation agreements not only with separate African countries, but also with the Supreme Council for Sports in Africa. Thus in 1982 Abraham Ordia, president of the council, signed with Sergei Pavlov in Moscow an agreement for the period 1983–84 to strengthen the unity of the international Olympic and sports movement, to exclude South Africa from international sports competitions, to fight against racism, apartheid, commercialism, and professionalism, and to facilitate the implementation of the final resolution of the Eleventh Olympic Congress.[107]

When in Moscow, members of the African sports delegations are expected to make certain declarations and statements, which usually praise the work of the Soviet specialists in Africa, the Soviet assistance in general, and the Soviet position on apartheid. Thus Abraham Ordia, president of the Supreme African Sports Council, went on record praising "the steady fight of Soviet representatives against racism," and supporting the "Soviet effort to bring about a further democratization of the IOC."[108] Tesafie Shevaikh, Ethiopian minister of sport, culture, and youth, praised the Moscow Olympic Games as a "victory of the forces of peace and progress";[109] and A. Ademola, a Nigerian member of the IOC executive committee, after watching the 1970 Spartakiade expressed his "admiration" for the "scale, planning and organization of physical education and sport in the USSR," as well as his regret that "many IOC members do not have a sufficiently clear idea of the level of sport in the Soviet Union."[110] This is just a random selection. There are hundreds of similar statements on record. Most of them use apparent Marxist concepts, denouncing various "reactionary forces," expressing support for the "forces of progress led by the USSR," and so forth. One cannot escape the conclusion that these statements were edited by the same hand, in order to incorporate them in various Soviet propaganda campaigns and turn them into an integral part of the Soviet propaganda effort to foster goodwill toward the USSR and develop positive attitudes toward the Soviet state and policy. Thus, inadvertently, African sports officials occasionally contribute to the Soviet propaganda effort.

The final political aspect of the USSR-African sports relations encompasses the struggle against apartheid. The Soviet Union has always been actively involved in this struggle. Soviet sports officials have repeatedly and consistently used various international forums, such as the IOC sessions and the Olympic congresses, to condemn apartheid. Instrumental in expelling South Africa and Rhodesia from international sports competition, the Soviet Union closely monitors South Africa's international sports relations and promptly condemns countries that compete against South African athletes. Thus in 1981 Great Britain was condemned for hosting a South African rugby team.[111] When in 1981 the South African Springboks rugby team visited the United States, Soviet officials defined the visit as "provocational" and pointed out that it contradicts regulation no. 3 of the Olympic Charter.[112] When in September 1982 some fifteen African countries decided to boycott the Commonwealth Games because of New Zealand's sports relations with South Africa, the USSR sports authorities were quick on the trigger and supported the boycott without any reservations.[113] This consistent anti-apartheid stand of the Soviet Union has been repeatedly acknowledged and greeted with gratitude by various African officials.

Since 1960 the Soviet Union has developed extensive sports relations with many African countries. Sports competitions and matches are only a small, almost negligible, part of these relations. Most important are extensive assistance in training African coaches, specialists, and athletes; material aid in various forms (equipment, facilities, stipends, and free travel to the USSR); extensive exchange of delegations of sports officials; annual sports cooperation agreements and protocols; and finally, joint participation in various political campaigns, such as anti-apartheid boycotts. These clearly political overtones apparently do not deter the African states. Their sports relations with the USSR grow annually, and in 1982 it was reported that seventeen developing countries (many of them African), had requested for the first time Soviet assistance in developing sport.[114]

It is impossible to discern any particular pattern in the Soviet-African sports relations, aside from the marked effort, on the part of the USSR, to use these relations for facilitating the implementation of its foreign policy goals. There seems, for example, to be no preference for former British or French colonies, or any particular predilection for Socialist or pro-Soviet regimes. It seems that all African countries (except the Republic of South Africa, of course) are welcomed by Moscow. However, if intensity of sports relations indicates particular political interest, then the Maghreb seems to be an area of special interest for the USSR. Algerian, Moroccan, and Tunisian gymnasts are permanent participants in the *Moscow News* and *Novosti* annual international gymnastics competitions.[115] The greatest number of Soviet sports specialists in Africa is concentrated in Algeria, where their total reached seventy in 1982.[116] At least one Soviet source pointed out that the regular activity of the Soviet physical culture institutes was affected by the substantial number of Soviet specialists in Algeria.[117] Whether these particularly intensified sports contacts are results of the special Soviet interest in the Mediterranean is a matter of speculation. The fact remains, however, that no other African country can compete with the Maghreb countries in everything related to sports contacts with the USSR.

Whatever the specific number of Soviet sports specialists or the geographical location and political system of the African country involved, Moscow's sports relations with African countries are perceived by the USSR as an instrument of political hegemony. These relations serve as a bridge toward developing cooperation in other areas, publicize and demonstrate various achievements of the Soviet political system (along with the Soviet successes in sport) as an example for the African states to follow. Furthermore, Soviet sources consistently describe sports relations with African countries as a part of the overall Soviet assistance to this countries, and as a "perfect example of the fruitful and selfless USSR cooperation with the developing countries."[118] It seems that the USSR also uses sports relations to transplant some (albeit peripheral) elements of its social system, such as the structure of the sport administration and the general attitude toward sport and physical culture, as well as to promote some more operative goals of Soviet foreign policy, such as founding and influencing the activity of societies for friendship with the USSR. Moscow makes no secret of this particular aspect of its sports relations with African countries and describes it in purely political terms: "Sports relations with African countries . . . make it possible to strengthen our ties still further, to stimulate the rapid development of sport in the newly-free countries, which are consolidating their indepen-dence";[119] "Soviet sport is an ambassador of peace";[120] "Sport is under-standing, peace and cooperation . . . new contacts and friendship, peace and solidarity";[121] "Sport is an important social phenomenon, which has a great role in instilling spiritual values and in forming a specific worldview."[122]

It seems that something from the Soviet attitude toward sport was trans-planted to Africa. Thus Anani Matthia, president of the Togolese National Olympic Committee and president of the Association of African National Olympic Committees, credits the USSR for helping to turn sport in Africa into an "important element of national pride and social development, and an important factor of national unity."[123]

Apparently, Soviet sports relations with Africa do serve their purpose and facilitate the development of relations in other areas as well as demonstrate the advantages of the Soviet political system. This conclusion seems ob-vious when one scrutinizes the statements of African officials on the impor-tance of sports relations with the USSR. Many of them stress the political aspects of these relations and their usefulness in many areas.

Marcel Koku, director of sports issues at Benin's ministry of youth and sport, said: "We want that in our country sport also serve the ideals of construction of the new socialist society and facilitate the upbringing of literate, politically mature and physically developed patriots."[124]

Hogan Bassey, coach of the Nigerian boxing team, remarked: "Some sixty years ago the Soviet state published the decree on peace and called for equality among nations and for friendship among people. The Soviet sport movement is consistently implementing these principles. . . . Our friend-ship with the Soviet boxers strengthened in joint training and competi-tion.[125]

Enrique Tofani, member of the Trainers' Council of the Republic of Guinea, said: "The unity of the African people in the struggle against racism strengthens every day. In this struggle we are being assisted by the USSR, the first country in which equality of people, regardless of their skin's color, social position and religion was proclaimed. These ideas were proclaimed by Great October and we witness how the Soviet representatives are con-sistently and consequently struggling against racial discrimination in sport. Many representatives of our country are visiting the USSR. There they feel themselves at home."[126]

Finally, noted Stephan Malonga, Congo, vice-president of the Union of African Sports Journalists: "Moscow is our hope. The hopes of Africa are linked to Moscow, which heads the world movement for peace."[127]

Regardless what the practical effect or political impact of these statements is, their propaganda value for the USSR is great. It is exactly such state-ments (widely amplified and publicized by the Soviet propaganda machine) that serve Moscow as a proof of its foreign policy's successes. Thus, in the final account, Soviet sports relations with Africa seek immediate propaganda effect and long-range political impact. In the short range they serve as another instrument of the Soviet propaganda machine, demonstrating the achievements of the Soviet system and promoting goodwill and admiration for the USSR. In the long range they serve purely political goals, such as facilitating the development of cooperation in other areas and transplanting to Africa various elements of the Soviet social system.

Notes

1. Antonín Himl, "Physical Culture is Part of Ideological Struggle," *Rudé Právo,* 12 April 1980.

2. V. Ivanin, *Sputnik Fizkulturnogo Rabotnika* (Moscow, 1977), 9–13.

3. *Sovetskiy Sport,* 2 July 1977.

4. *Olympiade-80,* no. 37 (1979): 28.

5. V. Ivonin, "Sport and Physical Culture in the USSR," *Moscow News,* no. 31 (1972): 3.

6. Y. Lomko, "Greetings to the Participants in the *Moscow News* Gymnastics Competition," *Moscow News,* no. 6 (1974): 16.

7. *Otechestven Front* (Bulgaria), 25 June 1977.

8. *Sovetskiy Sport,* 25 June 1977.

9. *Sovetskiy Sport,* 2 July 1977.

10. V. Solodivnikov, et al., eds., *Africa in Soviet Studies* (Moscow, 1976), 214.

11. Ibid., 219.

12. *KPSS V Rezolyutsiakh I Resheniyakh, 1898–1970,* (Moscow, 1970), III, 244.

13. *Pravda,* 15 November 1967.

14. Colin Legum, "The African Environment," *Problems of Communism* (January–February 1978): 3.

15. "CPSU CC Report to the 20th CPSU Congress," in Leo Grilow, ed., *Current Soviet Politics* (New York, 1957), II, 33.

16. David Albright, "Soviet Policy," *Problems of Communism* (January–February 1978): 33.

17. A. Chugunov, "Interesting Research of Contemporary African Problems," *Komunist,* no. 5 (March 1976): 126–27.

18. A. Shepilov, "Contacts Based on Truth and Friendship," *Olympisches Panorama,* no. 2 (1982): 12.

19. Sergey Pavlov, "Solidarity—Entirely Concrete Concept," *Olympisches Panorama,* no. 13 (1980): 40.

20. C. Andrianov, "Olympic Solidarity," *Sport in der UdSSR,* no. 10 (1977): 14.

21. Pavlov, 40.

22. Andrianov, 14.

23. Pavlov, 40.

24. Ibid.

25. Andrianov, 14.

26. S. Pavlov, "Unity is Our Goal," interview, *Sport in der UdSSR,* no. 9

(1979): 18.

27. S. Pavlov, "Solidarity . . .," 40.

28. Y. Lomko, 16.

29. *Otechestven Front*, 25 June 1977.

30. V. Ivonin, 5.

31. D. Prokhorov, "The Ties of Friendship Strengthen," *Sport in der UdSSR*, no. 12 (1977): 20.

32. V. Avilov, "Cooperation in All Areas," *Sport in der UdSSR*, no. 5 (1978): 25.

33. Unattributed, "Roads of Cooperation," *Sport in der UdSSR*, no. 5 (1978): 25.

34. Ibid.

35. V. Avilov, 25.

36. V. Avilov, "With Open Heart," *Sport in der UdSSR*, no. 3 (1980): 26–27.

37. *Komsomolskaya Pravda*, 23 November 1982.

38. Unattributed, "Gymnastics Gala at Moscow's Palace of Sports," *Moscow News*, no. 15 (1976): 8–9.

39. *Sovetskiy Sport*, 25 March 1983.

40. N. Cherepanova, "Olympic Attachés Have the Floor," *Sport in der UdSSR*, no. 5 (1979): 6.

41. Pavlov, "Solidarity," 40.

42. I. Rudoi, "Dialogue in Language of Sport," *Sport in der UdSSR*, no. 2 (1980), 22.

43. *Olympiade-80*, no. 40 (1980): 46.

44. V. Khavin, *Moskovskaya Olimpiada V Tsifrakh I Faktakh* (Moscow, 1982), 76–124.

45. S. Pavlov, "Solidarity," 40.

46. *Olympisches Panorama*, no. 12 (1980): 12.

47. *Sovetskiy Sport*, 7 October 1982.

48. C. Dudarev, V. Lagutin, "We Thank the Soviet Specialists," *Olympisches Panorama*, no. 2 (1982): 14.

49. *Sovetskiy Sport*, 7 October 1982.

50. P. Shirova, "A Coach in Tunisia," *Sport in der UdSSR*, no. 1 (1980): 10.

51. Shepilov, 13.

52. *Sovetskiy Sport*, 7 October 1982.

53. V. Ivonin, "A Beginning for 1980," *Sport in der UdSSR*, no. 11 (1978): 33.

54. Avilov, "With Open Heart," 26.

55. *Sovetskiy Sport*, 7 October 1982.

56. Shepilov, 12.

57. Unattributed, "To Strengthen Friendship in Cooperation," *Sport in der UdSSR*, no. 6 (1977): 15.

58. Dudarev and Lagutin, 14.

59. *Sovetskiy Sport*, 7 October 1982.

60. Ibid.

61. Avilov, "Cooperation," 18.

62. Zachavin, 38–39.

63. Avilov, "With Open Heart," 26.

BARUCH A. HAZAN

64. Ibid.

65. Vasiliyev, 10.

66. Y. Bolchov, "Concrete Solidarity," *Sport in der UdSSR*, no. 1 (1983): 15.

67. S. Bliznyuk, "Noble Mission," *Sport in der UdSSR*, no. 7 (1982): 22.

68. N. Cherepanova, 6.

69. Bliznyuk, 23.

70. *Sovetskiy Sport*, 12 February 1983.

71. Mikhail Grigoryev, "USSR–Africa: A Look at Sports Relations," *Moscow News*, no. 25 (1983): 11.

72. Ibid.

73. O. Yuruyeva, "Algerian Gymnasts in Moscow," *Sport in der UdSSR*, no. 12 (1982): 15.

74. *Sovetskiy Sport*, 23 October 1982.

75. *Sovetskiy Sport*, 19 October 1982.

76. Pavlov, "Unity," 18.

77. S. Pavlov, "Solidarity," 40.

78. Bolchov, 15.

79. Unattributed, "Roads of Cooperation," *Sport in der UdSSR*, no. 5 (1978): 24.

80. Rudoi, 23.

81. Y. Mitin, "Effective Cooperation," *Sport in der UdSSR*, no. 8 (1982): 35.

82. Ibid.

83. Bliznyuk, 22.

84. I. Denisov, "A Continent Striving toward the Future," *Sport in der UdSSR*, no. 7 (1979): 18–19.

85. A. Shepilov, "Geography of Cooperation or Sports Ambassadors to All Continents," *Sovetskiy Sport*, 7 October 1982.

86. *Olympiade-80*, no. 40 (1980): 46.

87. Moscow TASS in English, 0947 GMT, 24 January 1980, FBIS *Daily Report*, 25 Jan 1980.

88. *Olympiade-80*, no. 40 (1980): 46.

89. Vasiliyev, 10.

90. "Roads of Cooperation," 27.

91. Avilov, "With Open Heart," 27.

92. Unattributed, "I. Novikov Leads Delegation to ASSC General Assembly," *Sport in der UdSSR*, no. 10 (1978): 4.

93. *Olympiade-80*, no. 40 (1980): 46.

94. Vasiliyev, 11.

95. Rudoi, 23.

96. I. Denisov, 19.

97. *Olympiade-80*, no. 40 (1980): 46.

98. Avilov, "With Open Heart," 27.

99. Pavlov, "Solidarity," 40.

100. Mitin, 34.

101. Unattributed, "Sports Cooperation Agreement," *Sport in der UdSSR*, no. 4 (1977): 20.

102. *Sovetskiy Sport,* 23 November 1982.

103. Unattributed, "With Firm Belief in Success," *Sport in der UdSSR,* no. 8 (1979): 35.

104. *Sovetskiy Sport,* 21 April 1983.

105. "Sports Cooperation Agreements," 20.

106. Unattributed, "While the Competitions Were Taking Place," *Sport in der UdSSR,* no. 11 (1979): 22.

107. *Olympisches Panorama,* no. 3 (1982): 21.

108. "To Strengthen Friendship," 14.

109. *Sovetskiy Soyuz,* no. 9 (1980): 55.

110. *Soviet Union,* no. 1 (1971): 23.

111. Rudoi, 23.

112. Y. Mitin, "Operation Springboks," *Sport in der UdSSR,* no. 12 (1981): 30–31.

113. *Sovetskiy Sport,* 2 October 1982.

114. *Sovetskiy Sport,* 7 October 1982.

115. *Komsomolskaya Pravda,* 23 November 1982, and "Gymnastics Gala," 8–9.

116. Dudarev and Lagutin, 14.

117. *Sovetskiy Sport,* 7 October 1982.

118. *Sovetskiy Sport,* 10 November 1983.

119. V. Ivonin, "Sport and Physical Culture in the USSR," *Moscow News,* no. 31 (1972): 5.

120. S. Pavlov interview, *Sport in der UdSSR,* no. 2 (1982): 27.

121. S. Pavlov, "Holiday of Peace, Friendship and Spiritual Understanding," *Sport in der UdSSR,* no. 6 (1980): 6.

122. *Sovetskiy Sport,* 2 July 1977.

123. Interview with Anani Matthia, *Sport in der UdSSR,* no. 4 (1983): 15.

124. *Sovetskiy Sport,* 5 October 1980.

125. *Sport in der UdSSR,* no. 12 (1977): 20.

126. *Sport in der UdSSR,* no. 11 (1977): 14–15.

127. *1979 Sports Calendar* (Moscow, 1978), 59.

12

Political Games:
The Meaning of International Sport for Independent Africa

WILLIAM J. BAKER

Like their European and American prede-
cessors, Africa's nationalist independence movements disrupted traditional
patterns of authority and behavior. So long as colonial administrators,
troops, and merchants remained on the scene, African nationalists united in
opposition; once their focus of xenophobic fury was removed, chaos
reigned. Nationalist parties divided into factions. Native leaders struggled
for power and profits formerly enjoyed by their colonial masters. Various
ethnic, regional, economic, and ideological interests came to the fore.
Whether independence was won from British, French, Dutch, or Portuguese rule, whether it came by force or negotiation, whether it was
infused with capitalist or socialist ideology, new African nations all faced the
inevitable struggle for stability. They had to create and enforce new laws;
hastily they constructed manageable modes of political succession; they
eagerly sought capital and encouraged economic investment; as best they
could, they erected national networks of transport and communication.

Beyond these structures of stability lay the more difficult task of building
a *sense* of nationhood: an instinctive frame of mind that would subjugate
tribal loyalties and parochial interests to sentiments of respect for, and
allegiance to, the new nation–state. Unfortunately, no groups or institutions
lent themselves to this larger national focus. Unlike older European nations,
new African states had no national churches around which they could build
hierarchies and mythologies of national identity; trade unions and student
groups affected small portions of the population. A mythology of nationhood had to be created out of nothing.

In that mythmaking endeavor, Africans recovered their past in terms
altogether different from the dominant colonialist view that posited little
importance to anything African prior to its discovery and conquest by
Europeans. Now, independent Africans looked on the colonial era as an
aberration, not the genesis, of their heritage. In festivals and folk museums
they celebrated their links with ancient forebears and unique customs.
Through contemporary symbols of nationalism, they connected their past
to their future. For purposes of unity, they adapted a hallowed European

tradition of flags and anthems. In every school and at numerous public gatherings, respect for modern symbols of national identity was fostered.

The greatest instrument of integration was the national hero. At first, the hero invariably headed the nationalist political party. Heroes came in all sizes and shapes: the colorful, zealous Habib Bourguiba of Tunisia, Kwame Nkrumah of Ghana, and Abbé Fulbert Youlou of the Congo; the shrewd, analytical style of Sékou Touré of Guinea, Modibo Keita of Mali, Nnamdi Azikiwe of Nigeria, and Julius Nyerere of Tanzania; the cautious, quiet Sylvanus Olympio of Togo, Félix Houphouët-Boigny of the Ivory Coast, Léopold-Sédar Senghor of Senegal, and Ferhat Abbas of Algeria. Elevated as the incarnation of the new nation's values and aspirations, the hero legitimized the nation. "In short," as one contemporary remarked, "the hero helps to bridge the gap to a modern state. The citizens can feel an affection for the hero which they may not have at first for the nation. Insofar as the hero works in tandem with a party structure, he provides a very powerful mechanism for integration of the state."[1]

If political heroes came first, athletic heroes shortly followed. As African runners, especially, emerged to the forefront of the international arena in the 1960s, they proudly displayed their new nations' colors. Returning home, they received accolades previously reserved for the heads of new African states: triumphal tours and ceremonial receptions, omnipresent pictures and press publicity, troubadors singing their praises, and public works and streets named in their honor. By 1970, African athletes had become powerful symbols of national identity. Like heads of state, they were highly visible, but with the added advantage that their apolitical fame would not be toppled by a coup. Even more than political heroes, athletes represented a kind of success that was ostensibly within the reach of vast numbers of young Africans.

In the world at large, they served as unofficial ambassadors. For developing African nations desperately in need of foreign technological expertise and capital investment, athletes successful at European, British Commonwealth, and Olympic games meant international visibility and prestige. Tanzania's director of sport rightly referred to Filbert Bayi as "a roving ambassador, showing the strength and determination of our people." What cultural ambassadors and African representatives to the United Nations attempted, athletes achieved with apparent ease: publicizing an image of strength and success rather than poverty and instability. American runner Marty Liquori's exaggeration makes the point: "No one heard of Kenya until Kip Keino won in Mexico City. John Akii-Bua's victory in Munich drew attention to Uganda before Idi Amin."[2]

Athletics also play a large part in the latest and most important phase of pan-Africanism, the movement for supranational unity of newly independent African states as a means of achieving common economic and political goals. The growth of organized regional athletic gatherings in the late 1950s, and then of All-African games in the 1960s, coincided significantly with the joining of black African forces across regional and language barriers. The Organization of African Unity, founded in 1963, and the Supreme Council of Sports in Africa, begun three years later, today work in tandem for the larger interests of independent Africa.

Their common foe is the apartheid regime of South Africa. Until the recent emergence of Zimbabwe, Rhodesia also claimed attention. Much of the history of black African participation in the modern international arena of sport has to do with concerted efforts to isolate and ultimately to destroy the final bastions of European colonialism on the continent. Sport is a leverage for the moving of political mountains; it is, in George Orwell's well-worn phrase, war minus the shooting.

Like threads in a rich tapestry, the meaning of sport for national identity and unity, for international visibility and prestige, and for pan-African cohesion and leverage weaves in and out of the history of independent Africa. Artificial isolation of any one of these themes would create a misleading picture. In the following narrative they appear, subtly change, and reappear in new guises just as they do in the course of modern African history.

More than half a century ago the father of the modern Olympic Games, Baron Pierre de Coubertin, spoke of "the essential conflict, the struggle of the colonial mind against movement towards emancipation of the native peoples" of Asia and Africa. Politically, economically, and militarily, the prospect of colonial independence seemed "full of perils" for Europe's imperial powers. Of greater interest to Coubertin was the distant possibility of European and American athletic dominance being challenged in the quadrennial Olympic Games. Africa especially seemed full of athletic promise. Coubertin in 1920 stood convinced that "before long sporting Africa will organize itself in spite of everything."[3]

The little baron himself attempted to hasten the process. In cooperation with Angelo Bolanaki, an Egyptian member of the International Olympic Committee, Coubertin ambitiously planned for All-African Games to begin in Algiers in 1925, hoping that they would be held regularly thereafter at two-year intervals. Massive financial and organizational problems thwarted the scheme, forcing Coubertin and Bolanaki to push back the opening date to 1929 and to change the site to Alexandria. The Egyptian government provided large sums of money for a stadium and facilities; medals and flags were made ready. Just a few weeks before the games were to begin, however, British and French colonial administrators vetoed the scheme. A large gathering of black Africans seemed both too expensive and potentially explosive. Reluctantly, British authorities allowed regional East African

Games between Kenya and Uganda to begin in 1934, with Tanzania joining a year later. From the outset, organized sport in Africa was circumscribed by political considerations.[4]

All the more did African participation in the Olympic Games reflect the political history of Africa. The continent's first Olympic victor was a South African schoolboy, R. E. Walker. A member of an all-white sports club modeled on traditional European lines, Walker won the gold medal in the one hundred meters at the London Olympics in 1908. At Stockholm four years later, Ali Mohammed Hassanein of Egypt competed in the saber and foil events, but sixteen years intervened before two Egyptian athletes became Olympic medalists. Only South Africa and Egypt regularly represented the entire African continent in the Olympic Games until small teams from Nigeria and Ghana participated in the Helsinki games of 1952. Prior to 1960, in fact, merely fifteen South Africans, six Egyptians, and a handful of North Africans (such as marathoners A. B. El Quafi of Morocco in 1928 and Alain Mimoun of Algeria in 1956, both competing under the flag of France) won Olympic laurels.[5]

Finally in 1960 Abebe Bikila of Ethiopia ran the marathon barefoot through the streets of Rome to claim the first gold medal for a black African nation. Coming in second to Bikila was Ben Abdesselam Rhadi of Morocco, as four of the first eight places in the marathon went to Africans. In all, about 100 Africans participated in the Rome Olympics. At Tokyo four years later, 150 Africans competed. There Bikila won another marathon gold, Mohammed Gammoudi of Tunisia took a silver medal in the ten thousand meters, and Wilson Kiprugut of Kenya came in third in the eight hundred meters.[6]

This surge to Olympic visibility came squarely in the midst of the movement for African independence from European rule. Whereas only five autonomous African states existed prior to 1960, no fewer than sixteen nations claimed independence in the same year that Bikila first won an Olympic medal. The year 1960 was accurately dubbed "the year of Africa." Within the following decade, the total number of independent states climbed to forty-three, representing some 300 million Africans living under governments of their own people.[7] Again, dramatic athletic victories at the Mexico City games of 1968 symbolized the African emergence. In the thin air of Mexico City, thirteen African athletes took the victory stand to receive sixteen different medals, compared to only three medals each at the two previous Olympics.[8]

An overwhelming number of Africa's Olympic victors—Bikila, Kipurgut, Mamo Wolde, Kipchoge Keino, Miruts Yifter, Benjamin Jipcho, Nafutali Temu, Amos Biwott, Filbert Bayi, and John Akii-Bua, to name a few—have come from the ranks of police and army forces. Especially in the early days of independence, as African school and university facilities were woefully inadequate, police and army organizations provided athletic equipment as well as regular pay and a consistent emphasis on physical fitness. "Athletics is a discipline," noted a European in Africa in 1966, "and the army and police imitate that discipline with regular hours, regular meals and regular sleep, all of which are vital to top-class athletes."[9] The army and police were of crucial importance to the stability (or lack of the same) of emerging nations; they were also important for African athletic perform-ance.

So were foreign coaches. The American Mal Whitfield, for example, went to East Africa in 1953 just after winning gold medals in the eight hundred meters in two successive Olympics (London in 1948 and Helsinki in 1952), and administered American aid programs to Africa while also coaching national track teams.[10] Following in Whitfield's train in the 1960s were several Peace Corps volunteers such as John Manners, who taught and coached track at a secondary school in Kenya;[11] and Tim Hickey and Nick Wetter, who combined teaching at a college in Dar es Salaam with organiz-ing national track meets, coaching the Tanzanian women's track team, and taking them to the East African Games in 1967.[12] Yet for all their diplomatic interest in Africa during the era of the cold war, Americans had no monop-oly on the coaching of African athletes. A Swedish resident in Ethiopia, Onni Niskanen, originally coached the great Bikila.[13]

In Kenya, especially, British teachers and coaches remained long after independence. A Cambridge University graduate, David Lewis, instructed Ben Jipcho in his formative years. Another Englishman, Robert Hancock, taught in seconday schools, coached various track teams from 1966 to 1974, and served as the only foreigner on the staff of the Kenyan Olympic team in 1972.[14] Most impressive of all, though, was John Velzian. A graduate of London University and the Carnegie College of Physical Education, Velzian went to Kenya in 1958 as a physical education officer for the British government. Each year he traveled several thousand miles raising the stan-dards of athletic performances in Kenya's schools, all the while scouring the countryside for promising athletes. In 1962 he discovered Kip Keino run-ning a 4:21.8 mile on a grassy track in Nyeri. Seeing potential, Velzian coaxed and coached Keino toward his record-breaking mile at the Com-monwealth Games in London in 1966, which set him on the way to Olympic stardom. Other Kenyan runners who developed under Velzian's tutelage included Nafutali Temu, Wilson Kiprugut, Ben Kogo, John Owiti, and Daniel Rudisha.[15]

The presence of foreigners such as John Velzian is an appropriate reminder that modern African sport was, from the outset, international in character. For all their importance, however, foreign coaches merely facilitated African athletes. The motivating force, and thus the larger meaning, lay in indige-nous factors. As some social scientists explain it, sport at the international

British champion hurdler Jack Parker instructs Kenyan Korigo Barmo, 1950s.
Courtesy of Kenya Department of Information.

level provided instant recognition for new African nations, serving as an
informal, unofficial, but highly visible corollary to the transnational activities of official diplomats and formal negotiations.[16] Australian runner
Ron Clarke offers a simpler, much more vivid explanation: "As well as their
physical attributes, the Africans have the tremendous incentive of representing small, intensely proud, emerging nations. Rightly, they are regarded as
national heroes whose exploits win their countries more publicity and
prestige than dozens of rousing political speeches."[17]

Yet the international, political meaning of sport for emerging African
nations ultimately depends on the internal, social meaning of sport for
modern Africans. No simple explanation will suffice, nor can attention on a
single sport such as track adequately explain the significance of sport for
Africans in the international arena.

Amid all their constitutional changes, military coups, and civil wars, young
African nations adapted old European styles of government to suit their
own needs. For purposes of health and discipline, they also promoted

American Chuck Coker assists Kenyan shot-putter Ayo Orlando, 1950s. Courtesy of Kenya Department of Information.

Western athletic games and programs of physical education in their schools. They found sport to be an invaluable common denominator for the pulling together of numerous tribes with diverse customs and languages into single nations. This potential of sport as a unifying factor was nothing new to the continent. "Our Administration officers are welding tribes into a nation," commented an Englishman in Kenya in 1927, as he observed the political effects of British transport, communication, and football (soccer) on the African scene. "Football teams now travel hundreds of miles by train and steamer to play the teams of other tribes."[18] After Kenya's independence in 1963, colonial administrators left the scene; trains, steamers, and football remained, to the young nation's benefit.

Long established as a popular "people's game" in Britain and France, soccer's simple rules and inexpensive equipment made it readily accessible to Africans. Its requirements of agility, speed, and endurance rather than brute strength gave it popular appeal throughout the continent except in the white dominions of South Africa and Rhodesia, where rugby football dominated.[19] In 1957 the first Africa Cup of Nations, staged in Khartoum as a corollary to Kwame Nkrumah's pan-Africanism, became the prototype for several pan-African sporting events. That seven different nations won the first ten cups—Egypt, Ghana, and Zaire twice each, and Ethiopia, Sudan, Congo-Brazzaville, and Morocco once each—indicates the universal appeal of the game for Africans. In 1972 Ghana's national team, the Black Stars, reached the finals of the Munich Olympics. In West Germany two years later, the Zaire Leopards became the first team from south of the Sahara to represent Africa in the World Cup.[20]

An altogether different sport, boxing, is similarly popular in emergent Africa. Even more than football, boxing is "labor intensive" rather than "capital intensive" in its initial stage of learning, making it attractive to underprivileged African youths just as it is for American ghetto blacks. Moreover, pugilism provides a unique link with old tribal tests of masculine prowess, and with the African warrior tradition.[21] Whatever its social and psychological roots, boxing in modern Africa is a favorite means of achieving international recognition. In 1974 the National Sports Commission of Nigeria signed former light-heavyweight champion Archie Moore to a two-year contract as a trainer of Nigerian boxers for Olympic, Commonwealth, and All-African contests.[22]

Black Africa's first world champion was a boxer. In 1922 Senegal's Louis Phal, known as Battling Siki, briefly held the world's light-heavyweight title. More recently, Nigerian Dick Tiger won the middleweight crown just before his nation won its independence; Nigerian Hogan Bassey later became featherweight champion. In 1975 David Kotey of Ghana seized the featherweight title. Until three boxers from Kenya emerged as medalists in the Olympic Games of 1968 and 1972, African world-class boxing achievements seemed a West African monopoly. Still, at the All-African Games in Lagos in 1973, boxers from Nigeria, Ghana, and Uganda won exactly half of the forty-two medals, with the other twenty-one medals going to pugilists from eleven different nations.[23]

This uneven geographical distribution of top-flight boxers is characteristic of most sport in Africa. Sporting traditions, programs, and international successes vary greatly from nation to nation. Until recently, countries such as Botswana, Mozambique, Rwanda, Burundi, Somalia, Zaire, and Sudan had little or no organized sport. Although weak programs in Zambia and Malawi are exceptions to the rule, former British and French colonies generally have the strongest sporting traditions: Nigeria, Ghana, the Ivory Coast, Senegal, and Cameroon in the west; Kenya, Uganda, and Tanzania in the east; Tunisia, Algeria, and Morocco in the north. Similarly scattered throughout Africa are varieties of handball, hockey, judo, swimming, cycling, lawn tennis, wrestling, and table tennis programs.[24]

Two other competitive activities require mention as the fastest-growing of all African sports. One is basketball. In 1946 a Nigerian looked on basketball in his homeland as "more or less a feminine sport" that was "thought to be a mild game, and therefore left to the fair sex." Yet he rightly predicted that in a few years basketball would "attract boys and assume the intensity of fight and swiftness of feet it has attained in the United States."[25] American Olympian, collegiate All-American, and professional star Bill Russell contributed to that turnaround when he toured several African countries in 1959, teaching the game.[26] What Russell introduced, Peace Corps volunteers firmly established. Periodic reports in the *Olympic Review* indicate that in nation after nation basketball ranks right alongside soccer as the sport that is growing fastest and attracting the largest number of spectators.[27] The recent emergence of Nigeria's Akeem Abdul Olajuwon and Sudan's Manute Bol to basketball fame and fortune in the United States will no doubt fan the flame of African enthusiasm.[28]

Scarcely is any external stimulus necessary for the growth of track competition in Africa. One cannot speak of track and field, for as of yet there is little African competence in field athletics such as javelin and discus throwing, activities that require special equipment, formal coaching, and stylized discipline for success. Except for a few hurdlers and steeplechasers, Africa's track stars have all been of the middle-distance and long-distance variety. Distance running seems "natural" for Africans, who have known a minimum of mechanized, motorized transportation.

Success builds on success. An Englishman in rural Africa in the early 1960s frequently heard road runners on their way to and from work teasingly greet each other with the ultimate reference to speed and stamina, "Abebe Bikila." Bikila's breakthrough to world fame inspired athletic determination and confidence all over Africa.[29] In Kenya, Kipchoge Keino's four medals in the 1968 and 1972 Olympics had the same effect. So did the feats of Filbert Bayi, whose emergence in various African and world meets in the mid-1970s seemed, to one reporter, "just what Tanzania needs" for athletic development. "He will do the same thing for Tanzania that Kipchoge Keino did for Kenya: give the people a person to be proud of and to follow."[30]

As pride borders on religious adoration of those tribal representatives whose magical exploits provide commonly accepted symbols of excellence and models of achievement, Max Weber's concept of the charismatic leader is peculiarly applicable to the African scene.[31] Primarily concerned with political leadership, Weber insisted that the charismatic head of state is especially attractive to people whose styles of life and government are in transition from traditional to modern modes of behavior. "In short," as Lancine Sylla puts it, "charismatic governments are quite likely to emerge in societies that, like those of Africa, are undergoing profound cultural transformation."[32] As political theorists apply Weber's idea of the charismatic leader to the thorny question of political succession in modern African states, a similar model is appropriate for an understanding of the emergence of modern African sport.

Athletes stand tall alongside political leaders in the African definition of nationhood, new social values, and future goals. Until his tragic automobile accident in 1969 that left him paralyzed and prey to death four years later, Abebe Bikila remained a national hero who ranked "not far below the Emperor Haile Selassie in the hearts of his countrymen."[33] Bikila, after all, first won his laurels in the capital city of Italy, Ethiopia's hated conqueror under Mussolini. Bikila's reputation immediately took on epic proportions. According to folklore that still circulates in Addis Ababa, his prestige aroused the jealousy of the emperor himself. Rumor has it that the auto accident was arranged at Selassie's command, and that the emperor furthermore ordered the national radio to refrain from reporting Bikila's death and funeral arrangements in 1973. These tales might merely reflect antigovernment bias. Most certainly they suggest a godlike reputation of a national sports hero.

Announced or not, Bikila's funeral procession attracted thousands of spontaneous participants. At the head of the procession, mourners held aloft Bikila's trophies, medals, track shoes, and uniform. The rich imagery invites anthropological analysis. In a ritual strikingly reminiscent of the funeral rites accorded a chieftain in Bikila's tribe, wherein the tribal leader's bows, arrows, and hunting trophies were displayed, the charismatic Bikila received the honor due the great hunter who had gone into the distant forest, won his trophies, and brought them home to tribal acclaim.[34]

Without the tragic overtones, Kipchoge Keino similarly achieved charismatic status in Kenya, where nationalistic pride rolled easily off the tongue in the alliterative trinity of Kenya, Kenyatta, and Keino. At Mexico City in

1968, Keino dramatically captured his first gold medal on 20 October, Kenyatta Day in Kenya. He instantly won undying fame in popular verse and music. One song extolled his feats in the tribal tongue of Kiswahili, and two others in Kelenjin. A Nairobi street was named in his honor. In 1970 Keino received the Distinguished Service Medal from the hands of Kenyatta.[35]

Charismatic athletes provide models for African youths. Filbert Bayi and Suleiman Nyambi Mujaya, for example, represented new possibilities for Tanzanian hero-worshippers. "Our young people like to run, to compete. But all they have done in the past is run and they have been satisfied with beating whomever they happened to be racing against," observed Erasto Zambi, Tanzania's national coach, in 1976. "Now that there is talk of records and medals and trips abroad, they have something to aim for."[36]

Just a decade or so before black African athletes first set their sights on Olympic records and medals, Africans other than Egyptians and South Africans began competing internationally. Early in the 1950s, old French and British imperial connections opened some doors for athletic meets. To Bolebec, France, Tunisians and Algerians regularly went for international cross-country races. In the mid-1950s, several Ghanaian and Nigerian athletes competed at White City Stadium, London, in the British Commonwealth Games—but without much success. Black African runners seemed, to an English observer, "a bit of a joke." Starting off fast only to wither quickly, the African apparently lacked the discipline, patience, character, and intelligence necessary to win at high-level competitions: "The African was the clown at the court of the European athlete."[37]

Something good came of that bad situation. In Uganda a group of colonial administrators served as a British Empire Games Committee for the 1954 games in Vancouver, Canada. A year later they continued to exist as a group, but with a new name: the Ugandan Olympic Committee. They were officially recognized by the International Olympic Committee six years before Ugandan independence. In 1956 Uganda sent three athletes to the Melbourne Olympic Games.[38]

Prior to any Olympic triumphs, however, African sportsmen organized several regional meets on the order of the old East African Games. At first, intra-African athletic competition reflected regional divisions and rivalries roughly analogous to the political groups known as Brazzaville, Casablanca, and Monrovia blocs.[39] In 1959 the *Jeux Inter-Africains* began in Bangui, Central African Republic, as an athletic event open only to French-speaking nations. In the following year came the inaugural West African Games, founded in Lagos, Nigeria, as part of Nigeria's independence celebration, for English and French-speaking Africans alike. Of far greater importance were the *Jeux de l'Amitié,* begun in 1960 in Tananarive, Madagascar, as an event sponsored jointly by the French government and sixteen former French colonies. About eight hundred athletes competed in eight events at those first "Games of Friendship." At Abidjan of the Ivory Coast in the following year, English-speaking Nigerians and Liberians joined to swell the numbers of participants.

Finally in 1963 the Games of Friendship came of age. At Dakar, Senegal, twenty-four hundred athletes from France and twenty-four new African nations (including English-speaking Gambia, Ghana, Liberia, Nigeria, and Sierra Leone) participated in a full program of track-and-field events. For the first time ever in international competition, African women ran and jumped for laurels.[40] Even more noteworthy was the attendance of the world's leading official of amateur sport. The presence of Avery Brundage, president of the International Olympic Committee, gave an official stamp of approval to the Games of Friendship. Just a few months later, Brundage nominated Sir Adetokunbo Ademola of Nigeria as the first black African member of the International Olympic Committee.[41]

The Games of Friendship served as the basis for the larger All-African Games. Before leaving Dakar in 1963, several officials discussed the possibility of pan-African games that would include every independent African nation except the apartheid states of Rhodesia and South Africa. In February, 1964, representatives from twenty-two nations convened in Brazzaville, to elect a permanent committee for the planning of the *Jeux Africains* (All-African Games). They planned exceedingly well.

The first All-African Games, in Brazzaville in July 1965, were a huge success. Avery Brundage attended with several of his colleagues from the International Olympic Committee; Abebe Bikila of Ethiopia was an honored guest. The president of the Congo Republic, Alfonse Massamba Debat, artfully wove sport and politics together in his opening address. "The torch of African sport will not fade out," he confidently announced. "On the contrary, its flame has today reached every corner of our continent." Brazzaville was honored "to be able to brandish this torch on this historic occasion, when the whole of Africa is declaring and celebrating its entity." At the center of that celebration were exciting contests involving more than three thousand athletes from thirty independent African nations.[42]

For the coordination and promotion of pan-African sport, and of African athletes in the global arena, the creation of the Supreme Council for Sports in Africa (SCSA) was of crucial importance. A successor of the permanent committee that had planned the first All-African Games, the SCSA originated with representatives of thirty-two African nations in Bamaki, Mali, in December 1966. Its permanent headquarters were established in Yaoundé, Cameroon. The first elected officers were André Hombassa of Congo-Brazzaville, president; Abraham Ordia of Nigeria, vice-president; Badora

Sow of Mali, second vice-president; and Jean-Claude Ganga of Congo-Brazzaville, secretary-general. A kind of "communications centre and clearinghouse for sport," the SCSA was formally recognized by the Organization of African Unity (OAU) in 1967.[43]

The need for coordination of sport throughout Africa was great, but the primary motive for the creation of the Supreme Council of Sports in Africa was to assault the bastion of racially segregated sport in South Africa. From the outset, the SCSA resolved "to use every means to obtain the expulsion of South African sports organizations from the Olympic Movement and from International Federations should South Africa fail to comply fully with IOC rules." One of the earliest public pronouncements of the SCSA was a declaration that its members would participate in the 1968 Olympics only if "no racialist team from South Africa takes part."[44]

South African apartheid, of course, was no new problem. Long had a strict separation of whites and nonwhites been enforced in South Africa. In 1954 came the first official government ban against racially integrated sports, when a Natal provincial council forbade mixed sports in educational institutions supported by the council. In 1956 that local ban was extended to the entire nation, covering all kinds of South African teams and sporting events, at home and abroad. The South African National Olympic Committee (SANOC) quickly joined the parade, announcing in November 1957 that it would sponsor no racially mixed athletics with South Africa.[45]

Under pressure from the International Olympic Committee, SANOC agreed that all South African athletes, regardless of color, would be eligible for the 1960 Olympics in Rome. As several critics observed, however, nonwhites without top-level training and competition had little chance of making the national team. Still, a black weight lifter, Precious McKenzie, defeated all his white competitors in segregated trials, only to be disqualified on a technicality. SANOC sent an all-white team to Rome.[46]

A series of events then began the process of isolating South Africa from the entire sporting world. In withdrawing from the British Commonwealth in 1961, South Africa disqualified itself from the Commonwealth Games. Within a year, international football and cricket organizations banned South African teams. But the South African government merely dug in its heels. In February, 1962, a new minister of the interior, Jan de Klerk, reaffirmed the principle that "no mixed team should take part in sports inside or outside this country." The government cracked down ruthlessly on dissidents. In 1963 Dennis Brutus, the founder of an opposition group, the South African Non-Racial Olympic Committee, was shot and nearly killed by a police officer.[47]

In 1963 a general session of the International Olympic Committee was scheduled in Nairobi, the first time such a meeting was to be held in Africa.

By then, though, black African nations were adamantly united against South Africa. Under pressure from the Organization of African Unity, the Kenyan government announced that it would refuse admittance of South African delegates to the session. Fearful of divisiveness, the IOC shifted its meeting to Baden-Baden, West Germany. There they voted to withdraw South Africa's invitation to the forthcoming Tokyo Olympics unless South Africa presented evidence of "a modification of its policy of discrimination in sports matters and in competitions in its country" by 31 December 1963.[48] No evidence was forthcoming. In January 1964, the IOC voted to ban the South Africans from the Tokyo games.

That extraordinary event gave notice of the emerging strength of new African nations acting in unison. For all their different interests, economic needs, and political philosophies, they found common ground on the South African question. The controversy over South Africa also reflected the larger cold war conflict between the world's two superpowers, the United States and the Soviet Union. Avery Brundage said more than he meant when he observed that "Africa is today a battleground for conflicting political creeds."[49] For strategic, political reasons, Soviet officials firmly supported black African demands against South Africa, while the United States Olympic Committee attempted to avoid the issue. On one point, however, all agreed. As the head of the International Aid Committee stated the case in the early 1960s, "There is no doubt that the whole world is now turned toward Africa and that the interests of all kinds—in spirit as in quality—mingle there."[50]

The focus remained on South Africa, forcing SANOC to promise a nonracial team selected by a nonracial committee for the Mexico City Olympics of 1968. But the South African government's refusal to budge on their larger apartheid policies prompted Jean-Claude Ganga to declare to the executive board of the IOC in 1967 that "we do not want South African blacks to come dressed like apes at a fair, and when the fair is over to be sent back to their cages."[51] Aroused, the IOC appointed a three-man commission to investigate the South African situation firsthand. In September 1967, Lord Michael Killanin of Ireland, Sir Adetokunbo Ademola of Nigeria, and Sir Reginald Alexander of Kenya spent ten days in South Africa interviewing white and nonwhite athletes, administrators, and politicians. Then they went to Lausanne to talk with exiled South African sportsmen such as Dennis Brutus, Precious McKenzie, and Chris de Broglio. Finally, in late January 1968, the commission issued its report.[52]

Scarcely a complete whitewash, the report nevertheless conveyed much positive assurance that nonwhite athletes in South Africa had adequate facilities and coaching, and that SANOC would select a multiracial team for the Mexico City games. On the basis of that assessment, IOC officials recommended the readmission of South Africa and sent out a postal ballot to all its members. On 15 February Avery Brundage happily announced the verdict: South Africa would be invited to send a team to Mexico City.[53]

Black Africa was outraged. The Organization of African Unity immediately called for a boycott of the 1968 summer Olympics. Algeria and Ethiopia first announced their withdrawal; Uganda, Tanzania, Ghana, Guinea, Gambia, and Kenya quickly followed. Within two weeks of the IOC's announcement, all thirty-two members of the Supreme Council for Sports in Africa were committed to a boycott. Never had the modern Olympic movement encountered such a solid, immovable force of opposition.[54]

Global support for the proposed boycott mounted, especially among Islamic and Caribbean nations, and within the Communist bloc of nations led by the Soviet Union. American blacks, discontented with their own native version of racial discrimination, cast their lot with black Africans. Within the previous year, outstanding black American athletes such as baseballer Jackie Robinson, basketballer Oscar Robertson, and tennis player Arthur Ashe had signed a petition addressed to the president of the United States Olympic Committee, urging that South Africa be kept out of the Olympics.[55] Now a young California professor of sociology, Harry Edwards, mobilized angry black Olympic athletes in agreeing to boycott the Mexico City games if South Africa were permitted to participate.[56]

Avery Brundage and the IOC finally got the message. In late April 1968, the IOC executive board met to reconsider the South African issue. Reluctantly they agreed that "in view of all the information on the international climate," their prior invitation to South Africa should be withdrawn. Another poll by mail returned an overwhelming agreement. Only American, Australian, West German, and Scandinavian, IOC members held out in support of South Africa, but their efforts were in vain.[57] White South African athletes were spared the ordeal of witnessing black African runners win a fistful of medals at Mexico City.[58]

White Rhodesians, too, missed that spectacle, for Rhodesia was also absent from the 1968 Olympics. Salisbury's Unilateral Declaration of Independence from Britain in 1965 had resulted in a resolution by the United Nations Security Council that Rhodesian passports should not be honored. Under pressure from black Africans and their international web of support, Mexican officals had little difficulty preventing a Rhodesian team from entering their country. The Rhodesian issue was thus shelved for future controversy.[59]

For the moment, South Africa remained at the forefront of African political interest as expressed in athletic terms. In order to appease their sportsmen who had been excluded from Mexico City, Pretoria officials in 1969 accepted Shell Oil money for the sponsorship of South African Games, to which only white athletes from Europe and North America would be invited. Black Africa rose immediately to the challenge. Kenya and Nigeria threatened to boycott the Commonwealth Games of 1970 if any Commonwealth nations participated in the South African Games. The Supreme Council for Sports in Africa went further, promising that none of its members would participate in the 1972 Munich Olympics if West Germany sent a team to South Africa. Confronted with these threats, virtually all foreigners declined the South African invitation. Even American athletic organizations withdrew official support of their athletes; Britain sent a solitary token participant.[60]

The noose tightened around the neck of South African athletics. Between 1968 and 1970, South African judo, boxing, weight lifting, and gymnastics teams were barred from international competition. Wherever a South African track team appeared, black African nations boycotted the event. In the spring of 1970, South Africa was momentarily banned from Davis Cup playoffs shortly after the Pretoria government refused black American tennis star Arthur Ashe a visa to play in South Africa.[61] Simultaneously, a proposed South African cricket tour of England and Northern Ireland provoked demonstrations and riots in Britain, causing the British government to cancel the visit. Then the International Olympic Committee drove the final nail in the coffin. Meeting in Amsterdam in May 1970, the IOC voted, 35–28 with three abstentions, to expel South Africa from the Olympic movement. No less than 98 percent of the nonwhite delegates voted with the majority.[62]

Early in the 1970s, Rhodesia joined South Africa as the target of athletic black Africa's "war without weapons" against minority white rule. In 1971 an investigating team of IOC officials judged Rhodesian sport facilities, teams, and competitive meets to be acceptably multiracial, so in order to avoid the earlier problem of passports, the IOC invited Rhodesia to participate in the 1972 Munich games as British subjects flying their preindependence flag. But black African leaders bristled at this artificial arrangement, insisting that Ian Smith's government was a broadly based form of white supremacy.

Whatever the facts of equal or near-equal athletic opportunities for Rhodesian blacks, nothing short of exclusion from Munich would be acceptable to black Africa. Just two weeks prior to the opening of the games, Guinea, Ethiopia, Ghana, Zambia, Tanzania, Sierra Leone, Liberia, Sudan, and Kenya publicly announced their boycott intentions; other African teams privately decided to follow. Once again black American athletes supported their African "brothers." For altogether different reasons, the Communist bloc did the same. Hastily the IOC reviewed its decision. In a sterling example of "doubletalk and doublethink," they manufactured a transparent excuse to repeal their earlier contrivance: Rhodesians would not compete at Munich because they had no passports proving they were British subjects.[63]

Finally expelled from the IOC in May 1975, Rhodesia ceased being a crucial factor in African Olympic participation. The spotlight turned again to South Africa and its sporting contacts with other nations. In May 1976, tensions reappeared in the unlikely form of a New Zealand rugby tour scheduled in the land of the Springboks. Although rugby was not an Olympic sport, the Organization of African Unity and the Supreme Council for Sports in Africa threatened in unison to boycott the forthcoming Montreal Olympics if New Zealand were allowed to participate. Just forty-eight hours before the opening of the games, fifteen African nations sent the IOC a final ultimatum demanding New Zealand's ouster. Stunned, and by now impatient with African persistence, the IOC refused to act. "As the hours ticked by towards the opening ceremonies," recalled one witness, "nobody was disposed to make even token concessions."[64] In the largest Olympic boycott ever to that time, thirty African nations withdrew from the 1976 Montreal Olympics.[65]

Little immediate effect seems to have been made on the world's "sporting contact" with South Africa. But yet another African threat to boycott the 1978 Commonwealth Games in Edmonton, Canada, prompted the delegates at a Commonwealth conference in London to agree unanimously to "discourage contact or competition by their nationals with sporting organizations, teams or sportsmen from South Africa or from any other country where sports are organized on the basis of race, colour or ethnic origin."[66] To the dismay of Jean-Claude Ganga and his SCSA organization, this "Gleneagles Agreement" was soon circumvented by both Great Britain and New Zealand.

In conservative Olympic circles, where a strict separation of sport and politics was an enshrined myth for the friends and heirs of Avery Brundage, irritation often gave way to infuriation at the constant threat of African boycotts from 1964 to 1976. Yet one Olympic apologist, Geoffey Miller, admits that "the staunchest champions of Olympism must have felt some innate sympathy with the Africans, who still have much to fight for." Miller offers a reasonable explanation for the African tactic: "Demonstration in the sports world, unfortunately, is one of their few effective weapons. Economic sanctions would hurt only themselves and they have little technology to withhold from the world, but they do produce great sportsmen, particularly in track and field, who mean much to the watching public."[67]

Yet the recent history of African participation in the politics of international sport is not all Olympic boycotts, nor is it confined to track-and-field athletes. As in South America, African soccer matches are often highly charged with nationalistic passions. Several recent matches have ended in nasty displays of violence. At Addis Ababa in 1974, rough play and physical scuffles between Ethiopian and Kenyan players fired emotions to such an extent that spectators threw bottles, invaded the field, and provoked policemen to fire their pistols in the air. A Zairean referee called off the game as several people staggered away, bleeding profusely.[68]

Political passions made an even messier scene in Libya in 1978, as an Egyptian team defeated Libya in a quarterfinal match for the Africa Cup. Just prior to the match, Egyptian President Anwar Sadat had announced his peace initiative with Israel, a measure bitterly opposed by the Arab "rejectionist" nations of Libya, Algeria, Syria, Iraq, and South Yemen. At the end of the game, the Egyptian team was assaulted by Libyan players and fans. Two Egyptian players suffered broken arms, and several others came away with cuts and bruises to the head. As Egypt withdrew from the Africa Cup tournament, irate partisans smashed Libyan and Algerian airline offices in Cairo. The president of Egypt's Sports Council, Abdul Aziz el-Shafei, announced that Egyptian athletes would no longer compete in "rejectionist" countries.[69]

While the rest of the world scarcely knew of these soccer squabbles, Africa's most publicized sporting event to date was a world heavyweight championship bout between title-holder George Foreman and challenger Muhammad Ali in Kinshasha, Zaire, in the autumn of 1974. A mixture of economic and political motives prompted President Mobutu Sese Seko to welcome the fight to Zaire. Having come to power in 1965 in an army-backed coup, Mobutu needed to cleanse his nation's image as an unstable society in order to entice foreign capital for his copper, cobalt, and diamond mines. "The fight will create a favorable press," said a Zaire diplomat to an American reporter, "so that President Mobutu will not be thought of as the leader of a country where people eat each other."[70]

To achieve his purpose, Mobutu waived bothersome customs regulations, paved several roads, installed streetlights in Kinshasa, and imported two hundred new air-conditioned Mercedes buses to accommodate visitors. He also reserved hundreds of first-class rooms in Kinshasa's best hotels and university dormitories, and even forbade taxi drivers and prostitutes to hike up their prices. Unfortunately he met with mixed success. Kinshasa's heat, poverty, and primitive conditions shocked foreign visitors. Provoked by criticism, Mobutu only made matters worse by imposing censorship on information leaving the country. The fall of Foreman in the eighth round brought a decisive end to Africa's first exposure to the tawdry drama of modern commercial sport.[71]

Just two months after that event, a much less publicized athletic gathering in Accra, Ghana, symbolized the future of sport in Africa. The first All-Africa University Games, built on foundations laid by the Council of West Africa University Games (1965) and the Federation of African University Sports (1971), were held in December 1974. They represented an initial step toward the end of the domination of police and armed services over African sport. The All-Africa University Games also promised a diminution of the "muscle drain" of African athletes to American universities.[72] In 1974 about fifty male and female Africans on track scholarships in the United States signified a pattern that would change only as African universities improved their sports programs.[73]

Given the lack of American support for African Olympic boycott movements from 1964 to 1976, the American call for a boycott of the Moscow Olympics in 1980 seemed, to many Africans, a bad joke. Most ludicrous of all was a visit by boxer Muhammad Ali to Tanzania, Kenya, Nigeria, Senegal, and Liberia, seeking support for President Carter's policy. Confronted with hard questions about America's motives, and especially about the United States' unwillingness to stand by Africans in their past boycott efforts, Ali bumbled his mission. Tanzanians and Nigerians especially considered him an insult. In the end, the only Africans who supported the American boycott of the Moscow Games were those nations that had traditional links with the United States (such as Liberia) and those that depended heavily on Western aid and expertise (such as Zaire and Kenya).[74]

For all their varied responses to the Moscow boycott, however, Africans continued to agree on one fundamental premise: that sports and politics were, for them, inseparably joined. Not for them the Western attitude expressed best by a West German IOC member, Willi Daume, who railed against "political pressure on international sport and the Olympics." For Daume, Avery Brundage, and their kind, international sporting events were not "the place to resolve political disputes."[75] For Africans, on the other hand, Nigeria's Minister of Sport Sylvanus Williams in the late 1970s dismissed "the philosophy that sport and politics should not mix" as a "hypocritical" position. "Sporting achievements," added Williams, "today are used as a measure of our country's greatness."[76] So has it been for the past quarter-century; so will it continue into the indefinite future for the developing nations of Africa.

Notes

1. Immanuel Wallerstein, *Africa: The Politics of Independence* (New York: Vintage Press, 1961), 99.

2. Marty Liquori and Skip Myslenski, *On the Run: In Search of the Perfect Race* (New York: William Morrow, 1979), 30.

3. Quoted in Michael Killanin and John Rodda, eds., *The Olympic Games: 80 Years of People, Events and Records* (London: Barrie Jenkins, 1976), 141.

4. Abraham A. Ordia, *History of the All-African Games* (Lagos: National Sports Council of Nigeria, 1973), 5–6; and "The Arab Republic of Egypt and Olympism," *Olympic Review* 122–23 (November–December 1977): 692–703.

5. Muriel Horrell, *South Africa and the Olympic Games* (Johannesburg: South African Institute of Race Relations, 1968), 6–7; Ramadhan Ali, *Africa at the Olympics*

(London: Africa Books, 1976), 67–68, 117; and for a first-hand acount of the Nigerians at Helsinki, see B. A. A. Goubadia, *Our Olympic Adventure* (Lagos: Crownbird, 1953).

6. David Prokop, ed., *The African Running Revolution* (Mountain View, Cal: World Publications, 1975), 4; Ali, 68–69; "Ethiopia and Olympism,"*Olympic Review* 114 (April 1977): 253–58; and "Morocco and Olympism," *Olympic Review* 135 (January 1979): 35–41.

7. Donald George Morrison, et al., eds., *Black Africa: A Comparative Handbook* (New York: The Free Press, 1972), xxv; and John Hatch, *Africa Emergent: Africa's Problems since Independence* (Chicago: Henry Regnery, 1974), 1–31.

8. Ali, 152–53.

9. Martin Kane, "A Very Welcome Redcoat," *Sports Illustrated,* 19 December 1966: 81; and cf. Ali, 114. On Bikila's role as imperial bodyguard, see the *New York Times,* 5 March 1967; on Keino's work as police inspector, see the *New York Times,* 1 February 1969.

10. "They Say It's a Revolution," *Ebony* (August 1976): 199; and Ali, 135.

11. Prokop, 26.

12. *New York Times,* 3 May 1976.

13. Geoff Fenwick, "The African Approach to Competition," in Prokop, 24.

14. Prokop, pp. 5, 9.

15. Kane, 79–81.

16. Timothy M. Shaw and Susan M. Shaw, "Sport As Transnational Politics: A Preliminary Analysis of Africa," in Benjamin Lowe, David B. Kanin, and Andrew Strenk, eds., *Sport in International Relations* (Champaign, Ill.: Stipes, 1978), 386–99.

17. Ron Clarke, as told to Alan Trengone, *The Unforgiving Minute* (London: Pelham Books, 1966), 168.

18. Quoted in George Shepperson, "External Factors in the Development of African Nationalism," in P. J. M. McEwan, ed., *Twentieth-Century Africa* (London: Oxford University Press, 1968), 439; and cf. Ralph C. Uwechue, "Nation Building and Sport in Africa," in Lowe, et al., 538–50.

19. James Walvin, *The People's Game: A Social History of British Football* (Newton Abbot, England: Readers Union, 1975), 109–11; Nicholas Mason, *Football! The Story of All the World's Football Games* (London: Temple Smith, 1974), 223; and cf. Remi Cignet and Maureen Stark, "Modernization and Football in Cameroun," *Journal of Modern African Studies* 12, no. 3: 409–21.

20. Ali, 86, 90.

21. See Ali A. Mazrui, "Boxer Muhammad Ali and Soldier Idi Amin as International Political Symbols: The Bioeconomics of Sport and War," *Comparative Studies in Society and History* 19, no. 2 (April, 1977): 206.

22. Ali, 87.

23. *Sports Illustrated,* 19 December 1966: 58; Ali, 85–87, 160; and "Uganda and Olympism," *Olympic Review* 157 (November 1980): 657–63.

24. Geoff Fenwick, "History, Tradition in African Track" and "The Talent Distribution," in Prokop, 13–15, 19–22.

25. Mbonu Ojike, "Our Wondrous Society," in Barbara Nolen, ed., *Africa Is People: Firsthand Accounts from Contemporary Africa* (New York: E. P. Dutton, 1967, 19.

WILLIAM J. BAKER

26. See Bill Russell, *Second Wind: Memoirs of an Opinionated Man* (New York: Random House, 1979), 88–91, 177–79.

27. For examples, see "Zaire and Olympism," *Olympic Review* 143 (September 1979): 521–22; "Mali and Olympism," *Olympic Review* 134 (December 1978): 695–700.

28. Curry Kirkpatrick, "The Liege Lord of Noxzwema," *Sports Illustrated*, 28 November 1983: 106–34.

29. Fenwick, "African Approach to Competition," 24.

30. *New York Times*, 3 May 1976.

31. Max Weber, "Politics As a Vocation," in H. H. Gerth and C. Wright Mills, eds., *From Max Weber* (Oxford: Oxford University Press, 1946).

32. Lancine Sylla, "Succession of the Charismatic Leader: The Gordian Knot of African Politics," *Daedalus: Journal of the American Academy of Arts and Sciences* 3, no. 2 (Spring 1982): 11–28; and cf. John Okumu, "Charisma and Politics in Kenya," *East African Journal* 5, no. 2 (February 1968): 9–16.

33. Oscar O. Johnson, Jr., *All That Glitters Is Not Gold: The Olympic Game* (New York: G. P. Putnam's Sons, 1972), 257. For Ethiopia's adulation of Bikila following his triumph at Tokyo in 1964, see the *New York Times*, 1 November 1964, 14 March 1965; and John Underwood, "The Number Two Lion in the Land of Sheba," *Sports Illustrated*, 12 April 1965: 86–92.

34. For this data and interpretation, I am grateful to John MacAloon of the University of Chicago.

35. Francis Noronha, *Kipchoge of Kenya* (Nakuru: Elimu Publishers, 1970), 113, 150, 156–57. In Zambia in the early 1970s, however, Canadian Ross Kidd had to force Zambian runners to "shake off the impression of the Kenyan athletes as 'gods' endowed with a unique, mystical gift for running." Otherwise Zambians would not make the sacrifices necessary to train hard and long. See Ross Kidd, "In Zambia, A Different Picture," in Prokop, 59.

36. *New York Times*, 3 May 1976.

37. Ali, 89; and David Lewis, "An Elan, a Zest and a Grace," in Prokop, 9–10.

38. "Uganda and Olympism," *Olympic Review* 157 (November 1980): 657–63.

39. Imanuel Geiss, *The Pan-African Movement: A History of Pan-Africanism in America, Europe and Africa,* trans. Ann Keep (New York: Africana Publishing Co., 1968), 421.

40. Uwechue, "Nation Building and Sport," 546–47; Daniel Ogungbenjo Ogunbiyi, "The Development of Nigeria's Participation in International Sport Competition and Its Effect on the Nation," unpublished Ph.D. dissertation, Ohio State University, 1978, 153–58.

41. Allen Guttmann, *The Games Must Go On: Avery Brundage and the Olympic Movement* (New York: Columbia University Press, 1984), 230–31.

42. Ogunbiyi, 160–64; and Ali, 118–19.

43. Jean-Claude Ganga, *Combats pour un sport africain* (Paris: L'Harmattan, 1979), 176–78; and Ali, 119.

44. Richard Edward Lapchick, *The Politics of Race and International Sport: The Case of South Africa* (Westport, Conn.: Greenwood Press, 1975), 80.

45. Ibid., 20–26; and Horell, 9–10.

46.   Lapchick, 27–44; and Richard Espy, *The Politics of the Olympic Games; With an Epilogue, 1976–1980* (Berkeley: University of California Press, 1981), 69–70.

47.   Lapchick, 36–51; and cf. Richard Thompson, *Race and Sport* (London: Oxford University Press, 1964).

48.   "Minutes of the 60th Session," 14–20 October 1963, *Bulletin du C.I.O.,* no. 85, (15 February 1964) quoted in Guttmann, *The Games Must Go On,* 234.

49.   Letter from Brundage to the Marquess of Exeter, 28 November 1964, Brundage Papers, Box 55 (University of Illinois Archives), quoted in Espy, 84.

50.   Circular no. 214, Comte de Beaumont to IOC members, 18 January 1963, Brundage Papers, Box 70 (University of Illinois Archives), quoted in Espy, 88. On Soviet interests in sporting Africa, see 69–71, 87–89.

51.   Ganga, 198–99.

52.   Lapchick, 97–101. Lord Michael Killanin, *My Olympic Years* (London: Secker & Warburg, 1983), 32–43.

53.   Espy, 100–103; Lapchick, 110–11.

54.   *New York Times,* 18–28 February 1968.

55.   *New York Times,* 8 May 1967.

56.   See Harry Edwards, *The Revolt of the Black Athlete* (New York: The Free Press, 1969); and cf. William J. Baker, *Sports in the Western World* (Totowa, N.J.: Rowman and Littlefield, 1982), 289–95.

57.   Lapchick, 119–21; and Espy, 102–4. For a good overview of the South African question, see Philip Goodhart and Christopher Chataway, *War without Weapons* (London: W. H. Allen, 1968), 112–27.

58.   For the Mexico City games, see Christopher Brasher, *Mexico City, 1968* (London: Stanley Paul, 1968).

59.   Espy, 103.

60.   Ibid., 125–26; and *The Times* (London), 4, 15, 18, and 24 March 1969.

61.   For Ashe and South Africa, see Arthur Ashe, with Neil Amdur, *Off the Court* (New York: New American Library, 1981), 144–66.

62.   Killanin, 45–46; *New York Times,* 16 May 1970; Peter Hain, *Don't Play with Apartheid: The Background to the Seventy Tour Campaign* (London: Allen & Unwin, 1971).

63.   Dick Schaap, *An Illustrated History of the Olympics,* 3d ed. (New York: Knopf, 1975), 360; and Espy, 129–30.

64.   Geoffrey Miller, *Behind the Olympic Rings* (Lynn, Mass.: H. O. Zimman, 1979), 92; and cf. Killanin, 134–35.

65.   J. B. Ludwig, *Five Ring Circus: The Montreal Olympics* (Toronto: Doubleday Canada, 1976); and Pat Putnam, "It Was a Call to Colors," *Sports Illustrated,* 26 July 1976: 14–19.

66.   *The Times* (London), 16 June 1977.

67.   Miller, *Behind the Olympic Rings,* 93.

68.   *New York Times,* 20 May 1974.

69.   *New York Times,* 25 July 1978. For yet another example of tensions between African nations finding expression in sport, see "Kenya Halts Sport Events with Tanzanian Teams," *New York Times,* 1 February 1977.

70.   "It Takes a Heap of Salongo," *Newsweek,* 23 September 1974: 72.

71. Ibid., 73; and Ali, 90–91.

72. Ogunbiyi, 203–21; G. Benneh, *History of All-Africa University Games* (Accra: University of Ghana Press, 1975).

73. John Manners, "African Recruiting Boom," in Prokop, 62–69; and Ali, 115.

74. *Newsweek,* 18 February 1980: 58; David B. Kanin, *A Political History of the Olympic Games* (Boulder, Colo.: Westview Press, 1981), 142–43; Ron Fimrite, "Only the Bears Were Bullish," *Sports Illustrated,* 28 July 1980: 10–17.

75. *New York Times,* 7 January 1980.

76. *New York Times,* 27 July 1978.

Index

295

Columbia University, 83
Combes, J. T., 102
Commonwealth Games, 104, 124, 220, 240, 265, 273, 282, 284, 287–88
Commonwealth Institute, 189
Congo, 129, 184, 258–59, 267, 273; region, 23; river, 31
Congo-Brazzaville, 279, 284
Congo Republic, 283
Congress of Peoples of the East, First, 252
Conseia, João Carlos de, 264
Conseil International des Sports Militaires, 129
Conton, W., 165
Cooper, Frederick, 211
Cordell, E. A., 199–201, 206–7
Cornish, V. L., 102
Coryndon, Robert, 178–79, 187
Coubertin, Pierre de, 274
Council of West Africa University Games, 289
Cowling, B. S., 205–6
Cowrie shells, 51, 58, 65
Craik, Henry, 143
Cranworth, Lord, 88
Craven, 241
Cricket, 94ff., 128, 131, 147, 196, 199, 219, 225, 233–34, 240, 284
Cripps, Arthur Shearly, 155
Crispin, Paul, 222
Crocker, W. R., 101
Cromer, Lord, 85, 100, 143–44
Cumming, Gordon, 179
Currie, James, 143
Curzon, Lord, 102
Cycling, 256, 280

Dahmank, Mohamed Muldi, 260
Dahomey, 65, 225
Dakar, 283
Dale, Andrew Murray, 10
Damascus, 217
Dance, 4, 6–9, 13–17, 198; English country, 153; and manliness, 117; in Salisbury, 198, 202–3; in South Africa, 199, 233; and warfare, 16–17, 117, 120
Dar es Salaam, 101, 276
Darwinism, 116
Daume, Willi, 290
Davies, J. G., 101
Davis Cup, 287

Debat, Alfonse Massamba, 283
Debt-pawning, 66, 69
Denkyira, 68
Devonshire Rovers, 117
D'Hertfelt, M., 16
Dice, 49
Dictionary of National Biography, 83–84
Diola, the, 24, 38
Diplomatic Service, 93–94
District officer, 81–110, 140–41
Divination, 63–64, 118, 130
Dodd, William, 94
Dogon, the, 26, 39
D'Oliveira, Basil, 240
Douglas, Arthur, 154
Dress, 217
Duala, 31
Dual Mandate in British Tropical Africa, The, 141
Duif, Yasuf, 261
Duignan, Peter, 96
Durban, 199
Durban and District African Football Association, 199, 236, 238
Duri, 207
Dynamo Tfilisi, 256

East Africa Division, 119
East African Games, 282
East Africa Protectorate, 189
Eastern Cadet Service, 89, 93
East London, 118
Eaton Hall, 125
Edinburgh, University of, 89
Edmonton, 288
Education, 138–65; African reaction to, 159–65; imperial, 140ff.; Islamic, 218–19; missionary, 145–55; public school, 138–39. *See also* "Adaptation;" "Assimilation"
Educational Policy in British Tropical Africa, 163
Education as Cultural Imperialism, 142
Edward VII (king of England), 182
Edwards, Harry, 286
Effiong, Philip, 120
Egypt, 23, 49, 252, 275, 279, 289
Eko-chechi, 27–28
Ekoi, the, 30
Elgon, Mount, 12
Eliot, Charles, 185
Elitism, 130–33

Shangana-Tsonga, 9
Shari'a, 217
Sharpe, Alfred, 178, 180, 184, 187
Sharpeville, 238
Shavalkadze, Robert, 258
Shepilov, A., 258
Shimmin, Isaac, 181
Shira, 10
Shona, the, 173–74, 176, 182, 197
Shooting, 88–89, 99, 104, 175ff.
Shorthose, W. T., 88
Shell Oil, 286
Sierra Leone, 128–29, 148, 257, 283, 287
Sipes, R. G., 5, 18
Slavery, 63, 65
Smith, Edwin W., 10
Smith, Ian, 287
Smithsonian Institute, 179
Snow, C. P., 90, 100
Snoxall, R. A., 88
Soccer football, 5, 63–64, 97, 104, 117–18, 121–23, 125–29, 144, 152–53, 219, 256, 258, 262, 279, 284; and nationalism, 288–89; in Rhodesia, 188–89; in South Africa, 233–36, 238, 244–46. *See also* "Multinationalism"; Non-racial sport
Social control, 197, 202, 210–11
Social mobility: and African reaction to education, 162–63; and gambling, 67; and wrestling, 40–41
Society for the Propagation of the Gospel, 149, 155
Sokote Caliphate, 61
Somalia, 119, 280
Somaliland, 86, 119, 178
Songhai, the, 26
Soninke, the, 25
Sorcery, 118, 130
Sotho, the, 8, 9, 18, 198
Soul, C. N., 198
South Africa, 32, 89, 117, 182, 197, 229–47; and international sport, 232, 263, 265, 275, 279, 284–88; sports policy of, 230–31; University of, 205. *See also* Apartheid; Boycotts; International Olympic Committee; "Multinationalism"; Non-racial sport; Olympic Games; Soccer football
South African Amateur Athletics Board, 237

South African Amateur Athletics Union, 237
South African Breweries, 245
South African Council on Sport, 232, 241, 243, 245
South African Cricket Union, 241
South African Football Association, 244–45
South African Games, 286–87
South African National Football Association, 244–46
South African National Amateur Swimming Association, 242
South African National Olympic Committee, 284–85
South African Non-Racial Olympic Committee, 238, 243, 284
South African Rugby Board, 239
South African Rugby Union, 239
South African Soccer Federation, 244–45
South African Sports Association, 238
Southern Rhodesia, 187, 196–211
Southern Rhodesia Native Association, 198
Sovetskiy Sport, 252, 258, 261
Soviet Institute of Physical Education, 251
Soviet Olympic Committee, 254
Soviet Union, 130, 250–68, 285. *See also* Apartheid; Boycotts; Rhodesia
Sow, Badora, 283–84
Soweto, 235–36, 242
Spade and Sport in Pagan Land, 88
Spahis, the, 120
Spain, 217
Spartakiade, 256–57, 260, 264, 275
Spear fighting, 35
Spear throwing, 226
Speke, John, 88
Spicer, native Commissioner, 206–7
Sport and Service in Africa, 88
Sporting Trips of a Subaltern, 88
Sport in the Sociocultural Process, 14
Springboks, 246, 265, 288
Squash, 131
Stallybrass, W. T. S., 93
Stanley Falls, 31
Stayt, H. A., 10
Steele, Beryl, 96
Stevenson, Marion, 152–53